The COFFMAN COLLECTION

A History of Distinctive Rock & Roll Hits

Larry Coffman

ISBN: 978-1-7353285-0-8

DEDICATION

For Belen,
God's greatest blessing in my life

CONTENTS

ACKNOWLEDGMENTS

This book could not have been produced without the guidance and support of Ernie Abeytia, my editor/consultant. Special thanks to Patrick Palas for his inspiration.

Introduction

Why We Love Rock & Pop

When Rock and Roll began its occupation of popular music in America, all the existing voices of music first were threatened – then they assimilated. Elements of classical, jazz, folk, country, big band and blues all found a place in this distinctly American melting pot of music.

At first it was teenagers, but it was not long before every age group had a rock and roll favorite. Radio, television, and movies added Rock and Roll to their productions. Parents and even grandparents were willing to dance the Twist.

As a member of the Rock & Roll Generation, I remember listening to many of the first pop/rock songs when they were new.

I compiled my first list of favorite songs when I was 7, and it consisted of three titles. I don't remember what numbers 2 and 3 were, but I clearly recall that "Hound Dog" by Elvis Presley was No. 1. The year was 1956.

I had three older sisters, but they did not connect with pop music. So I kept listening casually to the songs of the day on the radio for the next five years, on the kitchen radio or in the family car. Our family didn't have money for luxuries like 45 rpm records, so my early audio pleasure did not include playing records on a phonograph.

Things changed dramatically when I entered 7th grade. At the ages of 12-13, my peers were listening to the current pop songs on the hip and powerful AM radio station WLS in Chicago – 50,000 watts transmitting 24 hours a day (except for midnight to 5 a.m. on Monday mornings.) To keep up with my schoolmates, I began to listen.

When I tuned in, a whole new world of musical delights opened up. The songs were entertaining, addictive and just plain fun. A soundtrack to my life had begun.

I got my first radio – a battery-powered portable radio encased in leather – as a Christmas present from my parents in 1961. Later, a friend gave me an old desk model radio that had tubes. It looked quirky because its outer case had been removed before my pal passed it on to me. I could see hose electrical tubes start to glow every time I turned it on.

I listened to my radios every night, usually while I did my school homework. The recording artists became my secret friends, and the WLS disc jockeys were like babysitters to me.

WLS printed a list of its top 40 songs each week. It was called the *Silver Dollar Survey.* One of the record shops in my hometown always had a stack of the current surveys next to the cash register, and I began to stop in each week to pick up a copy. Being a collector by nature, I saved these precious, colorful pieces of paper and didn't stop collecting them for the next 10 years. In mid-1967, the title changed to *Super Summer Survey* for four months. Then the name reverted to *Silver Dollar Survey* until Dec. 29, 1967, when it became the *WLS Hit Parade.*

When I entered Bradley University in Peoria, Ill., my survey collecting didn't have to stop. I found a record shop about three miles from campus that got *WLS Hit Parade* deliveries every week. This was 165 miles from Chicago.

I developed a fascination for the charts, constantly rooting for my current favorite song to reach No. 1. I marveled at the action, watching songs go up and down the list, some dying off much quicker than others.

The influence of WLS on me and many other kids cannot be understated. The station, located at 890 on the AM dial, began broadcasting in 1924 as an informational conduit for Midwestern farmers. It soon gained widespread attention for its wildly popular Saturday night program *National Barn Dance.* Since it was one of about a dozen stations using 50,000 watts, clear channel, it reached over two dozen states and could be heard on some ships at sea.

In 1960 the American Broadcasting Company (ABC) bought the station and soon changed its format to "Musicradio," which was pop/rock. The playlists also included country, rhythm & blues, adult contemporary and comedy/novelty records, which gave me an introduction to a wide spectrum of styles. I never tired of listening to WLS, and it pained me when I had to curtail my relationship with the station after I went off to college and then my career. Without WLS, I could not have become the music fan that I have been for about 60 years.

Sadly, in 1989 WLS jettisoned its music format and became a talk radio station.

In 1973 I discovered the *Billboard* charts and the incredibly informative syndicated radio program *American Top 40* with genial host Casey Kasem. This show not only provided me with a way of keeping track of current songs and their national ranking on a week-to-week basis, it injected interesting backstories into Kasem's narrative throughout the three-hour show.

The *Hot 100*, which included pop singles, was introduced in 1958. For many years *Billboard* compiled that chart by polling 100 record stores around the nation for their sales data, plus 54 radio stations for airplay data, to make up the weekly surveys. *Billboard* published its first chart, called a hit parade, in 1936. Nowadays, *Billboard* uses sales, radio airplay, digital downloads and streaming activity to rate the current songs.

Billboard HOT 100 FOR WEEK ENDING APRIL 11, 1970

★ STAR PERFORMER—Sides registering greatest proportionate sales progress this week. Ⓢ Record Industry Association of America seal of certification as million selling single.

This Week	1 Wk Ago	2 Wks Ago	3 Wks Ago	Title	Weeks on Chart
★	2	2	6	LET IT BE	4
★	4	6	14	ABC	5
3	3	3	4	INSTANT KARMA (We All Shine On)	7
★	6	8	13	SPIRIT IN THE SKY	7
Ⓢ 5	1	1	1	BRIDGE OVER TROUBLED WATER	10
6	5	5	8	LOVE GROWS (Where My Rosemary Goes)	8
7	7	11	15	HOUSE OF THE RISING SUN	10
8	9	10	23	COME AND GET IT	10
9	10	12	18	EASY COME, EASY GO	10
10	8	4	2	THE RAPPER	11
★	16	22	25	UP THE LADDER TO THE ROOF	6
Ⓢ ★	23	25	26	THE BELLS	10
13	13	19	19	CALL ME	13
★	20	29	38	LOVE OR LET ME BE LONELY	6
★	17	34	46	AMERICAN WOMAN/NO SUGAR TONIGHT	4
Ⓢ 16	14	14	5	RAINY NIGHT IN GEORGIA	14
17	12	9	3	GIVE ME JUST A LITTLE MORE TIME	13
18	18	17	9	EVIL WAYS	12
19	11	7	7	HE AIN'T HEAVY, HE'S MY BROTHER	17
20	15	15	17	CELEBRATE	7
21	24	26	35	SOMETHING'S BURNING	9
★	32	47	72	TURN BACK THE HANDS OF TIME	4
23	21	21	24	GOTTA HOLD ON TO THIS FEELING	8
★	33	37	41	YOU'RE THE ONE	7
★	30	33	39	SHILO	10
★	26	35	42	LONG LONESOME HIGHWAY	7
★	29	32	47	TENNESSEE BIRDWALK	7
Ⓢ 28	22	18	10	DIDN'T I (Blow Your Mind This Time)	14
29	19	13	12	MA BELLE AMIE	12
30	31	51	60	REFLECTIONS OF MY LIFE	5
31	25	16	16	KENTUCKY RAIN	9
32	27	28	34	ALL I HAVE TO DO IS DREAM	9
★	35	68	—	WOODSTOCK	3
★	37	41	87	YOU NEED LOVE LIKE I DO (Don't You)	4
★	36	61	77	GET READY	5
36	34	31	28	DO THE FUNKY CHICKEN	10
★	42	74	—	EVERYBODY'S OUT OF TOWN	3
★	75	98	—	VEHICLE	3
★	43	71	81	FOR THE LOVE OF HIM	5
★	58	70	82	LITTLE GREEN BAG	4
41	39	39	51	TEMMA HARBOUR	8
★	50	56	80	MY WOMAN MY WOMAN MY WIFE	5
43	45	53	73	MIGHTY JOE	6
44	40	40	53	WHO'S YOUR BABY	6
45	41	42	50	LET'S GIVE ADAM AND EVE ANOTHER CHANCE	6
46	52	79	84	I COULD WRITE A BOOK	4
47	54	62	62	CALIFORNIA GIRL	8
48	48	52	65	EASY TO BE FREE	6
49	44	43	40	JENNIFER TOMKINS	15
50	53	59	61	TO THE OTHER WOMAN	7
51	56	72	86	FUNKY DRUMMER (Part 1)	4
★	74	—	—	EVERYTHING IS BEAUTIFUL	2
53	46	45	45	GOTTA GET BACK TO YOU	8
★	62	83	95	CHILDREN	4
55	55	64	70	THE CAT WALK	8
★	—	—	—	LOVE ON A TWO WAY STREET	1
★	89	—	—	MAKE ME SMILE	2
58	57	63	71	COME TOGETHER	6
★	78	—	—	COME RUNNING	2
60	67	90	—	CAPTURE THE MOMENT	3
61	69	—	—	THE GIRLS' SONG	2
62	66	85	—	THE FUNNIEST THING	3
63	63	84	88	NOTHING SUCCEEDS LIKE SUCCESS	4
★	—	—	—	LOVE LAND	1
65	65	75	76	LIVIN' LOVIN' MAID (She's Just a Woman)	5
★	—	—	—	WHAT IS TRUTH	1
67	68	83	85	DEAR PRUDENCE	4
★	—	—	—	CECILIA	1
★	79	87	—	BUT FOR LOVE	3
70	73	80	94	IS ANYBODY GOIN' TO SAN ANTONE	5
71	71	—	—	DEEPER (In Love With You)	2
72	72	—	—	CRYIN' IN THE STREETS (Part 1)	2
73	76	100	—	WHICH WAY YOU GOIN' BILLY?	3
★	82	—	—	CHICKEN STRUT	2
★	—	—	—	SO EXCITED	1
76	77	77	79	RUN SALLY RUN	6
★	—	—	—	HEY LAWDY MAMA	1
78	81	86	—	BROWN PAPER BAG	3
★	—	—	—	HE MADE A WOMAN OUT OF ME	1
80	80	99	100	I GOT A THING, YOU GOT A THING	4
81	87	—	—	MISS AMERICA	2
★	90	—	—	DON'T STOP NOW	2
83	83	93	93	HITCHIN' A RIDE	4
84	84	—	—	CAN YOU FEEL IT	2
85	86	—	—	LOVE MINUS ZERO—NO LIMIT	2
86	88	—	—	BUFFALO SOLDIER	2
87	85	94	—	JULY 12, 1939	3
★	—	—	—	COME SATURDAY MORNING	9
★	—	—	—	VIVA TIRADO, Part I	1
★	—	—	—	AIRPORT THEME	1
91	94	—	—	MY WIFE THE DANCER	2
92	95	—	—	COLE, COOKE & REDDING	2
93	93	—	—	HANG ON SLOOPY	2
94	92	—	—	MISSISSIPPI QUEEN	2
95	—	—	—	OH HAPPY DAY	1
96	98	—	—	LUCIFER	2
97	—	—	—	YOU MAKE ME REAL/ROADHOUSE BLUES	1
98	91	97	—	IF I ONLY HAD MY MIND ON SOMETHING ELSE	3
99	—	—	—	I CAN'T LEAVE YOUR LOVE ALONE	1
100	—	—	—	ANGELICA	1

HOT 100—A TO Z—(Publisher-Licensee)

BUBBLING UNDER THE HOT 100

Compiled from national retail sales and radio station airplay by the Music Popularity Dept. of Record Market Research, Billboard.

Chart performances are important in identifying the relative popularity of a song against its peers that have been in stores and on radio playlists at the same time. While *Billboard's* charts are not the only national charts in the United States, they are considered the industry standard for accuracy and comprehensiveness.

The *Billboard Hot 100* is like a melting pot. It contains songs that fall into several different categories, like rock, country, rhythm & blues, adult contemporary, folk, jazz, etc. These songs may have widely different sounds, but they have certain things in common: they are well-liked by a large section of our population, they are played on radio stations across the nation and their records (or compact discs or digital downloads) sell many copies. Therefore, they are able to compete on the same national chart.

There also is a need for specialized charts, such as the ones that track songs in the genres of country, R&B, adult contemporary, etc.

Throughout years of careful listening, I have identified undercurrents throughout the history of popular music. As time has passed, many songs have taken on similar characteristics – a common thread to connect them. Rather than run down the timeline of pop music chronologically, or artist by artist, this book will separate some of the most notable songs according to their common thread.

The most common theme in pop music is love. Boy meets girl. Boy dates girl. Boy and girl have a spat and break up. Boy tries to win back girl. And on and on it goes. But in this book, we primarily will explore songs that go beyond love to promote other themes. Perhaps there are more than you realized. This will be a study of popular music and how it got to be that way.

You may have a song that you consider to be your favorite of all time. Mine is "Runaround Sue" by Dion. It is a song about a guy who laments that his girlfriend isn't true to him, and this tears him apart.

But the words are not what drew me to this record in 1961. I was only 12 years old when it was released, and I didn't know anything about love or girlfriends or broken hearts. Just the sound of the singer's voice, the tune, the instrumentation, the backing vocals and other intangibles turned me on. It was the reason I started being a rock and roll devotee. I dearly love that recording to this day.

Have you ever thought about what the most important date in rock history might be? I have. To me, that date is Nov. 22, 1963.

On that date, at approximately 12:30 p.m. CST, Pres. John F. Kennedy was shot while in his motorcade in Dallas, Texas. I was in German language lab as a high school freshman when I learned the news. He was pronounced dead at 1:00 p.m. From that moment on, for a period of about six weeks, the United States went into a period of mourning. Even after the President was laid to rest in Arlington National Cemetery on Nov. 25, it seemed like we weren't supposed to laugh, have fun or do anything enjoyable. The programming on radio and television was eerily sullen.

Coincidentally, the album "A Christmas Gift For You from Phil Spector," featuring one of the most revolutionary treatments of secular holiday songs, was released Nov. 22, 1963. One of the songs contained therein, "Sleigh Ride" by the Ronettes, got a lot of play on WLS and helped get me through a glum Christmas season.

Then we turned the page to a new year, 1964. There was a new sound on the radio – "I Want To Hold Your Hand" by the Beatles. This is the same Liverpool, England, band that had "Please Please Me" on American radio nine months earlier and was quickly rejected.

But now we were ready for the Beatles. And they were ready for us. It was the perfect way to end our mourning and get back to living. In America, the Beatles' first album release of 1964 was titled "Meet The Beatles," and all the songs on it were different from what we had been hearing in rock and roll's first 10 years. Our ears were reborn!

With their enormous success in the U.S., the Beatles opened the door for many other British musicians to send their songs our way. These included the Dave Clark Five, the Searchers, the Rolling Stones, Peter & Gordon, Chad Stuart & Jeremy Clyde, Billy J. Kramer & the Dakotas, Dusty Springfield, Gerry & the Pacemakers, Herman's Hermits, Petula Clark, the Zombies and the Kinks, to name a few. Rock and pop music would never sound the same. It truly was a change for the better.

Without a presidential assassination, would the Beatles have been able to make the kind of entrance that they made and get exposure for music that changed the course of rock? Perhaps not.

We love so many songs, but why is that so? We'll try to find answers.

Each song that is spotlighted in this study will be identified by title, songwriter(s), recording artist, complete lyrics and a summary of its performance on *Billboard Magazine's Hot 100* chart. If the song was not a single release, I will identify its album.

The Rock Era, like the Ragtime Era or the Big Band Era, is one of the most notable periods of music history. It began in 1955 with the song "(We're Gonna) Rock Around The Clock" by Bill Haley & His Comets. That record was the catalyst that sent popular music down the path of rock, and it was the first *Billboard* No. 1 song of the rock era.

Sources indicate that the song was written as early as 1952, and it was recorded in 1954. Decca Records released it in 1954 and again in '55. It received a big boost from its inclusion in the 1955 movie *The Blackboard Jungle.*

The music industry has experienced a boom during the Rock Era, as many talented musicians and songwriters have stepped forward to seek their fortune in an industry that is almost as much about pop culture as it is about music.

Along the way we will see many artists who managed to hit the charts just once. Despite their efforts to repeat this success, they were unable to "catch lightning in a bottle" again. We call these artists "one-hit wonders." They have dotted the pop music landscape in every year since 1955, and they represent the struggle that is involved in making a hit record.

Many rock songs have interesting backstories which tell remarkable tales of how songs got to be recorded, how records got to be hits and how singers got to be stars. This book seeks to tell those stories with the hope that readers will enjoy and appreciate the little-known facts behind the music that has dominated the industry for over half a century.

Chapter 1

All About Rock

Songs about rock music or the rock & roll lifestyle

Overview: Only two years into the Rock Era, songs that extoll rock and roll music began to surface. It was a little strange to hear hit songs on the radio that talked about hit songs that were on the radio.

But the music that was sweeping the nation was so seductive and addictive that several songwriters couldn't help but write about it. The result was a bevy of songs that surged up the charts over the span of about a quarter century.

It's interesting the way the writers took different approaches in delivering their message about the music.

To view the full lyrics of these songs, please log on to www.google.com, enter song titles & artist names and click Google Search.

To listen to these songs, please log on to www.youtube.com and enter song titles & artist names.

(We're Gonna) Rock Around The Clock [Bill Haley & His Comets] Rock and roll records had been recorded for a few years when this one came along. It didn't break new ground, so to speak, in the industry. But it got the kind of exposure and promotion that helped it become a catalyst in taking rock into the mainstream.

When it was inserted into the soundtrack of *Blackboard Jungle*, a movie about teen rebellion, it was adopted as an anthem of American youth. It spent an eye-popping eight weeks at No. 1 on the *Billboard Best Sellers* chart. It also topped the *Juke Box* and *Disc Jockey charts.* To this day, it is considered to be the first No. 1 song of the Rock Era.

The song had international appeal and was No. 1 on the United Kingdom pop chart. It was the best-selling song of the 1950s in the U.K.

The song's message is simple: let's rock, 24/7. We'll never tire of it.

What many people don't realize is that Bill Haley & His Comets had four highly charted singles before "Rock Around The Clock" found success. "Shake, Rattle And Roll" was the most prominent, rising to No. 7 in the U.S. while giving Haley his first gold record.

Another little-known quirk is that Sonny Dae & His Knights recorded "Rock Around The Clock" 23 days before Haley and his comrades recorded their version in spring of 1954. The Knights' recording became a regional hit.

Haley's "Rock Around The Clock" initially charted June 3, 1954, as the B-side behind "Thirteen Women (and Only One Man In Town") and did well enough for Decca Records to invoke the option on his contract. After the release of *Blackboard Jungle,* the record took off again and quickly went to No. 1.

Fate almost prevented Haley and the Comets from arriving at their recording session at Pythian Temple studios in New York City. The band was traveling by ferry from Philadelphia when the vessel temporarily got stuck on a sandbar.

The recording was produced by Milt Gabler, the uncle of actor Billy Crystal.

Twenty years later, when the 1950s nostalgia television situation comedy *Happy Days* used "Rock Around The Clock" over its opening credits, the record took on a new life. Boosted by the show's popularity, it ran up the charts again to a peak position of No. 39.

Elton John's "Crocodile Rock" took a jab at "Rock Around The Clock" in 1973. One line declares, "While the other kids were rockin' 'round the clock, we were hoppin' and boppin' to the Crocodile Rock."

"Rock Around The Clock" is in the National Recording Registry of the Library of Congress and has been cited as being "culturally, historically or artistically significant."

Haley, who had a knack for taking bluesy songs and giving them a rockabilly twist, didn't have a long career following "Rock Around The Clock." His fame was eclipsed by the phenomenal Elvis Presley, who used Haley's blueprint to create his mountain of popular music.

In 1981 Haley died at his home in Harlingen, Texas, at the age of 55. The nebulous cause of death on his death certificate was "natural causes, most likely a heart attack." According to *Legacy.com*, he struggled with alcoholism throughout his life. In 1980 it was revealed that he had a brain tumor.

Haley's official website calls him "The Father of Rock 'n' Roll."

(We're Gonna) Rock Around The Clock

Songwriters: Max C. Freedman, James E. Myers

Peaked at No. 1 on Billboard Best Sellers

July 9, 1955
July 16, 1955
July 23, 1955
July 30, 1955
Aug. 6, 1955
Aug. 13, 1955
Aug. 20, 1955
Aug. 27, 1955

Bill Haley & His Comets

Bill Haley (July 6, 1925-Feb. 9, 1981) guitar
Danny Cedrone (June 20, 1920-June 17, 1954) guitar
Marshall Lytle (Sept. 1, 1933-May 25, 2013) double bass
Billy Gussack (session player on "Rock Around The Clock") drums
Joey d'Ambrosio (March 23, 1934-) saxophone
Billy Williamson (Feb. 9, 1925-March 22, 1996) steel guitar
Johnny Grande (Jan. 14, 1930-June 3, 2006) piano
Formed in Bethel, Pa., in 1952

Bill Haley (center) and His Comets

Rock & Roll Music [Chuck Berry] – This song was written by the man who also has been called the "Father of Rock and Roll," Chuck Berry, and was recorded in May 1957 in Chicago. It was released as a single in September 1957. This is barely two years after the acknowledged beginning of the rock and roll era.

Berry was born in St. Louis, Mo., and lived his entire life in that area.

He may have had the concept for this song in mind in January of '57, when he recorded the song "School Days." At the end of that song, he sang the lines: "Hail, hail rock and roll, deliver me from the days of old. Long live rock and roll, the beat of the drums loud and bold. Rock, rock, rock and roll, the feeling is there, body and soul."

"Rock & Roll Music" peaked at No. 8 on *Billboard's* pop chart. While there were many covers of the song, prominent versions were recorded by the Beatles (1964) and Beach Boys (1976).

The lyrics tell of a guy who wants to dance to nothing but rock and roll, which is a unique salute to the music.

Rock and Roll Music

Songwriter: Chuck Berry

Peaked at No. 8 on Billboard Weekly Singles Chart

Dec. 23, 1957

Chuck Berry

Oct. 18, 1926-March 18, 2017

Born Charles Edward Anderson Berry in St. Louis, Mo., and died in Wentzville, Mo.

Chuck Berry

Rock And Roll Is Here To Stay [Danny & the Juniors] – On this recording, four fellows from Philadelphia fearlessly forecasted the future.

It was recorded in early 1958 as a follow-up to Danny & the Juniors' smash hit "At The Hop." The song peaked at No. 19 on *Billboard's* pop chart and spent seven weeks in the top 40.

The vocal quartet formed in 1955. Dave White Tricker, the first tenor of the Juniors, wrote this song and "At The Hop." Therefore, it's no surprise that "Rock And Roll Is Here To Stay" sounds a lot like its predecessor.

Danny & the Juniors were the first of many great rock acts to emerge from Philadelphia. Later there would be Bobby Rydell, Chubby Checker, Patti LaBelle, the Tymes, the Delfonics, the Stylistics, Jim Croce, Harold Melvin & the Blue Notes, Blue Magic, Daryl Hall & John Oates and others.

In the 1960s Tricker left the Juniors to concentrate on songwriting and production. He wrote such hits as "You Don't Own Me," which became a hit for Lesley Gore in 1963-64.

Lead singer Danny Rapp committed suicide on April 5, 1983, at the age of 41.

Rock And Roll Is Here To Stay

Songwriter: Dave White Tricker

Peaked at No. 19 on Billboard Pop Chart

March 24, 1958

Danny & the Juniors

Danny Rapp (May 9, 1941-April 5, 1983) lead vocalist
Frank Maffei (Dec. 15, 1939-) baritone/2nd tenor
Joe Terranova (Jan. 30, 1941-) baritone
Dave White Tricker (Sept. 1, 1939-) 1st tenor
Formed in Philadelphia, Pa., in 1955

Danny Rapp, Dave White Tricker, Frank Maffei, Joe Terranova

It Will Stand [Showmen] – A rhythm & blues quintet became cheerleaders for rock and roll music with this sweet soul song.

Written by General Norman Johnson of the Showmen, the song praises rock and identifies some of rock's elements, like "sax blowing sharp as lightning" and "drums beating loud as thunder."

One of my favorite parts is the chorus, in which we hear, "Some people don't understand it, that's why they don't demand it."

The gist of the message is that rock is here to stay. As for rock's doubters, the message takes a Biblical stance (Luke 23:34) by saying, "Forgive them, for they know not what they're doing."

The record stayed on the *Billboard Hot 100* for about three months, but it never rose higher than No. 61. Perhaps that is because listeners could not understand how an R&B vocal group would be singing about rock and roll.

The message resonated in Chicagoland, though, as the record reached No. 6 on the local charts in mid-February 1962.

"It Will Stand" was re-released in 1964 and charted at No. 80. But it had a substantial following in the Detroit area, where it peaked in the top 10 in Windsor on the Canadian side of the border.

Originally from Norfolk, Va., the Showmen found their way to New Orleans in 1961, where they were mentored by local music guru Allen Toussaint. Johnson wrote most of their material, as well as songs recorded by other artists (see Chapter 8, "Patches" by Clarence Carter). He also wrote several hits songs for the trio Honey Cone in the early 1970s, as well as "Bring The Boys Home" for Freda Payne (see Chapter 10, End The War!).

Johnson parted from the Showmen in 1968 and connected with Invictus Records (see Chapter 6, The Story of Motown) in Detroit as a songwriter and lead singer of the Chairmen of the Board.

It Will Stand

Songwriter: General Norman Johnson

Peaked at No. 61 on Billboard Hot 100

Jan. 20, 1962

The Showmen

General Norman Johnson (May 23, 1941-Oct. 13, 2010)
Milton "Smokes" Wells
Dorsey "Chops" Knight
Gene "Cheater" Knight
Leslie "Fat Boy" Felton
Formed in Norfolk, Va., in 1961

The Showmen

I Dig Rock And Roll Music [Peter, Paul & Mary] – The folk trio recorded this sarcastic song in 1967 for their album titled "Album 1700" on Warner Brothers Records. It was the first single from the album and reached No. 9 on *Billboard's Hot 100* in the fall.

It would be a full two years, however, before a second single would be released from "Album 1700," and that would be the trio's final top 40 hit and only No. 1 song, "Leaving On A Jet Plane."

The threesome formed in New York City in 1961. Peter Yarrow is from Brooklyn. Paul Stookey was born in Baltimore and moved to Birmingham, Mich., when he was 12. Mary Travers was born in Louisville but moved to Greenwich Village in Manhattan when she was 2.

Many of their songs promoted social change and various humanitarian causes.

"I Dig Rock And Roll Music" parodies the styles of three popular acts of the day: the Mamas & the Papas, Donovan and the Beatles.

Folk artists, in general, felt that their music was superior to rock. In a 1966 interview with the *Chicago Daily News,* Travers said of rock, "It's so badly written. When the fad changed from folk to rock, they didn't take along any good writers."

The writers of this song, Stookey, James Mason and Dave Dixon, apparently believed that folk was deep and thought provoking and that rock was shallow and appealed only to the lowest common denominator of record buyers.

This song's lyrics take on the biggest band of the day (and of all time), the Beatles, accusing them of being more interested in how much money their music was making than in what their songs were saying. The Beatles, a huge money-making machine, were passed off here as being phonies when it came to promoting love, peace and idealism.

The Mamas & the Papas were parodied for their vocal style, as was Donovan. The guitar swell on his "Sunshine Superman" also was replicated.

The final verse contends that important messages could be conveyed through rock, but if so, they would have to be severely cleaned up. Some rock lyrics of the 1960s carried foul language and references to illicit drug use.

A 1960s no-no is sneaked into the final verse – "I could really *get it on* that scene." Back then "get it on" referred to having sex.

Travers died in 2009 at the age of 72 of complications from chemotherapy for treatment of leukemia.

I Dig Rock And Roll Music
Songwriters: Dave Dixon, Paul Stookey, James Mason
Peaked at No. 9 on Billboard Hot 100
Sept. 23, 1967
Sept. 30, 1967

Peter, Paul & Mary
Peter Yarrow (May 31, 1938-)
Noel Paul Stookey (Dec. 30, 1937-)
Mary Travers (Nov. 9, 1936-Sept. 16, 2009)
Formed in New York City, N.Y., in 1961

Peter Yarrow, Mary Travers & Paul Stookey

Rock And Roll [Led Zeppelin] – This was written and recorded by the members of Led Zeppelin in 1971 for their untitled fourth album, commonly referred to as "Led Zeppelin IV."

The band was at a mansion they had rented for recording in Hampshire, England, and was struggling to finish a certain song for the album, "Four Sticks." Tensions were rising among the members and, in a pique of frustration, drummer John Bonham started playing something completely unrelated to the material on which they were working. It was a riff that was akin to Little Richard's 1957 song "Keep A-Knockin'." Jimmy Page added a guitar riff. Tape was rolling, and Led Zeppelin had the basis of a classic song within 15 minutes.

Page: "It actually ground to a halt after about 12 bars, but it was enough to know that there was enough of a number there to keep working on it." Robert Plant added lyrics. All four members of Led Zeppelin, including bassist John Paul Jones, received writing credit.

Page added, "… It was just so exciting that we thought, 'Let's just work on this.' The riff and the sequence was really immediate to those 12-bar patterns that you had in those old rock songs, like Little Richard, etc., and it was just so spur-of-the-moment the way that it just came together more or less out of nowhere."

The lyrics evoke buzzwords from some rock songs of the 1950s, such as "the stroll," "book of love" and "walk in the moonlight." This provides a retro feel that is married to a heavy, 1970s-style rock guitar sound.

"The Stroll" was a hit song for the Diamonds in 1957-58, as well as the name of a popular line dance. "Book Of Love" was a hit song for the Monotones in '58. The term "moonlight" is mentioned in decades-old songs such as "What A Little Moonlight Can Do," "Moonlight Becomes You" and "In The Chapel in the Moonlight." All were recorded by multiple artists.

Bonham, the guy who started the ball rolling on the song, died Sept. 25, 1980, at age 32. An excessive drinker, he quaffed four quadruple screwdrivers at breakfast on the day before he died. He continued to drink heavily at band rehearsals throughout the day. The band members went to Page's house afterward, whereupon Bonham fell asleep. Someone took him to bed and placed him on his side. He was found unresponsive the next afternoon.

An inquest showed that, within 24 hours, Bonham had consumed 1 to 1.4 liters of vodka (40 shots) and choked to death on vomit as he slept. No other drugs were found in his system, and the death was ruled accidental. At one time he had been a heroin user, it is rumored.

Rather than recruit another drummer, Led Zeppelin decided to disband. Bonham was widely considered one of the top drummers in all of rock.

"Rock And Roll" was used in a 2002 Cadillac automobile TV commercial campaign. The customer base of the luxury car brand gradually was dying off, and it wanted to appeal as a hip choice for young car buyers. The ads first appeared during the Super Bowl, and sales grew 16 percent in the ensuing year.

The single was released on Feb. 21, 1972, with "Four Sticks" on the flip side, and it peaked at No. 47 on the *Billboard Hot 100* (indicating that, for a song with retro lyrics, it was ahead of its time). It is a staple on classic rock radio stations around the world. The album, on the other hand, peaked at No. 2 on the *Billboard 200* chart and went on to sell about 37 million copies.

Rock And Roll

Songwriters: Jimmy Page, Robert Plant, John Bonham, John Paul Jones

Peaked at No. 47 on Billboard Hot 100

April 15, 1972

April 22, 1972

Led Zeppelin

Robert Plant (Aug. 20, 1948-) vocals

Jimmy Page (Jan. 9, 1944-) guitar

John Paul Jones (Jan. 3, 1946-) bass, keyboards, mandolin

John Bonham (May 31, 1948-Sept. 25, 1980) drums

Formed in London, England, in 1968

Led Zeppelin: John Paul Jones, Robert Plant, John Bonham and Jimmy Page

The Cover of "Rolling Stone" [Dr. Hook & the Medicine Show]– Humorist Shel Silverstein ("A Boy Named Sue") wrote this humorous song, and Dr. Hook and the Medicine Show recorded it in 1972. It was the band's third single release and second to hit the top 40. Silverstein had written some of their early songs, and he wrote all the songs for their second album, "Sloppy Seconds."

In the lyrics, the band pleads for *Rolling Stone Magazine* to complete their quest for fame by featuring them on the cover, and they proceed to detail the reasons why they deserve it. It is a somewhat comical view of the excess-riddled, superficial lives of modern rock stars.

What the band may not have expected was that *Rolling Stone* eventually did put a caricature of them on the cover of the March 29, 1973 edition. A caption underneath read, "What's-Their-Names Make the Cover."

The name of the group was shortened to Dr. Hook in 1975.

Rolling Stone, based in San Francisco, was founded in 1967 by publisher Jann Wenner and music critic Ralph Gleason. The pop culture publication quickly gained popularity and respect for its coverage of the music industry and the political reporting by Hunter S. Thompson. It apparently filled a niche that publications like *Billboard* and *Variety* failed to address.

The Cover Of "Rolling Stone"
Songwriter: Shel Silverstein
Peaked at No. 6 on Billboard Hot 100
March 17, 1973
March 24, 1973

Dr. Hook & the Medicine Show
Ray Sawyer (Feb. 1, 1937-) vocals
Dennis Locorriere (June 13, 1949-) vocals, guitar, harmonica
Billy Francis (Jan. 16, 1942-) vocals, guitar, keyboards
George Cummings (July 28, 1938-) guitar
John "Jay" David (Aug. 8, 1942-) drums
Jance Garfat (March 3, 1944-) bass
Rik Elswit (July 6, 1945-) guitar
Formed in Union City, N.J., in 1967

Dr. Hook & the Medicine Show

Caricatures on the cover of *Rolling Stone*

Life Is A Rock (But The Radio Rolled Me) [Reunion]– This amazing song represents the fastest-sounding 3½ minutes in the history of rock and was recorded by the studio group Reunion. Joey Levine (lead vocals), Paul DiFranco (composer), Norman Dolph (lyrics) and Marc Bellack were the primary musicians on the track, and the first three of those men co-produced it.

Reunion was not a band that played live shows. They got together only to record.

Levine had experience as a singer on the 1967 hit "Run Run Run" by the Third Rail, several hits by the Ohio Express (1968-69) and "Quick Joey Small" by the KK Singing Orchestra Circus ('68). In the 1970s he began to create and sing advertising jingles.

Here are some of the advertising campaigns Levine worked on: *Mounds & Almond Joy* – "sometimes you feel like a nut, sometimes you don't;" *Pepsi* – "the joy of cola;" "Gentlemen prefer *Hanes*;" "Just for the taste of it – *Diet Coke*;" "Orange you smart" – *orange juice*; "Come see the softer side of *Sears;*" *Chevy* – "the heartbeat of America;" *Dr. Pepper* – "you make the world taste better;" "You asked for it, you got it" – *Toyota*; "Who's that kid with the *Oreo* cookie;" "This *Bud's* for you" and "This is *Budweiser*, this is beer."

The lyrics are a lightning-fast nod to many names of disc jockeys, musicians, record labels, songwriters, producers, song titles, lyrics, places and pop culture figures of the first two decades of rock and roll.

In the fall of 1974, it spent 15 weeks on *Billboard's Hot 100*, and on Nov. 16 it peaked at No. 8. In my research I found nothing that indicates that the tape was speeded up in the mixing of the recording to make Levine's vocal sound artificially fast.

The following year Reunion released a song titled "Disco-Tekin," which failed to chart in the U.S.

Life Is A Rock (But The Radio Rolled Me)

Songwriters: Norman Dolph, Paul DiFranco, Joey Levine

Peaked at No. 8 on Billboard Hot 100

Nov. 16, 1974

Reunion

Joey Levine (May 29, 1947-)
Norman Dolph (April 1, 1939-)
Paul DiFranco (DOB unavailable)
Marc Bellack (DOB unavailable)

Joey Levine

Rock N' Roll (I Gave You The Best Years Of My Life) [Mack Davis] – This song is an acknowledgement of all the thousands of musicians who tried to make it big in the business but failed. It is a tough business, indeed.

By examining the lyrics, we can begin to understand why there are so many failed musicians scattered around the world.

Australian Kevin Johnson penned the song. His version of it was a No. 4 hit on an Aussie chart in 1973. It is one of the most covered Australian songs ever, with 27 versions recorded in 1975 alone. Canadian Terry Jacks ("Seasons In The Sun") recorded a notable rendition.

American country/pop singer Mac Davis made the recording that was the most successful in the U.S., which peaked at No. 15 in the winter of 1975.

Johnson wrote the early verses of the song about his own experiences and the later verses about those of other singers he had known. He said he wrote the song in two days and added, "I always draw on things I know, things around me, on everyday life for my songs."

The song reminds listeners of how important timing is in a musician's career. If your writing is too far ahead of musical trends or just a little behind, your songs can fail to achieve popularity.

Johnson's original lyrics of the last verse state: "She followed me when finally I sold my old guitar. She tried to help me understand that I'd never be a star."

His final chorus reads: "And though I never knew the magic of making it with you, I thank the Lord for giving me the little that I knew."

Davis's version leaves out the part that says, "I'd never be a star." Said Johnson, "There were a few people who wouldn't sing (that line) because in their minds they were big stars."

In 1979 the Eagles put a song titled "The Sad Café" on their album "The Long Run." The song recounts the early days of the band when they were unknown musicians playing in the Troubadour nightclub in West Hollywood, Calif.

At one point, the lyrics raise the question of why the Eagles made it big in the business while many of their peers did not. "Now I look at the years gone by and wonder at the powers that be," the song says. "I don't know why fortune smiles on some and lets the rest go free.

"Some of their dreams came true, some just passed away. And some of them stayed behind inside the Sad Café."

The language of success must be quite puzzling when even insiders like the Eagles can't decipher it.

Rock N' Roll (I Gave You The Best Years Of My Life)

Songwriter: Kevin Johnson

Peaked at No. 15 on Billboard Hot 100

Feb. 1, 1975

Mac Davis

Born Morris Mac Davis in Lubbock, Texas, on Jan. 21, 1942

Mac Davis

Shooting Star [Bad Company]– The song was recorded by the four-man British band Bad Company in 1975 for their second album, "Straight Shooter," which reached No. 3 on the *Billboard 200* album chart.

The band's lead singer Paul Rodgers wrote it, based on the drug and alcohol-related deaths of Jimi Hendrix, Janis Joplin and Jim Morrison. It features some heavy rock guitar solos by Mick Ralphs.

While there is some dispute over the details of **Hendrix's** demise, he seems to have spent his last full day, Sept. 17, 1970, in London with his girlfriend, Monika Dannemann. She has said that she cooked a late supper for them in her apartment, where they consumed a bottle of wine. She drove him to a friend's house at about 1:45 in the morning and then picked him up an hour later. They stayed up talking until 7 a.m. in her apartment and then went to sleep. Dannemann awoke around 11 a.m. on Sept. 18 to find Hendrix breathing but unresponsive.

An ambulance transported Hendrix to St. Mary Abbot's Hospital, where he was pronounced dead. The coroner ordered a post-mortem examination, and a forensic pathologist concluded that Hendrix had suffocated on his own vomit while intoxicated with barbiturates.

Later, Dannemann admitted that Hendrix had consumed nine of her prescription sleeping tablets, *Vesparax*, which was 18 times the recommended dosage.

Joplin was in Los Angeles, Calif., on Oct. 4, 1970, staying at the Landmark Motor Hotel in Hollywood. When she failed to show up for a session with the band Full Tilt Boogie at Sunset Sound Recorders, the band's road manager John Cooke went to the Landmark to check on her. He found her lifeless body on the floor next to the bed.

Joplin's death, ruled accidental, was caused by a heroin overdose, possibly compounded by consumption of alcoholic beverages. She was a known user of heroin throughout most of the time she was a famous singer.

After the Doors completed their album "L.A. Woman," **Morrison** and his girlfriend Pamela Courson went to Paris, France, in March 1971. On July 3, Courson found him dead in the bathtub of their apartment. Heart failure was listed as the official cause of death, although there was no autopsy performed since it was not required under French law and there were no signs of foul play.

The syndicated television program *Night Flight* contends that French aristocrat Jean de Breteuil was responsible for the deaths of Joplin and Morrison. He was a heroin dealer who allegedly sold extra strong China White heroin to Joplin and Morrison.

British singer/actress Marianne Faithfull, who was de Breteuil's girlfriend at the time, said in an interview with *Mojo Magazine* that her boyfriend was at Morrison's home the day he died. De Breteuil also sold heroin to Courson, she said.

Morrison had become known for his heavy consumption of alcoholic beverages, but his heroin habit was not well known. He was buried in Pére Lachaise Cemetery in Paris.

Hendrix, Joplin and Morrison all were 27 years old at the time of their deaths.

"Shooting Star" is a cautionary tale of what the rock and roll lifestyle can lead to, with touring, partying and various kinds of excesses (pills, booze, marijuana, etc.)

The song never was released as a single in the United States, but it appears on all of the band's greatest hits compilations.

Shooting Star

Songwriter: Paul Rodgers

Included on the album "Straight Shooter"

Peaked at No. 3 on Billboard 200

May 31, 1975

Bad Company

Paul Rodgers (Dec. 17, 1949-) vocals, keyboards, guitar

Simon Kirke (July 28, 1949-) drums, vocals

Mick Ralphs (March 31, 1944-) guitar, keyboards, vocals

Boz Burrell (Aug. 1, 1946-Sept. 21, 2006) bass, guitar, vocals

Formed in London, England, in 1973

Bad Company: Mick Ralphs, Paul Rodgers, Simon Kirke, Boz Burrell

Life's Been Good [Joe Walsh] – Joe Walsh wrote and recorded this song in 1978, when he had been a member of the Eagles for two years. At that time, the Eagles were still touring in support of the "Hotel California" LP and had not yet started the sessions that would produce the 1979 album "The Long Run."

"Life's Been Good" first appeared on the soundtrack of the movie *FM.*

Walsh attended Kent State University in Ohio and settled in Colorado after college.

The song also was contained in Walsh's solo album "But Seriously, Folks ..." Walsh appears on the cover, fully dressed at the bottom of a swimming pool, eating a meal underwater, which cemented his reputation as clown prince of rock (one of his nicknames). His other album titles included "The Smoker You Drink, The Player You Get" and "You Can't Argue With A Sick Mind."

This song takes a cynical, yet humorous look at the life of a typical rock star of the day and pokes fun at Walsh himself. Some of the things he says that he does, like "live in hotels, tear out the walls" were done by musicians like Keith Moon of the Who. He regularly trashed hotel rooms while on tour and was banned from the Holiday Inn chain for life after he drove his car into a hotel's swimming pool.

Walsh plays great rock guitar solos on the intro, middle and end of the track. The call and response lines at the end of the second and third verses feature producer Bill Szymczyk (call) and Walsh's future wife Jody Boyer (response).

The unusual keyboard sound on the instrumental break that accompanies Walsh's guitar came from an ARP synthesizer.

In 1979 the *Rolling Stone Record Guide* called the song "riotous" and "(maybe) the most important statement on rock stardom anyone has made in the late '70s."

An edited 4½-minute version of the song peaked at No. 12 on *Billboard's Hot 100* in the summer of 1978. The album version runs 8:04.

Life's Been Good

Songwriter: Joe Walsh

Peaked at No. 12 on Billboard Hot 100

Aug. 12, 1978

Aug. 19, 1978

Joe Walsh

Born Joseph Fidler in Wichita, Kan., on Nov. 20, 1947. At age 5 he took his adoptive stepfather's last name after his father was killed in a plane crash.

Joe Walsh

Old Time Rock & Roll [Bob Seger] – How do you increase the popularity of a great song without re-recording it? Wait a few years and insert it into a motion picture!

This rock standard was doing just fine as a popular part of Bob Seger's 1978 album "Stranger In Town." As the fourth single released from that LP, it attained a peak position of No. 28 on the *Billboard Hot 100* in 1979. It got a lion's share of airplay on album-oriented rock radio stations.

Then came the movie *Risky Business* in 1983, where "Old Time Rock & Roll" was featured in a memorable scene with Tom Cruise doing a lip sync number in a long-sleeved shirt and his tidy whities. The single got a new life and recharted at No. 48.

The lyrics take a fond look back at rock as a link to the narrator's past, as he accepts no substitutes from other genres to satisfy his need for music. It's the kind of dying devotion that songwriters expressed in the first decade of the rock era.

Seger's recording became so iconic that it was included as one of the "Songs of the Century," a list of treasured music from the 20th century as compiled by the Recording Industry Association of America, the National Endowment for the Arts and Scholastic Inc.

George Jackson and Thomas Jones are the credited songwriters. Seger polished up the lyrics but took no writing credit or royalties.

According to the *Songfacts* website, Seger said he was feeling generous at the time and that not claiming writing credit was "the dumbest thing I ever did." Seger claims he altered all of the original lyrics except the words in the title.

Old Time Rock & Roll

Songwriters: George Jackson, Thomas E. Jones III
Peaked at No. 28 on Billboard Hot 100
May 26, 1979
June 2, 1979

Bob Seger & the Silver Bullet Band
Bob Seger (May 6, 1945-) lead vocals, guitar, piano
David Teegarden (Nov. 15, 1945-) drums
Drew Abbott (Jan. 13, 1947-) guitar
Rick Manasa (Aug. 7, 1950-) keyboards
Alto Reed (May 16, 1948-) saxophone, flute
Chris Campbell (DOB unavailable) bass
Formed in 1974

Bob Seger (lower right) & the Silver Bullet Band

It's Still Rock And Roll To Me [Billy Joel] – A native of Hicksville, Long Island, N.Y., Billy Joel wrote and recorded the song in 1980.

As a teen he was an amateur boxer, winning 22 Golden Gloves bouts. He left the sport after his nose was broken during his 24th match.

It wasn't until his fifth album ("The Stranger," 1977) that Joel garnered national attention.

Two albums later he released "Glass Houses." Joel had taken flack in the press for cranking out "middle-of-the-road trash" so, being the fighter that he was, he struck back with his seventh album. The cover photo shows Joel's own house in Cove Neck, NY, which has a two-story front glass façade. Joel is standing a few feet away holding a sizeable rock with his arm cocked and ready to throw. The unspoken message to the media: people who live in glass houses shouldn't throw stones.

In 2014 Joel told radio host Howard Stern, "Sometimes the press gave me a hard time, and I liked giving them a hard time back. In my neighborhood, (if) somebody hits you, you hit them right back."

The album featured a harder edge with more pure rock songs than its predecessors. However, "It's Still Rock And Roll" has a quiet tone with emphasis on the lyrics. A raucous saxophone solo on the break by Richie Cannata is the loudest part.

The lyrics are laid out in the form of a dialogue between Joel and his manager. Joel believed that the current changes that had come to pop music in the form of punk, funk, new wave, etc., were likeable, but not anything new. They merely were a variation of the power pop that had been around since the 1960s. The fictional manager wants him to update his image to keep up with a changing scene, but Joel prefers to retain substance over style because his music is still relevant.

The "Miracle Mile" lyric refers to a mile-long stretch of road in Manhasset, Long Island, which features numerous stores near Joel's hometown.

The song occupied the No. 1 position on *Billboard's Hot 100* for two weeks and spent 11 weeks in the top 10. It was the first of three No. 1 songs by the artist known as "The Piano Man."

It's Still Rock And Roll To Me

Songwriter: Billy Joel

Peaked at No. 1 on Billboard Hot 100

July 19, 1980

July 26, 1980

Billy Joel

Born William Martin Joel in the Bronx, N.Y., on May 9, 1949

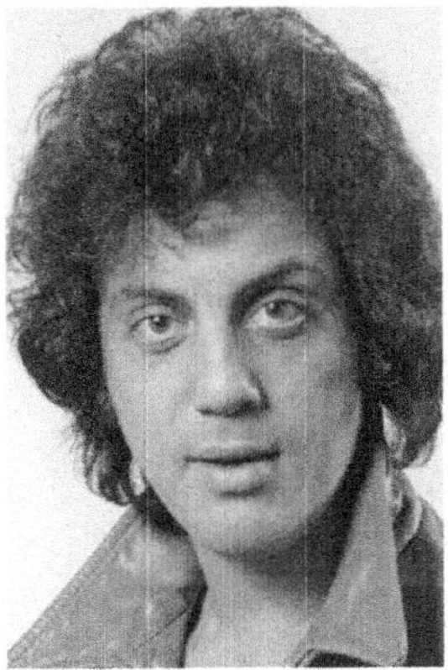

Billy Joel

I Wanna Rock [Twisted Sister] – Sure, the lyrics to this 1980s hair band classic are shallow. But, in a way, that's good. The title and its stark message are repeated many times throughout the song in a way that cuts through the clutter.

Twisted Sister saw their other notable single, "We're Not Gonna Take It," have a better chart performance, but this one gave rock fans a head-banger to hang their hats on.

Twisted Sister represented the hair band sub-genre well. The musicians not only had oversized hairdos but also used facial makeup and played heavy metal music. Such bands were an outgrowth of the 1970s glam rock movement.

"I Wanna Rock" was written by Twisted's front man, Dee Snider, who did most of band's writing. Snider described the thought process behind the song to *Songfacts* this way:

"'I Wanna Rock' was designed when I realized that Iron Maiden was having tremendous success with their sort of galloping metal rhythms, and then there was the anthemic thing that I like to do, which bands like AC/DC do, and one of my biggest influences … Slade. I thought that if I could combine the drive of a Maiden song with the anthemic quality of an AC/DC song, I'd have a (expletive) huge hit. And I was right."

The annals of the *Billboard Hot 100* don't indicate that the hit was outrageously huge, but it did peak at No. 68 for two weeks during a seven-week stay on the chart.

Surprisingly, the creators of *The SpongeBob SquarePants Movie* asked Snyder if they could use "I

Wanna Rock" at the end of the film. "I immediately lit up – licensing is fantastic!" Snider told *Blabbermouth.net.* There was only one stipulation – they wanted to change the song title to "Goofy Goober Rock." Snider was offered a lot of money, and he agreed.

The song also got prominent exposure in a TV advertisement for Facebook Groups during Super Bowl LIV in 2020.

The record found a friendly fan base in South Africa, where it charted at No. 3. In Norway it peaked at No. 5. In 2009, the VH1 TV network rated "I Wanna Rock" No. 17 on its list of 100 Greatest Hard Rock Songs.

I Wanna Rock

Songwriter: Dee Snider

Peaked at No. 68 on Billboard Hot 100

Nov. 10, 1984

Nov. 17, 1984

Twisted Sister

Daniel "Dee" Snider (March 15, 1955-) lead vocals

Eddie "Fingers" Ojeda (Aug. 5, 1955-) guitar, backing vocals

Jay Jay French (July 20, 1952-) guitar, backing vocals

Mark "The Animal" Mendoza (July 13, 1956-) bass, backing vocals

A.J. Pero (Oct. 14, 1959-March 20, 2015) drums, backing vocals

Formed in Ho-Ho-Kus, N.J., as Silver Star in 1972

Twisted Sister: Jay Jay French, Eddie Ojeda, Dee Snider, A.J. Pero, Mark Mendoza

Chapter 2

Rockin' Devotional

Songs with Biblical, Christian or spiritual themes

Overview: Starting with the infancy of rock, songs with spiritual themes started coming out of recording studios. It may have taken until the 1960s for them to establish a presence on the charts, but obviously there was a thirst among listeners for this kind of music.

To quench this thirst, some of the biggest names in the business stepped up and recorded many of those songs. Some were even written by the artists themselves.

Over time, there have been musical references to God and religion, but some songs were outright religious. There also is a strong connection between rock, pop, blues and gospel.

George Harrison, the quiet Beatle who had the most interest in spirituality, is represented in this chapter with two songs.

The charts bear witness that the songs were well received, and they live on today as inspirations that happen to be wrapped in very enjoyable melodies.

To view the full lyrics to these songs, please log on to www.google.com, enter song titles & artist names and click Google Search.

To listen to these songs, please log on to www.youtube.com and enter song titles & artist names.

Shadrack [Brook Benton] – Robert MacGimsey wrote this song in the 1930s. It was recorded by other musicians, such as Louis Armstrong, the Ames Brothers, Benny Goodman, Kay Starr, Phil Harris and Louis Prima.

The song is a retelling of Chapter 3 from the Book of Daniel, in which three godly immigrants, Shadrach, Meshach and Abednego, were persecuted in Babylon for not worshipping an idol, as the king had ordered. In the end, their unshakeable faith saved them from a fiery death.

Brook Benton's handling of the arrangement is pure gospel, with a choir providing backing vocals.

Originally from South Carolina, Benton moved to New York City at the age of 17 to perform with gospel groups and seek a career as a songwriter. Along the way, he became a solo vocal artist, too, and had many hit records on the R&B, pop, easy listening and Christmas music charts.

His last big pop chart success came in 1970 with the song "Rainy Night In Georgia," which peaked at No. 4.

Shadrack
Songwriter: Robert MacGimsey
Peaked at No. 19 on Billboard Hot 100
Feb. 17, 1962

Brook Benton

Sept. 19, 1931-April 9, 1988

Born Benjamin Franklin Peay in Lugoff, S.C., and died of pneumonia in New York City, having been weakened by spinal meningitis

Brook Benton

Crying In The Chapel [Elvis Presley] – This slow-paced gem was written by Artie Glenn in 1953 for his son Darrell to sing. Darrell recorded it with Artie's band the Rhythm Riders, and the single went to *Billboard* No. 6. Many cover versions were made that same year.

Elvis Presley recorded it on Oct. 30, 1960, for his gospel album "His Hand In Mine." But RCA held the song off the album and eventually released it as an Easter Special single in April 1965. In Britain, the single reached No. 1 for two weeks. It also was included as a bonus track on Presley's 1967 gospel album "How Great Thou Art."

The lyrics provide encouragement for prayer, which can lead to God's intervention in solving our problems.

The song soared to No. 3 and cemented Presley as a presence in the gospel music field. Presley had five albums appear on the *Billboard Top Christian Albums* chart. Before that chart was created, he placed four gospel albums on the *Billboard 200.*

Crying In The Chapel

Songwriter: Artie Glenn

Peaked at No. 3 on Billboard Hot 100

June 12, 1965

Elvis Presley

Jan. 8, 1935-Aug. 16, 1977

Born Elvis Aron Presley in Tupelo, Miss., and died in Memphis, Tenn.

Elvis Presley

Turn! Turn! Turn! (To Everything There Is A Season) [Byrds] – The lyrics of this song come from Ecclesiastes 3:1-8 and were turned into a song by folk artist Pete Seeger in the late 1950s. It was originally released on the Limelighters' 1962 album "Folk Matinee" and then several months later on Seeger's album "The Bitter and the Sweet."

In the U.S., it holds the distinction of being the No. 1 song with the oldest lyrics. Ascribed to King Solomon, the Old Testament book goes back to at least the 10th century B.C.

The song is about cycles of life, with a time designated for everything.

One of the backing musicians of the Limelighters was Jim McGuinn, who later became known as Roger McGuinn, one of the founding members of the Byrds. McGuinn sang lead vocals and played Rickenbacker 12-string guitar on the recording.

Reportedly, it took the Byrds 78 takes to finish the track. It was embraced by the American public as a cry for peace as the Vietnam War was beginning to escalate. Rock music and its relationship to war will be discussed in a later chapter.

Turn! Turn! Turn! (To Everything There Is A Season)
Songwriter: Pete Seeger
Peaked at No. 1 on Billboard Hot 100
Dec. 4, 1965
Dec. 11, 1965
Dec. 18, 1965

The Byrds
Roger McGuinn (July 13, 1942-) vocals, guitar, banjo
Gene Clark (Nov. 17, 1944-May 24, 1991) guitar, harmonica, tambourine, vocals
David Crosby (Aug. 14, 1941-) guitar, keyboards, vocals
Michael Clarke (June 3, 46-Dec. 19, 1993) drums, percussion
Chris Hillman (Dec. 4, 1944-) bass, guitar, mandolin
Formed in Los Angeles, Calif., in 1964

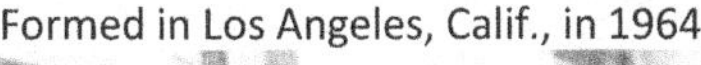

The Byrds: David Crosby, Chris Hillman, Roger McGuinn, Michael Clarke, Gene Clark

Oh Happy Day [Edwin Hawkins Singers] – Recorded in 1967 at the Ephesian Church of God in Christ in Berkeley, Calif., this is a gospel arrangement of an 18th century hymn. Edwin Hawkins, leader of the group, adapted the lyrics of English clergyman Philip Doddridge and produced the recording.

Dorothy Combs Morrison is the lead singer in this vocal group, which easily could be called a choir. It features the classic gospel call and response, which is a staple in black churches.

Released as a single in spring 1969, it rose to No. 1 in France, Germany and Netherlands. It peaked at No. 4 on the American pop chart.

Oh Happy Day

Songwriter: Edwin Hawkins, based on an 18th century hymn by Philip Doddridge

Peaked at No. 4 on Billboard Hot 100

May 31, 1969

June 7, 1969

Edwin Hawkins

Aug. 19, 1943-Jan. 15, 2018

Born Edwin Reuben Hawkins in Oakland, Calif., died in Pleasanton, Calif., of pancreatic cancer

The Edwin Hawkins Singers

Crystal Blue Persuasion [Tommy James & the Shondells] – Tommy James and his band were becoming Christians at the time the song was written in 1969. In an interview, James said that guitarist Eddie Gray came up with a guitar riff, and Tommy and Mike Vale wrote the lyrics.

James said in an interview, "It's out of the Bible. The imagery was right out of Chapter 19 of the Book of Revelation, about the lake of crystal, and just what John sees. The imagery was just right there. Crystal blue persuasion, although those words aren't used together, is what the image meant to me."

Rev. 14:6 seems to contain words that appear in the song lyrics ("And I saw another angel flying through the heavens, carrying the everlasting good news to preach to those on earth – to every nation, tribe, language and people.")

Rev. 21:10-27 talks about a vision in which the city of Jerusalem appears to glow like a precious gem, crystal clear like jasper. The city's foundation stones were inlaid with various gems: jasper, sapphire, chalcedony, emerald, sardonyx, sardus, chrysolite, beryl, topaz, chrysoprase, jacinth and amethyst.

The words "it's a new vibration" refers to James's budding Christian faith. Some observers incorrectly interpreted the words to contain drug references, such as crystal meth.

James: "Oh course, everybody thinks if they don't understand what you're talking about, that it must be about drugs. But it wasn't. We were going through an interesting time back then, and a very wonderful time. Everybody in the band, by the way, became Christian. And we're very proud of it. And 'Crystal Blue Persuasion' was sort of our way of saying that in a kind of pop record way."

According to James's manager, Tommy actually was inspired by the Book of Ezekiel, which he remembered speaking of a blue Shekhinah light that represented the Almighty God, and the Book of Isaiah and the Book of Revelation, which tell of a future age of brotherhood mankind, living in peace and harmony. However, the term Shekhinah is from rabbinic literature and does not occur in the Bible.

Ezekiel Chapter 10 mentions a throne of blue sapphire and "the court of the Temple was filled with the brightness of the glory of the Lord."

Crystal Blue Persuasion
Songwriters: Eddie Gray, Tommy James, Ritchie Cordell
Peaked at No. 2 on Billboard Hot 100
July 26, 1969
Aug. 2, 1969
Aug. 9, 1969

Tommy James & the Shondells
Tommy James (April 29, 1947-) vocals, guitar, tambourine
Eddie Gray (Feb. 27, 1948-) guitar
Peter Lucia (Feb. 2, 1947-Jan. 6, 1997) drums
Ron Rosman (Feb. 28, 1945-) keyboards
Mike Vale (July 17, 1949-) bass
Formed in Niles, Mich., in 1964

The Shondells: Peter Lucia, Mike Vale, Tommy James, Ron Rosman, Eddie Gray

That's The Way God Planned It [Billy Preston] – Having started piano at the age of 3, Billy Preston was a marvelously gifted musician. The Beatles thought so, as they had him contribute to some of their songs – even giving him artist credits.

This song was his first release on the Beatles' Apple label and preceded two No. 1 singles he would record in the 1970s. Apple press officer Derek Taylor, writing in the liner notes for the album "That's The Way God Planned It," said, "(Preston is) the best thing that happened to Apple this year. He's young and beautiful and kind, and he sings and plays like the son of God."

Preston, speaking at a fan convention in 1996, said that his inspiration for the song was Paul McCartney's "Let It Be."

The lyrics lay out some platitudes that Preston feels we should fulfill because it is God's will. The message was well received in the U.K., where the single reached No. 11 on the charts. On the *Billboard Hot 100,* it peaked at No. 62.

In 1979, Preston said in an interview that the success of the song in North America was cramped by Apple's lack of promotional experience. The label had been formed in 1968. "At that time, the company didn't really know how to promote – because you didn't have to promote a Beatle record."

The album version of the song runs 5 minutes 34 seconds, but the single was shortened to 3:22.

Sharon Davis, writing for *Blues & Soul Magazine,* said the song "really elevated Billy into the mainstream record market, bringing to the fore his remarkable pedigree."

In a 1975 interview with Andy Davis, Preston said, "I've never asked anybody to help me or give me a break. What I don't have now I believe will come. Why? I have to say it's God – the God in me."

Preston's life was one of paradoxes. As a musician he was entirely self-taught. He played organ behind Mahalia Jackson's gospel singing at age 10. He joined Little Richard's band as an organist in 1962, and he first met the Beatles in Hamburg, Germany, while on tour that year.

He was a devout Christian who later had bouts with alcohol and cocaine addiction. According to his manager, Joyce Moore, he was sexually abused as a boy when he was part of the touring production of *Amos 'n' Andy*.

Preston was devastated when his fiancée, Kathy Silva, left him for Sylvester Stewart, aka Sly Stone, whom she later wed in Madison Square Garden during a concert. This trauma apparently resulted in his homosexuality, which he kept secret until just before his death in 2006.

Suffering from chronic kidney disease brought on by hypertension, he received a kidney transplant in 2002. His health, however, continued to deteriorate. He was in a coma for over six months before he died at the age of 59.

That's The Way God Planned It
Songwriter: Billy Preston
Peaked at No. 62 on Billboard Hot 100
Aug. 23, 1969

Billy Preston
Sept. 2, 1946-June 6, 2006
Born William Everett Preston in Houston, Texas, and died in Scottsdale, Ariz.

Billy Preston

Jesus Is A Soul Man [Lawrence Reynolds] – Performed and co-written by Lawrence Reynolds, it was released in late summer of 1969. The title was a take-off of Sam & Dave's 1967 hit song "Soul Man," the lyrics of which tell why the singer(s) is a soul man. Example: "Got what I got the hard way, and I make it better each and every day."

In his version, Reynolds labels Jesus as a soul man in a different way, because Jesus dwells within us spiritually and has offered us salvation for our souls through His sacrifice on the cross.

Reynolds was a country music singer from Alabama, and this song was his only foray onto the pop music charts. It peaked at No. 28 on the *Billboard Hot 100*.

It got heavy rotation on Chicago's WLS radio playlist, however, spending seven weeks in the top 40 and reaching a peak position of No. 11 on Oct. 13 and 20, 1969, on the *Silver Dollar Survey*.

The song was adapted into several musical genres by other artists, such as Conway Twitty and Johnny Rivers.

Jesus Is A Soul Man
Songwriters: Lawrence Reynolds, Jack Cardwell
Peaked at No. 28 on Billboard Hot 100
Nov. 1, 1969

Lawrence Reynolds
July 13, 1944-Aug. 15, 2000
Born Lawrence Reynolds in St. Stephens, Ala., and died of coronary artery disease

Lawrence Reynolds

Spirit In The Sky [Norman Greenbaum] – Norman Greenbaum, an orthodox Jew, wrote and recorded this declaration of faith in heaven in late 1969.

He was inspired to write it after watching country music icon Porter Wagoner sing a gospel song on TV. "I thought, yeah, I could do that, knowing nothing about gospel music, so I sat down and wrote my own gospel song. It came easy. I wrote the words in 15 minutes."

The song's arrangement came in a studio in San Francisco. Greenbaum used a Fender Telecaster guitar with a fuzz box built into the body to achieve the signature sound. The total result was a melding of gospel and psychedelic rock with heavy drums, hand claps and tambourine. An Oakland-based gospel trio, the Stovall Sisters, did backing vocals.

Because of the unusual lyrics and style, Reprise Records (Greenbaum's label) was reluctant to release it. But after two other singles from the same album had poor sales, it was issued on 45 rpm in late winter 1970.

Greenbaum's lack of knowledge of an essential tenet of Christianity – that everyone is born a sinner – caused some controversy in the song's last verse. "You know, I flubbed that part," he said when someone asked him about that verse. "So what are you going to do?"

The song has been used in some 30 movies, and it's played at Angel Stadium when the Los Angeles Angels' starting lineup is announced before home baseball games.

Spirit In The Sky

Songwriter: Norman Greenbaum

Peaked at No. 3 on Billboard Hot 100

April 18, 1970
April 25, 1970
May 2, 1970

Norman Greenbaum

Born Norman Joel Greenbaum in Malden, Mass., on Nov. 20, 1942

Norman Greenbaum

Everything Is Beautiful [Ray Stevens] – Ray Stevens was primarily a writer of novelty/comedy songs, but in 1970 he wrote and recorded an inspirational song that praises God's creations.

The opening Sunday school verse was sung by children from Oak Hill Elementary School in Nashville, which includes Stevens's two daughters.

The record hit No. 1 and earned Stevens a 1971 Grammy Award for Best Male Pop Vocal Performance. Its lyrics would be very relevant today, as they deliver a message of racial equality and tolerance.

Until 1981, Stevens' first hit single in 1961 held the *Billboard* chart record for longest song title for 20 years: "Jeremiah Peabody's Polyunsaturated Quick-Dissolving Fast-Acting Pleasant-Tasting Green And Purple Pills."

In '81 the Dutch band Stars on 45 had a No. 1 hit with this record-breaking title: "Medley: Intro "Venus" - Sugar Sugar - No Reply - I'll Be Back - Drive My Car - Do You Want To Know A Secret - We Can Work It Out - I Should Have Known Better - Nowhere Man - You're Going To Lose That Girl."

Stevens was back at his comedic best in 1974 when he had another No. 1 hit, "The Streak," which was inspired by the fad of streaking.

Everything Is Beautiful

Songwriter: Ray Stevens

Peaked at No. 1 on Billboard Hot 100

May 30, 1970
June 6, 1970

Ray Stevens

Born Harold Ray Ragsdale in Clarkdale, Ga., on Jan. 24, 1939

Ray Stevens

My Sweet Lord [George Harrison] – The song was George Harrison's first single release following the break-up of the Beatles. In America, it was the first No. 1 song by an ex-Beatle, and it was No. 1 worldwide. In the U.K. it was the top-selling single of 1971.

The song was written in praise of the Hindu god Krishna. But the lyrics served as a call to abandon religious sectarianism by deliberately alternating the Hebrew word *hallelujah* with chants of *Hare Krishna*. The lyrics reflect Harrison's oft-stated desire for a direct relationship with God, expressed in simple words that all believers could affirm, regardless of their religion. Harrison himself did not belong to any religious organization.

Phil Spector was the producer, and Ringo Starr, Eric Clapton and "Fifth Beatle" Billy Preston appeared on the recording. "Isn't It A Pity" was the flip side, issued as a double-A side. A double-A side is a single on which both sides are promoted by the record company. In this case, it was Apple Records. Normally, a single has an A side and a B side, with the B side receiving no promotion. "Isn't It A Pity" ranked No. 1 with "My Sweet Lord" all four weeks.

Harrison used his popular slide guitar technique for the first time. He also provided backing vocals through the use of overdubbing.

A few years later the song was embroiled in controversy as the centerpiece of a copyright infringement lawsuit. Bright Tunes music publishing company claimed it had too much similarity to the 1963 hit "He's So Fine," sung by the Chiffons and written by Ronnie Mack (who died shortly after the record hit the charts). In 1976 a U.S. District Court in New York found Harrison guilty of "subconscious plagiarism," and he was forced to pay Bright Tunes $1,599,987 from the earnings of "My Sweet Lord" and the albums "All Things Must Pass" and "Best of George Harrison."

"I wasn't consciously aware of the similarity between 'He's So Fine' and 'My Sweet Lord' when I wrote the song, as it was more improvised and not so fixed," Harrison wrote in his autobiography *I Me Mine*. "Although when *my* version of the song came out and started to get a lot of airplay, people started talking about it, and it was then I thought, 'Why didn't I realize?' It would have been very easy to change a note here or there, and not affect the feeling of the record."

Harrison added, "I was inspired by the Edwin Hawkins' Singers' version of 'Oh Happy Day.'"

My Sweet Lord

Songwriter: George Harrison

Peaked at No. 1 on Billboard Hot 100

Dec. 26, 1970

Jan. 2, 1971

Jan. 9, 1971

Jan. 16, 1971

George Harrison

Feb. 25, 1943-Nov. 29, 2001

Born in Liverpool, England, and died in Los Angeles, Calif., of lung cancer that had spread to his brain

George Harrison

Put Your Hand In The Hand [Ocean] – This invitation to accept Jesus Christ was written by Canadian singer-songwriter Gene MacLellan, who was born in Quebec, raised in Toronto and eventually settled on Prince Edward Island.

Apparently suffering from depression, he committed suicide days before his 57th birthday in 1995. He had suffered from polio and a heart condition as a child, and he'd survived several car crashes. As an adult he had a failed marriage, but he reinvented himself as a gospel singer in the 1980s, performing in churches and prisons.

He was posthumously inducted into the Canadian Songwriters Hall of Fame.

The song first was recorded for Anne Murray's third album. It was the first hit song for Ocean, a quintet from Toronto. The song reached No. 2 in the U.S. and No. 10 in Canada. They never had another top 40 song in the U.S.

Ocean benefitted from huge sales of the record, but the band didn't "walk the walk" since the members didn't have a personal connection to the lyrics. In the book *Axes, Chops and Hot Licks,* keyboardist Greg Brown stated, "We were concerned that (releasing the song as a single) might give the group a gospel image."

And he was right. Ocean was pigeon-holed as a gospel rock band.

Put Your Hand In The Hand

Songwriter: Gene MacLellan

Peaked at No. 2 on Billboard Hot 100

May 1, 1971

Ocean

Greg Brown – vocals, keyboards
Jeff Jones – bass, vocals
Janice Morgan – vocals, guitar
Dave Tamblyn – guitar
Chuck Slater – drums
Formed in Toronto, Ontario, Canada, in 1970

Ocean

Mighty Clouds Of Joy [B.J. Thomas] – Billy Joe Thomas recorded in pop, country and gospel genres. He was raised in and around Houston, Texas. His first hit single was a cover of Hank Williams' "I'm So Lonesome I Could Cry" in 1966.

"Mighty Clouds of Joy" was his 22nd single release and was contained on his "Greatest Hits Volume Two." It represents a marriage of pop and gospel music and has a message of hope and redemption. On the U.S. adult contemporary chart, it attained a position of No. 8.

Four years after "Mighty Clouds Of Joy" climbed the charts, Thomas and his wife, Gloria Richardson, became Christians. Thomas had ended his dependency on drugs and alcohol, which helped save his marriage.

In 1996 Thomas released "Home Where I Belong," the first of his gospel albums. It was the first Christian album to earn platinum status (at least 1 million copies sold), which established him as the top contemporary Christian artist of the period.

Mighty Clouds Of Joy

Songwriters: Buddy Buie, Robert Nix

Peaked at No. 34 on Billboard Hot 100

Aug. 21, 1971
Aug. 28, 1971

B.J. Thomas
Born Billy Joe Thomas in Hugo, Okla., on Aug. 7, 1942

B.J. Thomas

Day By Day [Godspell] – The words are ascribed to 13th century English bishop Saint Richard of Chichester: *May I know Thee more clearly, Love Thee more dearly, Follow Thee more nearly.*

The simple prayer/song is from the 1971 musical *Godspell* and was sung by the original cast for the hit recording in 1972 and attributed to the group name of "Godspell." Robin Lamont was the lead singer.

It also was used in the 1973 film, which followed 1971's *Jesus Christ Superstar* in the God Rock musical/film genre.

An instrumental version was used as the theme music for NBC-TV's *Today Show* in the 1970s.

Day By Day
Songwriter: Stephen Schwartz
Peaked at No. 13 on Billboard Hot 100
July 29, 1972
Aug. 5, 1972

Godspell lead singer
Born Robin Lamont in Boston, Mass., on June 2, 1950

Robin Lamont

Speak To The Sky [Rick Springfield] – Rick Springfield was born in a suburb of Sydney, Australia. He learned guitar at age 13 and joined various bands in England, where his father was stationed 1958-1963 with the Australian Army. Rick moved to Hollywood, Calif., in 1972.

According to an interview in 2000, he said, "I was 17 when I wrote that. I think I was leaning toward a country (music) career."

In 1984 he commented, "It was just a song I wrote because my mother said, 'Why don't you write a happy song, Son?' I'd been writing all this stuff about suicide and love triads, and so I wrote a happy song." The lyrics offer encouragement to pray.

He was raised in the Church of England. In 2014 he remarked, "My concept of God goes through changes daily. I'm still very Christian."

Springfield's recording career kicked into high gear in 1981 with the No. 1 single "Jessie's Girl," for which he won a Grammy Award. He also forged a successful career as a television actor, originating the role of Dr. Noah Drake on *General Hospital.* He also has made guest appearances as an actor on other TV shows.

Speak To The Sky
Songwriter: Rick Springfield
Peaked at No. 14 on Billboard Hot 100
Oct. 7, 1972
Oct. 14, 1972

Rick Springfield
Born Richard Lewis Springthorpe in Balmain, Australia, on Aug. 23, 1949

Rick Springfield

Jesus Is Just Alright [Doobie Brothers] – This song of praise for the Savior was written by Arthur Reid Reynolds and was first recorded by his group The Art Reynolds Singers for their 1966 album "Tellin' It Like It Is." The 1960s slang term "alright" was used to mean cool, hip or very good.

The song was covered several times, including a version by the Byrds in 1969 (stalled at No. 97). It was contained on the Doobie Brothers' breakthrough album "Toulouse Street" in 1972 and featured an arrangement that was close to that of the Byrds'.

None of the Doobie Brothers' individuals were religiously inclined, but the song gained favor among Christians during the early 1970s, particularly those within the hippie counterculture who were involved with the Jesus movement. In this presentation, Jesus may be viewed as more of a cult leader than a savior.

The song was produced by Ted Templeman, who continued to produce Doobie Brothers music into the 1980s, along with stars like Van Halen, Carly Simon, Sammy Hagar, Van Morrison, Aerosmith and Eric Clapton.

Jesus Is Just Alright
Songwriter: Arthur Reid Reynolds
Peaked at No. 35 on Billboard Hot 100
Feb. 24, 1973

Doobie Brothers
Tom Johnston (Aug. 15, 1948-) vocals, guitar, harmonica
Patrick Simmons (Oct. 19, 1948-) vocals, guitar, piano, flute
Tiran Porter (Sept. 26, 1948-) bass, vocals
John Hartman (March 18, 1950-) drums, percussion
Michael Hossack (Oct. 17, 1946-March 12, 2012) drums
Formed in San Jose, Calif., in 1970

Doobie Brothers: Michael Hossack, Patrick Simmons, Tom Johnston, Tiran Porter, John Hartman

Give Me Love (Give Me Peace On Earth) [George Harrison] – This is the second solo hit by George Harrison that has a religious theme. Like the first ("My Sweet Lord"), the words are addressed directly to God. It is contained on his 1973 album "Living In The Material World."

When the song knocked the Paul McCartney song "My Love" from No. 1 to No. 2 on the *Billboard Hot 100* on June 30, 1973, it was the only time that two former Beatles occupied the top two spots during the same week in America.

Harrison produced the recording, which showed a marked departure from the complex sounds of his earlier solo albums produced by Phil Spector and demonstrated a scaled-back, simpler approach. He also played a series of slide guitar solos on the track, which was becoming his trademark technique.

He described the song as "a prayer and personal statement between me, the Lord, and whoever likes it." The writing of it followed Harrison's work in 1971-72 with assisting refugees of the Bangladesh Liberation War.

In his lyrics, Harrison expresses his vision for life in the physical world. Following the opening instrumental passage, the song begins with a chorus in which he first pleads for a life without the karmic burden of rebirth, or reincarnation. "Give me love, give me love, give me peace on earth / Give me light, give me life, keep me free from birth."

As stated in *Wikipedia,* these lyrics bear a simple, universal message, one that, in the context of the day, related as much to the "peace and love" idealism of the 1960s as it did to Harrison's personal spiritual journey.

Give Me Love (Give Me Peace On Earth)
Songwriter: George Harrison
Peaked at No. 1 on Billboard Hot 100
June 30, 1973

George Harrison
Feb. 25, 1943-Nov. 29, 2001
Born in Liverpool, England, and died in Los Angeles, Calif.

George Harrison

The Lord's Prayer [Sister Janet Mead] – This unique song was recorded in 1973 by Australian nun Sister Janet Mead, to a melody written by Arnold Strals. She was known in her homeland for pioneering the use of contemporary rock music in celebrating Catholic mass and for her weekly radio programs. It could be considered a seed for what germinated into the genre known as contemporary Christian music.

After it reached No. 3 in Australia, it went on to become an international hit, selling nearly 3 million copies as it charted in Canada, Japan, Brazil, Germany and the U.S.

It was picked up for American distribution by A&M Records and was certified gold (1 million in sales). It entered the *Billboard Hot 100* on Feb. 23, 1974, and spent 13 weeks on the chart. It reached its peak position of No. 4 during Easter Week in April.

It became the only song to hit the top 10 whose entire lyrical content originated from the Bible, and the only top 10 hit whose words were attributed to Jesus Christ.

The song earned Mead a Grammy nomination for Best Inspirational Performance. She lost to Elvis Presley's "How Great Thou Art."

Sister Janet studied piano at Elder Conservatorium of music before joining the Sisters of Mercy order. She also taught music at Saint Aloysius College in Adelaide.

The Lord's Prayer
Songwriters: Jesus Christ, Arnold Strals
Peaked at No. 4 on Billboard Hot 100
April 13, 1974

Sister Janet Mead (also known as Sister Marietta)

Born Janet Mead in Adelaide, South Australia, in 1938

Sister Janet Mead

The Old Rugged Cross [Johnny Cash] – Johnny Cash was a Christian. He was arrested seven times for misdemeanors – and he conquered drug addiction – but his faith stayed with him for a lifetime.

In the introduction to his 1986 novel about the life of the Apostle Paul, "Man In White," he wrote, "Please understand that I believe the Bible, the whole Bible, to be the infallible, indisputable Word of God. I have been careful to take no liberties with the timeless Word."

He recorded 11 gospel albums throughout his stellar country/pop career.

Methodist evangelist George Bennard wrote "The Old Rugged Cross" over the span of several weeks as he traveled to revival meetings. In his memoirs he wrote, "I seemed to have a vision … I saw Christ and the cross as inseparable."

The melody came easily to him, but the words took him longer. He wrote the first verse in the fall of 1912 as a response to ridicule he received at a revival. He completed the refrain and three other verses between Dec. 29, 1912, and Jan. 12, 1913, in Sturgeon Bay, Wis. It was first published in 1915 and popularized by Billy Sunday in his evangelic campaigns and national radio broadcasts. Two members of his campaign staff, Homer Rodeheaver and Virginia Asher, are believed to be the first to record it in 1921.

Cash recorded the song four times for various albums, including duet versions with Jessi Colter and June Carter Cash.

He acted in seven movies and hosted his own television variety show on ABC 1969-1971. He hosted the television special "All My Friends Are Cowboys" in 1998. Eleven of his albums reached No. 1 on the *Billboard Country Chart.*

The Old Rugged Cross

Songwriter: George Bennard

Included on the album

"Johnny Cash Sings Precious Memories"

1975

Did not chart

Johnny Cash

Feb. 26, 1932-Sept. 12, 2003

Born J.R. Cash in Kingsland, Ark., and died of complications of diabetes in Nashville

Johnny Cash

What A Friend We Have In Jesus [Dolly Parton] – Irish-born Joseph Scriven wrote the words to this traditional hymn near Port Hope, Ontario, in 1855. His life was filled with difficulties, poor health forcing him to give up his ambition for a career in the army.

In 1844 his fiancée died in a drowning accident on the eve of their wedding. Looking for a new life as a teacher, he moved to Canada. But his plans for marriage were dashed once again when his bride-to-be died following a short illness. Scriven wrote this hymn to console his mother in Dublin.

According to *Wikipedia,* Scriven originally published it anonymously in Horace Hastings' 1865 "Social Hymns, Original and Selected." Charles Crozat Converse, a U.S. attorney who also worked as a composer of church songs, set the words to music three years later. Scriven finally received credit for the hymn in Hastings' 1886 "Songs Of Pilgrimage," but the same year he drowned in Rice Lake.

Dolly Parton is a Christian, and she has said, "God is in everything I do, and all my work glorifies Him." She recorded the song at a concert in her amusement park, Dollywood.

She hosted the syndicated television variety show "Dolly!" in 1976-77, as well as a similar show, "Dolly" in 1987-88. She has acted in movie and TV roles.

Parton had two pop No. 1 singles: "9 To 5" and "Islands In The Stream."

What A Friend We Have In Jesus

Songwriters: Joseph M. Scriven, Charles C. Converse

Included on the album

"Heartsongs: Live From Home" recorded on stage at Dollywood

Peaked at No. 87 on Billboard 200

Oct. 29, 1994

Dolly Parton

Born Dolly Rebecca Parton in Locust Ridge, Tenn., on Jan. 19, 1946

Dolly Parton

Chapter 3

Reality meets pop

Songs that feature real people, places or events

Overview: Writing a song can be hard. But for a songwriter to take a real person, place or event and write a song that stays true to the facts – that's got to be even harder.

Several such songs have shown up on the charts over the years. They are marvelous in the way that they incorporate reality in the lyrics, and their chart success is a testament to that.

What a great songwriter will do is stick to historical facts and minimize the use of poetic license. Some of the songs in this chapter will include fantasy along with reality, and that's all right because music is, after all, entertainment.

One song that you'll read about is "We're An American Band." It provides a glimpse into the seldom-seen world of a band on tour, after hours. I think a lot of music fans appreciated that, since most of us get to see the musicians only when they're on stage.

When a catchy melody is applied to the lyrics, it makes for pure magic. Included here are some of the best reality-drenched songs I could find.

To view the full lyrics to these songs, please log on to www.google.com, enter song titles & artist names and click Google Search.

To listen to these songs, please log on to www.youtube.com and enter song titles & artist names.

Tom Dooley [Kingston Trio] – This highly revered folk song by the Kingston Trio of San Francisco spent one week atop the *Billboard Hot 100.* It was their only No. 1 song.

The song's true story is based on the 1866 murder of Laura Foster in North Carolina, allegedly by Tom Dula (pronounced "Dooley"). A local poet named Thomas Land wrote a song about the incident shortly after Dula was hanged on May 1, 1868.

The words that Land wrote were handed down through the years and were recorded with various changes to the original lyrics. It's safe to say that the Kingston Trio's version probably has its own quirks injected to make the song marketable.

Foster was stabbed to death with a large knife, and Confederate war veteran Dula was her lover and father of her unborn child. The case is somewhat complicated, but Dula made an enigmatic statement from the gallows, saying that he had not harmed Foster but still deserved punishment.

In the lyrics, arranged by Trio member Dave Guard, Dooley declares that he took the woman's life. This is just poetic license.

The man in the song named "Grayson" sometimes has been characterized as a romantic rival of Dula's (hence, the mention of the "eternal triangle") or a vengeful sheriff.

After the song hit No. 1, Dula's forgotten grave in North Carolina was restored, and steps were taken to give him an official pardon.

Tom Dooley

Songwriter: Thomas Land (arranged by Dave Guard)

Peaked at No. 1 on Billboard Hot 100

Nov. 17, 1958

Kingston Trio

Dave Guard (Oct. 19, 1934-March 22, 1991)
Bob Shane (Feb. 1, 1934-Jan. 26, 2020)
Nick Reynolds (July 27, 1933-Oct. 1, 2008)
Formed in Palo Alto, Calif., in 1954

Nick Reynolds, Dave Guard, Bob Shane

El Paso [Marty Robbins] – This song's fictional story takes place in a real town – El Paso, Texas – and it was the seventh top 40 hit for Marty Robbins on the pop charts and his only No. 1.

It was the longest song (4 minutes 40 seconds) to rank No. 1 at that time. It was so long that Columbia Records rejected Robbins' request to release it as a single. They mutually agreed to release it on the album "Gunfighter Ballads and Trail Songs." Public response to the song was so strong that label executives relented and released it as a single late in 1959.

The lyrics tell of an Old West gunslinger (in the first person) who falls in love with a beautiful young Mexican woman, Feleena, who is a dancer at Rosa's Cantina. When the narrator sees a handsome cowboy sharing a drink with Feleena, he goes into a jealous rage and challenges the stranger to a gunfight. The stranger draws first but isn't quick enough to avoid being hit by a fatal shot.

Fearing a charge of murder, or retribution from the cowboy's friends, the protagonist flees. Perhaps his only crime is stealing a horse from the hitching post behind the cantina – a hanging offense in the Old West.

Grady Martin played the signature Spanish guitar on the track. Bobby Sykes and Jim Glaser added backing harmonies.

The character of Feleena was inspired by a real person – the 5th grade schoolmate of Robbins named Fidelina Martinez. Robbins has said that he was fascinated by the city of El Paso and its name since he was a child, as it has been considered the beginning of the American West.

His career started out with producer Mitch Miller mentoring him as a pop singer, but he began to indulge his passion for Western music in 1959. While driving through El Paso from Nashville to Phoenix for the third time, he got the inspiration for his soon-to-be-famous song. By the time he arrived in Deming, N.M., he had finished the song in his head.

One of the lines sung by the protagonist is particularly poignant: "My love is stronger than my fear of death." This passion draws him out of hiding in the "badlands of New Mexico" to return to El Paso and be reunited with his beloved.

El Paso

Songwriter: Marty Robbins

Peaked at No. 1 on Billboard Hot 100

Jan. 4, 1960

Jan. 11, 1960

Marty Robbins

Sept. 26, 1925-Dec. 8, 1982

Born Martin David Robinson in Glendale, Ariz., and died in Nashville, Tenn., six days after undergoing quadruple coronary bypass surgery

Marty Robbins

Dead Man's Curve [Jan & Dean] – This action-filled song was written by Brian Wilson of the Beach Boys, Capitol Records vice president Artie Kornfeld, radio personality/lyricist Roger Christian and singer Jan Berry.

The lyrics tell the story of a late-night street race in Los Angeles between a young man driving a Corvette Sting Ray and another driving a Jaguar XK-E that ends in a horrific crash.

Real streets in the Los Angeles area are mentioned (Sunset, Vine, La Brea, Crescent Heights, Doheny), as well as the famous Schwab's Drug Store. Sound effects of screeching tires add some realism to the recording.

The song carried the banner for the "car song" genre that was popular in the early 1960s, following up Jan & Dean's "Drag City." It peaked at No. 8 on the *Billboard Hot 100* for two weeks in May 1964 and was No. 1 in Chicago for a week.

There is debate on the actual location of the curve mentioned in the song, but it could well have been the part of Sunset just past North Whittier Drive, where the pavement makes a turn of nearly 90 degrees.

The song foreshadowed Berry's own fate. He crashed his Corvette Sting Ray into a parked truck on Whittier near Dead Man's Curve on April 12, 1966, and suffered severe head injuries that put him in a coma for more than two months. His recovery from brain damage and partial paralysis took years and cost him virtually the rest of his music career. He died of a seizure on March 26, 2004, eight days before his 63rd birthday.

The duo met while they were students at Emerson Junior High School in Westwood, and they formed their musical alliance in 1958. After Jan's accident, Dean Torrence went on to become a successful graphic designer.

Dead Man's Curve

Songwriters: Brian Wilson, Artie Kornfeld, Roger Christian, Jan Berry

Peaked at No. 8 on Billboard Hot 100

May 9, 1964

May 16, 1964

Jan & Dean

Jan Berry

April 3, 1941-March 26, 2004

Born William Jan Berry in Los Angeles, Calif.

Dean Torrence

Born Dean Ormsby Torrence in Los Angeles, Calif., on March 10, 1940

Jan Berry & Dean Torrence

The Great Airplane Strike [Paul Revere & the Raiders] – One of the fun-loving bands of the 1960s, Paul Revere & the Raiders took a humorous look at a big labor dispute with this hit song.

On July 9, 1966, 35,400 members of the International Association of Machinists (IAM) went on strike against five airlines in the United States, crippling 60 percent of domestic air travel. United, Northwest, National, Eastern and Trans World were affected for 43 days.

To move into the jet age, airlines had invested in technology and equipment in the late 1950s and early '60s. During this time, workers such the IAM members had their wages frozen. Despite the highly skilled nature of their jobs, their wages lagged behind other industries.

Airlines were running "in the red" as late as 1964, but then the new jet technology began to pay off. Contract negotiations with the IAM stretched out for a year before the membership hit the picket lines at 230 airports. Some airlines leased planes to try to keep service going, but members of the Transport Workers Union (ground service workers, flight attendants, etc.) refused to work on any plane that was leased by their airline during the strike.

About 150,000 travelers per day were left scrambling for trains, buses and rental cars.

A proposal by President Lyndon Johnson for a raise of 4.5 percent for each of the next three years was rejected by the IAM by a margin of almost 3-to-1.

In Congress, the Senate passed a measure that would have ordered the unionists back to work. Before the House of Representatives could vote on the bill, the machinists agreed to a new contract with a 6 percent wage hike.

The debacle made good fodder for Revere, Mark Lindsay and Terry Melcher, who wrote the song about the hassles of traveling without normal airline service. Melcher also arranged and produced the recording, which climbed as high as No. 20 on the *Billboard Hot 100.*

The Great Airplane Strike
Songwriters: Paul Revere, Mark Lindsay, Terry Melcher
Peaked at No. 20 on Billboard Hot 100
Oct. 29, 1966

Paul Revere & the Raiders
Paul Revere (Jan. 7, 1938-Oct. 4, 2014) keyboards
Mark Lindsay (March 9, 1942-) lead vocals
Phil "Fang" Volk (Oct. 25, 1945-) bass
Michael "Smitty" Smith (March 27, 1942-March 6, 2001) drums
Jim "Harpo" Valley (March 13, 1943-) guitar
Drake "The Kid" Levin (Aug. 17, 1946-July 4, 2009) guitar, backing vocals
Formed in Boise, Idaho, in 1958

Paul Revere & the Raiders

Snoopy vs. The Red Baron [Royal Guardsmen] – German air warrior Manfred Albrecht Freiherr von Richthofen (May 2, 1892-April 21, 1918) is the real person in this song. The producer of the recording, Phil Gernhard, was one of the writers.

The storyline has comic strip dog Snoopy (of "Peanuts" fame) stopping the Red Baron's rampage during World War I, during which he downed 80 enemy planes for the German Luftwaffe. Von Richthofen was the ace of aces, but eventually he was shot down and killed at Moriancourt Ridge near Vaux-sur-Somme in northern France.

Freiherr is a title of nobility, often translated as "baron." He had his aircraft painted red, which led to the moniker of Red Baron.

The Royal Guardsmen, from Ocala, Fla., took their name from a model of Vox amplifier, the Royal Guardsman. They liked the name because it sounded British and they wanted to give the illusion of being part of the British Invasion, which started in 1964 and still had an impact on the rock music scene when they formed in 1965.

There is an organ riff after the fourth verse that mimics the melody of the McCoys' "Hang On Sloopy" from 1965 (see Chapter 8, Hard Times). This riff fueled speculation that the Royal Guardsmen actually were the McCoys, which is not true.

In the storyline of the comic strip, Snoopy took on the persona of a "World War I flying ace." He liked to sit on the roof of his doghouse, pretending it was a Sopwith Camel biplane. It's one of many fantasy identities that Snoopy adopted during the 50-year run of "Peanuts." The first such appearance was Oct. 10, 1965.

The first TV appearance of Snoopy as the WWI flying ace was Oct. 27, 1966, in the animated special "It's The Great Pumpkin, Charlie Brown." The Great Pumpkin was the Halloween equivalent of Santa Claus.

In the show, Linus Van Pelt writes his annual letter to the Great Pumpkin. While all the other kids are trick-or-treating on Oct. 31, Linus goes to the pumpkin patch to wait for the Great Pumpkin. When Linus sees a shadowy figure rising from the moonlit patch, he thinks the Great Pumpkin has arrived and he faints. It turns out to be Snoopy. Ultimately, Linus vows that the G.P. will come to the pumpkin patch next year. Linus is the only "Peanuts" character who believes in the Great Pumpkin.

The song struck a strong chord with pop music fans and spent an incredible four weeks at No. 2 on the *Billboard Hot 100.*

Snoopy vs. The Red Baron

Songwriters: Phil Gernhard, Dick Holler

Peaked at No. 2 on Billboard Hot 100

Dec. 31, 1966
Jan. 7, 1967
Jan. 14, 1967
Jan. 21, 1967

<u>The Royal Guardsmen</u>

Chris Nunley – vocals
Bill Balough – bass
John Burdett – drums
Tom Richards – guitar
Billy Taylor – keyboards
Barry Winslow – guitar, vocals
Formed in Ocala, Fla., in 1965

The Royal Guardsmen: Chris Nunley, Barry Winslow, Billy Taylor, John Burdett, Bill Balough, Tom Richards

Penny Lane [Beatles] – The lyrics of this song come straight from Paul McCartney's memories of sights, sounds and experiences he had as a lad growing up in Liverpool, England.

The title references a depot where youths like McCartney changed buses to access practically every part of the metropolis. The street Penny Lane runs through the southern suburb of Mossley Hill.

Writing of the song commenced late in 1966, and the song originally was targeted for inclusion in the album that would become "Sgt. Pepper's Lonely Hearts Club Band." However, the Beatles' British label, Parlophone, pressed the band for a single early in 1967, since they hadn't had one since late summer of '66. It became part of a Double A release along with "Strawberry Fields Forever." Meanwhile, writing and recording for "Sgt. Pepper" continued through spring of '67.

The two songs would not appear on an album until "Magical Mystery Tour" was released at the end of 1967.

John Lennon had penned a nostalgic piece about a year earlier, "In My Life," and this was McCartney's answer to that song.

According to the *Beatles Bible,* McCartney wrote the song in the music room at his London home, 7 Cavendish Ave., near Abbey Road Studios. It was composed on an upright piano which artist David Vaughan had painted in psychedelic rainbow patterns.

After McCartney got stuck while writing the third verse, Lennon stepped in to help. It is believed that Lennon contributed the line "four of fish and finger pies," which has a dual reference: a small serving (fourpence) of fish and chips, and the act of teen boys massaging girls' vaginal areas while making out (finger pie).

According to *Songfacts,* the barber mentioned in the lyrics was James Bioletti, who cut hair for McCartney, Lennon and George Harrison in the days of their youth.

The part about the barber showing photographs of all his customers was made up. The photos actually were pictures of models displaying various hairstyles.

Unlike many Beatles songs that were guitar driven, this one mainly featured piano. Lennon and producer George Martin shared the duties of tickling the ivories. The cheery horn part was played by session musician David Mason on piccolo trumpet. A fire alarm was mimicked by Ringo Starr on handbell.

On one pressing of the record, Mason played a seven-note outro. But that pressing was sent only to radio stations, making disc jockeys the only possessors of a rare collector's item.

In the U.S., "Penny lane" was available only as a monaural recording until 1980, when the "Rarities" album was released. That album pressing did include Mason's seven-note piccolo trumpet ending.

The track became the Beatles' 13th No. 1 single on the *Billboard Hot 100.* It also charted at No. 1 in Australia, Canada, Netherlands, New Zealand and West Germany. A promotional film for the record showed the Beatles wearing mustaches for the first time.

McCartney told writer Barry Miles, "When I came to write it, John came over and helped me with the third verse, as often was the case. We were writing childhood memories, recently faded memories from eight or ten years before, so it was a recent nostalgia, pleasant memories for both of us. All the places were still there, and because we remembered it so clearly, we could have gone on."

"Penny Lane" was backed with "Strawberry Fields Forever," another song about a real location in Liverpool. It was a double A disc, and both songs received strong radio play. When the two songs entered the *Billboard Hot 100,* "Strawberry Fields" had a slight lead. But "Penny" soon surged ahead. "Strawberry" eventually would crest at No. 8.

Penny Lane

Songwriters: John Lennon, Paul McCartney

Peaked at No. 1 on Billboard Hot 100

March 18, 1967

The Beatles

Paul McCartney (June 18, 1942-) vocals, piano, bass
John Lennon (Oct. 9, 1940-Dec. 8, 1980) piano, backing vocal, congas
George Harrison (Feb. 25, 1943-Nov. 29, 2001) guitar, backing vocal, handclaps
Ringo Starr (July 7, 1940-) drums, handbell
Formed in Liverpool, England, in 1960

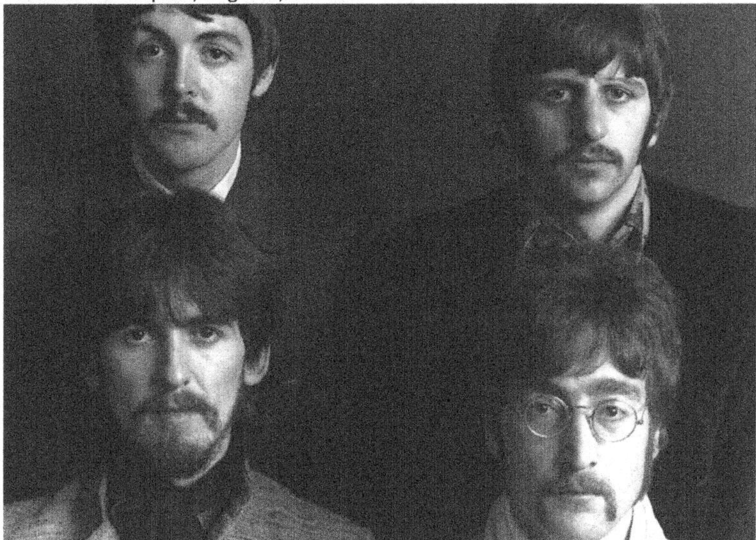

The Beatles – Top: Paul McCartney, Ringo Starr
Bottom: George Harrison, John Lennon

Creeque Alley [The Mamas and The Papas] – As far as I know, the Mamas and the Papas were the only group who had a hit song that chronicled their own history. The lyrics were written by the married couple in the band, John and Michelle Phillips. How more realistic can you get than having a history written by the people who lived it?

The title (pronounced "creaky") is the name of a thoroughfare in St. Thomas, Virgin Islands, where the Phillipses spent time when they were playing with the New Journeymen. It was a time when money was scarce and they had to charge daily necessities to their American Express credit card in order to survive.

John Phillips, born and raised on the East Coast, met Michelle in San Francisco while he was playing folk music gigs with the Journeymen and she was a 17-year-old model. He left his wife and children to marry Michelle, and he brought her into the music business.

Cass Elliot, who was born Ellen Naomi Cohen in Baltimore, Md., and Denny Doherty, from Halifax, Nova Scotia, Canada, met John and Michelle in New York City and eventually formed the Mamas and the Papas.

The real people and places mentioned in the "Creeque Alley" lyrics include:

- Zal (Zalman "Zal" Yanovsky, a Halifax native who would eventually join the Lovin' Spoonful)
- McGuinn (Jim "Roger" McGuinn, who was a founding member of the Byrds)
- McGuire (Barry McGuire, a member of the folk group New Christy Minstrels who had a No. 1 solo hit with "Eve Of Destruction")
- Sebastian (John Sebastian, who played in the folk music scene and played with the Mugwumps before joining the Lovin' Spoonful)
- Night Owl (the Night Owl Café, a small music venue in Greenwich Village, New York)

- Mugwumps (a New York group that played jug band music)
- Duffy's (a club on Creeque Alley owned by Hugh Duffy)

There is a repeated line, "No one's getting fat except Mama Cass." While Elliot was a plus-size woman, there also was a time before the Mamas and the Papas formed when she was making more money than John, Michelle and Denny – hence, she was assigned the term "fat."

Despite dire financial straits, the quartet managed to leave St. Thomas for the mainland and went to Los Angeles, Calif. They played some of the songs they had written for record producer Lou Adler, who liked them and got them signed to Dunhill Records.

Their first single, "Go Where You Wanna Go," failed to chart. The follow-up, "California Dreamin'," peaked at No. 4, before "Monday, Monday" became a No. 1 song.

Creeque Alley

Songwriters: John Phillips, Michelle Phillips
Peaked at No. 5 on Billboard Hot 100
June 30, 1967

The Mamas and The Papas

John Phillips (Aug. 30, 1935-March 18, 2001) guitar, vocals
Denny Doherty (Nov. 29, 1940-Jan. 19, 2007) vocals
Cass Elliot (Sept. 19, 1941-July 29, 1974) vocals
Michelle Phillips (June 4, 1944-) vocals
Formed in Los Angeles, Calif., in 1965

The Mamas and The Papas: John Phillips, Cass Elliot, Michelle Phillips, Denny Doherty

The Ballad of Bonnie and Clyde [Georgie Fame] – Englishman Georgie Fame recorded this tale about American outlaws in late 1967. His first American top 40 hit was "Yeh, Yeh" in 1965.

Real Depression-era robbers Bonnie Parker and Clyde Barrow are the subjects of the lyrics.

The song was inspired by, but not included in, the 1967 movie *Bonnie And Clyde.* The writers were Englishmen Mitch Murray and Peter Callander. Their lyrics are flawed by the mention of Savannah. Bonnie and Clyde met in Dallas, Texas, and never traveled as far east as Georgia. Also, the music is played in ragtime style, another error because ragtime was finished by 1917 whereas

Bonnie and Clyde began their crime spree in 1932.

Murray: "We had a good example of bad research working well for us with 'Bonnie and Clyde.' We had 'dewlap bag' instead of 'burlap bag.'"

The lyrics also state that Bonnie and Clyde were "walking in the sunshine" at the time of their deaths, but they were in a car when a four-man posse shot them dead.

The recording features sounds of police sirens, screeching tires and gunfire, which firmly delivers the mood of the criminals' flight from law enforcement. There also are replicated sounds of the final shootout that resulted in Bonnie and Clyde's death at Bienville Parish, La., on May 23, 1934.

The Ballad Of Bonnie and Clyde

Songwriters: Mitch Murray, Peter Callander

Peaked at No. 7 on Billboard Hot 100

April 13, 1968

Georgie Fame

Born Clive Powell in Leigh, Lancashire, England, on June 26, 1943

Georgie Fame

Folsom Prison Blues [Johnny Cash] – The song is about a real institution – Folsom State Prison. It was written by Johnny Cash in 1953 when he was in the U.S. Air Force, stationed in West Germany. He was inspired to write it after watching the 1951 movie *Inside The Walls of Folsom Prison.* His first version was recorded in 1955.

A live version of the song was recorded Jan. 13, 1968, during a concert at the prison in Folsom, Calif. It was released as a single later that year and became a No. 1 song on the *Billboard Country Chart* while peaking at No. 32 on the pop chart. The live version is more up-tempo than the original studio recording. It was a No. 1 country hit in Canada, and in the U.S. it was rated the top country single of 1968. It also garnered a Grammy Award for Cash.

The song conveys the pain and remorse of a man in prison for murder. The question remains, why is a man who committed murder in Reno, Nevada, serving time in a California prison?

The song is partially plagiarized. The opening line is from a Gordon Jenkins song titled "Crescent City Blues." Cash reportedly settled out of court to compensate Jenkins $100,000.

Cheering from prisoners was added in post-production. A documentary on the concert indicates that prisoners were careful not to cheer Cash's comments about the prison, fearing reprisals from guards.

The most famous line in the song – "I shot a man in Reno just to watch him die" – resulted from Cash trying to think of the worst possible reason for killing another person.

Cash was a long-time advocate of prisoners and performed about 12 free prison concerts a year. Other than overnight stays in jail for drunkenness, reckless driving, drug possession and picking flowers on private property, Cash was never imprisoned.

Cash: "I don't see anything good come out prison. You put them in like animals and tear out the souls and guts of them, and let them out worse than when they went in."

The album "Live From Folsom Prison" provided a career boost for Cash, who hadn't had a song on the *Billboard* top 40 since 1964's "Understand Your Man." He got his own TV show in 1969, and it lasted three years.

Called "The Man in Black," he didn't always wear black clothing, but when he did, he said it was for all the people in the world who were oppressed. His black-clothing image had solidified by the 1970s, and he regularly performed clad in black during those years.

His real name was J.R. Cash and had to add the first name John when he enlisted in the military.

In the mid-1970s he and his wife June completed a course in Bible study through Christian International Bible College in Columbus, Ohio, and he became an ordained minister.

Folsom Prison Blues

Songwriter: Johnny Cash

Peaked at No. 32 on Billboard Hot 100

July 6, 1968

Johnny Cash

Feb. 26, 1932-Sept. 12, 2003

Born J.R. Cash in Kingsland, Ark., and died of complications of diabetes in Nashville, Tenn.

Johnny Cash

Woodstock [Crosby, Stills, Nash & Young] – The focus of this 1970 hit by Crosby, Stills & Nash is a real event – the 1969 Woodstock Festival.

The saga of the Woodstock Music and Art Fair is one of those true stories that is stranger than fiction.

The iconic festival, which nearly was scrubbed because it lost its venue three weeks before it was to begin, hosted an astonishing 450,000 guests in rural New York and, against all odds, lived up to its advertised billing of "three days of peace and music."

Four New Yorkers were the principal players in the creation of the Woodstock event. Michael Lang and Artie Kornfeld, both originally from Brooklyn, met by happenstance in 1968 when Lang contacted Capitol Records in Hollywood in an effort to get a recording contract for The Train, a resident Woodstock, N.Y., band he was managing. Kornfeld was a vice president at Capitol, and he was a songwriter/producer with more than 75 charted songs to his credit. A deal never came to fruition, but Lang and Kornfeld struck up a friendship and began hanging out together.

John Roberts and Joel Rosenman, both from wealthy families in the New York metro area, met on a golf course in 1966. They had Ivy League educations and became roommates on Manhattan's upper eastside. Since they hated their respective jobs in the financial world, they quit and became partners as venture capitalists. Roberts was an heir to the Polident fortune and received large payments from a family trust fund. Roberts and Rosenman bought an ad in the Wall Street Journal, claiming to be "young men with unlimited capital looking for legitimate and interesting business proposals."

Lang had promoted a small music festival in Miami, Fla., having moved there after dropping out of New York University. After he moved to Woodstock, he wanted to create a recording studio there because a number of music luminaries like Janis Joplin and Bob Dylan had taken up residence. "We felt it would be a great place to have a retreat for artists to go up there and record," Kornfeld told the VH-1 documentary Behind The Music.

Lang and Kornfeld had worked with attorney Miles Lurie, who brought them together with Roberts and Rosenman, who also were his clients and had financed the successful Media Sound recording studio in Manhattan. The four formed Woodstock Ventures, Inc., and set out to create a studio in Woodstock, about 100 miles north of New York City.

Attached to the bottom of Lang and Kornfeld's proposal was the sentence, "Woodstock, being the home of a lot of famous artists, we think we can get some of them to do a small concert to celebrate the opening of the recording studio."

"We decided to do the concert first," Rosenman said, "and with the proceeds we would build the recording studio." The highly successful Monterey Pop Festival of 1967 was a model for the event they sought to produce.

A festival site never really existed at Woodstock, however, because there wasn't enough open land. A site at Wallkill, NY, was located 40 miles south, and a deal was signed with the city in March 1969, to hold the festival on Aug. 15-17.

While Rosenman and Roberts took care of finances and Kornfeld handled promotion and advertising, Lang took care of production and set out to sign musical acts. The typical fee for top rock bands in 1969 was $5,000. But Lang's strategy was to offer $12,000 in order to ensure enough popular bands would play. Rosenman and Roberts estimated that $250,000 in financing from a bank would be needed, and ticket sales would cover the rest.

Ticket prices were set at $7 for one day, $13 for two days or $18 for all three days.

Jimi Hendrix was the highest paid star at $32,000. His contract stipulated that no act could follow him on stage. In all, $180,000 was spent on musical talent.

But as the size of the event grew, so did the apprehension of the Wallkill townsfolk. They were filled with mistrust and a fear of thousands of hippies descending on their conservative, little town. Wallkill went to court to cancel the deal, and on July 15 the festival was without a home. By then 100,000 tickets had been sold.

Woodstock Ventures thought about cancelling the festival but discarded the idea and frantically set out to find a new site. They even employed a helicopter to scour the countryside from the air.

In White Lake, 42 miles west of Wallkill, Elliot Tiber had a small resort hotel and a permit to run a music festival in the neighboring town of Bethel, population 3,900. But his 15 acres were largely swampy and unsuitable as a site for the fair. As depicted in the 2009 film *Taking Woodstock*, Tiber referred Woodstock Ventures to Bethel dairy farmer Max Yasgur.

Yasgur saved the event by offering his 600-acre alfalfa field. The land had a gently sloping bowl shape with a small rise at the bottom where a stage could be established. A pond sat behind the rise.

The organizers had agreed to pay Wallkill $7,500 for use of land there, but Yasgur asked for 10 times that amount. Relieved that they had a place to stage the festival, Roberts and Rosenman gladly agreed to terms, and Yasgur cleared the land himself. Contracts for use of land surrounding Yasgur's farm cost another $25,000.

A full-page ad in the *New York Times* announced Bethel as the new site. White Lake and Bethel were part of the Catskill Mountains Borscht Belt resort area, catering to city dwellers during the summer months. Most of the inns had their heyday in the 1930s through early '70s.

With three weeks to go, Woodstock Ventures had a home for its event, but there were no telephones or electricity and no easy access. The logistics were staggering, but preparations surged at a fever pitch.

Filmmaker Michael Wadleigh had hopes of shooting a movie of the festival. But documentaries were dubious money makers, and he could not find backing. Kornfeld made Warner Brothers an offer it couldn't refuse, though, and secured $100,000 to buy film. The contract was hand-written and signed at the 11th hour.

A deal to bring in New York City police to work security fell through at the last minute, and the best the festival could do was hire about 300 anonymous off-duty cops who were paid in cash.

Two days before the festival was to begin, construction workers were joined by about 50,000 early arrivals. The issue of fencing the property had been stalled until the last minute because of milking schedules for cows in neighboring pastures. With so many people already on the infield, the organizers had the choice of herding them out so that they could start collecting money or avoid a riot and take the loss. A decision to maintain good public relations won out.

As seen in Wadleigh's footage, fences that already were erected in a slipshod manner easily were breached by many on the festival's opening day. A lame attempt at shoring up the perimeter came too late, and a majority of the concertgoers got in free.

The week before the event, Woodstock Ventures already was over $1 million in debt, so things had gone from bad to worse. Thoughts turned to keeping the guests safe and giving them the time of their lives.

As thousands of rock fans swarmed the Bethel area, two-lane Rt. 17B quickly clogged. Traffic backed up some 20 miles, and concertgoers began to abandon their cars on the road to walk the rest of the way.

Eventually, the New York Thruway handled so much concert traffic that two exits had to be closed. It is estimated that for every person who got to the festival there were two who tried and failed.

The first day of music was to have started at noon on Aug. 15, but there was a three-hour delay before opening act Richie Havens took the stage. He was supposed to play 20 minutes, but the organizers coaxed him back out again and again for two hours because the following acts were late. Ultimately, helicopter lifts were the only way to move musicians in and out of the site.

With the size of the crowd being four or five times the expected size, the scene was rife with possibilities for disaster. There was insufficient food and water, there was no way to service the portable toilets and no way for an ambulance to access the site.

The four men of Woodstock Ventures, who were aged 24-27, began to wonder what would happen if rioting occurred or if security overreacted to crowd misbehavior. They were begging bands to play double sets because they didn't want the crowds to have a moment without entertainment. A number of heavy rainstorms soaked the fields, and there were hundreds of thousands of kids who were cold, wet, hungry and stoned. The situation could have exploded.

New York Gov. Nelson Rockefeller phoned Roberts and told him he was thinking of sending in 10,000 national guardsmen. "I was on my knees begging and pleading with Gov. Rockefeller not to send in troops," Roberts said. He tried to explain that things were going pretty well, and the only thing that could fracture the status quo would be for "half a million youngsters to see armed troops with rifles pointed at them."

A major concern came from the passage of people over the muddy festival grounds, which threatened to uncover buried electrical cables that carried power to the stage. With wet bodies packed tightly throughout the field, a mass electrocution became possible.

"I was just thinking about doing a business venture earlier in the year," Rosenman said, "and now I was wondering whether I was going to go down as a person who had electrocuted 50,000 people."

While no mass tragedy occurred, there were three deaths during the four days: a guest died from a burst appendix, another suffered a heroin overdose and a third was in his sleeping bag when he accidentally was run over by a tractor.

Wavy Gravy (Hugh Romney), the founder of the Hog Farm commune in California, had been brought in to set up free kitchens and a place to provide help for kids on bad LSD trips. He and his crew may have saved many other lives.

Rains that plagued the event turned into an unexpected career boost for singer Melanie Safka, a New York resident. On the first day, Melanie took the stage at 11 p.m. for a seven-song set because The Incredible String Band refused to play in the rain. After the festival she wrote and recorded the song "Lay Down (Candles In The Rain)" about her experience at Woodstock. In 1970 it became her first top 40 hit in the U.S.

Weather delays forced the three-day festival into a fourth day, which was anchored by Jimi Hendrix starting at 9 a.m. on Monday, Aug. 18. Since most of the crowd had already departed, only about 80,000 people were left to witness his 19-song set.

In all, there were 32 musical acts that performed, including super group Crosby, Stills and Nash, who played together in public for only the second time.

On Day 3 an exhausted Kornfeld accepted a pill from a stranger that he thought would help keep him awake. It turned out to be an LSD tab, which sent Kornfeld on his first hallucinogenic high.

Legend has it that a baby was born at the festival, but there is no confirmation. Marion Vassmer, who was Sullivan County registrar at the time, said there were no recorded births in Bethel that weekend.

After the grounds were empty Lang stayed behind to help with clean-up and Roberts, Rosenfeld and Kornfeld returned to New York City for a meeting at Citibank. The bank chairman was furious over the losses, which pushed upward of $1.6 million.

Later, Lang and Kornfeld went back to Warner Brothers in an effort to renegotiate the film deal. The studio refused, but eventually a new deal was signed in which the four Woodstock Ventures principals gave up their 50-50 profit split in exchange for $1 million cash. The film was a huge success and won an Academy Award in 1970 for best documentary.

Woodstock Ventures had vowed never to declare bankruptcy, and they kept their promise.

While many of the top musical acts of the day were on the concert bill (such as John Sebastian, the Grateful Dead, Creedence Clearwater Revival, Janis Joplin, Sly & the Family Stone, the Who and the Jefferson Airplane), Bob Dylan never was in serious negotiations. He had signed in July to appear at the Isle of Wight Festival on Aug. 31 and left for England on Aug. 15.

Canadian folk rock star Joni Mitchell originally was scheduled to perform, but she canceled at the urging of her manager in order to avoid missing a scheduled appearance on the Dick Cavett TV show. Despite her absence, she wrote a song about the event, "Woodstock," which became a big hit for Crosby, Stills and Nash the next year, joined by Neil Young.

Woodstock

Songwriter: Joni Mitchell

Peaked at No. 11 on Billboard Hot 100

May 9, 1970

May 16, 1970

Crosby, Stills, Nash & Young

David Crosby (Aug. 14, 1941-)

Stephen Stills (Jan. 3, 1945-)

Graham Nash (Feb. 2, 1942-)

Neil Young (Nov. 12, 1945-)

Formed in Los Angeles, Calif., in 1969

Graham Nash, Stephen Stills, David Crosby, Neil Young

Killing Me Softly With His Song [Roberta Flack] – This song was inspired by an accomplished pop performer and was first recorded by a singer who flew under the radar her whole career.

Los Angeles native Lori Lieberman, working with her songwriting team, issued the first rendition of "Killing" in 1971 and then watched helplessly as Roberta Flack's version became an international No. 1 hit two years later. Reportedly, Lieberman's folk-oriented version was gaining traction with radio stations when Flack's recording overtook it.

Lieberman was 22 when she made a guest appearance on the syndicated *Mike Douglas* TV talk show in 1973 and remarked, "It was written for me. The people who wrote the songs for my album ('Becoming') are ... Charles Fox and Norman Gimbel, and Norman writes the words to the songs, and he had the title 'killing me softly with his song.'

"I went to see Don McLean perform at a club and I was so moved by his performance, and we talked about this and that's how the song came about."

McLean was on the verge of stardom in 1971 when he played at the Troubadour nightclub in West Hollywood, Calif. Lieberman was in the audience, scribbling notes on a cocktail napkin.

"Hearing Don McLean perform his song, 'Empty Chairs,' affected me deeply. I wrote a poem about how I felt right then and there. Later that night, I called Norman and read him my poem. He thought it would match one of the titles he had written in his notebook of ideas."

The title was "Killing Us Softly With Some Blues." A little tweaking resulted in the existing title and lyric.

"She (Roberta Flack) was very creative with it, but for me it was just a folk song," Lieberman said in a 2011 interview with *FaceCulture*. "She was really very brilliant. That's when music was changing from James Taylor and Carole King to disco, and it was a really hard time for me. I couldn't relate to the business at all. I didn't know where to turn. My kind of music really wasn't the kind people were playing and enjoying."

When Lieberman performed the song for Douglas, she accompanied herself on acoustic guitar. Flack, on her recording, accompanied herself on electric piano and added some scat vocals at the end.

Disillusioned, Lieberman left the music business in the late 1970s but returned in 1994. She released her latest album "Takes Courage" in 2010. That album contained a new version of "Killing Me Softly."

"As the years went by, I kind of disclaimed (the song), as though it weren't a part of me. And now I recorded it on this record because I'm so proud of it. I'm *very* proud of it, actually."

Flack had *Billboard's* top-ranked single of 1972, "The First Time Ever I Saw Your Face." She had three No. 1s in a stellar 20-year career on the singles chart.

"In 1972, I was on a flight from New York to Los Angeles and was listening to the plane's music channels," Flack told the *Wall Street Journal*. "That's where I first heard Lori Lieberman's version of 'Killing Me Softly.' I probably heard it four times on the flight.

"The lyrics were haunting and the chord changes were lush. I could feel the song and knew I could tell the song's story my way.

"Parts of the song reminded me of my life, of the pain that comes with loving someone deeply, of feeling moved by music, which is the universal language. More than anything, music makes us feel. As I listened, I jotted down the lyrics on a napkin. I also wrote down music lines and made notes on how I was going to arrange the song."

McLean, who had a huge No. 1 hit with "American Pie" in late 1971 and early '72, told the *New York Daily News*, "I'm absolutely amazed. I've heard both Lori's and Roberta's version and I must say I'm very humbled about the whole thing. You can't help but feel that way about a song written and performed as well as this one is."

Flack's version earned two Grammy Awards. As a hip hop-tinged album track for the Fugees in 1996, it charted at No. 2 for three weeks on the *Billboard Hot 100 Airplay* list and bagged a best R&B performance Grammy in 1997.

Killing Me Softly With His Song

Songwriters: Norman Gimbel, Charles Fox

Peaked at No. 1 on Billboard Hot 100
Feb. 24, 1973
March 3, 1973
March 10, 1973
March 17, 1973
March 31, 1973

Roberta Flack

Born Roberta Cleopatra Flack in Black Mountain, N.C., on Feb. 10, 1937

Roberta Flack

Rocky Mountain High [John Denver] – Real life experiences as a young man form the backbone of this folk-rock classic. John Denver wrote the words, and he was assisted by Mike Taylor in composing the melody. It took him nine months to complete the song, in which he refers to himself in the third person.

Factual information in the lyrics includes:

- "He was born in the summer of his 27th year." That was Denver's age when he had the experiences that inspired the song.
- "Coming home to a place he'd never been before." Denver and his wife Annie had recently moved to Aspen, Colo.
- "On the road and hanging by a song." Denver was just getting his career started by playing concerts on tour.
- "I've seen it rainin' fire in the sky." This is what a meteor shower looked like to him.
- "The shadow from the starlight ..." He was camping in the mountain wilderness where the sky was so clear and the stars so bright that a stand of trees cast a shadow.
- "He lost a friend but kept a memory." A friend who was visiting him from Minnesota was accidentally killed while riding Denver's motorcycle.
- "Why they try to tear the mountains down to bring in a couple more." Denver was concerned about talk of bringing the 1972 Winter Olympics to the Rocky Mountains. Those Olympic games were awarded to Sapporo, Japan, as it turned out.

In a career that spanned 30 years, Denver embraced the beauty and tranquility of the Rockies while railing against city life. In 2007 the Colorado General Assembly made "Rocky Mountain High" one of two official state songs.

Denver's father was a captain in the U.S. Army Air Forces, and he moved the family often.

By the time he was attending college, the budding singer-songwriter changed his surname in honor of the capital of his favorite state.

Rocky Mountain High
Songwriters: John Denver, Mike Taylor
Peaked at No. 9 on Billboard Hot 100
March 3, 1973
March 10, 1973

John Denver
Dec. 31, 1943-Oct. 12, 1997
Born Henry John Deutschendorf Jr. in Roswell, N.M. He died when the experimental airplane he was piloting crashed into Monterey Bay near Pacific Grove, Calif.

John Denver

Doolin-Dalton [Eagles] – This is the only song in this chapter that was not released as a single. It was written by Glenn Frey, Don Henley and Jackson Browne for the Eagles' album *Desperado,* and it's about real people – the Dalton gang that robbed banks and trains.

The 1973 album, the Eagles' second, was tied together by Old West themes. In its ninth week on the *Billboard 200 album chart,* it peaked at No. 41. The success of later Eagles albums spurred sales of "Desperado," and it was certified double platinum (sales over 2 million).

The lyrics of "Doolin-Dalton" tell part of the story of the Dalton gang, which formed in the Oklahoma Territory in 1890. Accordingly, the album features photos of the band members dressed in period costumes. This was the only Eagles' album in which the band members were pictured on the outer jacket.

Members of the Dalton gang included Bill, Bob and Emmett Dalton, George "Bitter Creek" Newcomb, Bill Doolin, Charley Pierce, "Blackfaced" Charlie Bryant, Dick Broadwell and Bill Power. Gratton Dalton joined in 1891.

A double bank robbery attempt on Oct. 5, 1892, in Coffeyville, Kan., brought on the demise of the gang as four members were killed in a shootout and another, Emmett, was captured (after being shot 23 times) and sentenced to prison. Doolin, Newcomb and Pierce were not part of the attempted heist.

The lyric "two brothers lying dead" refers to Bob and Grat.

The 1800s Old West theme belied the setting in which the album was recorded – Island Studios in London with Englishman Glyn Johns producing. Henley sang lead on the song with Frey contributing a few lines.

A songwriting contributor to the album's songs, J.D. Souther said, "We were quite taken with the idea of being, or at least portraying, outlaws. It was a serviceable metaphor for our story. Generally, I thought there were limitations to the metaphor of musicians as gunslingers."

Doolin-Dalton
Songwriters: Glenn Frey, Don Henley, Jackson Browne
Included on the album
"Desperado"
Peaked at No. 41 on Billboard 200
June 30, 1973

Eagles
Glenn Frey (Nov. 6, 1948-Jan. 18, 2016) vocals, guitar, keyboards
Don Henley (July 22, 1947-) vocals, drums, percussion
Randy Meisner (March 8, 1946-) vocals, bass, acoustic guitar
Bernie Leadon (July 19, 1947-) vocals, guitar, banjo, mandolin, pedal steel guitar
Formed in Los Angeles, Calif., in 1971

The Eagles: Bernie Leadon, Randy Meisner, Don Henley, Glenn Frey

Smoke On The Water [Deep Purple] – This song is about a real disaster – a casino fire in Switzerland. The song was written by the members of the British band Deep Purple, who made it a hit recording in 1973.

On Dec. 4, 1971, Deep Purple was in Montreux, Switzerland, to record an album in the Rolling Stones Mobile Studio, which was rented from the Rolling Stones band, at the entertainment complex that was part of the Montreux Casino.

On the eve of a recording session, Frank Zappa & the Mothers of Invention played a concert at the casino's theater. It was to be the theater's final show before the casino closed down for annual winter renovations, which would enable Deep Purple to record there.

Someone in the audience fired a flare gun toward the rattan-covered ceiling, igniting a fire. The entire complex was consumed, including the Mothers' equipment.

Deep Purple bassist Roger Glover is credited with coming up with the song's title, which related how the fire's smoke spread over Lake Geneva as members of Deep Purple watched from their hotel. Glover said the phrase came to him in a dream.

The "Funky Claude" in the lyrics refers to Claude Nobs, director of the Montreux Jazz Festival. He helped some of the audience escape the burning building.

"Smoke On The Water" was included on Deep Purple's album "Machine Head," which was recorded in the Montreux sessions. It became their most commercially successful LP, topping the album charts in several countries. It was released as a single in May 1973, reaching No. 4 on *Billboard's Hot 100.* It soared to No. 2 in Canada.

Deep Purple, with an expensive mobile unit ("Rolling truck Stones thing" in the lyrics) but no place to record, had to scout the town for another venue. Nobs found a promising place, a local theater called the Pavilion. But soon after the band started to record, neighbors complained of the noise, and the band was able to lay down instrumental tracks for only one song before police forced them to shut down.

After about another week of searching, they rented the nearly empty Montreux Grand Hotel and converted its hallways and stairwells into a makeshift studio.

Because of the exposure Montreux received from "Smoke On The Water," an international hit, the town formed a lasting bond with Deep Purple. The song is honored by a sculpture on the lake shore with the band's name, the song's title and the signature riff in musical notes.

"Deep Purple" was the favorite song of Ritchie Blackmore's grandmother, which inspired him to name the hard rock band after it. The song was first published in 1933 as a piano composition. Lyrics were added in 1938.

Smoke On The Water

Songwriters: Ritchie Blackmore, Ian Gillan, Roger Glover, Jon Lord, Ian Paice

Peaked at No. 4 on Billboard Hot 100

July 28, 1973

Aug. 4, 1973

Deep Purple

Ritchie Blackmore (April 14, 1945-) guitar

Jon Lord (June 9, 1941-July 16, 2012) keyboards

Ian Paice (June 29, 1948-) drums

Roger Glover (Nov. 30, 1945-) bass

Ian Gillan (Aug. 19, 1945-) vocals

Formed in Hertford, Hertfordshire, England, in 1968

Deep Purple: Roger Glover, Ian Gillan, Ritchie Blackmore, Jon Lord, Ian Paice

We're An American Band [Grand Funk] – Real places and real people are mentioned in the lyrics of this song by Grand Funk Railroad from Flint, Mich. Their name was shortened to Grand Funk in 1973 for legal reasons. The lyrics, written by drummer Don Brewer, also were inspired by real experiences of the band while out on tour.

Mark Farner and Mel Schacher were the other original members who formed GFR in 1969, and keyboardist Craig Frost joined in 1972.

Little Rock and Omaha are the cities mentioned, and legendary groupie "Sweet Connie" Hamzy from Arkansas and blues guitarist Freddie King are the people. King, who died in 1976 at age 42, toured with Grand Funk as an opening act. The song is a tribute to groupies, who have followed rock stars on tour for years.

According to writer Dave Marsh, a tour in early 1973 had Grand Funk on the same bill with English band Humble Pie. After one show, members of the two bands were drinking together in a bar when an argument about British rock vs. American rock broke out. Brewer stood up, bragged about rock heroes such as Jerry Lee Lewis, Fats Domino, Little Richard and Elvis Presley and proclaimed, "We're an American band!"

The next morning he turned his patriotism into inspiration and wrote the song that would become a No. 1 hit on Sept. 29, 1973, guitarist Mark Farner's 25th birthday.

We're An American Band
Songwriter: Don Brewer
Peaked at No. 1 on Billboard Hot 100
Sept. 29, 1973

<u>Grand Funk Railroad</u>
Mark Farner (Sept. 29, 1948-) vocals, guitar
Don Brewer (Sept. 3, 1948-) drums, vocals
Mel Schacher (April 8, 1951-) bass
Craig Frost (April 20, 1948-) keyboards
Formed in Flint, Mich., in 1969

Grand Funk Railroad: Craig Frost, Mel Schacher, Don Brewer, Mark Farner

Rock And Roll Heaven [Righteous Brothers] The soulful duo from Southern California had been absent from the singles chart for four years when they scored this hit in 1974. It was a cover of a song that had been recorded by Climax a year earlier but had failed to chart.

With the lyrics slightly retooled, "Rock And Roll Heaven" became a huge success for the Righteous Brothers because it brought back into the public consciousness some beloved rockers who were deceased. In the song, they were identified by first name only, with brief phrasing to connect them to their music.

Those musicians were Jimi Hendrix, Janis Joplin, Otis Redding, Jim Morrison, Jim Croce and Bobby Darin. All were in their 20s when they died, except Croce (30) and Darin (37). References to

Buddy Holly and Ritchie Valens were removed from the original version.

One of the songwriters was Alan O'Day, who later would write two No. 1 songs – "Angie Baby" by Helen Reddy and his own "Undercover Angel."

Righteous Brother Bill Medley said he and Bobby Hatfield were skeptical of their recording's chances for success because they didn't think it had the "old Righteous Brothers feel." Public acceptance came quickly, however, as the single shot up to No. 3.

"We liked 'Rock And Roll Heaven'," Medley told *Songfacts*, "but we knew it wasn't going to be necessarily a great Righteous Brothers record. We knew it wasn't going to be the kind of song that people were going to get dressed up and come out to watch you perform."

Rock And Roll Heaven

Songwriters: Alan O'Day, John Stevenson

Peaked at No. 3 on Billboard Hot 100

July 20, 1974

July 27, 1974

The Righteous Brothers

Bill Medley

Born William Thomas Medley in Santa Ana, Calif., on Sept. 19, 1940

Bobby Hatfield

Aug. 10, 1940-Nov. 5, 2003

Born Robert Lee Hatfield in Beaver Dam, Wis., and died in Kalamazoo, Mich.

Bill Medley and Bobby Hatfield

The Wreck Of The Edmund Fitzgerald [Gordon Lightfoot] – The song is about another disaster – a shipwreck on Lake Superior. Canadian folk artist Gordon Lightfoot wrote and sang it.

The *Edmund Fitzgerald* sank during a colossal storm on Nov. 10, 1975. The freighter originally was launched June 7, 1958. It was owned by the Northwest Mutual Life Insurance Co. of Milwaukee and was named after its president and chairman.

The song ironically was contained on Lightfoot's 1976 album "Summertime Dream," but the lyrics depict a setting that is neither summery nor dreamy.

The ship was bound for Detroit, not Cleveland as the lyrics specify, to discharge taconite iron ore pellets before a planned docking in Cleveland for the winter. The last radio transmission by Capt. Ernest McSorley stated that the crew were "holding our own." No distress signal was received.

The "old cook" mentioned in the lyrics actually was a replacement for the regular chef, who was too ill to make the trip. The ship began its fateful voyage from Superior, Wis., on Nov. 9, 1975.

The ship sank like a rock after the moisture-absorbing iron ore pellets took on water and dramatically increased the vessel's weight. It hit bottom hull-first and broke in two. It had needed to travel another 17 miles to reach the safety of Whitefish Point. The *Edmund Fitzgerald* was found on

Nov. 14, 1975, 530 feet under water, but it took several months to identify it. At the time Lightfoot recorded the song, very few details were known of the sinking, and much of his writing was done on speculation. The only part of the ship to be salvaged was the 200-pound bell.

With a value of $24 million, the ship's financial loss was the greatest in Great Lakes sailing history. Between 1816 and 1975 at least 240 ships sank in the Whitefish Point area of Lake Superior.

The Ojibwe (Chippewa) tribe calls Lake Superior "gichi gami." Henry Wadsworth Longfellow wrote it as "Gitche Gumee" in *The Song Of Hiawatha* in 1855. It means "great sea."

The "Maritime Sailors' Cathedral" in the last verse actually is the Mariners' Church of Detroit. After a parishioner complained about the adjective "musty," Lightfoot changed the lyric to "rustic" in subsequent live performances.

The Wreck Of The Edmund Fitzgerald

Songwriter: Gordon Lightfoot

Peaked at No. 2 on Billboard Hot 100

Nov. 20, 1976

Nov. 27, 1976

Gordon Lightfoot

Born Gordon Meredith Lightfoot Jr. in Orillia, Ontario, Canada, on Nov. 17, 1938

Gordon Lightfoot

Same Old Lang Syne [Dan Fogelberg] – The story told by the lyrics is based on an actual chance meeting that singer/songwriter Dan Fogelberg had with a former girlfriend on Christmas Eve, 1975.

There have been many songs recorded in the rock era that tell a story. But the crème de la crème of true-life tales is "Same Old Lang Syne" by Fogelberg. It became his signature song.

The song is a compelling account of two former lovers who have a chance meeting in a grocery store on Christmas Eve. They had dated in high school and are now adults who have not seen one another in a few years. Their efforts to take their conversation from the market to a bar are foiled when they find that all the taverns are closed. So they stop at a neighborhood liquor store, buy some beer and sip while they chat in the woman's car.

After Fogelberg died of cancer on Dec. 16, 2007, Jill Greulich stepped forward to reveal she is the woman whom he encountered on that snowy night in Peoria, Ill. Greulich, now living with her second husband in suburban St. Louis, Mo., grew up in Peoria and attended Woodruff High School with Fogelberg from 1965 to '69. Her account of the Christmas Eve event first appeared in the *Peoria Journal-Star*.

It's such a small world – Jim Greulich, Jill's current husband, was a schoolmate of mine in Des Plaines, Ill. Jim met Jill when he was a commercial pilot and she was a flight attendant.

Fogelberg and Greulich, who was Jill Anderson back then, dated intermittently during their high school years. After he departed for the University of Illinois and she for Western Illinois University, they kept in touch and even dated occasionally. But the romance was finished when he left the state to pursue his music career. Dan was playing coffeehouses in Champaign, Ill., when he was discovered by schoolmate and fledgling agent Irving Azoff, who sent the budding star to Los Angeles and then Nashville to sharpen his skills.

Jill, meanwhile, relocated to the Chicago area to work as an elementary school teacher and flight attendant. A man she met there became her first husband.

In December 1975, Jill and her husband were in Peoria for a visit. During a family gathering the night of the 24th, her mother asked her to get some eggnog from a nearby store. She ended up at the Convenient Food Market, where Dan, also home for the holidays, had gone to purchase whipped cream to make Irish coffees.

As they sat in Jill's car with beer in hand, they caught up on the years that had passed since their last meeting. There were some bittersweet moments, as told by Dan's skillful lyrical crafting. The two finally ran out of things to talk about and went back to their respective families.

The song ends on a melancholy note, with Dan reliving the high school days he spent as Jill's lover and feeling the pain of their break-ups. As they part, an idyllic winter night is soured when falling snow "turned into rain."

Five years later the song, which would appear on the album "The Innocent Age," was released. Jill heard it on the radio one morning as she was driving to work and thought it sounded like Dan's singing. Then she absorbed the lyrics and thought, "Oh my gosh! That really happened!"

The song is factual – to a point. The words say that Dan told Jill, "...her eyes were still as blue." But in reality, her eyes are green. Chalk that up to poetic license. They also say that Jill told Dan she had married an architect when her then-husband actually was a physical education teacher. It's unlikely that Dan knew what Jill's husband did for a living and just thought "architect" sounded good, she said.

The memory of the event is one that Jill treasures. She explained that she sat on the secret for so long because "it wasn't about me, it was about Dan. It was Dan's song."

The melody at the beginning of each verse comes from Tchaikovsky's "1812 Overture."

The recording features Fogelberg on acoustic piano, bass and electric piano, and he overdubbed his backing vocals. Russ Kunkel played drums, and the late Michael Brecker played the closing solo snippet of "Auld Lang Syne" on soprano saxophone.

"Auld Lang Syne" is a Scottish poem written by Robert Burns in 1788 and set to the tune of a traditional folk song. Translated, the title means "old long since," "long long ago" or "days gone by."

Band leader Guy Lombardo often is credited with popularizing the use of the song on New Year's Eve through his annual broadcasts on radio and TV dating back to 1929. He also recorded it in 1939 and '47.

"Same Old Lang Syne" was not the only song Dan wrote from his personal life. "Leader Of The Band" was about his father, Lawrence Fogelberg, who was an educator and band leader at Woodruff and Pekin high schools. He began an eight-year stint as band director at Bradley University in 1951, the year Dan was born. On his website, Dan wrote, "I was so gratified that I gave him that song before he passed on."

Dan's mother, Margaret, emigrated from Scotland as a child and was classically trained as a pianist while attending Bradley in the 1940s.

The liner notes from "The Innocent Age" include a thank you from Dan to "my father for his gift of music and my mother for her gift of words."

Same Old Lang Syne

Songwriter: Dan Fogelberg

Peaked at No. 9 on Billboard Hot 100

Feb. 21, 1981

Feb. 28, 1981

Dan Fogelberg

Aug. 13, 1951-Dec. 16, 2007

Born Daniel Grayling Fogelberg in Peoria, Ill., and died of prostate cancer in Deer Isle, Maine

Dan Fogelberg

We Didn't Start The Fire [Billy Joel] – Veteran rocker Billy Joel wrote and recorded this rapid-fire, chronological, 40-year world history that runs almost 5 minutes in length.

He strung together words, phrases and short sentences to connect 1949, the year of his birth, to 1989, which is the year the recording was made and released.

Many of the names, places and events mentioned are references to the Cold War, which pitted the Soviet Union against Western nations (mainly the United States) from the end of World War II to about 1990. That is when the Soviet Union began to dissolve into its component republics.

The idea for the song came to Joel after he had a conversation with a young man in a recording studio. The man contended that 1989 was "a terrible time to be 21" and added that Joel's generation had it easy because "everybody knows that nothing happened in the '50s."

Joel's retort was, "Wait a minute, didn't you hear of the Korean War or the Suez Canal crisis?" These talking points led Joel to begin writing the lyrics, and the melody came later. This was the opposite of Joel's normal writing pattern.

The title and the lyrics in the chorus suggest that the Baby Boomer generation wasn't responsible for the events mentioned in the song, but the Boomers had to cope with them and try to make improvements in the face of post-war situations.

The song hit No. 1 in America, but Joel was critical of his own tune. "... I don't think it was really that good to begin with, melodically," he said in the documentary film *Billy Joel: Shades Of Grey.*

"It's terrible musically," Joel told *Billboard.* "It's like a mosquito buzzing around your head." The tune came from an old melody he had written that he called "Jolene."

Joel told author Fred Bronson that he tried to keep his lyrical images in the order in which they happened. "I started jotting these images down," he said, "these flashes of newspaper headlines that occurred to me. I actually tried to write them down in chronological order, like it was a mental exercise. It wasn't meant to be a record at the time.

"I went home and checked my encyclopedia to see how close I was to the chronology of events. As it turned out, I was almost dead on the money. I'd say about three or four changes came from reading the encyclopedia."

Since there are 119 historical items in the lyrics, Joel has had trouble remembering all of them when performing the song in concert. According to *Songfacts,* in these instances he has looked for help to fans in the audience who are mouthing the words.

The timing of the song was fortuitous for Joel. It started a two-week stay at No. 1 on Dec. 9, 1989, after the East German government had announced one month earlier that all Berliners could travel between the communist and free sectors of the city. Official demolition of the Berlin Wall began the following June. Within weeks, the Cold War was over.

We Didn't Start The Fire
Songwriter: Billy Joel
Peaked at No. 1 on Billboard Hot 100
Dec. 9, 1989
Dec. 16, 1989

Billy Joel
Born William Martin Joel in The Bronx, New York City, N.Y., on May 9, 1949

Billy Joel

Chapter 4

Crime and punishment

Songs about crime, punishment or both

Overview: It's rather amazing how many times rock songwriters have turned to the subjects of crime and criminals throughout the years.

But, let's face it, crime is a fact of life, and rock music reflects life. I applaud songwriters who can deliver a message that may contain this negativity but can make an entertaining song out of it. Both male and female singers tried their hand at singing these songs.

Since the 1950s the charts have been peppered with songs about criminals – some who got caught by law enforcement and some who didn't.

To view the full lyrics to these songs, please log on to www.google.com, enter song titles & artist names and click Google Search.

To listen to these songs, please log on to www.youtube.com and enter song titles & artist names.

Jailhouse Rock [Elvis Presley] – Elvis Presley combined singing and acting to create this monster hit, since it came from his 1957 film of the same name. The single was released about two months before the release of the movie. It was written by the highly successful New York City song writing team of Jerry Leiber and Mike Stoller (see Chapter 7, Brill Building).

Some of the characters in the lyrics are named for real people. Shifty Henry was a Los Angeles musician; the Purple Gang was a real crime mob; and Sad Sack was a U.S. Army term in World War II for a person who was a loser in life.

The lyrics make great use of poetic license. For example:

- What county jail has a warden?
- Why would a person who runs a jail throw a party for the inmates when they're supposed to be incarcerated to pay for their crimes?
- Why would any inmate pass up a chance at escape just to stay and enjoy the party?
- There seems to be an instance of gay romance when one inmate tells another "You're the cutest jailbird I ever did see" (assuming this wasn't a co-ed jail.)

This was Presley's ninth No. 1 pop song and was one of his most decorated hits. It hit No. 1 in the U.K., becoming the first record ever to enter the British chart at No. 1. In the USA, it was No. 1 on the following charts:

- Billboard Weekly Singles (7 weeks)
- Billboard Country & Western
- Billboard Rhythm & Blues
- Billboard Best Sellers in Stores
- Billboard Most Played by Disc Jockeys
- Cashbox Top Country & Western Singles

It is ranked No. 67 on the *Rolling Stone Magazine* list of 500 greatest songs of all time.

In the story line of the film, Presley plays the part of Vince Everett, a convict who is encouraged by his cellmate to pursue a singing career after appearing in a televised prison talent show. Presley himself choreographed the scene in which he sings the title song. Stoller has a cameo as the piano player in the band.

Jailhouse Rock

Songwriters: Jerry Leiber, Mike Stoller

Peaked at No. 1 on Billboard Weekly Singles chart

Oct. 21, 1957
Oct. 28, 1957
Nov. 4, 1957
Nov. 11, 1957
Nov. 18, 1957
Nov. 25, 1957
Dec. 16, 1957

Elvis Presley

Jan. 8, 1935-Aug. 16, 1977

Born Elvis Aron Presley in Tupelo, Miss., and died of cardiac arrest in Memphis, Tenn.

Elvis Presley

The Tijuana Jail [Kingston Trio] – This was the trio's follow-up hit to the No. 1 song "Tom Dooley," breaking into the *Billboard* top 40 in March 1959. The song would peak at No. 12.

The story of the lyrics comes in a month after the narrators were arrested in Tijuana, Mexico, for participating in an illegal craps game in a cantina. The police raided the joint and took the protagonists to the local jail. They couldn't raise the bail of $500, so they are remaining incarcerated for an undetermined time.

Their simple request: "Just send our mail to the Tijuana jail."

For many decades Tijuana has been a popular place for residents of Southern California to spend a day or two shopping, attending bull fights or participating in activities that are illegal in the United States.

The members of the Kingston Trio at that time were Dave Guard, Bob Shane and Nick Reynolds. Personnel changes began in 1961.

The song was recorded during the sessions for the album "At Large," which was the trio's first stereo recording. However, it was not included on that album.

This song is possibly the only one in the rock era that specifically tells of a crime committed on foreign soil. Built in the 1950s, the putrid Tijuana jail of which the Kingston Trio sang was closed in October 2010.

The Tijuana Jail

Songwriter: Denny Thompson

Peaked at No. 12 on Billboard Hot 100

April 20, 1959

Kingston Trio

Dave Guard (Oct. 19, 1934-March 22, 1991)
Bob Shane (Feb. 1, 1934-Jan. 26, 2020)
Nick Reynolds (July 27, 1933-Oct. 1, 2008)
Formed in Palo Alto, Calif., in 1954

Nick Reynolds, Dave Guard, Bob Shane

Chain Gang [Sam Cooke] – Written and recorded by soul singer Sam Cooke, this record about punishment was released June 26, 1960. It peaked at No. 2 on the *Billboard Hot 100* and the *Hot R&B Sides* chart. In the U.K. it reached No. 9.

It was Cooke's second most successful hit record, behind the 1957 No. 1 smash "You Send Me."

While on tour in 1959, Cooke's bus came upon a chain gang on a highway in Georgia. Cooke had the bus driver stop because he felt sorry for the prisoners, and he and his brother Charles got out, shook a few hands and gave the prisoners several cartons of cigarettes.

Chain gangs were unique to the American South as a way to have prisoners who were chained together perform physical labor for little or no pay on building repair, road projects or farming. They were on the decline by 1955, with Georgia the final state to employ them.

However, during the regime of Sheriff Joe Arpaio in Maricopa County, Ariz. (1993-2016), chain gangs were revived at the county jail, mostly for pick-up of trash along highways and desert areas.

The song brought attention to the plight of the chain gang detainees, but it wouldn't be long before the institution disappeared throughout the South.

Unfortunately, Cooke had more than chain gangs to grieve about. In 1963 his 18-month-old son drowned in the family's swimming pool. That led to depression and a broken marriage.

On Dec. 11, 1964, he was fatally shot by the manager of the Hacienda Motel in Los Angeles and died at the age of 33. A trial found that Cooke had been "drunk and disorderly," and the manager got off with a verdict of justifiable homicide from the coroner's jury.

Cooke was born in Clarksdale, Miss., and his family moved to Chicago when he was 2.

Chain Gang

Songwriter: Sam Cooke
Peaked at No. 2 on Billboard Hot 100
Oct. 3, 1960

Sam Cooke

Jan. 22, 1931-Dec. 11, 1964

Born in Clarksdale, Miss., and died in Los Angeles, Calif., of a gunshot wound to the chest

Sam Cooke

I Fought The Law [Bobby Fuller Four] – Here's a song about crime that was written by Sonny Curtis of the Crickets, who penned it in 1958 and then recorded it in 1959 after he took the place of his late bandmate Buddy Holly on guitar.

The song was on their 1960 album "In Style With the Crickets" and in 1961 served as the B side of their recording "A Sweet Love." But it received no airplay.

After two unsuccessful cover versions were recorded by other artists, Texan Bobby Fuller and his group recorded the song in 1965. The following year it rose to No. 9 on *Billboard's Hot 100,* and received a top ranking of No. 11 on the Canadian chart. It was their first nationwide smash.

The Bobby Fuller Four's version contains a strong flavor of the rockabilly sound that the Crickets popularized. In 2004 the Rock and Roll Hall of Fame named it one of the 500 songs that shaped rock.

The lyrics are sung by a protagonist who has made his living through armed robbery. It states that "the law won," but it does not specify how the robber was punished.

Fuller was born in Baytown, Texas, and moved with his family to Salt Lake City as a young child. They relocated to El Paso in 1956.

Capitalizing on the success of "I Fought The Law," the Bobby Fuller Four made the round of TV music shows and even appeared as Nancy Sinatra's band in the beach movie *The Ghost In the Invisible Bikini.*

The 23-year-old Fuller was found dead in the front seat of his mother's automobile outside his apartment building in Hollywood, Calif., on July 18, 1966, his body doused with gasoline, according to *Wikipedia.* The deputy medical examiner's report stated that Fuller had petechial hemorrhages on his face, likely caused by gasoline vapors and the summer heat. He found no bruises, no broken bones and no cuts – no evidence of a beating. Boxes on the report form for "accident" and "suicide" were checked, but next to those boxes were question marks.

Fuller's death has been profiled in an episode of TV's *Unsolved Mysteries.* The official cause of death was changed from suicide to accidental asphyxiation. His family reportedly planned to have the body exhumed in hopes that modern technology will determine the cause of his death.

"Love's Made A Fool of You" (a Buddy Holly song) was the Bobby Fuller Four's final top 40 hit.

I Fought The Law

Songwriter: Sonny Curtis

Peaked at No. 9 on Billboard Hot 100

March 5, 1966

March 12, 1966

Bobby Fuller Four

Bobby Fuller (Oct. 22, 1942-July 18, 1966) guitar, vocals
Randy Fuller (Jan. 29, 1944-) bass
Jim Reese (Dec. 7, 1941-Oct. 26, 1991) guitar
DeWayne Quirico (DOB unavailable) drums
Formed in Texas in 1962

The Bobby Fuller Four

Green Green Grass of Home [Tom Jones] – Written by Claude "Curly" Putman, this song about punishment was first recorded by Johnny Darrell and first popularized by Porter Wagoner in 1965. Jerry Lee Lewis also recorded a version, and Tom Jones learned the song from Lewis's version.

Jones recorded his version late in 1966, and it rose to a peak position of No. 11 on the *Billboard Hot 100* in 1967. It was a No. 1 song in the U.K., Ireland, Norway and Australia. It hit No. 2 in New Zealand and Austria.

The first two verses of the song are filled with warm and pleasant imagery, as a man tells of returning to his hometown to be reunited with his parents, his sweetheart and the house in which he grew up. Then the lyrics take a downturn as the narrator finds that he has awoken from a dream. In reality, he is a condemned prisoner who is about to be executed.

His mortal crime is never revealed. His body will be returned to his hometown only for his burial after the execution has been completed.

Jones possesses an extremely expressive voice, which convincingly carries the story from one mood to another.

Jones: "It made me think of Wales (his native country) when I recorded it – 'the old hometown looks the same.' When I went back to Pontypridd in those days, getting off the train from London, those words would ring true. It seems like a lot of people relate the sentiment to their home, too."

The song helped Jones establish a long, successful career. One of the perquisites was having adoring female fans throw panties and hotel room keys at him as he performed on stage.

Putman died of congestive heart and kidney failure at age 85 on Oct. 30, 2016.

Green, Green Grass Of Home

Songwriter: Curly Putman

Peaked at No. 11 on Billboard Hot 100

Feb. 18, 1967

Tom Jones

Born Thomas John Woodward in Treforest, Pontypridd, Glamorgan, Wales, on June 7, 1940

Tom Jones

Delilah [Tom Jones] – Here's another crime song from Tom Jones. This time we find out what the crime is, but there is no time to mention the subsequent punishment.

The song was released in 1968 and was written by Britons Barry Mason (lyrics) and Les Reed (music).

The song is the story of a betrayed lover who watches as his girlfriend Delilah, silhouetted behind a window shade, makes love to another man at night. Although he realizes that she is no good for him, the narrator goes crazy at the sight. After the paramour leaves at daybreak, the protagonist knocks on the door, which the girlfriend opens and proceeds to laugh in his face. The laughter is cut short when he stabs her to death.

Coming to his senses after the slaughter, the narrator begs Delilah's forgiveness before the police come to break down the door and take him into custody. Hence, we have a crime, but punishment is yet to be determined.

The song went to No. 1 in Germany, Switzerland, Ireland and Finland. In the U.S. it peaked at No. 15 on the *Billboard Hot 100* on June 8, 1968.

It is written in the style of an old drinking song, in which many who are congregated can sing along with the chorus. Toward that end, it is a popular song at some European sports stadiums.

In 2014 Dafydd Iwan, a folk singer and former head of the Party of Wales, called for Welsh rugby supporters to stop singing the song at games because it trivializes violence against women. Jones responded in a BBC interview, "It's not a political statement. This woman is unfaithful to him, and he just loses it. It's something that happens in life. If it's going to be taken literally, I think it takes the fun out of it."

In 2001 Mason told the British newspaper *The Sun* that he based the lyrics on a woman he met while on vacation in Blackpool, England, when he was 15. They had a summer fling but, when it came time for her to return home to North Wales, she told Barry that she had a boyfriend there and it was over between them.

"I was shattered," Mason reportedly said. "I never shook it off, and I became sick with jealousy and a whole lot of pain. She had dark hair and brooding eyes, and she was really feisty. If there's a typical Welsh girl, she was the one."

Mason said her name was Delia, which was impossible to integrate into a song. A decade later, working with Reed, he got the idea to change her name to Delilah, and they completed the song. "I just got more and more worked up with each line," Mason said. "I put my heart and soul into that song, and that's how 'Delilah' was born."

Jones went on to be knighted by Great Britain for his excellence in recording and live performance.

Delilah

Songwriters: Barry Mason, Les Reed

Peaked at No. 15 on Billboard Hot 100

June 8, 1968

I've Gotta Get A Message To You [Bee Gees] – Written by all three of the Bee Gees – Barry, Robin and Maurice – this is a song about pending punishment.

It was the brothers' second U.K. No. 1 single and first top 10 entry in the U.S. It peaked at No. 8 on *Billboard's Hot 100* on Sept. 28 and Oct. 5, 1968. The record also hit No. 1 in Ireland and Italy.

The lyrics tell a story of a condemned murderer who is in prison and about to be executed. Quoted in *Wikipedia,* Robin said, "This is about a prisoner on death row who only has a few hours to live. He wants the prison chaplain to pass on a final message to his wife. There's a certain urgency about it. Myself and Barry wrote it. It's a bit like writing a script. Sometimes you can sit there for three hours with your guitar and nothing will happen. Then in the last ten minutes something will spark."

He added that the man's crime was the murder of his wife's lover, although the lyrics do not explicitly identify the victim or the motive for the crime.

Robin sings the first and third verses, while Barry handles the second.

Not long after this record was on the charts, the Bee Gees broke up for about a year and a half. After they reconciled and became a team again, they charted nine No. 1 singles in America, including an incredible six in a row in 1977-79.

All of the Bee Gees were born on the Isle of Man. Barry, 71, is the lone surviving Gibb brother. Maurice died in 2003 at the age of 53 in a Miami Beach hospital of complications of a twisted intestine. Robin, his twin, died in 2012 of liver and kidney failure. He suffered from the same condition that killed Maurice, and he developed colorectal cancer that metastasized in his liver.

Their younger brother Andy, a solo artist who was born in Manchester, died at age 30 of myocarditis. All four brothers were raised in Australia after the family moved there in 1960. They returned to England as young men to begin their recording career under the wing of producer Robert Stigwood.

I've Gotta Get A Message To You

Songwriters: Barry Gibb, Robin Gibb, Maurice Gibb

Peaked at No. 8 on Billboard Hot 100

Sept. 28, 1968

Oct. 5, 1968

Oct. 12, 1968

Oct. 19, 1968

Bee Gees

Barry Gibb, vocals, guitar (Sept. 1, 1946-)
Robin Gibb, vocals, keyboards, guitar (Dec. 22, 1949-May 20, 2012)
Maurice Gibb, vocals, bass, piano, guitar (Dec. 22, 1949-Jan. 12, 2003)

The Bee Gees: Barry, Maurice and Robin

Indiana Wants Me [R. Dean Taylor] – Written, produced, arranged and sung by Toronto native R. Dean Taylor in 1970, this song was released on Rare Earth Records, a new division of Motown that was promoting rock acts. Taylor already had been a successful songwriter for Motown.

Taylor explained the inspiration for the song in an issue of *Melody Maker* magazine. "I was living in a fleabag hotel, and one night I heard these sirens, and somebody was breaking in a store below. I looked out and police had surrounded this store, and I turned my tape recorder on. I saw *Bonnie And Clyde* a couple of times and, with those two things, that's how I came to write "Indiana Wants Me."

The song is narrated as a letter to his wife by a fugitive who killed a man who insulted her. The crime occurred in Indiana, and now he's on the run to avoid being captured and returned to that state. There is much fear and trepidation in the voice of the man on the lam.

The song opens with the sound of a police siren, which was very realistic sound effect for that period. Because radio listeners in their cars were pulling over and looking for squad cars when the record began to play, the label sent an edited copy to radio stations with the opening siren taken out.

After a voice on a bullhorn advises the narrator that he is surrounded, the sounds of a gun battle can be heard. From that, we can surmise that he would rather go out in a blaze of glory than be tried for his crime.

The song reached a peak position on the *Billboard Hot 100* of No. 5 on Nov. 7 and 14, 1970. It was No. 2 in the U.K., Ireland and Canada.

Indiana Wants Me

Songwriter: R. Dean Taylor
Peaked at No. 5 on Billboard Hot 100
Nov. 7, 1970
Nov. 14, 1970

R. Dean Taylor

Born Richard Dean Taylor in Toronto, Ontario, Canada, on May 11, 1939

R. Dean Taylor

The Night The Lights Went Out In Georgia [Vicki Lawrence] – This song was written by accomplished songwriter Bobby Russell in 1972 and recorded by his then-wife Vicki Lawrence, a comedienne and actress. It was her only fling at being a recording artist.

Russell, who had very marginal success as a singer, was married to Lawrence a scant two years.

The lyrics tell a story (told in the person of the victim's sister) of an unnamed man who returns to his hometown after two weeks away to be informed by his best friend Andy that the man's wife has been unfaithful, sleeping with both Andy and a third man, "that Ames boy, Seth." The man goes home and, noting his wife is not home, heads to Andy's house with a gun. When he arrives, he finds Andy's dead body.

In an attempt to flag down the Georgia State Patrol, the man fires a shot into the air, only to realize too late that the combination of circumstances (the dead body, holding a smoking gun and an audible gunshot) make him look like the killer.

The sheriff arrests the man, a swift show trial is held and the man is convicted and quickly hanged. In the song's epilogue, the man's younger sister (the narrator) confesses that she killed Andy as well as the man's wife, whose body was disposed where it would never be found. The little sister blames the Georgia criminal justice system for her brother's death, warning in each chorus "the judge in the town's got blood stains on his hands." If she ever faced justice for the killings, listeners never are informed.

Russell was reluctant to record even a demo of the song because he didn't like it. According to Lawrence, she believed it was destined to be successful and recorded the demo herself. The publishers and the Bell record label did not quite know how to pitch the song, as it was not really a country or a pop song. The first thought was to offer the song to actress/singer Liza_Minnelli. Eventually it was offered to Cher, but her then-husband and manager Sonny Bono reportedly refused it, as he was said to be concerned that the song might offend Cher's southern fans. Cher didn't find out until years later that the song had been offered to her.

Without a singer to record the song, Lawrence went into a studio and recorded it professionally herself, with the instrumental backing of L.A. session musicians from the Wrecking_Crew. Then she pressed the label to release it as a single.

The song was the basis for a movie by the same name in 1981.

While the song languished at No. 36 on the *Billboard* Country chart, it occupied the No. 1 spot on *Billboard's Hot 100* for two weeks in 1973. It went to No. 1 in Canada, also.

The Night The Lights Went Out In Georgia

Songwriter: Bobby Russell

Peaked at No. 1 on Billboard Hot 100
April 7, 1973
April 14, 1973

Vicki Lawrence

Born Victoria Ann Lawrence in Inglewood, Calif., on March 26, 1949

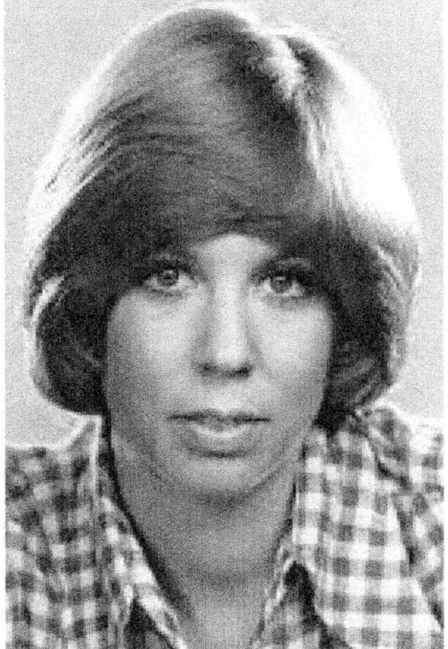

Vicki Lawrence

Dark Lady [Cher]– This grim tale was written in 1973 by Johnny Durrill, the keyboard player for the Ventures. It was the first single released from Cher's 1974 album of the same name. Snuff Garrett, who produced "The Night The Lights Went Out In Georgia," was the producer.

According to *Songfacts,* Durrill said, "I spent a week in his (Garrett's) office playing him songs, one of which Cher recorded. Later, when I was on tour in Japan with the Ventures, I was writing an interesting song. I telegraphed the unfinished lyrics to Garrett. He said to 'make sure the bitch kills him.' Hence, in the song both the lover and fortune teller were killed."

The "Dark Lady" of the song's title is a gypsy fortune teller in New Orleans with a history of misandry (the narrator of the song describes seeing scratches on the inside of the teller's limousine from her previous conquests). The narrator follows the fortune teller's limousine to her lair and pays money for a fortune. As a result of the fortune, she learns that her lover has been unfaithful to her with "someone else who is very close to you."

Advised to leave the fortune teller's parlor, never to return, and to forget she has ever seen the fortune teller's face, the narrator returns home in a state of shock. She is unable to sleep, and then she realizes to her horror that she had once smelled, in her own room, the perfume the fortune teller had been wearing. Sneaking back to the fortune teller's parlor with a gun, she catches her boyfriend and the fortune teller "laughing and kissing" and shoots them both to death, presumably in a fit of rage.

At that point, the song ends, leaving us to ponder whether the shooter would get off with a verdict of temporary insanity or whether a prosecutor could succeed with a charge of second-degree murder.

A gypsy violin solo in the intro lends credence to the "gypsy queen" storyline.

The song was No. 1 on the *Billboard Hot 100* the week of March 23, 1974, and spent 16 weeks on the chart.

Dark Lady

Songwriter: Johnny Durrill
Peaked at No. 1 on Billboard Hot 100
March 23, 1974

Cher

Born Cherilyn Sarkisian in El Centro, Calif., on May 20, 1946

Cher

The Night Chicago Died [Paper Lace] – A Windy City gang war is the premise of this chart topper written in 1974 by – guess who! – that English songwriting team of Mitch Murray and Peter Callander. We talked about them in Chapter 3 during the "Ballad of Bonnie And Clyde" segment.

Earlier in '74 they had written a song titled "Billy, Don't Be A Hero" for the Nottingham band Paper Lace. It became a No. 1 hit in England. While they were trying to make a deal with an American label for release in the U.S., producer Steve Barri heard the song and got Cincinnati band Bo Donaldson & the Heywoods to record it. Their version was sped to market and spent two weeks atop the *Billboard Hot 100* in early summer. Meanwhile, Paper Lace's version stalled at No. 96 in America.

With "The Night Chicago Died" the producers rushed out the recording by Paper Lace before anyone had a chance to cover it. The result was a U.S. No. 1 hit for the Brits on Aug. 17, 1974.

The story is told through the voice of a youngster whose father was a Chicago policeman. His daddy survives the onslaught of gang violence, although the family is sick with worry. Musical instruments are used effectively to replicate the sound of police sirens in the intro.

As quoted in *Songfacts,* Murray said, "Our research was a little bit slipshod. We wrote this fictional story about Al Capone and his men having a shoot-out with the police, which of course never happened. And we used the phrase 'East Side of Chicago.' They claim there is no east side of Chicago!"

The song peaked at a disappointing No. 3 in Britain, even though it was written for domestic consumption. "Our song was written for the English market," Murray said. "If you sit down and try to write an international hit, you get nowhere."

After watching the song climb the American charts, Paper Lace's manager got the idea to write to Chicago Mayor Richard Daley, hoping to arrange a civic reception to congratulate the band. Instead of getting the key to the city, the group received what Murray termed "a rather rude letter." The mayor ended it with, "And one more question – are you nuts?"

A member of Daley's staff was quoted as saying that Paper Lace should "jump into the Chicago River, placing your heads under water three times and surfacing twice."

The Night Chicago Died

Songwriters: Mitch Murray, Peter Callander

Peaked at No. 1 on Billboard Hot 100

Aug. 17, 1974

Paper Lace
Philip Wright (April 9, 1948-) vocals, drums
Mick Vaughan (July 27, 1950-) guitar, arrangements
Cliff Fish (Aug. 13, 1949-) bass
Chris Morris (Nov. 1, 1954-) guitar, vocals
Formed in Nottingham, England, in 1967

Paper Lace

I Shot The Sheriff [Eric Clapton] – Jamaican reggae star Bob Marley wrote this song about a conflict with police in 1973 and recorded it that year with his band the Wailers.

Eric Clapton's version was the most successful on the charts, peaking at No. 1 on the *Billboard Hot 100* for one week and also hitting No. 1 in Canada and New Zealand.

It's about a man who claims he shot a sheriff in self-defense. He is wanted by the law for killing a deputy, which he denies. We never get to find out whether the narrator gets his day in court or if he faces punishment for his deed. The record's melody is faithful to the reggae style in which it originally was written.

The song was the headliner of Clapton's successful album *461 Ocean Boulevard,* the first recording he made after he kicked a two-year addiction to heroin.

A member of Clapton's band played the Marley album for him and convinced him to record the song. Clapton didn't want to use it on his album, but his band members and management told him that not only should he record it but also release it as a single. It became his only No. 1 single in America.

Clapton discussed the song in a phone call with Marley. "I asked him (Marley) what the song was all about but couldn't understand much of his reply," Clapton said. "I was just relieved that he liked what we had done."

The song can be viewed as a message of freedom vs. law, confessional statement seeking redemption and pride in being "wanted" and having notoriety.

I Shot The Sheriff
Songwriter: Bob Marley
Peaked at No. 1 on Billboard Hot 100
Sept. 14, 1974

Eric Clapton

Born Eric Patrick Clapton in Ripley, Surrey, England, on March 30, 1945

Eric Clapton

Take The Money And Run [Steve Miller Band] – Veteran rocker Steve Miller wrote and produced this song and recorded it with his band in 1976. Miller was very successful in the 1970s and '80s at writing his own songs and turning them into hit recordings.

This song was the first single released from the highly acclaimed album "Fly Like An Eagle." On July 24, 1976, it peaked at No. 11 on the *Billboard Hot 100.*

In the lyrics Miller tells a tale of two young slackers, Billy Joe and Bobbie Sue (probably Texans) who get bored with their do-nothing lives. So they go to El Paso and stage a home invasion, whereupon Billy Joe shoots the homeowner. His accomplice takes stolen money and flees.

The story is open-ended. The lyrics declare, "They headed down south, and they're still running today." The crime is clear enough, but we never find out whether the perpetrators get punished. We don't even know whether the wounded homeowner survives.

The story loosely resembles the plot of the 1972 Steve McQueen movie *The Getaway.*

Although born in Milwaukee, Miller moved to Texas in 1950 when he was 7.

Miller wrote the number as a road trip song. As a child, he went on long road trips with his parents during which they listened to the radio all the while and sang along with their favorite songs. In the 1970s FM radio allowed for clear sound and stereo transmission. Miller wrote many of his songs as road trip anthems with multiple layers of sound. He made these songs upbeat and fun, like the ones he enjoyed as a kid.

Another characteristic of Miller's songs was the mention of various places around the nation. This one features El Paso. Another song on the same album ("Rock 'N Me") mentions Phoenix, Tacoma, Philadelphia, Atlanta and L.A.

In 2011-12 Miller was an artist-in-residence at the University of Southern California's Thornton School of Music, where he taught students in the popular music and music industry programs.

There have been 25 different members who rotated through the Steve Miller Band over the years, starting in 1966 when it was known as the Steve Miller Blues Band.

Take The Money And Run

Songwriter: Steve Miller

Peaked at No. 11 on Billboard Hot 100

July 24, 1976

Steve Miller

Born Steven Haworth Miller in Milwaukee, Wis., on Oct. 5, 1943

Steve Miller Band (circa 1976)

Renegade [Styx] – Written by Styx guitarist Tommy Shaw in 1978 for the band's album "Pieces Of Eight," "Renegade" was released as a single in 1979.

The song is a first-person account of an outlaw who is about to be hanged for his crimes, which are not detailed. He cries out to his mother in his time of fear and anguish. He refers to himself a "renegade," but in fact he is just a common criminal who committed capital crimes.

Shaw handles the lead vocal. Although he and fellow Styx guitarist James Young usually played lead guitar on their own compositions, Young asked Shaw if he would play lead on this song.

When Shaw did the original writing on the song, it was a dirge with minor keys and three-part harmony. Keyboard player Dennis DeYoung suggested that Shaw sing the intro *a cappella.*

Reportedly, the Pittsburgh Steelers adopted the song in 2001 to be played in their stadium during games and, in the 2008 season that saw Pittsburgh win the Super Bowl, the defense was unscored upon nine out of 10 times the song was played.

Styx is from Chicago, and the members are from the Roseland section of the far south part of the city. The first name they chose for themselves in 1963 was the Tradewinds but, when another group by that name had a national hit, they changed it to TW4 (There Were 4). Three members attended Chicago State University.

After they signed with Wooden Nickel Records in 1972, they changed their name to Styx, the name of the river in Greek mythology over which dead souls were ferried to reach Hades. A&M Records became their home during the years in which they had their greatest success. Styx's lone No. 1 single, "Babe," hit the top of the *Billboard Hot 100* on Dec. 8, 1979.

Renegade

Songwriter: Tommy Shaw

Peaked at No. 16 on Billboard Hot 100

June 9, 1979

Styx
Dennis DeYoung (Feb. 18, 1947-) vocals, keyboards
Chuck Panozzo (Sept. 20, 1948-) bass, vocals
John Panozzo (Sept. 20, 1948-July 16, 1996) drums
Tommy Shaw (Sept. 11, 1953-) vocals, guitar, mandolin, autoharp, synthesizers
James Young (Nov. 14, 1949-) guitar, keyboards, vocals
Formed in Chicago, Ill., in 1972

Styx: Tommy Shaw, John Panozzo, James Young, Dennis DeYoung, Chuck Panozzo

Ride Like The Wind [Christopher Cross] – Christopher Cross wrote this song about a callous outlaw for his debut album in 1979. He is the son of an Army pediatrician who was stationed at Walter Reed Army Hospital in the 1950s. Cross's father was the physician for President Dwight Eisenhower's grandchildren.

The first single released from Cross's eponymous first album, "Ride Like The Wind" spent four weeks at No. 2 behind *Billboard's* top record of 1980 – "Call Me" by Blondie.

The song is sung in the first person by a man who is riding his horse as fast as he can to escape the pursuit of authorities on his way to the safety of Mexico. That premise is flawed since the United States has had an extradition treaty with Mexico since 1861. The man admits in the lyrics that he has killed 10 men ("lived nine lives, gunned down ten"), and he has been condemned to hang.

Michael McDonald, who was lead singer of the Doobie Brothers at the time, contributed great backing vocals.

"I grew up with a lot of cowboy movies – serials and stuff like the *Lone Ranger* – where they were always chasing the bad guy," Cross told *Songfacts*. "And I lived in San Antonio near Mexico, so there was always this anarchistic allure that, if you could get to Mexico, you could escape the authorities. Also, Mexico was a place where you could go down there and drink and do all this debauchery that, as a kid, sounds really cool. So, getting to the border of Mexico was a fascinating thing to me."

The follow-up single was Cross's first No. 1 single, "Sailing" (see Chapter 17, Ramble On). The debut album sold double platinum and won five Grammy Awards:

- Album of the year
- Record of the year ("Sailing")
- Song of the year ("Sailing")
- Best instrumental arrangement accompanying vocalist ("Sailing")
- Best new artist

Cross scored his second No. 1 single in 1981, "Arthur's Theme (Best That You Can Do)." But his mellow adult contemporary pop style didn't fit well with the flourishing MTV format that was sweeping the music world at that time, and he was unable to crack the top 40 after 1983. He has continued to release albums, as recently as 2014, without regaining the attention he received early in his career.

Ride Like The Wind

Songwriter: Christopher Cross

Peaked at No. 2 on Billboard Hot 100

April 26, 1980
May 3, 1980
May 10, 1980
May 17, 1980

Christopher Cross

Born Christopher Geppert in San Antonio, Texas, on May 3, 1951

Christopher Cross

Smuggler's Blues [Glenn Frey] – Glenn Frey and his songwriting partner, Jack Tempchin, wrote this graphic song/story about drug trafficking. I attended a Glenn Frey concert in 1992. The musician who was originally scheduled to be the opening act of the show couldn't make it, and Tempchin filled in.

Tempchin had a hand in writing a several of Frey's songs, as well as Eagles hits "Peaceful Easy Feeling" and "Already Gone," and he recorded a number of solo albums.

On Feb. 1, 1985, an episode of NBC-TV's *Miami Vice* featured Frey in the role of a drug smuggler. Fittingly, the episode was titled "Smuggler's Blues." His song by the same name was played over part of the action.

Frey had a good showing on videos of his solo songs over the previous three years, and this would be the first of several TV acting jobs for him.

The song was contained on the album *The Allnighter,* and it subsequently was released as a single after the TV show aired. It peaked at No. 12 on *Billboard's Hot 100* on June 16, 1985.

The lyrics are sung by a smuggler who deals in "heroin, cocaine or hash." In the song he doesn't get busted, but his business is fraught with danger from police and criminals who would kill him to take his money or his goods. He speaks his message to a girlfriend who is his accomplice.

Frey landed a starring role in the 1993 CBS drama *South of Sunset,* playing the part of a private detective. The series last one episode before it was canceled. His successful solo singing career was shelved the following year when the Eagles got back together for recording and touring.

He never had a solo No. 1 hit in America, but two of his songs peaked at No. 2.

Smuggler's Blues
Songwriters: Glenn Frey, Jack Tempchin
Peaked at No. 12 on Billboard Hot 100
June 16, 1985

Glenn Frey
Nov. 6, 1948-Jan. 18, 2016
Born Glenn Lewis Frey in Detroit, Mich., and died in New York City, N.Y., of complications from rheumatoid arthritis, acute ulcerative colitis and pneumonia

Glenn Frey

Chapter 5

Sex $ells

Songs that contain overt sexual messages

Overview: Everybody loves sex. Sex is fun, interesting and all around us. We would not exist without it.

Sexual content can help sell records, but is it a good idea to blatantly put this content up front? Apparently, quite a few writers, singers and producers have thought it is. Hence, we have enough songs with overt sexual messaging to fill an entire chapter.

We're not forgetting that the phrase "rock and roll" originally was a euphemism for the sex act. But standards for content of songs that are broadcast on the public airwaves long have been held to a certain standard of decency. There should be a difference between being sexy and being trashy.

Read the lyrics of these 16 songs carefully and decide for yourself if the presentation of sex is too raw, or maybe just right. A dichotomy exists, with what's obscene opposing what is entertaining. The tastes of each individual listener can be unique and different from those of others.

Whatever the case, these records certainly rang the cash registers in a lot of music shops.

To view the full lyrics to these songs, please log on to www.google.com, enter song titles & artist names and click Google Search.

To listen to these songs, please log on to www.youtube.com and enter song titles & artist names.

Sixty Minute Man [Dominoes] – The group that recorded this song in 1951 also went by the name of Billy Ward and his Dominoes. Ward was the group's piano player, manager and songwriter and was a classically trained vocal coach. His business partner Rose Marks was a white New York talent agent, and she received co-writing credit.

The blues-rooted song was a candidate for being the first ever rock and roll song. A tour guide at Sun Studio in Memphis, Graham Winchester, says that honor goes to "Rocket 88" by Jackie Brenston and his Delta Cats, a song that also emerged in 1951.

In the 10 or 15 years after 1951, most songs that fit into the pop/rock genre were ditties about innocent, young love. The words of "Sixty Minute Man," however, form a strong statement of sexual prowess. The narrator breaks down his love-making routine into 15-minute segments that total one hour.

The fourth segment, "15 minutes of blowing my top," refers to – well, you can guess what that means. The narrator says, "They call me Lovin' Dan," which is a reference to "Dan, The Back Door Man," a song recorded in 1937 by Georgia White. Dan was the lover of a married woman and would slip out of her house via the back door as her husband entered through the front.

The record rose to No. 17 on the *Billboard Jukebox Hits* chart and was one of the top songs of the year. It was No. 1 on the Rhythm & Blues Chart for 14 weeks. Ultimately, it was banned by many radio stations and remained a novelty song. For years it did not inspire any other songs with its gritty lyrics.

Later in 1951 the song was recorded as a rockabilly duet by Hardrock Gunter and Roberta Lee and again by the York Brothers.

One of the Dominoes, Clyde McPhatter, later became famous as a member of the Drifters and as a solo performer.

Ward, who served in the U.S. Army during World War II, and his partner Marks owned the name "The Dominoes" and had the power to hire and fire singers. They paid their singers a salary – allegedly $100 a week, minus deductions for taxes, food and hotel bills. Ward, a strict disciplinarian, was known to levy fines for such things as sloppiness, growing a mustache and leaving the hotel without permission.

Sixty Minute Man

Songwriters: Rose Marks, Billy Ward

Peaked at No. 23 on Billboard Best Sellers chart

Sept. 22, 1951

Dominoes

Billy Ward (Sept. 19, 1921-Feb. 16, 2002)
Bill Brown (1936-2004)
Clyde McPhatter (Nov. 15, 1932-June 13, 1972)
Charlie White (1930-2005)
Joe Lamont (died 1998)
Formed in New York City, N.Y., in 1949

Billy Ward (top) and the Dominoes

Rhapsody In The Rain [Lou Christie] – Fifteen years after "Sixty Minute Man," this song became a lightning rod for censorship. Basically, it's about two young people who had sex in a car on a date during a rainstorm. They had drifted apart, and the boy now wants to get back together with the girl and do it again.

Lou Christie told *Goldmine Magazine,* "I had priests and nuns calling to complain. Even *Time Magazine* did an article on it, saying I was corrupting the youth."

Gene Taylor, program director at radio station WLS in Chicago, said in the article that lines in the lyrics and the mention of windshield wipers could only mean that the couple was having sex in time with the wipers.

With stations across the nation pulling the plug on the song's airplay, MGM Records rushed out an amended version. "Makin' out in the rain" was changed to "we fell in love in the rain," and "our love went much too far" was altered to say, "our love came like a falling star."

But it was too late – the record's momentum had been stalled. It spent only four weeks in the *Billboard* top 40, topping out at No. 16. It must have been at that point that radio stations were yanking the song because it dropped five positions the following week and quickly plummeted off the charts.

Writing credit for "Rhapsody" is shared by Twyla Herbert, Christie's long-time collaborator. They met at an audition in a church basement in his hometown of Glenwillard, Pa., when he was 15 and she was 36. She was a self-described clairvoyant and mystic, whom Christie said was a "bohemian gypsy, psychic and former concert pianist."

Christie has commented, "Twyla is a genius. She was going to be a concert pianist, but we started writing rock and roll. The hardest part was that we had too many ideas. If we wanted to write a song, it would never stop."

Herbert died in Phoenix on July 11, 2009, at the age of 87.

The song inspired a stage production known as "A Rhapsody In The Rain."

Christie, along with Del Shannon and Frankie Valli of the Four Seasons, was one of the major artists of the 1960s who prominently used the falsetto style of singing.

He grew up in suburban Pittsburgh and studied music and voice in high school while serving as student conductor of the choir. After graduation in 1961, he traveled to New York City and worked as a session vocalist before he cut his own record and changed his name.

Soon after his first single "The Gypsy Cried" became a regional hit around Pittsburgh, he was signed to Roulette Records.

A veteran New Jersey girl trio known as the Delicates provided the backing vocals. They have been honored for their singing accomplishments in their hometown of Belleville with a spot on the city's "Wall of Recognition," and they have a plaque on a wall at Belleville High School next to one that honors another alum, Connie Francis. The auditorium in Grammar School #8 is named for them.

Rhapsody In The Rain

Songwriters: Lou Christie, Twyla Herbert

Peaked at No. 16 on Billboard Hot 100

April 30, 1966

Lou Christie

Born Lugee Alfredo Giovanni Sacco in Glenwillard, Pa., on Feb. 19, 1943

Lou Christie

Honky Tonk Women [Rolling Stones] – About three years after Lou Christie's lyrical misstep, Mick Jagger and Keith Richard were on vacation at a ranch near Sao Paulo, Brazil. Out in the country with horses all around, they sat on the porch of their ranch house feeling just like cowboys.

The two Rolling Stones songwriters started to put together a twangy song on acoustic guitar to fit the mood they were in. After they returned to England in early January 1969, Jagger and Richards polished up the song. In March, the Stones recorded an acoustic song they titled "Country Honk." On June 8 they finished recording "Honky Tonk Women," a song about sexual adventures with a prostitute in Memphis and a divorcee in New York City, which had similar structure to "Country Honk." There was also a reference to cocaine use (she blew my nose …).

Guitarist Brian Jones, who was the leading force in forming the band in 1962, participated in some of the recording sessions. But his overindulgence in recreational drugs was making him useless to the group. The others recruited guitarist Mick Taylor from John Mayall's Bluesbreakers, and then they told Jones that he was fired from the band.

The single was released in Great Britain on July 4, the day after Jones's dead body was found at the bottom of his swimming pool.

The highly suggestive lyrics of the song were tempered just enough to keep it from getting banned by radio stations. In Chicago, Gene Taylor had been promoted to station manager at WLS. But there were no cries of righteous indignation from him as the song ascended to the No. 1 position on the WLS *Hit Parade* for five weeks. It also spent five weeks at No. 1 in the U.K. and was the Stones' last No. 1 hit in their homeland.

The distinctive cowbell intro was played by Jimmy Miller, who served as producer of the recording.

Throughout the years the Stones have made a few personnel changes, and the band has gone on hiatus from time to time. But they remain the longest-running rock act ever and have three original members still on board. Bassist Bill Wyman retired from the band in 1993 and never was officially replaced.

Honky Tonk Women

Songwriters: Mick Jagger, Keith Richards

Peaked at No. 1 on Billboard Hot 100

Aug. 23, 1969
Aug. 30, 1969
Sept. 6, 1969
Sept. 13, 1969

Rolling Stones

Mick Jagger (July 26, 1943-) lead vocals
Keith Richards (Dec. 18, 1943-) guitar, backing vocals
Charlie Watts (June 2, 1941-) drums
Bill Wyman (Oct. 24, 1936-) bass
Brian Jones (Feb. 28, 1942-July 3, 1969) guitar
Formed in London, England, in 1962

The Rolling Stones: Bill Wyman, Mick Jagger, Keith Richards, Charlie Watts, Brian Jones

Pillow Talk [Sylvia] – This is the first rock-era song by a female artist that delivered a blatantly sexual message. She wouldn't be the last. It basically consists of 3 and a half minutes of whispering, cooing, coaxing, moaning, pleading and heavy breathing.

Sylvia had been laying low as a recording artist for years before she cut this track. She was part of the duet Mickey & Sylvia that scored a hit with "Love Is Strange" in 1957. They released six more low-charting songs between 1957 and '61. Then Mickey broke up the act when he moved to France.

Sylvia (married name: Robinson) and Michael Burton had written "Pillow Talk" in hopes that Al Green would record it. But Green, an ordained minister who sang gospel-tinged soul songs, turned it down because he thought it was too risqué.

So, Sylvia recorded it herself and released it in 1973. It made a serious run at the No. 1 spot on the *Billboard Hot 100* before stopping at No. 3. It spent two weeks at No. 1 on the *Billboard Soul Chart*, and it peaked at No. 3 in Canada and No. 14 in the U.K.

Curiously, Sylvia eventually became better known for something other than her singing. In 1974 she and her husband Joe Robinson formed Sugar Hill Records, and they released the first ever rap recording in 1979, "Rapper's Delight" by the Sugarhill Gang. This earned her the nickname "Mother of Hip-Hop."

Sylvia dropped out of school at the age of 14 and began recording music in 1950 under the name Little Sylvia. In 1954 she began teaming with Kentuckian Mickey Baker. She began her brief solo career in 1972.

She died at Meadowlands Hospital in Secaucus, N.J., from congestive heart failure.

Pillow Talk

Songwriters: Sylvia Robinson, Michael Burton

Peaked at No. 3 on Billboard Hot 100

June 9, 1973

June 16, 1973

Sylvia

May 29, 1935-Sept. 29, 2011

Born Sylvia Vanderpool in Harlem, New York City, N.Y., and died in Secaucus, N.J.

Sylvia

I'm Gonna Love You Just A Little More Baby [Barry White] – Composer Barry White had produced a hit record for the girl group Love Unlimited in 1972. The following year he was ready to stand in front of the microphone and record his own hit song. He also did the writing and producing.

"I'm Gonna Love You Just A Little More Baby" would serve as a kind of blueprint for White's vocal career. It was soft, smooth, sultry and sexy and had seductive lyrics. His hit songs that followed for the next 20 years had the same basic elements.

The song's lyrics were very suggestive, but public reception was positive as the record topped the *Billboard Soul Chart* for two weeks and peaked at No. 3 on the pop chart. In Canada it hit No. 10.

White was overweight for most of his adult life, but his bass-baritone voice enabled his image as a sexy crooner to thrive. His familiar nickname was "The Walrus of Love."

His parents never married, so his mother gave him her last name. Later he took on the surname of his father, Melvin A. White. He grew up in South Central Los Angeles, Calif., where he listened to his mother's classical music collection and tried to emulate on piano what he heard on the records. He was jailed for four months at the age of 16 for stealing $30,000 worth of automobile tires. While incarcerated he heard "It's Now Or Never" by Elvis Presley on the radio, an experience he credited with changing the course of his life.

He died at Cedars-Sinai Medical Center in Los Angeles following a severe stroke. He had been undergoing dialysis and was waiting for a kidney transplant.

He amassed 106 gold albums (500,000 in sales) worldwide and 20 gold and 10 platinum singles.

I'm Gonna Love You Just A Little More Baby
Songwriter: Barry White
Peaked at No. 3 on Billboard Hot 100
June 23, 1973

Barry White
Sept. 12, 1944-July 4, 2003
Born Barry Eugene Carter in Galveston, Texas, and died in Los Angeles, Calif.

Barry White

Let's Get It On [Marvin Gaye] – Starting in 1963, Marvin Gaye had a nice recording career going with Motown Records. He had a clean-cut image and sang innocent love songs, some of them great duets with female singers (see Chapter 6, The Story of Motown).

Then in 1970 he took about a year off, and when he came back, he was fully bearded as he released an album of protest songs. He sang about the Vietnam War, the ecology and inner-city strife. His persona took on a whole new dimension.

In the spring of 1973, his career took another turn with the recording of an album and single titled "Let's Get It On." According to the Urban Dictionary, "get it on" is a euphemism for having sex, and Gaye's song popularized that meaning and sent it into the mainstream of pop culture.

The song is a lengthy, sensual pleading by a guy to a girl to have sex with him. Since this was the more permissive 1970s, the record was not hassled by censors or radio station executives.

Ed Townsend, a one-hit recording artist from the 1950s, co-wrote the song and conceived it after his release from an alcoholism rehab center to express his desire to get on with life. It originally had a religious theme. But Gaye's confidante, Kenneth Stover, changed the words to give it a political meaning. Then Gaye and Townsend reworked the lyrics again to arrive at the final product.

The erotic recording seemly went against the grain of Gaye's upbringing. His father was an apostolic preacher in Washington, D.C., and Marvin Jr. started singing in his father's church choir at age 4.

Gaye befriended jazz guitarist Slim Gaillard and had fallen in love with Gaillard's 17-year-old daughter Janis. It is believed that Janis was in the recording booth when Gaye laid down the track, since they were smitten with each other. They soon began dating, and they married in 1977.

While the record spent two weeks atop the *Billboard Hot 100*, it notched eight weeks at No. 1 on *Billboard's Soul Chart*. It became Motown's biggest selling single in the United States at that time, selling over two million copies in its first six weeks. *Billboard* ranked it as the No. 4 single for the year 1973.

Gaye's parents were a Pentecostal minister and a domestic worker. At 17 he dropped out of school and enlisted in the U.S. Air Force. Disappointed in his role in the service, he faked mental illness and was discharged shortly thereafter.

He relocated to Detroit in 1960 and, after signing a recording contract with Motown subsidiary Tamla Records, he changed the spelling of his last name because of the teasing he got about it.

Gaye was shot dead by his father in the family's Los Angeles home after he intervened in a fight between his parents.

Let's Get It On

Songwriters: Marvin Gaye, Ed Townsend

Peaked at No. 1 on Billboard Hot 100

Sept. 8, 1973

Sept. 22, 1973

Marvin Gaye

April 2, 1939-April 1, 1984

Born Marvin Pentz Gay Jr. in Washington, D.C., and died in Los Angeles, Calif.

Marvin Gaye

Lady Marmalade [Labelle] – It may be sung in French, but the buzz phrase from this song leaves no doubt as to the song's meaning. *Voulez-vous coucher avec moi ce soir* translates to "do you want to sleep with me tonight?"

The context of the lyrics of "Lady Marmalade" is a New Orleans prostitute propositioning a potential customer. The ensuing encounter is related tastefully, but the sexual tone of the song is obvious. We hear "itchi gitchi ya ya da da" a few times, along with the mention of *boudoir* and black satin sheets.

The three-member vocal group Labelle was from Philadelphia, but the song's co-producer, Allen Toussaint, was from New Orleans, where he was an influential musician, songwriter, arranger and producer.

Kenny Nolan and Bob Crewe wrote the song, which was inspired by Crewe's experiences with prostitutes in New Orleans. It was first recorded by a disco group called the Eleventh Hour. Crewe showed the song to Toussaint, who decided to record it with Labelle.

In a quirk of chart history, with "Lady Marmalade" Nolan and Crewe became the third songwriting team to succeed themselves in the *Billboard Hot 100's* No. 1 position. Their composition "My Eyes Adored You" by Frankie Valli was No. 1 the week before.

Nolan explained , "I had one part of the song here and one part there, and it still needed something. Bob and I came up with the idea of '*voulez-vous couchez avec moi ce soir.'* It was like a puzzle that finally fit together."

In a 1986 interview with *NME* magazine, lead singer Patti LaBelle said, "That song was taboo. I mean, why sing about a hooker? Why not? I had a good friend who was a hooker, and she died. She never took the mic out of my hand, and I never took the mattress from under her. She was a friend, doing her thing. It'd be like discriminating because you're white and I'm black, or you're gay and someone's straight. I don't believe in separating people. If your job is a hooker, more power to you."

When Labelle performed the song on television, the trio was prohibited from singing the chorus as written. So, they sang the French equivalent of "do you want to **dance** with me?"

The song also was No. 1 on the *Billboard Soul Chart*, and it hit No. 1 in Canada and the Netherlands.

The group originated as the Ordettes and soon changed their name to the Blue Belles.
One of the original members, Cindy Birdsong, joined the Supremes in 1967. In 1971 they altered their appearance and musical direction with the name change to Labelle. The members went their separate ways at the conclusion of a tour in 1976.

"Lady Marmalade" appeared as part of a medley in the movie *"Moulin Rouge!"* A single recorded by Christina Aguilera, Lil' Kim, Mya and Pink topped the *Billboard Hot 100* for five weeks in 2001.

Lady Marmalade

Songwriters: Bob Crewe, Kenny Nolan

Peaked at No. 1 on Billboard Hot 100

March 29, 1975

Labelle

Patti LaBelle [born Patricia Louise Holt] (May 24, 1944-)

Nona Hendryx (Oct. 9, 1944-)

Sarah Dash (Aug. 18, 1945-)

Formed in 1962 in Philadelphia, Pa.

Labelle: Nona Hendryx, Patti LaBelle, Sarah Dash

Chevy Van [Sammy Johns] – This song provides a classic example of casual sex and comes to us in the form of a little tale.

The narrator is driving from city to city in his Chevy van in parts untold. He picks up a hitchhiker – an attractive young female. She is tired, so she lies down in the rear of the vehicle to take a nap. At some point she wakes and returns to the driver's area where she "took me by the hand, we made love in my Chevy van."

There is no seduction or provocative talk. No double entendres, no heavy breathing. The scene is laid out in a matter-of-fact way, but we are left with no doubt of what these two people are doing in the vehicle.

Eventually the girl gets out at her destination, a very small town, and walks away. The narrator doesn't expect to return there or see her again.

This fanciful story portrays the kind of scenario that a typical young man fantasizes about.

The song was recorded in 1973 and was included on Sammy Johns' eponymous first album. The GRC record label held it back until after the release of the first single, "Early Morning Love," which peaked at No. 68 on the *Billboard Hot 100.*

Rolling Stone called the song "the song of the '70s."

According to an anecdote read by disc jockey Casey Kasem on *American Top 40,* Johns toured the U.S. just to thank personnel at the radio stations that played "Chevy Van" and helped make it a hit.

Future remakes of "Chevy Van" by other artists were given more of a country music treatment.

Johns founded his first band, the Devilles, when he was a teenager. He moved to Atlanta, Ga., in the early 1970s, where he signed with GRC Records. He wrote songs that became No. 1 country hits for Waylon Jennings, Conway Twitty and John Conlee. Johns had drug and alcohol problems throughout his life and had four failed marriages.

He died in Gaston Memorial Hospital in Gastonia, N.C. It was speculated that he suffered a stroke or was electrocuted while repairing an old lamp.

Chevy Van

Songwriter: Sammy Johns

Peaked at No. 5 on Billboard Hot 100

May 3, 1975

Sammy Johns

Feb. 7, 1946-Jan. 4, 2013

Born Sammy Reginald Johns in Charlotte, N.C., and died in Gastonia, N.C.

Sammy Johns

Love Won't Let Me Wait [Major Harris] – With the smooth and soulful Philly Sound, Major Harris scored a big hit with this sexy song. Just one year earlier in 1974, he had left the Delfonics to pursue a solo career.

The lyrics are not blatantly sexual, for the most part, but there is seduction in Harris's voice. As a bonus, female vocalist Barbara Ingram offers some whispering, moaning and groaning to let everyone know that she has taken the bait and is all in on the conquest. Carla Benton and Yvette Benson were the other backing singers.

We know that the narrator plans to spend the night with the girl at her place, so I hope she has the makings for a nice breakfast in her kitchen!

Besides earning a top five ranking on the pop chart, the song spent one week at No. 1 on *Billboard's Soul Chart. Billboard* ranked it as the No. 24 song of 1975.

Harris sang with such groups as the Charmers, the Teenagers, the Jarmels and Nat Turner's Rebellion early in his career. In the early 1970s he replaced Randy Cain as a member of the Delfonics, which was one of the top proponents of the Philadelphia soul sound.

Harris died in a Richmond hospital of congestive heart and lung failure.

Love Won't Let Me Wait

Songwriters: Vinnie Barrett, Bobby Eli

Peaked at No. 5 on Billboard Hot 100

June 21, 1975

June 28, 1975

July 5, 1975

Major Harris

Feb. 9, 1947-Nov. 9, 2012

Born Major Harris III in Richmond, Va., and died in his hometown

Major Harris

Love To Love You Baby [Donna Summer] – Boston native Donna Summer was living in Europe for eight years, doing musical stage productions. She had one album under her belt when this song was created.

She suggested the title lyric to Italian musician Giorgio Moroder in 1975, and he turned it into a full disco song before he asked her to record it. Since the lyrics were explicit, Summer agreed to record it only as a demo to give to someone else. However, Summer's embellishment of the vocal impressed Moroder so much that he convinced her to release it as her own song, whereupon it became a modest hit in the Netherlands.

A tape of the song was sent to Casablanca Records president Neil Bogart in the U.S., and he played it over and over. He contacted Moroder and wanted him to make the track longer – up to 20 minutes. Summer had reservations about doing that, but she decided to put herself in the role of an actress to play the part of someone in sexual ecstasy.

The lights in the studio were turned off to create the proper mood, and she let fly with more than 16 minutes of "Love To Love You." When it was released in November 1975 for worldwide distribution, the word "baby" was added to the end of the title. The song took up the entire first side of an album by the same name.

It became a disco smash, and *Billboard* ranked it No. 1 for four weeks on its *Dance Club Songs* chart. On the *Hot 100* it rose to No. 2, and it was No. 1 in Canada.

Over in England, the BBC refused to play or promote the record, noting that the full-length version contained 23 "orgasms." Still, the song reached No. 4 on the U.K. singles chart.

Summer was tagged "the first lady of love," but later would become a born-again Christian. Thereafter she omitted "Love To Love You Baby" from her concert playlists for the next 25 years.

She was raised in the Boston neighborhood of Mission Hill. In 1967, weeks before high school graduation, she moved to New York City and joined the blues rock band Black Crow. She later auditioned and won the role of Sheila in the musical *Hair,* and agreed to take the role in the Munich, Germany, production of the show.

She married Austrian actor Helmuth Sommer in 1973 and gave birth to a daughter the same year. She recorded an album in 1974 and, due to an error on the record jacket, she became Donna *Summer* – the name stuck.

Summer died of lung cancer at her home in Naples, Fla. She believed that the disease resulted from inhaling dust and toxic fumes in New York City on Sept. 11, 2001.

Love To Love You Baby

Songwriters: Donna Summer, Giorgio Moroder, Pete Bellotte

Peaked at No. 2 on Billboard Hot 100

Feb. 7, 1976

Feb. 14, 1976

Donna Summer

Dec. 31, 1948-May 17, 2012

Born LaDonna Adrian Gaines in Boston, Mass., and died in Naples, Fla.

Donna Summer

Afternoon Delight [Starland Vocal Band] – So what does a clean-cut quartet do after it has a hit with a song about having sex in the afternoon? Go on TV with its own nighttime summer variety show, that's what.

"Afternoon Delight" was No. 1 for two weeks in the summer of 1976, and times had changed since the 1960s. Not only did the song get unfettered airplay, the singers were rewarded with the TV show a year later.

The title came from a P.M. menu section from Clyde's restaurant in the Georgetown section of Washington, D.C. Bill Danoff, who formed Starland Vocal with his wife Taffy and future newlyweds Jon Carroll and Margot Chapman, had a different idea of what an afternoon delight should be.

"I didn't want to write an all-out sex song," Danoff told the *Los Angeles Times.* "I just wanted to write something that was fun and hinted at sex. It was one of those songs that you could have a really good time writing.

"If the song had been banned, it would have been a real injustice. The lyrics are subtle and sophisticated and not at all raunchy. It might have been banned years ago, but not today."

Bill Danoff had met John Denver at the Cellar Door club in Washington in the late '60s, and together they wrote songs that included "Take Me Home, Country Roads." The Danoffs and their band Fat City sang back-up on Denver's recording of the song.

After the Starland Vocal Band was formed, they were the first act signed to Denver's label, Windsong Records. Their calling card was terrific harmonizing.

"Afternoon Delight" was No. 1 in Canada and No. 5 in New Zealand but peaked at only No. 18 in the U.K. Starland Vocal Band and their smash hit won the Grammy for Best Arrangement of Voices in 1977.

The marriages of the Danoffs and the Carrolls both eventually ended in divorce. The quartet was active until 1981. All of the band members went on to have undistinguished solo careers.

Afternoon Delight
Songwriter: Bill Danoff
Peaked at No. 1 on Billboard Hot 100
July 10, 1976
July 17, 1976

Starland Vocal Band
Bill Danoff (May 7, 1946-)
Taffy Danoff (Oct. 25, 1944-)
Jon Carroll (March 1, 1957-)
Margot Chapman (Sept. 7, 1957-)
Formed in Washington, D.C., in 1976

Starland Vocal Band: Jon Carroll, Margot Chapman, Taffy Danoff, Bill Danoff

Tonight's The Night (Gonna Be Alright) [Rod Stewart] – Here's another super hit that had an overt sexual message. But public acceptance was phenomenal.

The record spent eight consecutive weeks at No. 1 on the *Billboard Hot 100* at the end of 1976, with the first week of 1977 included. Because of the way *Billboard* configures its year-end rankings, the song was declared the No. 1 song of 1977.

The slow-tempo melody is accompanied by lyrics that have the narrator seducing a woman with promises of love and pleasure. At one point, he calls the girl an angel and invites her to "spread your wings and let me come inside." Not very subtle, eh? That line got the song banned by the BBC but, due to public pressure, the ban was later lifted and the single rose to No. 5 in the U.K.

The phrase "sex rock" had entered the public domain in 1975, due in part to an article in *Time Magazine* about the rise of songs like this one. With a new genre clearly defined, there were protests from various social groups like Jesse Jackson's Operation PUSH, which contended that such music was corrupting the nation's youth.

Oddly, the roots of "Tonight's The Night" go back to an evening Rod Stewart spent at the home recording studio of Dan Peek, a Christian who was a member of the trio America. "I played 'Today's The Day,' the song I had been working on," Peek said. "Rod said that he liked it and that it gave him an idea for a song. Of course, after his recording of 'Tonight's The Night' came out, I laughed when I remembered what he'd said. I'm sure I probably smacked my forehead and said, 'Why didn't I think of that?'"

"Today's The Day" became a No. 1 hit on the *Billboard Adult Contemporary* chart and peaked at No. 23 on the *Hot 100* during the summer of 1976.

Swedish actress Britt Ekland, who was Stewart's girlfriend at the time, provided the French words whispered at the end of the track. Stewart said she did not want to do it, but he plied her with alcoholic beverages to get her to comply. She also appears in a promo video for the song, although her back is always to the camera.

While much of the recording was done at Muscle Shoals, Ala., Stewart's final vocal was recorded at Caribou Ranch Studios in the Colorado Rockies. The result of recording at high elevation was a pitch that was one octave higher than that at sea level.

The song hit No. 1 in Canada, No. 2 in New Zealand and Ireland and No. 3 in Australia.

Stewart had a Scottish father and an English mother. He developed a love for soccer at an early age. His introduction to rock and roll was hearing Little Richard on record and seeing Bill Haley & His Comets in concert.

His ambition was to be a professional soccer player, but he went unsigned after participating in tryouts in 1960. Thereafter, he concentrated on music as a career. He sang with several bands before he established his solo career in 1971.

Tonight's The Night (Gonna Be Alright)

Songwriter: Rod Stewart

Peaked at No. 1 on Billboard Hot 100

Nov. 13, 1976
Nov. 20, 1976
Nov. 27, 1976
Dec. 4, 1976
Dec. 11, 1976
Dec. 18, 1976
Dec. 25, 1976
Jan. 1, 1977

Rod Stewart

Born Roderick David Stewart in Highgate, North London, England, on Jan. 10, 1945

Rod Stewart

Physical [Olivia Newton-John] – Entering 1981 Olivia Newton-John had four No. 1 hits in America, totaling eight weeks at the top spot. By the end of that year, she would surpass that total with one mega-hit that topped the *Billboard Hot 100* for 10 weeks.

Also, up to that time her image had been carefully crafted by songwriter/producer John Farrar and her other handlers to be pure and pristine throughout her 10-year recording career. But suddenly she appeared to be a bit naughty.

When ONJ invited listeners to "get physical," it's safe to say that she didn't mean to do so by just holding hands. The song's video showed her in workout togs, trying to help overweight men lose weight in a health club. But that was just a G-rated diversion.

The song was written by Steve Kipner and Terry Shaddick, who originally intended to offer it to Rod Stewart. They did offer it to Tina Turner, who declined it.

"Physical" was banned or censored for its suggestive lyrics in some markets. The line "there's nothing left to talk about unless it's horizontally" was particularly offensive to some radio station programmers.

Nonetheless, the record was much decorated. *Billboard* ranked it No. 6 on its all-time top 100 list; No. 1 on its Top 50 Sexiest Songs Of All Time; and No. 1 on its list of Top 100 songs of the 1980s. It was rated the No. 1 song of 1982, since chart data for that year started in Nov. 1981. It hit No. 1 in Australia, Belgium, Canada, New Zealand and Switzerland, but in the U.K., it peaked at No. 7.

"I just wasn't in the mood for tender ballads," ONJ told *People Magazine.* "I wanted peppy stuff because that's how I'm feeling. We thought it was a great title because of the keep-fit craze that is going on.

"I think the song has a double entendre. You can take it how you want to. But it's meant to be fun … it's not meant to be taken too seriously."

One radio music director commented in *Billboard*, "Once the words sank in, it caused an uncomfortableness among listeners."

Born in England, Newton-John's family emigrated to Melbourne, Australia, where her father became professor of German and then Master of Ormond College at the University of Melbourne. She broke into show business at age 14 when she formed an all-girl vocal group. Her first international hit as a solo artist was "If Not For You" in 1971.

Physical

Songwriters: Steve Kipner, Terry Shaddick

Peaked at No. 1 on Billboard Hot 100
Nov. 21, 1981
Nov. 28, 1981
Dec. 5, 1981
Dec. 12, 1981
Dec. 19, 1981
Dec. 26, 1981
Jan. 2, 1982
Jan. 9, 1982
Jan. 16, 1982
Jan. 23, 1982

Olivia Newton-John

Born Olivia Newton-John in Cambridge, England, on Sept. 26, 1948

Olivia Newton-John

Touch Me (I Want Your Body) [Samantha Fox] – This song doesn't describe the actual act of sex, but it does go a little over the top with the female narrator describing her bawdy feelings and her search for a lover.

What is a bit confusing about Samantha Fox doing this song is the fact that she was a beautiful 20-year-old British singer, model and actress at the time. She didn't have to put on an act of desperation, as she surely had many gentlemen suitors at the time. Her image wasn't totally clean, however, as she became a topless model for a British tabloid newspaper when she was 16. In 1996 she posed for the October issue of *Playboy Magazine.*

This was her first single as a recording artist, and it became a worldwide hit. It preceded her other songs with similar subject matter, such as "Do Ya Do Ya (Wanna Please Me)" and "Naughty Girls (Need Love Too)."

If you're looking for irony in Fox's life, you won't be disappointed. Rumors about her sexuality began to surface in 1999, and sometime later she admitted that she was gay. Her manager, Myra Stratton, joined her in a civil union, but Stratton died of cancer in 2015 at age 60.

Through most of Fox's modeling, acting and singing career, she was managed by her father, Patrick Fox. In 1991 she hired accountants to trace over £1 million that she believed had been embezzled from her accounts. She sued her father and was awarded a court settlement of £363,000. He died in 2000.

"Touch Me" hit No. 1 in Australia, Canada, Finland, Norway, Sweden and Switzerland.

Touch Me (I Want Your Body)

Songwriters: Jon Astrop, Mark Shreeve, Pete Q. Harris
Peaked at No. 4 on Billboard Hot 100
Feb. 14, 1987

Samantha Fox

Born Samantha Karen Fox in Mile End, London, England, on April 15, 1966

Samantha Fox

Shake You Down [Gregory Abbott] – This song has lots of sex appeal, but I think it represents a good side of sex rock. It's a seduction of sorts, but it comes across as a smooth, catchy love ballad.

As sweet rhythm & blues songs, "Pillow Talk" and "Let's Get It On" could have been like this if they had toned down the lyrics and assorted vocal noises.

One might assume that "shake you down" means someone trying to borrow money from you or ask for a hand-out. But Gregory Abbott, who wrote and produced the song, gave the phrase a different meaning.

"I think I might have coined a new phrase," Abbott said. "The song was my attempt to express how men feel when they see a woman they like. Emotionally, the phrase 'shake you down' made sense to me and, when I repeated it to a lady friend of mine, she definitely understood what I was saying. So that became the hook of the song.

"Now I hear women saying, 'Yeah, he really shook me down last night,' or 'I'd sure like to shake him down.'"

It was a quantum leap for a guy from Harlem, N.Y., to go from choirboy to the holder of the No. 1 spot on both the *Billboard Hot Black Singles* and *Hot 100* charts. Abbott, who got his first piano lessons from his mother, sang in the St. Patrick's Cathedral Choir in Manhattan. He went on to earn a bachelor's degree in psychology from Boston University and a master's degree from California State University at San Francisco. He did graduate work in literature at Stanford and taught various courses at UC Berkeley. He interrupted work on his doctorate degree to pursue a music career.

Abbott's parents were from Venezuela and Antigua. He was married to R&B singer Freda Payne, 1976-79.

"Shake You Down" was Abbott's only hit single, and it reached No. 2 in Canada and No. 3 in Netherlands and New Zealand. *Billboard* ranked it as the No. 3 song of the year 1987.

The song received one million air plays faster than any other song in history, thanks in part to its status as a pop/soul crossover hit.

Shake You Down

Songwriter: Gregory Abbott

Peaked at No. 1 on Billboard Hot 100

Jan. 17, 1987

Gregory Abbott

Born Gregory Joel Abbott in New York City, N.Y. on April 2, 1954

Gregory Abbott

I Wanna Sex You Up [Color Me Badd] – Like the previous one, this song is sonically pleasant. But it might have had more mass appeal if the lyrics had been toned down. Who would have thought that a quartet of young men from conservative Oklahoma City would release a song with such a title for their first hit?

Reportedly, some radio disc jockeys referred to the song on air as "I Wanna Love You Up" in deference to the feelings of their audiences.

The song was featured prominently in the 1991 movie *New Jack City.* The producers wanted a song that had the modern R&B sound, which became known as "New Jack Swing." Contemporary artists like Bobby Brown and Jody Watley had been proponents of the budding genre.

You may not be able to hear it, but a line in the background is repeated several times, "I *know* you're not gonna sing *that* song." That line comes from an anecdote related by singer Betty Wright. She once told a concert audience that she was planning to sing a song titled "Tonight Is The Night," which chronicles a young woman's first intimate encounter with a man. Wright's mother, who was mortified by the song's subject matter, exclaimed, "I *know* you're not gonna sing *that* song!"

Color Me Badd did not ask for Wright's permission to sample her voice on the final mix of the recording. She eventually found out that her cousin was managing the band. "My mother and their mother worked it out, and lawyers didn't have to work it out. I just wanted what was mine," Wright said on the TV documentary *Unsung.*

"I Wanna Sex You Up" spent four weeks at No. 2 on the *Billboard Hot 100* and hit No. 1 in the U.K. and New Zealand, as well as the *Billboard Hot R&B* and *Hot Dance Music* charts. *Billboard* ranked it as the No. 2 song of the year 1991.

Sam Watters named the group after a racehorse known as Color Me Bad. The original four members met at Northwest Classen High School in Oklahoma City and were members of the school choir.

I Wanna Sex You Up

Songwriter: Elliot Straite

Peaked at No. 2 on Billboard Hot 100

June 8, 1991
June 15, 1991
June 22, 1991
June 29, 1991

Color Me Badd

Bryan Abrams (Nov. 16, 1969-)
Mark Calderon (Sept. 27, 1970-)
Sam Watters (July 23, 1970-)
Kevin Thornton (June 17, 1969-)
Formed in Oklahoma City, Okla., in 1985

Color Me Badd: Kevin Thornton, Sam Watters, Mark Calderon, Bryan Abrams

Chapter 6

Motown

The story of a successful independent record label

Overview: The Motown aggregate of record labels is important in the music industry because it represents the efforts of an independent, private company to compete in the recording business with the goal of advancing one specific kind of music.

The company attained its goal and succeeded, probably beyond its founder's wildest dreams. The artists and their recordings became famous around the world, and the rhythm & blues genre that they promoted became known as the "Motown Sound." The impact on public consciousness and pop culture has been enormous.

No other record label that started out as a small, independent competitor can claim to have the kind of success and industrial impact as Motown.

Prologue: Berry Gordy Jr. (born Nov. 28, 1929) of Detroit, Mich., is the founder of Motown Records. In the 1950s he briefly held a job making $86.40 a week as an assembly line worker in a Lincoln-Mercury plant. He hated the work and aspired to enter the music business.

Before he became an autoworker, Gordy served in Korea for the U.S. Army and then opened the 3-D Record Mart. The store went bankrupt in 1955.

In 1959, Gordy's sisters Gwen and Anna, along with Billy Davis, launched Anna Records, and they asked Berry Gordy to serve as president. He had shown talent as a songwriter, but he was dissatisfied with the paltry amount of royalties he was getting.

With $800 he borrowed from his family and royalties earned from writing songs for rising star Jackie Wilson, Gordy opened Tamla Records on Jan. 12, 1959. That same year he bought the property at 2648 West Grand Blvd., Detroit, which would house his family, the company's offices and a recording studio. Also in 1959, Gordy started his own music publishing company, Jobete Publishing. It was named for his children Hazel Joy, Berry and Terry.

Anna Records was absorbed by Motown in 1961.

Quote: "Every day I'd watch how a bare metal frame rolling down the line would become a spanking brand-new car. What a great idea! Maybe I could do the same with my music – create a place where a kid off the street could walk in one door an unknown, go through a process and come out a star." ~ *Berry Gordy Jr.*

Detroit had an abundance of musical talent, and Gordy had a large pool of singers and musicians to tap. A group known as the Matadors had unsuccessfully auditioned for Jackie Wilson's manager, Nat Tarnopol, in 1958. Gordy liked them, however, and struck up a close friendship with the lead singer, William "Smokey" Robinson. The Matadors soon changed their name to the Miracles, who would have the first hit record on Tamla. It was Robinson who talked Gordy into starting his own label, and he would become a vice president of the company.

Gordy's vision was to racially integrate the artist make-up on the pop charts and expose black music to the whole world. He did that, largely, by finding talented singers in Detroit's black churches and musicians in the bars and nightclubs of the city.

Quote: "Berry's concept in starting Motown was to make music with a funky beat and great stories that would cross over." ~ *Smokey Robinson*

Barrett Strong recorded a song Gordy wrote, "Money (That's What I Want)," in 1960. Fledgling Tamla was not equipped to handle a major hit, however, and the song went to the Anna label. It rose to No. 23 on the *Billboard Hot 100* chart.

Late in 1960 Tamla released "Shop Around" by the Miracles, and it peaked at No. 2 on the national pop chart. By that time Gordy had set up the Motown Record Corporation, Hitsville USA and Berry Gordy Enterprises. Recordings were henceforth issued on the Tamla, Gordy and Motown labels and a plethora of minor labels.

Mary Wells had the first of her 12 top 40 pop hits in the summer of 1961. But the real eye-opener came on Dec. 11, 1961, when the Marvelettes hit No. 1 with "Please Mr. Postman."

That led to a three-month bus tour of Motown artists Marvin Gaye, the Contours, Martha & the Vandellas, the Supremes, the Marvelettes, Mary Wells and Little Stevie Wonder in late '62.

Quote: "Until Motown, in Detroit, there were three big careers for a black girl – babies, the factories or daywork." ~ *Mary Wells*

By the end of 1966, Motown had over 450 employees and an annual gross income of $20 million. In 1967 the corporation bought Golden World Records of Detroit and turned its recording studio into Motown Studio B (Studio A was in the W. Grand Blvd. property).

The Funk Brothers: This was the informal name given to the house band that played the instruments on most of Motown's hits from 1959 to '72, after which the corporation moved its headquarters to Los Angeles, Calif.

Except for Stevie Wonder (multiple instruments), Marvin Gaye (drums) and Junior Walker (saxophone), the Motown stable of artists did vocals only in the 1960s. Bands that featured members who could play instruments were signed in the 1970s and thereafter.

Many articles have been written about the role of the band in the success of the Motown label, as well as notations in a documentary film and a book. The members have been honored with a Grammy Lifetime Achievement Award and a star on the Hollywood Walk of Fame. The documentary claims that the Funk Brothers played on more No. 1 hits than Elvis Presley, the Beatles, the Beach Boys and the Rolling Stones combined.

The Funk Brothers often moonlighted for other labels in Detroit and elsewhere.

Some of the key musicians were:

Joe Hunter, bandleader and keyboards (replaced by Johnny Griffith in 1964)
Earl Van Dyke, piano and organ (became bandleader in '64)
Clarence Isabell, double bass
James Jamerson, bass guitar and double bass
Benny "Papa Zita" Benjamin and Richard "Pistol" Allen, drums
Paul Riser, trombone
Robert White, Eddie Willis and Joe Messina, guitar
Jack Ashford, tambourine, percussion, vibraphone, marimba
Jack Brokensha, vibraphone, marimba
Eddie "Bongo" Brown, percussion
Uriel Jones, drums
Bob Babbitt, bass
Dennis Coffey, guitar

Some members of the ensemble learned of their dismissal in '72 from a notice left on the studio door after Berry Gordy closed the facility and moved operations to Los Angeles. Others followed management to L.A. but found the environment to be uncomfortable. Members of a session coalition known as the Wrecking Crew did much of the instrumental work in L.A.

Jamerson and Benjamin have been inducted into the Rock & Roll Hall of Fame, and the Funk Brothers have been inducted into the Musicians Hall of Fame (2007) and the Rhythm & Blues Hall of Fame (2013).

The Andantes: This is the trio of back-up singers who, starting in 1962, regularly added vocals to Motown hit recordings. Their names were Marlene Barrow, Louvain Demps and Jackie Hicks.

Their efforts were used to embellish and smooth out the vocals of the label's stars. On Supremes' records, they sometimes replaced the vocals of Mary Wells and Cindy Birdsong in 1968-69.

Among the honors that were bestowed upon the Andantes was induction into the Rhythm & Blues Hall of Fame in 2013. Barrow died in 2015 at the age of 73.

Holland-Dozier-Holland: They were a songwriting and production team that created many of the songs that defined the Motown Sound 1962-67. The members were Brian Holland, Lamont Dozier and Eddie Holland. Dozier and Brian Holland acted as composers and producers, while Eddie Holland wrote the lyrics and arranged the vocals. Most of their great songs ended up being hits for the Supremes and the Four Tops.

Eddie Holland worked with Berry Gordy prior to the formation of Motown Records and had a modest recording career as a singer. His brother Brian was co-composer of "Please Mr. Postman." Dozier was a recording artist for several labels in the late 1950s and early '60s, including Anna Records.

The three came together as a team to create material for themselves and other artists, but they soon found that they preferred being songwriters and producers.

The end of their tenure at Motown was centered around a dispute with Berry Gordy over royalties and profit sharing. They created their own labels, Invictus and Hot Wax, and had modest success.

Quote: "The chemistry between the three of us working was just very rare, because there are a lot of thoughts and everybody wants to do their own thing, but somehow we just clicked. We went into these songs with the idea of making the best possible music we could make." ~ *Lamont Dozier*

Since they were legally contracted to Motown's publishing arm, they could not use their own names on the songs they wrote after 1967, and they used the names Wayne-Dunbar and Edythe Wayne. Litigation between Holland-Dozier-Holland and Motown concluded in 1977.

Broadcast Music Inc. (BMI), a music industry advocacy group, has bestowed many awards upon the trio. They also were inducted into the Rock & Roll Hall of Fame (1990) and Michigan Rock and Roll Legends Hall of Fame (2010).

The Motown Finishing School: Starting in 1964 Maxine Powell became an important member of the Motown staff when she opened a charm school for the performing artists. Her goal was to polish the singers' public images.

Powell's official title was artist development, but her duties were to teach the young artists how to present themselves charmingly during performances, interviews and off-stage appearances. Each mandatory two-hour session taught public speaking, posture, walking, stage presence, etiquette and personal grooming.

Cholly Atkins was brought on board in 1964 to serve as choreographer for the Temptations, Supremes, Four Tops and others.

Quote: "When I opened up … the finishing school, the purpose was to help the artists become class, to know what to do on stage and off stage, because they did come from humble beginnings. Some of them from the projects and some of them using street language. Some were rude and crude, you understand, but with me it's not where you come from, it's where you're going." ~ *Maxine Powell*

Powell, who toured with the artists occasionally, had a background as an actress, model, manicurist and cosmetologist. She had founded a finishing school/modeling agency for blacks and had studied at the renowned Madam C.J. Walker training school in Indianapolis, Ind.

Quote: "Mrs. Powell was always a lady of grace, elegance and style, and we did our best to emulate her. I don't think I would have been successful at all without her training." ~ *Martha Reeves.*

Powell left Motown in 1969 and passed away in October 2013.

The Motown Museum: The corporation moved operations to Los Angeles in 1972 because Berry Gordy wanted a piece of the action in the television and film industries. But Gordy did not sell the property at 2548 West Grand Blvd. His sister, Esther Gordy Edwards, refused to move to California with the others, and she was put in charge of the buildings that had been dubbed "Hitsville U.S.A." She received requests to receive visitors at Hitsville, so she and her secretary put posters and gold records on the walls and carefully preserved Studio A.

The Motown Museum was created in 1985 in three of the buildings on W. Grand. It contains photos, costumes and records from Motown's golden era. The Gordys' upstairs apartment has been made a part of the museum tours and has been decorated as it was in the 1960s. Tour guests also get to enter Studio A, where 90 percent of Motown's hits were recorded.

In 2016 the museum announced plans for a $50 million expansion plan to create interactive displays, a performance theater, meeting space, expanded retail area and recording studios.

According to the museum's website, "the (non-profit) Motown Museum tells the story of how a man's vision turned into one of the largest, most successful record companies of all time and how the music—the Motown Sound —captured the hearts of young people, not only in America, but across the globe."

Guided tours are available each day the museum is open and begin every 30 minutes.

The Major Artists of the 1960s

The Miracles – They were the first successful act for the Motown corporation. They started as the Five Chimes in 1955 when Smokey Robinson, Warren "Pete" Moore, Ronnie White and Bobby Rogers united as a vocal group. Rogers' sister Claudette would join them later, along with Marv Tarplin. Two years later they changed their name to the Matadors. In 1958 they became the Miracles, and Smokey and Claudette married in 1959.

In an audition with Jackie Wilson's manager, Nat Tarnopol, they were rejected because he thought they sounded too much like the Platters.

With Smokey writing most of their songs, they scored several hits on the rhythm & blues chart and easily crossed over to the pop chart.

In 1967 they changed their name to Smokey Robinson & the Miracles and had their biggest hit since 1960 with "I Second That Emotion" (No. 4 on *Billboard's Hot 100*).

A song that was included on their 1967 album, "The Tears Of A Clown," had an instrumental track that was written by Stevie Wonder and Henry Cosby. They didn't like the lyrics they had written for it, though, and asked Smokey to help. The sound of a calliope on the track reminded him of Pagliacci the sad Italian clown, and he took the lyrics in that direction. Three years later Motown's British division released "The Tears Of A Clown" as a single, and it went to No. 1 in the U.K. Late in 1970 it was released as a single in the U.S. with the same result.

It was at this time that Smokey tried to leave the group to spend time with his young family. The success of "Clown" led him to stay on another two years. In 1974 he had his first top 40 song as a solo artist. Billy Griffin replaced him as lead singer of the Miracles, and they scored a No. 1 hit with "Love Machine" in 1976.

The Miracles classic lineup

William "Smokey" Robinson (Feb. 19, 1940-)
Claudette Rogers Robinson (June 20, 1942-)
Bobby Rogers (Feb. 19, 1940-March 3, 2013)
Ronnie White (April 5, 1939-Aug. 26, 1995)
Warren "Pete" Moore (Nov. 19, 1938-Nov. 19, 2017)

Miracles: Smokey Robinson, Claudette Robinson, Ronnie White, Bobby Rogers, Pete Moore

Significant songs:

Shop Around
You've Really Got A Hold On Me
Going To A Go-Go
I Second That Emotion

What's So Good About Good-by
Mickey's Monkey
That's What Love Is Made Of
Ooo Baby Bay
The Tracks Of My Tears
If You Can Want
Baby, Baby Don't Cry
The Tears Of A Clown
I Don't Blame You At All
Love Machine (Part 1)

Mary Wells – Dubbed the "Queen of Motown," her story was one of rags to riches to rags. She was the first female singer signed by the company to make an impact on the pop charts.

She was born in Detroit to a single mother who worked as a domestic. Mary contracted spinal meningitis at the age of 2 and was beset by deafness in one ear, partial blindness and temporary paralysis. At the age of 10 she contracted tuberculosis. But by the age of 12 she was well enough to assist her mother in cleaning houses.

Quote: "Daywork they called it, and it was damn cold on hallway linoleum. Misery is Detroit linoleum in January – with a half froze bucket of Spic and Span." ~ *Mary Wells*

She started singing in church and in the high school choir and went on to perform in local nightclubs. She aspired to write songs and penned "Bye Bye Baby" for Jackie Wilson to record. When she got a meeting with Berry Gordy to present the song to him, he had her sing it and he signed her to a recording contract on the spot.

Wells established several firsts for the new Motown label. She was the first to record on Motown, the first to have Smokey Robinson for a writer/producer, the first to have a top 10 pop song on Motown and the first to give the label a No. 1 song. She also was the first star to leave the Motown corporation.

Her recording of "I Don't Want To Take A Chance" peaked at No. 33 in June 1961, and she hit the top 10 three times in 1962.

Mary's trademark song, "My Guy," written and produced by Robinson, hit No. 1 in spring of 1964. At a time when the Beatles had a choke hold on the American charts, she was hailed as "the girl who beat the Beatles."

She was 21 and at the peak of her career, and it was time to renegotiate her contract with Motown, which was signed when she was 17. She was jealous that profits from "My Guy" were being used to promote the Supremes (much as money from her label mates' records had been used to promote Wells). She also sought to gain a larger share of the royalties from earlier in her career.

In the end, she invoked a clause that allowed her to leave the label. Part of the terms of termination were that she could receive no royalties from her past work with the label and she could not use her own likeness to promote herself. Early in 1965 she signed a $200,000 contract with 20th Century Fox Records.

In short, the rest of Wells' career was a struggle, and she never matched the success of her heyday at Motown. She recorded for the Atco, Jubilee, Reprise and Epic labels, and she had two failed marriages.

A heavy smoker for years, Wells was diagnosed with laryngeal cancer in 1990. Treatments caused her to lose her voice. Further, since she had no medical insurance, her illness wiped out her savings.

With a weakened immune system, she was hospitalized with pneumonia in 1992. She died at the age of 49.

Mary Wells

May 13, 1943-July 26, 1992

Born Mary Esther Wells in Detroit, Mich., and died in Los Angeles, Calif.

Mary Wells

Significant songs:

You Beat Me To The Punch
Two Lovers
The One Who Really Loves You
Laughing Boy
Your Old Standby
What's Easy For Two Is So Hard For One
My Guy
What's The Matter With You Baby [with Marvin Gaye]
Once Upon A Time [with Marvin Gaye]
Use Your Head

The Marvelettes – This girl group was responsible for the first No. 1 pop hit for the Tamla label.

The girls started singing together in the glee club at their high school in suburban Inkster, Mich. Gladys Horton enlisted Katherine Anderson, Georgeanna Tillman, Juanita Cowart and Georgia Dobbins to become a vocal group in 1960. Dobbins would leave the group before they were signed by the Motown Corp.

They called themselves the "Casinyets," a contraction of the self-effacing phrase "can't sing yet." They entered a school competition with an audition with Motown executives on the line for the top three finishers, but they placed fourth. Nonetheless, two of their teachers felt that they were good enough to go to the audition, and they sang in front of Brian Holland and Robert Bateman, who were songwriters and producers. This led to a second audition in front of more staff, including Smokey Robinson and Berry Gordy, who asked them to come back with an original composition.

Dobbins contacted a local songwriter she knew, William Garrett, to see if he had any material the Casinyets could use. He had a blues song titled "Please Mr. Postman." Though inexperienced in writing songs, Dobbins took the song home and overnight totally rewrote the lyrics. Then she taught Horton how to sing it, because Dobbins was leaving the group to care for her sick mother. Garrett allowed usage of his song on the condition he would receive a writing credit if it became a hit.

After another audition with Gordy, he signed them and changed their name to the Marvelettes. "Please Mr. Postman" was polished up by Holland, Bateman and Freddie Gorman, and Tamla released the recording on Aug. 21, 1961. It took an agonizingly long 15 weeks to reach the top of the *Billboard Hot 100.*

The Marvelettes would have four more hits in 1962 before they slumped for a while. They came back with hit singles in 1966, '67 and '68. They disbanded in 1970.

Tillman, who had been diagnosed with sickle cell anemia as a child, began to suffer from lupus in 1963. She had to retire from the group in 1965, leaving the Marvelettes to carry on as a trio. She died from her health issues in 1980 at age 35.

The Marvelettes classic lineup
Gladys Horton (May 30, 1945-Jan. 26, 2011)
Katherine Anderson (Jan. 16, 1944-)
Georgeanna Tillman (Feb. 6, 1944-Jan. 6, 1980)
Juanita Cowart (Jan. 8, 1944-)

The Marvelettes: Gladys Horton, Juanita Cowart, Georgeanna Tillman, Katherine Anderson

Significant songs:

Please Mr. Postman
Twistin' Postman
Playboy
Beechwood 4-5789
Too Many Fish In The Sea
I'll Keep Holding On
Don't Mess With Bill
The Hunter Gets Captured By The Game
When You're Young An In Love
My Baby Must Be A Magician

Marvin Gaye – Born and raised in Washington, D.C., Marvin Gay moved to Detroit in 1960 with Harvey Fuqua, who'd fronted a group called the Moonglows. Gaye signed on with Tri-Phi Records as a session drummer, but he performed at Berry Gordy's house during the 1960 holiday season. Impressed with Gay's singing, Gordy bought out his contract and put him on the Tamla label. Soon afterward, Marvin added the "e" to the end of his last name in response to teasing.

His first recordings for Tamla were unsuccessful, and he spent most of his time over the next two years drumming on recordings of other artists in the Motown family.

Gaye's break-out hit was "Stubborn Kind Of Fellow" late in 1962, and his first entries on the pop top 40 came the next year. In 1964 he had a hit single and album as a duet with Mary Wells, the first of many collaborations with some of Motown's female stars. His best-known duets were with Tammi Terrell, who died in 1970 of a malignant brain tumor.

He married Berry Gordy's sister Anna in 1963, and they separated in 1973. Anna filed for divorce in 1975, and it became final in 1977. In October of '77 he married Janis Hunter, a union that lasted until 1981.

Gaye's biggest hit on the pop charts was "I Heard It Through The Grapevine," a song that spent seven weeks atop the *Billboard Hot 100* at the end of 1968. His greatest triumph on the soul chart was 1982's "Sexual Healing," with spent 10 weeks at No. 1. He thus earned the nicknames "Prince of Motown" and "Prince of Soul."

With a four-octave vocal range, Gaye racked up 28 romantic top 40 hits through 1970. Then he changed his physical appearance and recorded an album of songs that voiced a social conscience – songs like "What's Going On," Mercy Mercy Me (The Ecology)" and "Inner City Blues (Make Me Wanna Holler)." They were a great success in 1971.

The album titled "What's Going On" made it onto the Library of Congress's National Recording Registry.

In 1982 Gaye left Motown because he was unhappy with the label's treatment of his album "In Our Lifetime?" He made his last recordings on the Columbia label.

Throughout his life Gaye was plagued by depression and drug and alcohol abuse. When he completed his final concert tour in 1983, he was sick and suffering from cocaine induced paranoia, so he moved into his parents' home in Los Angeles.

On April 1, 1984, Marvin intervened in a fight between his father and mother. Minutes later his father, Marvin Gay Sr., shot Gaye in the heart and shoulder, killing him. The physical confrontation between the father and son was a scene that had played out many times when Marvin was in his youth.

Quote: "I record so that I can feed people what they need, what they feel. Hopefully, I record so that I can help someone overcome a bad time." ~ *Marvin Gaye*

Marvin Gaye

April 2, 1939-April 1, 1984
Born Marvin Pentz Gay Jr. in Washington, D.C.

Tammi Terrell

April 29, 1945-March 16, 1970
Born Thomasina Winifred Montgomery in Philadelphia, Pa. She changed her first name to Tammy at age 12 after seeing the film *Tammy and the Bachelor* and hearing its theme song, "Tammy." Berry Gordy changed her name after she signed with Motown to shorten it and give it sex appeal. She died in Philadelphia following her eighth operation for cancerous brain tumors.

Marvin Gaye and Tammi Terrell

Significant songs:

Hitch Hike
Try It Baby
Pride And Joy
Can I Get A Witness
You're A Wonderful One
Baby Don't You Do It
Chained
Your Unchanging Love
I'll Be Doggone
Ain't That Peculiar
You're A Special Part Of Me [with Diana Ross]
Come Get To This
Ain't No Mountain High Enough [with Tammi Terrell]
Your Precious Love [with Tammi Terrell]
Ain't Nothing Like The Real Thing [with Tammi Terrell]
You're All I Need To Get By [with Tammi Terrell]
If I Could Build My Whole World Around You [with Tammi Terrell]
That's The Way Love Is
What's Going On
Mercy Mercy Me (The Ecology)
Inner City Blues
Trouble Man
Keep On Lovin' Me Honey [with Tammi Terrell]
How Sweet It Is To Be Loved By You
I Heard It Through The Grapevine
Too Busy Thinking About My Baby
Let's Get It On
It Takes Two [with Kim Weston]
My Mistake (Was To Love You) [with Diana Ross]
Distant Love
Got To Give It Up (Pt. 1)
Sexual Healing

Martha & the Vandellas – The roots of this all-girl group go back to 1957. Detroit teens Annette Beard and Rosalind Ashford sang together in a group called the Del-Phis. The group originally had six members, but Alabama native Martha Reeves was added after one of them dropped out. They briefly recorded for Checkmate Records.

Reeves left to perform as a solo act and took on the name Martha LaVaille. Motown staffer Mickey Stevenson noticed her singing at a prominent Detroit nightclub and offered her an audition, which she missed by showing up at her appointment on the wrong day. Stevenson ended up hiring her as his secretary, and she was responsible for helping acts audition for the label.

Quote: "I was never a secretary. I was a singer who could type." ~ *Martha Reeves*

By 1961 the Del-Phis were known as the Vels and were supplying backing vocals for emerging Motown star Marvin Gaye. With Reeves doing lead vocals, the group did a demo of "I'll Have To Let Him Go," and Berry Gordy was so impressed with it that he offered them a recording contract in 1962. One of the members, Gloria Williams, backed out because she dreaded the rigors of a show business career.

The remaining three – Reeves, Beard and Ashford – became Martha & the Vandellas, a name cobbled from Detroit's Van Dyke Street and Reeves' favorite singer, Della Reese. They were assigned to the Gordy label.

The spring of 1963 saw their single "Come And Get These Memories" charge into the pop top 40, and they finished the year with "(Love Is Like A) Heat Wave" and "Quicksand" reaching the top 10.

Their biggest single was "Dancing In The Street," which spent two weeks at No. 2 in fall of 1964. Beard, with a young child and marriage plans, dropped out about that time, and Betty Kelly replaced her.

There was some infighting among the members, particularly between Kelly and Reeves, and Kelly was fired in 1967, replaced by Reeves's sister Lois. That same year the group's name was officially changed to Martha Reeves & the Vandellas, conforming to name changes of other Motown groups like Diana Ross & the Supremes and Smokey Robinson & the Miracles.

Martha & the Vandellas found themselves in the same shoes as some other Motown acts, with good recording material hard to find since the corporation was heavily promoting the Supremes and, later, the solo career of Diana Ross. They also were hurt by the departure of Stevenson in '67 and the songwriting team of Holland-Dozier-Holland in '68.

In their final fling on the pop top 40, their song "Honey Chile" peaked at No. 11 early in 1968. The group disbanded after a farewell concert at Detroit's Cobo Hall on Dec. 21, 1972.

Martha & the Vandellas

Martha Reeves (July 18, 1941-)
Rosalind Ashford (Sept. 2, 1943-)
Annette Beard (July 4, 1943-)

Martha Reeves, Annette Beard, Rosalind Ashford

Significant songs:

Come And Get These Memories
Heat Wave
Quicksand
Wild One
Nowhere To Run
You've Been In Love Too Long
Dancing In The Street
My Baby Loves Me
I'm Ready For Love
Dancing In The Street
Jimmy Mack
Wild One
Love Bug Leave My Heart Alone
Honey Chile

Stevie Wonder – Born Stevland Hardaway Judkins in Saginaw, Mich., he was a child prodigy who was the third of six siblings born to a mother who was a songwriter. He was born six weeks premature and became blind shortly after birth due to retinopathy of prematurity.

When he was 4 years old, his mother divorced his father and moved her children to Detroit. She later changed her son's last name to Morris, partly because of relatives, and he has legally maintained that surname ever since.

He began playing instruments such as piano, harmonica and drums at a young age and did his first singing at the Whitestone Baptist Church.

In 1961, at age 11, he sang his own composition "Lonely Boy" to Ronnie White of the Miracles, and that got him an audition at Motown. Before signing him to a contract, producer Clarence Paul gave him the nickname Little Stevie Wonder. The label drew up a rolling five-year contract that would hold Stevie's royalties in trust until he was 21. He and his mother were given a weekly stipend of $2.50, and he was given a tutor when he went out on tour.

Under Paul's care Stevie worked on two albums, neither of which was commercially successful. In 1962 his first single peaked at No. 101 and then fell out of sight.

Early in 1963, while on tour with the Motortown Revue at Chicago's Regal Theater, Wonder's 20-minute performance was recorded and turned into a live album. A single, "Fingertips Pt. II," was released and went to No. 1 on the *Billboard Hot 100.* At age 13 Stevie Wonder became the youngest recording artist to top the chart and the first to have a single *and* the album that spawned it in the No. 1 slot.

More singles would follow throughout the remainder of the 1960s, and it provided a steady stream of hits for Wonder and the Tamla label.

As the 1970s came along and Wonder matured, his music took on a more artistic and sophisticated style. He wrote and recorded several albums and singles that topped the charts. When he turned 21, he allowed his Motown contract to expire, and he negotiated a new, 120-page contract that gave him a much higher royalty rate. He also received his own production and publishing companies, staffed with his own people.

Wonder has been married three times – the first when he was 20 when he wed singer and former Motown secretary Syreeta Wright. Fashion designer Kai Millard was his second wife, and he currently is married to Tomeeka Bracy.

His most successful album probably was 1976's "Songs In The Key of Life," which topped the *Billboard 200* chart and produced two No. 1 singles. The double album was No. 1 in Canada, Netherlands and France, as well.

Wonder's work in the 1980s was equally impressive, earning more chart-topping albums and singles and accolades.

With musical tastes in the 1990s lilting towards rap and hip hop, Wonder was largely absent from the pop music charts. His brief North American tour of 2007 was his first in 10 years. He has done songs for a movie soundtrack and contributed to other artists' records.

The only hit recordings that Wonder has had on labels outside the Motown family are a duet with Paul McCartney ("Ebony And Ivory" on Columbia Records) and a collaboration with Dionne Warwick, Gladys Knight and Elton John ("That's What Friends Are For" on Arista).

His legacy is untarnished, and he is one of the top 60 artists of all time in record sales.

Quote: "Stevie Wonder is in every sense of the word … an absolute genius." ~ *Dionne Warwick*

Stevie Wonder

Born Stevland Hardaway Judkins in Saginaw, Mich., on May 13, 1950

Stevie Wonder

Significant songs:

Fingertips Pt. 2
Uptight (Everything's Alright)
A Place In The Sun
I Was Made To Love Her
I'm Wondering
Shoo-Be-Doo-Be Doo-Da-Day
For Once In My Life
My Cherie Amour
Yester-Me, Yester-You, Yester-Day
Signed, Sealed, Delivered I'm Yours
Heaven Help Us All
If You Really Love Me
Superstition
You Haven't Done Nothin'
Boogie On Reggae Woman
Isn't She Lovely
I Wish
Sir Duke
Send One Your Love
Master Blaster (Jammin')
I Ain't Gonna Stand For It
That Girl
Ebony And Ivory [with Paul McCartney]
Do I Do
I Just Called To Say I Love You
Love Light In Flight

You Are The Sunshine Of My Life
Higher Ground
Living For The City
Don't You Worry 'Bout A Thing
That's What Friends Are For [with Dionne Warwick, Gladys Knight & Elton John]
Part-Time Lover
Go Home
Overjoyed

The Temptations – This vocal group – basically consisting of five members at a time over the years, became one of the mainstays of the Gordy label.

Eddie Kendricks and Paul Williams sang together in church as children in Birmingham, Ala. With a third member, they formed the Cavaliers and then relocated to Detroit in 1957. Their friend left the alliance and was replaced by Milton Jenkins, and they became the Primes.

Meanwhile, Texas teenager Otis Williams moved to Detroit to be with his mother. He formed his own vocal group, the Distants, and brought in Montgomery, Ala., native Melvin Franklin.

Ultimately, Otis Williams recruited Paul Williams, Kendricks, Franklin and Al Bryant for a group to be known as the Elgins. They auditioned for Motown in March 1961. Berry Gordy was prepared to sign them, but he found out that there already was another group named the Elgins. On the front steps of Hitsville U.S.A., the members started tossing around ideas for a new name, and they finally hit upon Temptations.

Their first two singles were released on the Miracle label, which Gordy then shut down. The Temptations were assigned to the Gordy label. Their first eight singles met with minimal success before they began working with songwriter/producer Smokey Robinson.

Local singer David Ruffin aspired to join the quintet and began following the group around. After Bryant expressed frustration with their lack of success and was involved in altercations with other members, he was fired. Ruffin became a Temptation in January 1964.

Thus began the golden era of the Temptations. They scored three top 40 singles in '64, and then hit No. 1 with the Robinson-penned "My Girl" in '65. By 1967 they had enough material for their first greatest hits album. The group dazzled concert audiences for years with their on-stage dance routines, performed while singing their soulful pop songs.

Unfortunately, the status quo didn't last. Ruffin, who took over lead vocals on most songs, began to demand special treatment. His boorish behavior began to irritate the others, especially when he caused friction with Berry Gordy. Ruffin, who had begun using cocaine regularly, demanded an accounting of the group's earnings, and he wanted the Temptations renamed in the fashion of Diana Ross & the Supremes.

The Temptations decided he had crossed the line when he missed a gig to attend a show by his new girlfriend, Barbara Martin (Dean Martin's daughter). They fired him on June 27, 1968, and replaced him the next day with Dennis Edwards of Motown group the Contours.

Ruffin was popular with the Temptations' fans, but the group carried on fine without him. They amassed three more No. 1 singles and maintained a solid chart presence into the mid-1970s. Ruffin went on to have a modest solo career.

Kendricks had been wanting to leave the group for years, as he preferred the old ballads to the new psychedelic soul songs that the group began doing in the late '60s. After he recorded his lead vocal for "Just My Imagination" early in 1971, he negotiated his release from the group and began a solo career. Damon Harris replaced him.

Paul Williams, who suffered from sickle cell anemia, also had problems with alcohol abuse and depression. In 1973, after being replaced in the lineup by Richard Street, he committed suicide.

In the late 1960s Franklin was diagnosed with rheumatoid arthritis, and he regularly used cortisone so that he could continue performing on stage. The drug weakened his immune system, however, and he developed diabetes in the early '80s. Then he contracted necrotizing fasciitis. On Feb. 15, 1995, Franklin collapsed into a coma and remained unconscious until his death eight days later at the age of 52.

Otis Williams has kept the Temptations going for years by plugging in new, young members. They are the Temptations in name only, and the only songs most fans remember are the ones recorded in the 1960s and '70s. As of 2019 Williams, at age 77, was still performing with the Temptations but concentrated on being the group's leader and organizer and the "baritone in the middle."

The Temptations classic lineup

David Ruffin [born Davis Eli Ruffin] (Jan. 18, 1941-June 1, 1991)
Eddie Kendricks [born Edward James Kendrick] (Dec. 17, 1939-Oct. 5, 1992)
Otis Williams [born Otis Miles Jr.] (Oct. 30, 1941-)
Melvin Franklin [born David Melvin English] (Oct. 12, 1942-Feb. 23, 1995)
Paul Williams (July 2, 1939-Aug. 17, 1973)

The Temptations: David Ruffin, Melvin Franklin, Paul Williams, Otis Williams, Eddie Kendricks

Significant songs:

The Way You Do The Things You Do
Girl (Why You Wanna Make Me Blue)
It's Growing
Since I Lost My Baby
My Baby
My Girl
Get Ready
Ain't Too Proud To Beg
Beauty Is Only Skin Deep
(I Know) I'm Losing You
All I Need
You're My Everything
(Loneliness Made Me Realize) It's You That I Need
I Wish It Would Rain
I Could Never Love Another (After Loving You)
Please Return Your Love To Me
Cloud Nine
I'm Gonna Make You Love Me [with the Supremes]
Runaway Child, Running Wild
I'll Try Something New [with the Supremes)
I Can't Get Next To You
Psychedelic Shack
Ball Of Confusion (That's What The World Is Today)
Superstar (Remember How You Got Where You Are)
Just My Imagination (Running Away With Me)
Papa Was A Rollin' Stone
Masterpiece
Shakey Ground

The Supremes – The original four members all were from the Brewster-Douglass housing project in Detroit. Their names are Florence Ballard, Mary Wilson, Diana Ross (original name Diane Earle) and Betty McGlown.

In 1958 Ballard met Paul Williams and Eddie Kendricks when their singing group was called the Primes. Williams's girlfriend McGlown also was a singer, and the Primes' manager, Milton Jenkins, decided to form a sister group to be called the Primettes. Ballard recruited her best friend Wilson, who in turn recruited her classmate Ross.

Funded and mentored by Jenkins, the Primettes began performing at sock hops, social clubs and talent shows around the Detroit area. For the most part, Ross, Ballard and Wilson equally shared lead vocals. After a while guitarist Marvin Tarplin was added to the group.

In 1960, when the girls were still in high school, Ross asked her old neighbor Smokey Robinson to help the Primettes get an audition with the upstart Motown company. He agreed, but he lured

Tarplin to become part of the Miracles.

After witnessing an *a cappella* audition, Berry liked them but wanted to wait until they finished school before signing them. Later that year they recorded a single for LuPine Records, but it failed to find an audience. Shortly thereafter McGlown became engaged to be married and left the Primettes. Barbara Martin promptly replaced her.

Determined to keep Gordy's attention, the girls dropped by Hitsville U.S.A. almost every day after school and eventually were allowed to do hand claps and backing vocals for Motown singers. Gordy offered them a contract in January 1961, under the condition that they change their name. Ballard was given a list of choices, and she picked Supremes. Ross disliked it because she thought it sounded too masculine, but the name stuck. In spring of 1962 Martin left to start a family, and the Supremes remained a trio.

It took a full two years for them to score their first hit, as their first six singles failed to crack the top 40. "When The Lovelight Starts Shining Through His Eyes" peaked at No. 23 for them early in 1964. Finally, they were given a song written by Holland-Dozier-Holland (and rejected by the Marvelettes), "Where Did Our Love Go." With Ross singing lead, it zoomed up to No. 1 for two weeks, and the Supremes were on their way. Their next four singles also went to No. 1.

Ross remained the lead vocalist on subsequent Supremes' songs, and Gordy helped them cultivate a glamorous image with signature wigs and sparkling gowns. The best songs written by Holland-Dozier-Holland were fed to them, too.

On Oct. 22, 1965, their "Supremes A' Go-Go" became the first No. 1 album on the *Billboard 200* chart by an all-female group. By the time the *Billboard Hot 100's* last edition of the 1960s came out, the Supremes had amassed 12 No. 1 singles – the most of any American vocal group.

While the success of the Supremes opened doors in the entertainment industry for other Motown acts, there also was jealousy among the Motown family because of the focus that Berry lavished on the trio. Gordy eventually would have an affair with Ross. Early in 1967 the name was changed to the Supremes with Diana Ross before being changed again that summer to Diana Ross and the Supremes.

With the focus on Ross, Ballard felt pushed aside. She started drinking heavily and gaining weight, until she no longer could comfortably fit into her stage costumes. She began missing recording dates and would come to live shows too inebriated to perform. Marlene Barrow of the Andantes replaced her for some shows.

In May 1967 Ballard returned to the group, slimmed down and sober, thinking she was on probation. Actually, Gordy had already planned to replace her as soon as he could buy out the contract of Cindy Birdsong of the Blue Belles.

The breaking point for Ballard came in July 1967 while the Supremes were at the Flamingo Hotel in Las Vegas for a series of shows. Ballard discovered an extra set of costumes for Birdsong and she reacted badly, going on stage for a show while drunk. She revealed her belly during a dance routine on stage when she purposefully thrust it forward. Gordy, enraged, quickly had her sent back to Detroit and permanently dismissed her from the group. Birdsong soon was added in her place.

Things returned to normal for the Supremes until early in 1970, when Gordy was ready to send Ross on her solo career. Jean Terrell replaced her as lead singer.

Without Ross the group lacked the sizzle to hit No. 1 again, but eight of their singles entered the top 40 from 1970 through 1976.

Ross had a sterling stint as a solo performer, collecting five No. 1 singles among her 27 that reached the top 40, plus a No. 1 duet with Lionel Richie. She expanded her talents to acting in films, and *Billboard Magazine* named her the female entertainer of the 20th century.

Tragically, Ballard fell on hard times after her dismissal from the Supremes. An attempted solo career with ABC Records fizzled quickly, and she entered a marriage that soon resulted in separation. She was receiving government aid to feed her three children by 1975. She died of cardiac arrest on Feb. 22, 1976, at age 32.

The 2006 movie "Dreamgirls" is loosely based on the story of the Supremes.

Quote: "Someone said, and I agree with him, that the Supremes were such a crossover for young black and white males in our country because there were three black girls and they could openly enjoy them and even lust for them without thinking what color they were." ~ Diana Ross

The Supremes classic lineup

Diana Ross (March 26, 1944-)
Mary Wilson (March 6, 1944-)
Florence Ballard (June 30, 1943-Feb. 22, 1976)

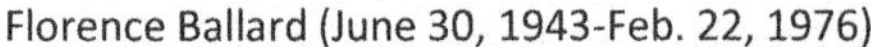

The Supremes: Florence Ballard, Mary Wilson, Diana Ross

Significant Supremes songs:

Let Me Go The Right Way
When The Lovelight Starts Shining Through His Eyes
Where Did Our Love Go
Baby Love
Come See About Me
Stop! In The Name Of Love
Back In My Arms Again
Nothing But Heartaches
I Hear A Symphony
My World Is Empty Without You
Love Is Like An Itching In My Heart
You Can't Hurry Love
You Keep Me Hangin' On
Love Is Here And Now You're Gone
The Happening
Reflections
In And Out Of Love
Forever Came Today
Some Things You Never Get Used To
Love Child
I'm Livin' In Shame
The Composer
No Matter What Sign You Are
Someday We'll Be Together
Up The Ladder To The Roof
Stoned Love
Nathan Jones
Floy Joy

Significant Diana Ross solo songs:

Reach Out And Touch (Somebody's Hand)
Ain't No Mountain High Enough
Remember Me
Reach Out I'll Be There
Good Morning Heartache
Touch Me In The Morning
You're A Special Part Of Me [with Marvin Gaye]
Last Time I Saw Him
My Mistake (Was To Love You) [with Marvin Gaye]
Theme From Mahogany (Do You Know Where You're Going To)
Love Hangover
The Boss
Upside Down
I'm Coming Out
It's My Turn
Endless Love [with Lionel Richie]
Why Do Fools Fall In Love
Mirror, Mirror
Muscles
All Of You [with Julio Iglesias]
Swept Away
Missing You

The Four Tops – Like most of Motown's luminaries, this quartet started singing together as teenagers. The original four are Levi Stubbs, Abdul "Duke" Fakir, Renaldo "Obie" Benson and Lawrence Payton, and their first gig was at a local Detroit birthday party in 1953. What is not typical of this group is that their lineup would remain unchanged for 44 years.

Their first name was the Four Aims, and they signed with Chess Records in 1956. But they changed to Four Tops to avoid confusion with the Ames Brothers. Stubbs became the lead singer, and the group's sound was defined by his vocals.

The Four Tops bounced from label to label for the next seven years and polished their stage routine to become a successful supper club act. In 1963 Berry Gordy recruited them into the Motown family. At first, they recorded jazz standards for the company's Workshop label.

The Holland-Dozier-Holland team came up with an instrumental track in 1964, and they didn't know what to do with it. They ended up developing it into a pop song for the Four Tops – "Baby I Need Your Loving." The record rose to No. 11 on the *Billboard Hot 100*, and the group was on its way to stardom. The following year they had their first No. 1 hit, "I Can't Help Myself (Sugar Pie, Honey Bunch)."

The next few years saw them using the songs of Holland-Dozier-Holland to pepper the charts with hit after hit. It was the Motown sound at its finest – simple, distinctive melodies and rhymes with augmentation from the Funk Brothers and the Andantes.

Their fortunes dropped with the departure of their main songwriting team in 1967. Their hit formula was changed with the addition of other songwriters, and they went without a top 40 entry in all of 1969.

Also, the Motown corporation was changing, moving aside older acts to concentrate on younger stars and a solo Diana Ross. There also was the move to California, during which Gordy decreed that all of his artists had to move with the corporation. The Four Tops were among those who chose to stay in Detroit, and they switched to ABC-Dunhill Records in 1972.

Quote: [On signing with ABC-Dunhill] "We got more than what we were asking from Motown. It was a good contract that lasted 4 or 5 years. We loved the writers. So, we had a couple of hits." ~ *Duke Fakir*

Two top 10 hits soon followed, and the group carried on the best it could with a new production team. They had a top 40 hit in 1981 with Casablanca Records and one in 1988 with Arista. Starting in the late '80s they concentrated on tours and live shows.

In 1997 Payton died of liver cancer at age 59, and Benson died of lung cancer at age 69 in 2005. Stubbs also became a cancer victim at age 72 in 2008.

The Four Tops

Levi Stubbs [born Levi Stubbles] (June 6, 1936-Oct. 17, 2008)
Abdul "Duke" Fakir (Dec. 26, 1935-)
Renaldo "Obie" Benson (June 14, 1936-July 1, 2005)
Lawrence Payton (March 2, 1938-June 20, 1997)

The Four Tops: Duke Fakir, Obie Benson, Levi Stubbs, Lawrence Payton

Significant songs:

Baby I Need Your Loving
I Can't Help Myself
Ask The Lonely
It's The Same Old Song
Something About You
Shake Me, Wake Me (When It's Over)
Reach Out I'll Be There
Standing In The Shadows Of Love
Bernadette
7 Rooms Of Gloom
You Keep Running Away
Walk Away Renee
If I Were A Carpenter
It's All In The Game
Still Water (Love)
River Deep - Mountain High [with the Supremes]
Just Seven Numbers (Can Straighten Out My Life)
Keeper Of The Castle
Ain't No Woman (Like The One I've Got)
Are You Man Enough
Sweet Understanding Love
When She Was My Girl

The Jackson 5 – This was Motown's youngest vocal group to become stars. They set a chart record by becoming the first act ever to hit No. 1 with all their first four singles.

Joe and Katherine Jackson raised nine children in Gary, Ind. Joe desired to have a career as a musician, but he found he couldn't support the family that way. Instead, he took a job operating a crane in a local steel mill.

One day Joe caught son Tito playing with his old guitar, and he endeavored to find out how much talent the 9-year-old boy had. Joe was impressed enough to buy Tito his own guitar. Soon brothers Jackie and Jermaine joined Tito in a three-man group, with Michael and Marlon coming on board later.

Joe would serve as the group's manager for many years, although he was notorious for being a strict disciplinarian and later was accused of physical and emotional abuse of his children.

With victories in several talent competitions under their belt, Joe started booking the kids at venues on the "chitlin' circuit." After they won a contest at Harlem's Apollo Theater in 1967, Gladys Knight sent their demo tape to Motown Records. The tape was rejected and sent back.

This led the Jackson 5 to sign with Steeltown Records, a small label in Gary. Their first two singles were released in 1968, but they failed to draw much notice.

After they did a week of shows at Chicago's Regal Theater as the opening act for Bobby Taylor & the Vancouvers, Taylor escorted the Jackson 5 to Detroit for a Motown audition on July 23, 1968. Once again, they were turned down since Berry Gordy was lavishing attention on Stevie Wonder. But Gordy changed his mind later, and the group was signed to Motown on March 11, 1969.

Gordy brought the boys to Hollywood for several months of intensive rehearsals. In August they began opening shows for the Supremes. Then they began recording their first album with songs written by the Corporation, a consortium of songwriters and producers who were assembled to create songs for the Jackson 5 consisting of Gordy, Alphonso Mizell, Freddie Perren and Deke Richards.

"I Want You Back" was their first single release and took the nation by storm, hitting No. 1 on Jan. 31, 1970. By the end of that year, "ABC," "The Love You Save" and "I'll Be There" also became chart toppers. At age 11, Michael sang lead on the first three hits, and he was 12 by the time the fourth reached the charts.

Many more hits would follow over the next 14 years, although there would be no more No. 1s. Late in 1971, Michael released his first solo effort, "Got To Be There," which rose to No. 4. He didn't officially leave the group until 1984, after having recorded a number of mega-successful solo albums and singles.

In 1976 the group left Motown for Epic Records, which offered them a royalty rate of 20 percent. Motown had been paying them only 2.8 percent. Jermaine opted to stay with Motown, since he was married to Berry Gordy's daughter Hazel. Randy Jackson, the youngest brother, replaced him. The group assumed the new name The Jacksons, since Motown owned the name Jackson 5.

"Torture," a No. 17 hit in 1984, was the final piece of musical relevance for the Jacksons as a recording act.

Michael kept on recording and performing, though, and finished the 1980s as the top charting act of the decade with eight No. 1 singles and a duet with Paul McCartney ("Say Say Say") that spent six weeks at No. 1.

After Michael Jackson's death on June 25, 2009, many pundits proclaimed that he was the greatest entertainer in history. Michael died at his home in Los Angeles, Calif., of cardiac arrest induced by acute propofol and benzodiazepine intoxication.

Sister Janet Jackson had a highly successful recording career of her own, and she also dabbled in acting. The other two sisters, Rebbie and La Toya, briefly took a shot at singing careers.

Quote: [On Michael performing onstage at age 10] "Michael was tiny. I felt so sorry for him because it was a nightclub. I said this little kid's gonna go out and (the audience is) gonna murder him. Michael went out there and brought the house down." ~ *Freddie Perren*

The Jackson 5

Sigmund Esco "Jackie" Jackson (May 4, 1951-)
Toriono Adaryll "Tito" Jackson (Oct. 15, 1953-)
Jermaine La Jaune Jackson (Dec. 11, 1954-)
Marlon David Jackson (March 12, 1957-)
Michael Joseph Jackson (Aug. 29, 1958-June 25, 2009)

The Jackson 5: Jackie, Marlon, Michael, Tito and Jermaine

Significant Jackson 5 songs:

I Want You Back
ABC
The Love You Save
I'll Be There
Mama's Pearl
Never Can Say Goodbye
Maybe Tomorrow
Sugar Daddy
Little Bitty Pretty One
Lookin' Through The Windows
Corner Of The Sky
Dancing Machine
I Am Love
Enjoy Yourself
Shake Your Body (Down To The Ground)
State Of Shock

Significant Michael Jackson solo songs (only the first 5 were recorded on Motown Records):

Got To Be There
Rockin' Robin
I Wanna Be Where You Are
Ben
Just A Little Bit Of You
Don't Stop 'Til You Get Enough
Bad
The Way You Make Me Feel
Man In The Mirror
Dirty Diana
Another Part Of Me
Smooth Criminal

Rock With You
Off The Wall
She's Out Of My Life
The Girl Is Mine [with Paul McCartney]
Billie Jean
Beat It
Wanna Be Startin' Somethin'
Human Nature
Say Say Say [with Paul McCartney]
P.Y.T. (Pretty Young Thing)
Thriller
I Just Can't Stop Loving You
Black Or White
Remember The Time
In The Closet
Jam
Heal The World
Who Is It
Will You Be There
Scream [with Janet Jackson]
You Are Not Alone
They Don't Care About Us
You Rock My World
Butterflies

Motown's Biggest Number 1 Record

"Endless Love" by Diana Ross & Lionel Richie – This movie theme spent an incredible nine weeks on top of the *Billboard Hot 100* in 1981. It also was No. 1 on the R&B and Adult Contemporary charts.

How big of a song was it? *Billboard* named the Ross/Richie version the greatest duet of all time. It was the second-best selling single of the year behind "Bette Davis Eyes" by Kim Carnes.

The song came from the movie by the same name. Directed by Franco Zeffirelli, it was an adaptation of a novel by Scott Spencer and starred Brooke Shields.

Richie, who was the primary songwriter and lead singer for the Motown band the Commodores, wrote the song and produced the recording. Zeffirelli originally asked him to write an instrumental theme for the soundtrack and later requested lyrics. Then the director suggested that the song be sung as a duet, with the inclusion of Ross.

With No. 1 ballads like "Three Times A Lady" and "Still" already on his resumé, Richie was up to the task. And when it came time to recommend a male singer to accompany Ross, he was no shrinking violet. He eagerly stepped into that role, too.

Ross and Richie both recorded the song individually for their respective solo albums that came later. Their duet was nominated for an Academy Award for Best Original Song, and they sang it at the Oscar presentations in 1982.

The movie's soundtrack peaked at No. 9 on the *Billboard 200* chart and was certified platinum. It was released on the Columbia label.

Mariah Carey and Luther Vandross recorded a version of "Endless Love" in 1994, and Richie joined Shania Twain for a remake of the duet in 2011.

Ross and Richie would record together once more. In 1985 they were part of an ensemble of established artists recording under the name USA For Africa on the song "We Are The World," which was co-written by Richie and Michael Jackson.

Endless Love

Songwriter: Lionel Richie

Peaked at No. 1 on Billboard Hot 100

Aug. 15, 1981
Aug. 22, 1981
Aug. 29, 1981
Sept. 5, 1981
Sept. 12, 1981
Sept. 19, 1981
Sept. 26, 1981
Oct. 3, 1981
Oct. 10, 1981

The Ross/Richie version spent 27 weeks on the Billboard Hot 100.

Diana Ross

Born Diane Ernestine Earle Ross in Detroit, Mich., on March 26, 1944. A clerical error at Hutzel Women's Hospital resulted in the name "Diana" to appear on her birth certificate.

Lionel Richie

Born Lionel Brockman Richie Jr. in Tuskegee, Ala., on June 20, 1949. He first gained fame as a member of the Commodores, who signed with Motown Records in 1972. He left the group in 1982 to pursue a solo career. His 1983 album "Can't Slow Down" sold over 20 million units and became the best-selling album in Motown history at the time.

Diana Ross and Lionel Richie

Epilogue: During the 1970s Motown became the target of a backlash by some fans of rock. Music with a harder edge began to emerge then, and punk rock had gotten a toehold, as well. But there still was a group of popular artists in the company's stable. Life was good for Motown, but artists continued to leave the label for better deals at other record companies as their contracts expired.

By the mid-1980s Motown began to lose money. Gordy sold his interest in the corporation to Boston Ventures and MCA Records (which had begun a distribution deal with Motown in '83) for $61 million in June 1988. He sold Motown Productions TV/film operations to Motown executive Suzanne de Passe in 1989.

Gordy feared that he may have sold for too low a price, and that was confirmed in 1993 when MCA sold Motown to Polygram for about $330 million. Today Motown is a subsidiary of Capitol Records.

All told, 326 acts have been under contract to Motown through the years.

Of the 15,000 songs in the Jobete Publishing catalogue, Gordy wrote or co-wrote 240 of them. In 1994 he published an autobiography, *To Be Loved*, which is the title of a song he wrote for Jackie Wilson.

Chapter 7

The Brill Building

The big influence of one building on pop music history

Overview: While some may regard it as just a stack of bricks, mortar and steel, I prefer to look at the Brill Building as a monument to a golden age in the history of pop music.

Like so many structures in Manhattan, New York, the office building at 1619 Broadway underwent major renovation in the 21st century. According to the guard in the lobby, only two floors were occupied by tenants at one point.

But from about 1957 to 1965, the Brill was a happening place in the music industry. Although many publishing companies, music agencies and record labels were based in New York and spread across the city, the Brill was ground zero for the industry.

History: Built in 1931 as the Alan E. Lefcourt Building, the building got its current name from a clothing store on the ground floor. Originally just tenants, the Brill Brothers eventually bought the place. Broadway Realty LLC has owned it since June 2013.

You might say that the Brill Building picked up where Tin Pan Alley (which was on West 28th St.) left off. Tin Pan Alley was the world's hub of music publishing and songwriting from 1885 through the 1920s. The origin of the name is thought to have been a reference that a *New York Herald* writer made to the collective sound made by "cheap upright pianos" up and down the street.

The final demise of Tin Pan Alley likely was brought about by the rise of rock and roll music in the 1950s, when the Brill Building supplanted it as the global music headquarters.

A plaque in the sidewalk on W. 28th St. identifies the former location of Tin Pan Alley

By 1962 the Brill housed 165 music-related businesses on its 11 floors. In the early '60s, without leaving the building, you literally could write a song, find a publisher to buy it, find an arranger, have it printed and copied at the duplication office, buy an hour of studio time, hire musicians and backing singers and cut a demo.

Then you could take the song to record companies, artists' managers or even the artists themselves. If a record deal was made, there were radio promoters in the building to sell it.

Some of the most prolific American songwriters worked in the Brill, usually in teams of composers and lyricists. Typically, they occupied small cubicles that included only an acoustic upright piano with bench and a chair and perhaps a table or desk. With many of these teams working within earshot of one another, songs tended to acquire the same sound – the Brill Building sound.

Among the legendary songwriters who called the Brill home were Burt Bacharach and Hal David; Gerry Goffin and Carole King; Ellie Greenwich and Jeff Barry; Jerry Leiber and Mike Stoller; Barry Mann and Cynthia Weil; Neil Sedaka and Howard Greenfield; Doc Pomus and Mort Shuman; Tommy Boyce and Bobby Hart; Phil Spector; Neil Diamond; Laura Nyro, and Paul Simon. Spector collaborated with Greenwich and Barry on occasion.

After their songs went to the recording studio, most were produced in an uncomplicated manner using acoustic piano, upright bass, drums, acoustic and electric guitars with perhaps backing vocals, Latin-style percussion, a trumpet, saxophone or trombone thrown in. Many of the songs were so good that they didn't need much instrumental embellishment.

Some of the famous musicians who were headquartered at the Brill were Elvis Presley, Bobby Darin, Connie Francis, Lesley Gore, Darlene Love, Tony Orlando, Gene Pitney, the Ronettes, the Shangri-Las, the Shirelles, the Four Seasons and Dionne Warwick.

Influence of the British Invasion: The music that came out of the Brill Building was enormously influential to the careers of many musicians. Even the bands that participated in the 1964 "British Invasion" recorded some of the songs.

It's not hard to imagine that John Lennon/Paul McCartney songs like "I Saw Her Standing There," "Do You Want To Know A Secret" or "I'm Happy Just To Dance With You" could have been born in the Brill.

Brill writers also influenced the Detroit songwriters. For example, the sensitivity and soulfulness of "Spanish Harlem," penned by Spector, Leiber and Stoller in 1959, could be heard in many Motown songs in the years that followed.

Unfortunately, when the English groups put their stamp on the same Brill songs that American artists first recorded, something was lost in the interpretation, so to speak. Tempos were changed, the emotions sometimes were sterilized, and the songs began to sound like assembly line pop. Thus, the British Invasion began to compromise the essence of the Brill sound.

Certainly, the British artists had listened to all of the major pop records that were generated from the Brill. But when it came time to record their own versions, they were delivering their own inflections, playing electrified instruments and generally sounding British.

Take for example the song "Chains," written by Goffin and King. The black female quartet the Cookies from Brooklyn made the original recording and made a No. 17 hit out of it late in 1962.

The Beatles, looking to fill out the album "Please Please Me," recorded it in February 1963. Whereas the Cookies' version was warmed by a soulful vocal rendering and minimal instrumentation (piano, sax, acoustic bass, drums), the Beatles' had a George Harrison lead vocal, Paul McCartney and John Lennon backing vocals, drums, harmonica and electrified guitars and bass. The Beatles' version wasn't bad – it was just the Beatles being themselves trying to cover a song that wasn't written for them.

Before long, the Brill's songwriters faced "extinction," since the upcoming bands of the latter half of the '60s wrote most of their own material.

Notable hit songs: Here are some examples of songs written by Brill writers along with artists who recorded them:

Neil Sedaka/Howard Greenfield
Where The Boys Are (Connie Francis)
Stupid Cupid (Connie Francis)
Where The Boys Are (Connie Francis)
Fallin' (Wanda Jackson)
Another Sleepless Night (Jimmy Clanton)
Breaking Up Is Hard To Do (Neil Sedaka)
Happy Birthday Sweet Sixteen (Neil Sedaka)
Next Door To Ann Angel (Neil Sedaka)
Crying In The Rain (Everly Brothers)
Foolish Little Girl (Shirelles)
It Hurts To Be In Love (Gene Pitney)
Puppet Man (5th Dimension)
Love Will Keep Us Together (Sedaka, The Captain & Tennille)

Burt Bacharach/Hal David
My Little Red Book (Manfred Mann)
(The Man Who Shot) Liberty Valance (Gene Pitney)
Only Love Can Break A Heart (Gene Pitney)
Twenty Four Hours From Tulsa (Gene Pitney)
What The World Needs Now Is Love (Jackie DeShannon)
Walk On By (Dionne Warwick)
Anyone Who Had A Heart (Dionne Warwick, Cilla Black)
Alfie (Dionne Warwick)
Do You Know The Way To San Jose (Dionne Warwick)
I Say A Little Prayer (Dionne Warwick, Aretha Franklin)
Make It Easy On Yourself (Jerry Butler, the Walker Brothers)
This Guy's In Love With You (Herb Alpert)
Raindrops Keep Falling On My Head (B.J. Thomas)
(They Long To Be) Close To You (Carpenters)
One Less Bell To Answer (5th Dimension)

Gerry Goffin/Carole King
Chains (Cookies, Beatles)
Don't Say Nothin' Bad About My Baby (Cookies)
Will You Love Me Tomorrow (Shirelles)
The Loco-Motion (Little Eva, Grand Funk Railroad, Kylie Minogue)
Take Good Care Of My Baby (Bobby Vee)
Up On The Roof (Drifters)
Go Away Little Girl (Steve Lawrence, Donny Osmond)
One Fine Day (Chiffons)
I Can't Stay Mad At You (Skeeter Davis)
Hey Girl (Freddie Scott)
I'm Into Something Good (Herman's Hermits)
Don't Bring Me Down (Animals)
(You Make Me Feel Like) A Natural Woman (Aretha Franklin)
Pleasant Valley Sunday (Monkees)

Ellie Greenwich/Jeff Barry
Do Wah Diddy (Exciters, Manfred Mann)
Da Doo Ron Ron (Crystals)
Then He Kissed Me (Crystals)
What A Guy (Raindrops)

The Kind Of Boy You Can't Forget (Raindrops)
Wait 'Til My Bobby Gets Home (Darlene Love)
Be My Baby (Ronettes)
Baby, I Love You (Ronettes)
Chapel Of Love (Dixie Cups)
I Wanna Love Him So Bad (Jelly Beans)
Maybe I Know (Lesley Gore)
I Have A Boyfriend (Chiffons)
Look Of Love (Lesley Gore)
Leader Of The Pack (Shangri-Las)
Wait 'Til My Bobby Gets Home (Darlene Love)
Hanky Panky (Tommy James & the Shondells)
River Deep – Mountain High (Ike & Tina Turner, Supremes/Four Tops)

Jerry Leiber/Mike Stoller
Kansas City (Wilbert Harrison, Beatles)
Stand By Me (Ben E. King, John Lennon)
Hound Dog (Big Mama Thornton, Elvis Presley)
Smokey Joe's Café (Robins)
Young Blood (Coasters, Bad Company)
Charlie Brown (Coasters)
Yakety Yak (Coasters)
Poison Ivy (Coasters)
Jailhouse Rock (Elvis Presley)
Don't (Elvis Presley)
Love Potion No. 9 (Clovers, Searchers)
Ruby Baby (Drifters, Dion)
Drip Drop (Drifters, Dion)
There Goes My Baby (Drifters)
The Reverend Mr. Black (Kingston Trio)
Love Potion No. 9 (Clovers, Searchers)

Barry Mann/Cynthia Weil
Bless You (Tony Orlando)
Uptown (Crystals)
My Dad (Paul Petersen)
Blame It On The Bossa Nova (Eydie Gorme)
On Broadway (Drifters)
Walking In The Rain (Ronettes)
I'm Gonna Be Strong (Gene Pitney)
Looking Through The Eyes Of Love (Gene Pitney)
You've Lost That Lovin' Feeling (Righteous Brothers)
We Gotta Get Out Of This Place (Animals)
Kicks (Paul Revere & the Raiders)
Hungry (Paul Revere & the Raiders)
I Just Can't Help Believing (B.J. Thomas)
Here You Come Again (Dolly Parton)
Somewhere Out There (Linda Ronstadt/James Ingram)

Pomus/Shuman
Turn Me Loose (Fabian)
A Teenager In Love (Dion & the Belmonts)
(Marie's the Name) His Latest Flame (Elvis Presley)
Sweets For My Sweet (Drifters)
This Magic Moment (Drifters, Jay & the Americans)
I Count The Tears (Drifters)

Save The Last Dance For Me (Drifters)
Seven Day Weekend (Gary U.S. Bonds)
Surrender (Elvis Presley)
Little Sister (Elvis Presley)
Suspicion (Elvis Presley, Terry Stafford)
Can't Get Used To Losing You (Andy Williams)
Viva Las Vegas (Elvis Presley)

Tommy Boyce/Bobby Hart
(Theme From) The Monkees
Last Train To Clarksville (Monkees)
I Wanna Be Free (Monkees)
Tomorrow's Gonna Be Another Day (Astronauts, Monkees)
(I'm Not Your) Steppin' Stone (Paul Revere & the Raiders, Monkees)
Valleri (Monkees)
I Wonder What She's Doing Tonight (Boyce & Hart)
Out And About (Boyce & Hart)
Alice Long (You're Still My Favorite Girlfriend) (Boyce & Hart)
She (Monkees)

Neil Diamond *(all recorded by Neil Diamond except where noted)*
Sunday And Me (Jay & the Americans)
Solitary Man
Cherry, Cherry
I'm A Believer (Monkees)
A Little Bit Me, A Little Bit You (Monkees)
Girl, You'll Be A Woman Soon
Thank The Lord For The Night Time
Kentucky Woman (Neil Diamond, Deep Purple)
Red Red Wine (Neil Diamond, UB40)
Brooklyn Roads
Brother Love's Traveling Salvation Show
Sweet Caroline
Holly Holy
Cracklin' Rosie
I Am, I Said
Song Sung Blue
Longfellow Serenade
If You Know What I Mean
You Don't Bring Me Flowers (Neil Diamond/Barbra Streisand)
Love On The Rocks
Hello Again
America
Heartlight

Laura Nyro
Flim Flam Man (Laura Nyro)
Eli's Coming (Three Dog Night)
And When I Die (Blood Sweat & Tears)
Blowing Away (5th Dimension)
Wedding Bell Blues (5th Dimension)
Stoned Soul Picnic (5th Dimension)
Sweet Blindness (5th Dimension)
Save The Country (5th Dimension)
Stoney End (Barbra Streisand)

***Paul Simon** (all recorded by Simon & Garfunkel, except where noted)*
The Sounds Of Silence
Homeward Bound
I Am A Rock
The 59th Street Bridge Song
Red Rubber Ball (Cyrkle)
A Hazy Shade Of Winter
At The Zoo
Fakin' It
Mrs. Robinson
The Boxer
Bridge Over Troubled Water
Cecilia
El Condor Pasa (If I Could)
My Little Town
Mother And Child Reunion (Paul Simon)
Me And Julio Down By The Schoolyard (Paul Simon)
Kodachrome (Paul Simon)
Loves Me Like A Rock (Paul Simon)
50 Ways To Leave Your Lover (Paul Simon)
Slip Slidin' Away (Paul Simon)

Paul Simon held most of his songs for the recording career of Simon & Garfunkel. Perhaps his most famous gem is "Bridge Over Troubled Water," which was the top charting single of 1970.

After Neil Diamond broke through as a vocal artist, the same was true for him. One of his early numbers, "Red Red Wine," was covered by UB40 as a reggae song two decades later. Deep Purple had a successful cover of his song "Kentucky Woman."

Target audience: The Brill sound identifies an era in pop-rock music when the vast majority of songs had a theme of boy-girl relationships and had a playing time of less than 3 minutes. Most of the songs were written for teen consumers. Teenagers who had an allowance from Dad and Mom or a part-time job formed the bulk of the record-buying public. They listened to pop radio stations and bought most of the products that were advertised on the air. They also had niche television programs like *American Bandstand* aimed at them.

Consumers aged 15-19 were immersed in their first romances, and the subject matter of most pop songs explored that theme extensively.

The teens who first supported rock in the '50s were becoming adults by 1965. To satisfy their changing tastes, sophistication and added length crept into the songs over the years. Examples of successful records that had exceptional length are "Like A Rolling Stone" (6:00) by Bob Dylan in 1965; "MacArthur Park" (7:20) by Richard Harris in 1968, and "Hey Jude" (7:11) by the Beatles in 1968.

In a building with marble floors, mirrored hallways and brass plated doors, the tenant directory when I visited there in 2015 included names like Above Average Productions, Broadway Video, Filmcore Distribution, Paul Simon Music and Sound One Corporation.

But the Brill carries historical significance for its important role in the history of pop, when great music bubbled from a fountain that took years to dry up.

It is worth noting that a nearby building also housed several music industry offices.
That was the structure at 1650 Broadway, a building that lacked a name and didn't have the panache of the Brill. Major tenants were Al Nevins and Don Kirshner, who ran Aldon Music, a music publishing company.

Kirshner owned three labels in the '60s – Chairman Records, Calendar Records and Kirshner Records. He hired songwriters Boyce and Hart to create hits for a made-for-TV band, the Monkees. He also became a household name in the 1970s with his popular, syndicated *Don Kirshner's Rock Concert* series on late night television.

Record labels located at 1650 Broadway included Bang, Bell, Buddah, Diamond, Gamble, Scepter/Wand and Just Sunshine. Allegro Sound Studios also were housed therein.

Brill Building entrance at 1619 Broadway, New York, N.Y.

Chapter 8

Hard Times

Songs about poverty and other social problems

Overview: Life is full of problems, and poverty ranks close to the top for many people.

As I have said before, pop music mirrors life. Numerous songs have been written and recorded with poverty as the central theme. And pop songwriters have incorporated other social problems into their work, including racial discrimination, interracial romance, child molestation and low self-esteem.

Each one of the following songs was a hit recording, proving that the sad subject matter was not a roadblock to success for the songwriters and recording artists.

To view the full lyrics to these songs, please log on to www.google.com, enter song titles & artist names and click Google Search.

To listen to these songs, please log on to www.youtube.com and enter song titles & artist names.

Patches [Dickey Lee] – The song is sung from the viewpoint of a young man who is in love with a girl who lives in the "old shanty town" part of his city. The two lovers plan to marry when summer comes, but his parents forbid it.

The story takes a sobering turn when the young man learns that his beloved was found dead in a nearby river – an apparent suicide. He counters this development with the revelation that he intends to join her by killing himself. The suicide angle caused many radio stations to banish the record from their playlists. However, it still sold over a million copies and was the No. 1 song for one week in Chicagoland on the *WLS Silver Dollar Survey*.

Romance across class boundaries is a theme that we will visit several times in this chapter.

New York songsmith Barry Mann (see Chapter 7, Brill Building) was one of the writers. The cadence is waltz time, which contains 84-90 beats per measure. The first beat of a measure is strongly accented.

This song also fits into the genre of "teen tragedies," which is another recurring theme throughout the history of pop.

Memphis native Dickey Lee started his music career in the late 1950s, writing songs in the country and pop genres. "Patches" was his biggest pop success. He had a No. 1 country hit, "Rocky," in 1975.

Patches

Songwriters: Barry Mann, Larry Kolber

Peaked at No. 6 on Billboard Hot 100

Oct. 6, 1962

Dickey Lee

Born Royden Dickey Lipscomb in Memphis, Tenn., on Sept. 21, 1936

Dickey Lee

Midnight Mary [Joey Powers] – Native Pennsylvanian Joey Powers became a one-hit wonder with this song, recorded in 1963.

He won a wrestling scholarship to Ohio State University, where he matriculated before returning to Pennsylvania to begin his recording career in 1958.

The demo of "Midnight Mary" was heard by Paul Simon (then known as Jerry Landis), who recommended it to Amy Records label owner Larry Uttal. The song had been written for the Everly Brothers, who turned it down. An album to showcase Powers' version was recorded the week of President John Kennedy's assassination.

The song's lyrics paint a picture of a young man who has disfavor with the father of his lover – possibly because of his social status ("your daddy says I'm a bad boy"). To hide their relationship he can meet Mary only at midnight, and he cautions her not to tell anyone.

In the final verse we learn a surprise – they already have secretly married.

Co-writer Artie Wayne revealed that the character of Mary was inspired by a girl named Jamela, the beautiful daughter of a deposed Iranian general who was exiled to the USA. Wayne dated her secretly in the early 1960s.

Jeannie Thomas provided the beautiful backing vocals on the track.

Midnight Mary

Songwriters: Artie Wayne, Ben Raleigh

Peaked at No. 10 on Billboard Hot 100

Jan. 4, 1964

Jan. 11, 1964

Joey Powers

Dec. 7, 1934-Jan. 20, 2017

Born Joseph S. Ruggiero in Washington, Pa., and died in his hometown

Joey Powers

Rag Doll [4 Seasons] – This was the fourth No. 1 hit for the 4 Seasons, who altered their name in 1964 to The 4 Seasons Featuring the Sound of Frankie Valli. The New Jersey group toiled for several years before their break-through song "Sherry" topped the charts in 1962. After that, their success didn't slow down for years – even through the years of the British Invasion.

The words of this song depict a poor, shabbily clad girl who is the object of the singer's love. His parents forbid him to wed her ("they say that she's no good.") 4 Seasons' keyboard player Bob Gaudio came up with the idea for the lyrics via true life experience.

Gaudio was on his way to a recording studio in New York City one day, driving on the West Side Highway in Manhattan. He stopped at a red light near 10th Ave., where there was a chronically long wait for cars who got stopped there. Because of that extraordinary length, neighborhood kids would approach stopped cars and offer to wash their windows for a few cents apiece.

A little girl wearing tattered clothes gave Gaudio's car this service and stood waiting for some change. He searched and searched and realized he had no coins. In a panic, he asked himself what he was going to give her. Finally, he found a $5 bill – the only money he had. Momentarily torn as to whether to hand it to the girl, he decided that he couldn't give her nothing. With the $5 bill in her hand, the little girl was so stunned that she couldn't even say "thank you." As Gaudio drove away he could see her in the mirror, standing in the street in disbelief.

"That whole image stayed with me," Gaudio said. "A rag doll was what she looked like."

After working on the song for a long time, Gaudio sought assistance from writer/producer Bob Crewe. Finishing it was so difficult that they considered dumping the song. But they persevered and finally completed it. But that wasn't the end of their travails.

On a Sunday, with the 4 Seasons scheduled to leave town for a tour the next day, the song had to be recorded in a rush. But they couldn't get into their normal studio and had to record in the basement of a demo studio in Manhattan. They couldn't use their engineer and had to use staff that they'd never worked with before.

Crewe, a New Jersey native, was a distinguished songwriter whose name appeared in Chapter 5 as co-writer of "Lady Marmalade." As a recording artist, he did the instrumental song "Music To Watch Girls By" as the Bob Crewe Generation in 1966.

"Rag Doll" was released about four months after the 4 Seasons had a similar song on the charts – "Dawn (Go Away)." In that song, a poor boy tells his well-to-do girlfriend to leave him so that her life will be better. He pleads, "Think what the future would be with a poor boy like me … go away back where you belong; girl, we can't change the places where we were born."

That song, too, was a huge success, rising to No. 3 on the *Billboard Hot 100.* Only the Beatles' first two American hits kept it out of the No. 1 spot.

Rag Doll

Songwriters: Bob Gaudio, Bob Crewe

Peaked at No. 1 on Billboard Hot 100

July 18, 1964

July 25, 1964

4 Seasons featuring the Sound of Frankie Valli

Frankie Valli [born Francesco Castellucio] (May 3, 1934-) lead vocals
Bob Gaudio (Nov. 17, 1942-) keyboards, tenor vocals
Tommy DeVito (June 19, 1928-) guitar, baritone vocals
Nick Massi [Nicholas Macioci] (Sept. 19, 1927-Dec. 24, 2000) bass guitar
Formed in 1956 in Newark, N.J., as the Four Lovers and evolved into the 4 Seasons

4 Seasons: Frankie Valli, Tommy DeVito, Nick Massi, Bob Gaudio

King Of The Road [Roger Miller] – This song takes a light-hearted look at the freewheeling lifestyle of the American hobo, a breed of homeless people who used to travel for free on freight trains and look for hand-outs to fill their bellies. They became common during the Great Depression of the 1930s.

Miller was a country singer/songwriter who penned hits for others before he broke through with his own recordings, which crossed over from country to pop in 1964. "King Of The Road" earned him five Grammy Awards in 1965, and its album "The Return of Roger Miller" won another. The song topped the *Billboard Country* and *Easy Listening* charts and was No. 1 in the U.K. and Norway. Many other artists covered the song.

The lyrics are upbeat, as is the title. But how many homeless people today would proudly declare that they are "king of the alley" or "king of the garbage dumpster?" I guess times have gotten rougher. We will look at another song that deals with homelessness later in this chapter.

Miller has related conflicting accounts of how he was inspired to write the song. At any rate, it seems that somewhere at some time he saw a sign that read "trailers for sale or rent," and he acquired a small statue of a hobo.

The success of the song led to *The Roger Miller Show*, a music variety show on NBC-TV in 1966. In the 1970s he opened two King of the Road Motor Inns – one in Valdosta, Ga., and one in Nashville (now part of the Clarion Hotel chain). They were upscale motels with a modern motif.

King Of The Road

Songwriter: Roger Miller

Peaked at No. 4 on Billboard Hot 100

March 20, 1965

Roger Miller

Jan. 2, 1936-Oct. 25, 1992

Born in Fort Worth, Texas, and died of lung and throat cancer in Los Angeles, Calif.

Roger Miller

Down In The Boondocks [Billy Joe Royal] – *Dictionary.com* defines "boondocks" as a remote rural area. Therefore, being a "hick from the sticks" is the stigma for the narrator of this song.

The love of his life is the daughter of his boss. So he is fighting an uphill battle in winning acceptance from his girlfriend's parents. What lies ahead of him is hard work to gain respect and improve his finances so that he can take his romance public and elevate his self-esteem. For now, she has to "steal away" to see him secretly at night. This probably is a common struggle in our society, today as it was in the mid-1960s when this song was released.

The writer was Joe South, an Atlanta native who wrote numerous popular songs, including some with social commentary in the lyrics.

The intro and the melody are almost identical to that of "Twenty Four Hours from Tulsa" by Gene Pitney, which was on the charts about 18 months earlier.

Down In The Boondocks

Songwriter: Joe South

Peaked at No. 9 on Billboard Hot 100

Aug. 28, 1965

Billy Joe Royal

April 3, 1942-Oct. 6, 2015

Born in Valdosta, Ga., and died in his sleep at his home in Morehead City, N.C.

Billy Joe Royal

Hang On Sloopy [McCoys] – A number of name changes frame this hit song. The band that recorded it changed their name from the Rick Z. Combo to Rick & the Raiders to the McCoys. The lead singer changed his name from Rick Zehringer to Rick Derringer. And the song title changed from "My Girl Sloopy" to "Hang On Sloopy."

The song was first recorded under its original title by the Vibrations, a black quintet from Los Angeles.

The Strangeloves from New York City wanted to record it but were riding high on the success of their hit "I Want Candy." They thought it could be a big rock hit if another band – a quartet that sported Beatle haircuts – recorded it. They found that band when Rick & the Raiders, from Union City, Ind., were the opening act on their concert tour stop in Dayton, Ohio.

The song tells of a girl known only as Sloopy, who lives in the slums. Her boyfriend loves her, nonetheless. In the face of put-downs by others, he calls encouragement to her throughout the song. To him, her social status is irrelevant.

By the final verse, the lyrics turn into a passionate love song. But the structure of the storyline is clear: it doesn't matter that this girl lives in a bad part of town or that she has to wear old clothing. She is loved intensely.

The McCoys went on to place two more songs in the national top 40 – "Fever" and "Come On Let's Go." After they broke up, Derringer went on to have a successful solo career.

The song is wildly popular in Ohio, especially at Ohio State University, where it is the signature song of the marching band.

In 1985, "Hang On Sloopy" was named the official rock song of the state of Ohio. According to the resolution, John Tagenhorst, then an arranger for the Ohio State University marching band, created the now-famous arrangement of "Sloopy," which was first performed at the Ohio State vs. Illinois football game on October 9, 1965.

The resolution reads: WHEREAS, "Hang On Sloopy" is of particular relevance to members of the Baby Boom Generation, who were once dismissed as a bunch of long-haired, crazy kids, but who now are old enough and vote in sufficient numbers to be taken quite seriously; and

WHEREAS, Adoption of this resolution will not take too long, cost the state anything, or affect the quality of life in this state to any appreciable degree, and if we in the legislature just go ahead and pass the darn thing, we can get on with more important stuff; and

WHEREAS, Sloopy lives in a very bad part of town, and everybody, yeah, tries to put my Sloopy down; and

WHEREAS, Sloopy, I don't care what your daddy do, 'cause you know, Sloopy girl, I'm in love with you; therefore be it resolved, that we, the members of the 116th General Assembly of Ohio, in adopting this Resolution, name "Hang On Sloopy" as the official rock song of the State of Ohio.

Hang On Sloopy

Songwriters: Wes Farrell, Bert Russell

Peaked at No. 1 on Billboard Hot 100

Oct. 2, 1965

The McCoys

Rick Derringer [born Ricky Dean Zehringer] (Aug. 5, 1947-) guitar, lead vocals
Randy Zehringer (Nov. 21, 1949-) drums
Bobby Peterson (DOB unavailable, died July 21, 1993) keyboards
Randy Jo Hobbs (March 22, 1948-Aug. 5, 1994) bass
Formed in Union City, Ind., in 1962

The McCoys

Poor Side Of Town [Johnny Rivers] – This song puts a unique twist on the romance-across-class-lines theme. The male narrator, a man of modest means from the wrong side of the tracks, had a girlfriend from his neighborhood. She left him to date a rich guy, who apparently has dumped her.

An unspoken value that the poor guy possesses is the ability to forgive, as he says, "Welcome back, baby, to the poor side of town." He asks only if the girl is going to stay with him this time.

The song is about redemption, hope and optimism. With his girl by his side, he is sure that the two of them can escape their poverty.

I understand this concept. In my own marriage, the sum of the partners is greater than the individual components. With two of us working together toward a common goal, with God's help and guidance, we have been able to accomplish great things.

This beautiful ballad was written by Rivers and legendary Hollywood record producer Lou Adler (see Chapter 3, Reality Meets Rock). The people at Rivers' record label were unhappy to see him depart from his go-go style of rock songs, which had been very successful over a three-year span.

Rivers said, "I had this tune I'd been working on, and I kept playing it for Lou. It took me about six months to finish. I did my vocals live with the band. I sat and played my guitar with the band (in the studio). There weren't any overdubs. We said it could use some singers and maybe some strings."

Marty Paich, who died in 1995 at age 70, was a pianist, composer, arranger and conductor, and he provided the arrangement for strings. The Blossoms, a vocal trio consisting of Darlene Love, Fanita James and Jean King, did the backing vocals.

The song became the only No. 1 single in Rivers' stellar recording career. It topped the Canadian chart, as well.

Born in New York City, Rivers grew up in Baton Rouge, La. He moved to Los Angeles in 1961 and got a big break three years later when he was hired on a one-year contract to play shows at the Whisky A Go Go nightclub in West Hollywood. That led to a record deal and widespread popularity.

Poor Side Of Town
Songwriters: Johnny Rivers, Lou Adler
Peaked at No. 1 on Billboard Hot 100
Nov. 12, 1966

Johnny Rivers
Born John Henry Ramistella in New York City, N.Y., on Nov. 7, 1942

Johnny Rivers

Skip A Rope [Henson Cargill] – In case you were wondering whether small children would be involved in a song with a strong message, this was one.

The song points at social issues as seen through the eyes of kids. The lyrics indicate that a lot can be learned about the issues to which children are exposed by listening to them as they play. It holds parents accountable for what they teach their children, intentionally or otherwise.

The activity of skipping rope or "jump rope," goes back to the 19th century and primarily is a girls' game. It requires two participants to swing the rope while a third jumps over the rope while chanting a rhyme, singing or counting.

The kids portrayed in "Skip A Rope" are rhyming the things they see and hear from their parents. We hear about marital discord (which gives a little sister nightmares), racism, tax evasion, a win-at-all-costs philosophy and personal betrayal. These are issues that can become values for kids after they become adults.

The game goes on and on without emotion for the kids, who accept the social issues as part of everyday life.

The song became a No. 1 hit for Henson Cargill for five weeks on *Billboard's Hot Country Singles* chart and crossed over to the pop chart, where it peaked at No. 25. Cargill was nominated for a Grammy Award (best country vocal performance, male) but lost to Johnny Cash, who was nominated for "Folsom Prison Blues" (see Chapter 3, Reality Meets Rock).

The Jordanaires, who backed Elvis Presley on several recordings, provided backing vocals.

Cargill left his job as Oklahoma City deputy sheriff to start a career as a country singer in Nashville in the mid-1960s. Producer Don Law helped him get a recording contract with Monument Records and guided him through "Skip A Rope," which was Cargill's first single.

Jack Moran and Glenn Douglas Tubb, nephew of country star Ernest Tubb, wrote the song. Cash had
looked at the song but rejected it because he was skeptical about its chances for success.

Cargill had marginal success over the remainder of his recording career. Eventually he returned to Oklahoma and opened a nightclub. He died at age 66 from complications following surgery.

Skip A Rope

Songwriters: Jack Moran, Glenn Douglas Tubb

Peaked at No. 25 on Billboard Hot 100

Feb. 10, 1968

Feb. 17, 1968

Henson Cargill

Feb. 5, 1941-March 24, 2007

Born Henson Cargill in Oklahoma City, Okla., and died there

Henson Cargill

Love Child [Diana Ross & the Supremes] – The female narrator of the song, who started her life in the poverty of slum life, is talking to her boyfriend, asking him not to pressure her into having pre-marital sex and thus creating an unwanted child. This was a brave message for ghetto youngsters and others.

Escaping the poverty of a ghetto is nearly impossible because of the repeating pattern of teens becoming single parents. The lyrics' narrator reveals that she herself was a love child.

The song debuted on a season-opening episode of CBS-TV's *Ed Sullivan Show,* Sept. 29, 1968. Instead of their normal, spangled gowns, the Supremes came out dressed differently that night – Ross wore a sweatshirt with the words "Love Child" emblazoned on the front and the other two Supremes wore leisure suits. All three were barefoot.

The single was released the next day.

The year 1967 was a year of change for Motown Records' veteran female trio. Shortly after "The Happening" became their 10th No. 1 single, the label fired Florence Ballard. Then the group's name was altered to elevate Ross to headliner, and Cindy Birdsong replaced Ballard. The next single release, "Reflections," went to No. 2, but the success of their records was lackluster in the first half of 1968.

So, Motown president Berry Gordy called a special meeting for a team of writers and producers at the Ponchartrain Hotel in Detroit. Absent were the stellar songwriting team of Brian Holland, Lamont Dozier and Eddie Holland, who had quit Motown over dissatisfaction with their share of royalties. (See Chapter 6, Story of Motown)

The result was "Love Child," which was a marked departure from the standard love songs that had defined the Supremes' catalog. Public response was immediate and very positive. The song topped the *Billboard Hot 100* for two weeks and also was No. 1 in Canada.

Mary Wilson and Birdsong did not provide backing vocals on the record, but a group known as Andantes (Jackie Hicks, Marlene Barrow and Louvain Demps) did. (See Chapter 6, Motown.) This was a normal practice on songs by Diana Ross & the Supremes.

Wilson said that giving Ross top billing over the others was a way of prepping her to go solo. She was right – at the dawn of 1970, Ross broke from the group and began a lengthy, successful solo career.

Love Child

Songwriters: R. Dean Taylor, Frank Wilson, Pam Sawyer, Deke Richards
Peaked at No. 1 on Billboard Hot 100
Nov. 30, 1968
Dec. 7, 1968

Diana Ross & the Supremes

Diana Ross (March 26, 1944-)
Mary Wilson (March 6, 1944-)
Cindy Birdsong (Dec. 15, 1939-)
Formed in Detroit, Mich., in 1959 as the Primettes

Supremes: Diana Ross, Mary Wilson (seated) and Cindy Birdsong

Cloud Nine [Temptations] – This was the first song by the Temptations to feature the "psychedelic soul sound," also known as black rock. Other such songs would follow, cementing the veteran Motown vocal group as one of the top acts on the pop and soul charts for years.

Co-writers Norman Whitfield and Barrett Strong and the Temptations have denied that the song is about drugs, but who are they trying to kid? The lyrics are laid out by a character who grew up in a large, poor family that lived in the slums. Broke, unemployed and despondent, he turns to "Cloud Nine." There is a fairly detailed list of "benefits" as the song progresses.

To me, the song glorifies the use of illicit drugs. I'm a little surprised that the Temptations and the songwriters didn't catch more flak for this overt message. But, undeniably, the scenario described by the lyrics is a common part of ghetto life.

This was the first Temptations' song fronted by Dennis Edwards after Motown yanked the talented but egotistical David Ruffin from the lineup. For details on Ruffin's dismissal, see Chapter 6.

Whitfield and Strong nicely filled the vacuum created by the departure of the Holland/Dozier/Holland songwriting team, which had fed many hits to the Temptations and other Motown artists. Details on the Holland-Dozier-Holland move out of Motown also appear in Chapter 6.

This was the first Motown song to feature guitar with wah-wah pedal, which was a new technological breakthrough at the time. It is a foot-activated device that gives the guitar player the ability to modulate the sound of his licks in a fluid manner, resulting in a "wah-wah" kind of sound.

Detroit guitarist Dennis Coffey brought it to a Motown workshop and played it for Whitfield as he was arranging the song. Whitfield loved the way it sounded, and he drafted Coffey into the Motown house band for the recording of the song.

Cloud Nine

Songwriters: Barrett Strong, Norman Whitfield

Peaked at No. 6 on Billboard Hot 100

Jan. 4, 1969

Jan. 11, 1969

Temptations

Dennis Edwards (Feb. 3, 1943-Feb. 1, 2018)

Otis Williams [born Otis Miles Jr.] (Oct. 30, 1941-)

Eddie Kendricks (Dec. 17, 1939-Oct. 5, 1992)

Melvin Franklin (Oct. 12, 1942-Feb. 23, 1995)

Paul Williams (July 2, 1939-Aug. 17, 1973)

Formed in Detroit, Mich., in 1960 as the Elgins

The Temptations: Paul Williams, Dennis Edwards, Melvin Franklin, Eddie Kendricks, Otis Williams

In The Ghetto [Elvis Presley] – We're staying in the ghetto, literally, for this song. Written by Mac Davis, it capsulizes the life of a Chicago ghetto-born boy who is a product of his environment. At a young age he steals a car and is shot dead trying to evade the police.

With back-up singers Jeannie Greene and Donna Thatcher echoing the song's title, the placid song lays bare the harsh realities of people who are born in the rough parts of big cities like Chicago. The original title was "The Vicious Circle." It was Presley's first single that contained a socially conscious message, but he didn't stop there. His next single was "Clean Up Your Own Backyard," also written by Davis (see Chapter 1, All About Rock).

According to the *Elvis Information Network* website, Presley's long-time friend Marty Lacker said, "At one point, in the beginning of the session, Elvis was concerned about recording 'In The Ghetto.'

He had never done what might be considered a message song and had often said he didn't want to get into this type of music. We discussed the matter quite thoroughly, and I finally said to Elvis, 'I really don't think it will hurt you. It's a good song … Elvis agreed."

Reaching No. 3, it was Presley's highest charting hit and first in the top 10 since "Crying In The Chapel" in 1965, signaling a true comeback for "the King of Rock & Roll." It was recorded during his sessions in Memphis, which produced several other hit singles. Nashville and Los Angeles had been his recording homes for years.

The song referenced a black kid that Davis knew in his hometown of Lubbock, Texas. Davis' friend Freddy Weller showed him the guitar lick that became the song's signature.

The song hit No. 2 in the U.K. and Canada and was No. 1 in West Germany, Ireland, Norway, Australia and New Zealand.

In The Ghetto

Songwriter: Mac Davis

Peaked at No. 3 on Billboard Hot 100

June 14, 1969

Elvis Presley

Jan. 8, 1935-Aug. 16, 1977

Born Elvis Aron Presley in Tupelo, Miss., and died of cardiac arrest in Memphis, Tenn.

Elvis Presley

Patches [Clarence Carter] – The song was recorded on the Invictus label, which was created by the songwriting team of Holland-Dozier-Holland after they left Motown. The writers were: General Johnson, lead singer of the Chairmen of the Board vocal group, which recorded on Invictus; and Ron Dunbar, who was a producer and artist & repertoire man for Invictus. The song was first recorded by the Chairmen of the Board as an album track early in 1970.

The story of the song is one of poverty and hard times for a family in rural Alabama. The oldest son has been given the nickname "Patches" because of the raggedy clothing he has to wear. After his father dies, the boy is saddled with the responsibility of running the family farm while still going to school. The family barely makes ends meet, and he gets to see his younger siblings grow to adulthood. This is a theme that is unique throughout the history of pop.

The music is a form of country soul, which combines blues, country and early rock. The song won a Grammy Award in 1971 for Best Rhythm and Blues Song. Much of the song is spoken, which punctuates the story. This technique was a staple throughout the recording career of Clarence Carter's recordings.

Carter has been quoted as saying, "I heard it on the Chairmen of the Board LP and liked it, but I had my own ideas about how it should be sung. I thought, initially, that it would be degrading for a black man to sing a song so redolent of subjugation." Producer Rick Hall persuaded him to record the song, as it related to Hall's personal history as he was growing up.

Carter's vocal was so convincing that he received letters from listeners who thought he was telling his own life story, praising him for his dedication to his family and for being an inspiration to them.

Born blind, Carter attended the Alabama School for the Blind in Talladega, and he earned a Bachelor of Science degree in music from Alabama State College.

The song peaked at No. 2 on the U.S. R&B chart and was No. 2 in the U.K.

Patches

Songwriters: General Norman Johnson, Ronald Dunbar

Peaked at No. 4 on Billboard Hot 100

Sept. 19, 1970

Sept. 26, 1970

Clarence Carter

Born Clarence George Carter in Montgomery, Ala., on Jan. 14, 1936

Clarence Carter

Indian Reservation [Raiders] – It was improbable that the "Trail of Tears" would somehow find its way into the lyrics of a pop song, but that is what happened.

The "Trail of Tears" was the forced relocation of Cherokee, Creek, Chickasaw, Choctaw and Seminole (among other tribes) living in Michigan to Florida to territory west of the Mississippi River. The Indian Removal Act of 1830 was signed by President Andrew Jackson and was motivated by lust for land and gold by settlers in the eastern states.

In 1835 the Treaty of New Echota was signed by a minority of Cherokees, but the Cherokee Nation rejected it. From 1836 to '39 federal soldiers and state militia rounded up 16,000 Cherokees from Tennessee, North Carolina, Georgia and Alabama, put them in stockades and then forced them to walk to the Oklahoma Territory. At least 4,000 died during this ordeal.

The song "Indian Reservation" was written by Nashville singer/songwriter John D. Loudermilk in the 1950s. It was first recorded by Marvin Rainwater in 1959 and was released on MGM Records under the title of "The Pale Faced Indian." It failed to attraction any attention.

In 1968 Englishman Don Fardon recorded a cover version, and it reached No. 20 on the *Billboard Hot 100* and No. 3 in the U.K.

At the end of the 1960s, the recording fortunes of American band Paul Revere & the Raiders were flagging. Lead singer Mark Lindsay had placed a couple of songs on the charts as a solo artist, and it was his intention to do the same with "Indian Reservation."

Lindsay said, "At the time, the Raiders had no material out there. As producer of the Raiders, I also produced 'Indian Reservation,' and it was my choice to put it out under the name Raiders. I'm about one-sixteenth Cherokee, so I suppose there was something that prompted me to tell about the injustice."

In short, the injustice includes taking the Cherokees' land, way of life and language.

The Raiders, who officially shortened their name in 1970, added a higher level of production than the previous versions of the song, including keyboards and strings.

The song made a strong march up the *Billboard Hot 100* and spent two weeks at No. 2 before taking over the No. 1 spot on July 24, 1971. Then it spent two more weeks at No. 2. By the time its chart run was over, it was the biggest-selling single ever for Columbia Records.

Indian Reservation (The Lament of the Cherokee Reservation Indian)

Songwriter: John D. Loudermilk

Peaked at No. 1 on Billboard Hot 100

July 24, 1971

The Raiders

Paul Revere [born Paul Revere Dick] (Jan. 7, 1938-Oct. 4, 2014) keyboards
Mark Lindsay (March 9, 1942-) vocals, saxophone
Mike "Smitty" Smith (March 27, 1942-March 6, 2001) drums
Freddy Weller (Sept. 9, 1947-) guitar
Keith Allison (Aug. 26, 1942-) bass
Formed in Boise, Idaho, in 1958 as the Downbeats and became Paul Revere & the Raiders in 1960

The Raiders

Ghetto Child [Spinners] – This song doesn't detail how life was growing up in a ghetto but, rather, relates the consequences. The narrator tells of the shame of being raised in poverty and the ridicule he received from his peers.

The beauty of the melody and the vocals belies the seriousness of the message.

To me, the key line is "I was just a boy being punished for a crime that was not mine." The narrator was born into a life of poverty. His parents tried to provide for their family the best they could, but they were not able to improve their lot. He finds that the best solution for him is to run away from home at the age of 17.

The Spinners were with the Motown Corp., 1963-72, after their contract with Tri-Phi Records was bought out. In 1972 they signed a contract with Atlantic Records, another label that had a stable of rhythm & blues artists.

Their career went into overdrive almost immediately, and their involvement with Jamaican-born producer Thom Bell was partly responsible. Under his guidance, the Spinners put seven songs in the top five of the pop charts, including a No. 1, "Then Came You," a collaboration with Dionne Warwick.

Ghetto Child

Songwriters: Thom Bell, Linda Creed
Peaked at No. 29 on Billboard Hot 100
Sept. 15, 1973
Sept. 22, 1973

The Spinners
Bobby Smith (April 10, 1936-March 16, 2013)
Purvis Jackson (May 17, 1938-Aug. 18, 2008)
Henry Fambrough (May 10, 1938-)
Philippe Wynne (April 3, 1941-July 14, 1984)
Billy Henderson (Aug. 9, 1939-Feb. 2, 2007)
Formed in Ferndale, Mich., as the Domingoes in 1954. They also have been known as the Detroit Spinners and the Motown Spinners.

The Spinners

Brother Louie [Stories] – The social issue in this song is interracial dating. It was a much touchier subject in 1973, when this song was on the charts, than it is now.

The band Stories recorded the song after lead singer Ian Lloyd found the master copy of the original version by the British band Hot Chocolate in a Buddah Records office.

"I went through a lot of demo tapes and discs," Lloyd told the *Forgotten Hits* website. "When I heard the chorus to 'Louie' I told Bob (Reno), 'This is a Number One record, let's do it.' At the time I did not know that I was listening to Hot Chocolate's finished master.

"I thought it was just another demo. I think both versions were released around the same time. The rest is rock history."

Two members of Hot Chocolate, Errol Brown and Tony Wilson, wrote the song. Their version peaked at No. 7 on the U.K. singles chart but didn't catch on in the U.S. It was longer and had some spoken parts. The racial epithets "honky" and "spook" are used in the original.

Hot Chocolate had to wait until 1975 to have a hit in America, when they charted to No. 8 with "Emma."

"Brother Louie" is about a white boy who is dating a black girl, and their relationship is spurned by his parents.

Stories, a New York-based band, saw their version top the *Billboard Hot 100* for two weeks, and it was ranked the No. 13 single of 1973. Kenny Aaronson was responsible for the pounding, funky bassline that drove the beat. Guitarist Steve Love gave the wah-wah pedal a good workout. "Brother Louie" made them a one-hit wonder.

Brown was proud that Hot Chocolate was England's first multi-racial band. "That was deliberate," he told London's *The Mail on Sunday*. "I wanted to show the world that we could work together, whatever our color or creed. It may sound idealistic, but bigotry and prejudice have always offended my sensibilities. I thought it important to show that we were all God's children and needed to respect each other. This is my philosophy of life. It's the way I've tried to live."

Brother Louie

Songwriters: Errol Brown, Tony Wilson

Peaked at No. 1 on Billboard Hot 100

Aug. 25, 1973

Sept. 1, 1973

Stories

Ian Lloyd – lead vocals

Steve Love – guitar

Bryan Madey – drums

Kenny Aaronson – bass

Formed in New York City, N.Y., in 1972

Stories: Ian Lloyd, Bryan Madey, Kenny Aaronson, Steve Love

Half-Breed [Cher] – This is another song that deals with racial hardships among native Americans. In this case, the narrator is a woman who is half white and half Cherokee, and she is snubbed throughout her life by members of both races.

The mixed-race girl is taunted by other children. This leads to a persecution complex, and she leaves home at the age of 19. The rest of her life becomes a series of movements, including her love life. At the end, she admits in despair that she cannot escape who she is. Cher delivered a passionate, heart-felt performance on the recording.

I can't help but think that this song could not have been made in the politically correct atmosphere of the 21st century. The song title is a slur that is not tolerated anymore.

For years Cher performed the song in her Las Vegas stage shows wearing an Indian headdress. She has taken a fair amount of criticism for that. She claims that her mother has some Cherokee blood, as well as Irish, English and German. Her father was Armenian-American.

Lyricist Mary Dean reportedly wrote the lyrics especially for Cher. Producer Snuff Garrett declared, "I said from the lyrics, it's a smash for Cher and for nobody else … to me, nobody else could do that song but Cher."

The song was readily accepted in 1973 and didn't stop climbing the *Billboard Hot 100* until it reached No. 1. It also hit No. 1 in Canada and New Zealand and peaked at No. 3 in Australia.

Half-Breed

Songwriters: Al Capps, Mary Dean

Peaked at No. 1 on Billboard Hot 100

Oct. 6, 1973

Oct. 13, 1973

Cher

Born Cherilyn Sarkisian in El Centro, Calif., on May 20, 1946

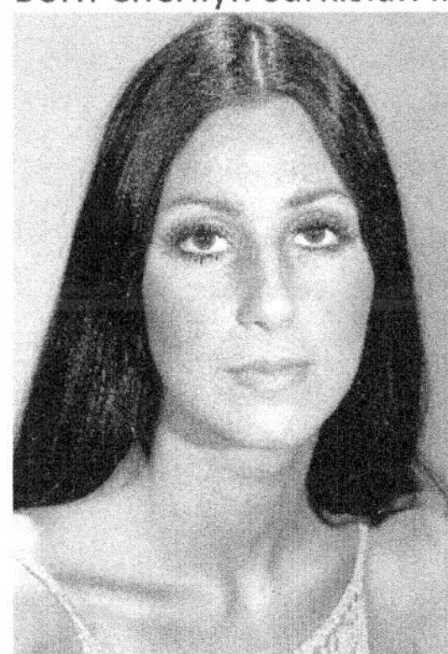

Cher

At Seventeen [Janis Ian] – This song is by a singer/songwriter who was suffering from a severe deficiency of self-esteem. In the lyrics she laid bare her feelings about her lack of beauty, confidence, boyfriends and popularity as a teen. She referred to herself as an "ugly duckling." She must have needed a team of psychiatrists to work through these feelings of inferiority.

And there must have been legions of listeners who heard these words and thought the song was about them. In a highly competitive period on the pop charts, "At Seventeen" surged to No. 3 in the summer of 1975.

Janis Ian, writing from the perspective of adulthood, made a major commentary on society's beauty standards, saying that "love was meant for beauty queens who married young and then retired."

She said the song, written over the course of three months in 1973, was inspired by a newspaper article about a former debutante who learned the hard way that being popular didn't solve all her problems. Included in the article was the quote, "I learned the truth at eighteen." Ian found that the word "seventeen" worked better with the tune she had composed.

She said that initially she did not want to perform or record the song because it was too personal to share, but she changed her mind after she added the final verse.

"At Seventeen" became quite a decorated recording, ascending to No. 1 on the *Billboard Adult Contemporary* chart and the Canadian pop chart. *Billboard* ranked it as the No. 19 song of 1975, and in 1976 it won a Grammy Award for Best Female Pop Vocal Performance.

She admitted that the song was the most likely to give her the artistic immortality that she says is every songwriter's dream.

Ian, who had recorded her first hit single at age 14, married Portuguese filmmaker Tino Sargo in 1978. In her autobiography, she detailed physical and emotional abuse during the union, and they divorced in 1983. She met Patricia Snyder in Nashville in 1989, and she came out as a lesbian in 1993. She and Snyder married in Toronto in 2003.

At Seventeen

Songwriter: Janis Ian
Peaked at No. 3 on Billboard Hot 100
Sept. 13, 1975
Sept. 20, 1975

Janis Ian

Born Janis Eddy Fink in New York City, N.Y., on April 7, 1951

Janis Ian

Another Day In Paradise [Phil Collins] – This song stands out as perhaps the only one in rock history that deals head-on with the problem of homelessness. It was well received and became the last *Billboard* No. 1 song of the 1980s and the first of the 1990s.

The fictional story laid out by the lyrics has a homeless, ailing woman approaching a man on the street to ask for help. The man pretends that he doesn't see or hear her and moves on in embarrassment. The message is this: with the blessings that most of us have been given, our lives are paradise compared to the misfortune that some others have to endure.

Short of taking one of these people into our home and providing for them, there's not much we can do. My wife and I contribute to charities that help the homeless, but some needy people refuse to accept this help.

In the bridge, Collins appeals directly to God: "Oh Lord, is there nothing more anybody can do? Oh Lord, there must be something you can say."

Collins took a lot of criticism for the song, despite winning a 1991 Grammy Award for Record of the Year. He was accused of exploiting the subject to further his success and for singing about the poor when he was very wealthy.

He responded in a *New York Times* interview, "When I drive down the street, I see the same things everyone else sees. It's a misconception that, if you have a lot of money, you're out of touch with reality."

Collins said he got the idea for the song when he was visiting Washington, D.C., where he saw "people living in boxes" and sleeping on grates in the street to keep warm.

It was Collins's seventh and final No. 1 song on the American charts (that doesn't count one No. 1 song with his band, Genesis). The song also hit No. 1 in Belgium, Canada, Finland, Germany, Italy, Norway, Sweden, Switzerland and Zimbabwe. In his native U.K. it peaked at No. 2.

Another Day In Paradise

Songwriter: Phil Collins

Peaked at No. 1 on Billboard Hot 100

Dec. 23, 1989
Dec. 30, 1989
Jan. 6, 1990
Jan. 13, 1990

Phil Collins

Born Philip David Charles Collins in Chiswick, West London, England, on Jan. 30, 1951

Phil Collins

Janie's Got A Gun [Aerosmith] – Minor children get more attention in this 1990 hit by Boston band Aerosmith. Instead of kids imitating what they hear from their parents (a la "Skip A Rope,") the subject matter is incest and child abuse. The end result is a revenge killing.

Janie, a girl of undetermined age, is the victim who gives her father some payback for molesting her.

The subject matter was a departure from the pattern of love songs that had formed the platform of Aerosmith's recording career, which was 15 years old at that point. Lead singer Steven Tyler wrote the song with help from bass player Tom Hamilton.

According to a 2020 story in *Rolling Stone,* Tyler claims that articles in *Time* and *Newsweek* about gun violence and child abuse in affluent suburbs, respectively, inspired him to pen the lyrics.

One of Tyler's original lines was "he raped a little bitty baby …" In order to get the song played on radio stations and MTV, Tyler changed "raped" to "jacked." An edited version replaced "put a bullet in his brain" with "left him in the pouring rain."

Tyler told *Rolling Stone,* "I'd heard this woman speaking about how many children are attacked by their mothers and fathers. It was [expletive] scary. I felt, man, I gotta sing about this. And that was it. That was my toe in the door."

In a frank admission to a *Rolling Stone* reporter, Tyler said he had an attraction to his daughter, actress Liv Tyler. "How can a father not be attracted to his daughter, especially when she's a cross between the girl he married and himself," he remarked. "All a man has to do is be totally honest with himself, and he can see it.

"However, the real man knows that's just a place to never go. Instead, he celebrates it by telling his daughter how beautiful she is and what a precious child of God she is. There's ways to love it without making love to it. I wrote "Janie's Got A Gun" about fathers who don't know the difference."

The result was Aerosmith's first ever win at the 1991 Grammy Awards.

Janie's Got A Gun

Songwriters: Steven Tyler, Tom Hamilton

Peaked at No. 4 on Billboard Hot 100

Feb. 10, 1990

Aerosmith

Steven Tyler [born Steven Victor Tallerico] (March 26, 1948-) lead vocals
Joe Perry (Sept. 10, 1950-) lead and rhythm guitar
Tom Hamilton (Dec. 31, 1951-) bass
Brad Whitford (Feb. 23, 1952-) lead and rhythm guitar
Joey Kramer (June 21, 1950-) drums
Formed in Boston, Mass., in 1970

Aerosmith: Tom Hamilton, Joey Kramer, Steven Tyler, Joe Perry, Brad Whitford

Chapter 9

It's All Greek To Me

Songs sung in foreign languages

Overview: In the late 1950s, the pop music landscape in America was on fire with new artists. Each year saw the release of hundreds of new songs that were influenced by the fledgling phenomenon called rock and roll.

But musicians in other parts of the world were taking notice, and they were able to create songs in their own languages that came to America's shores. And, one by one, they began to compete very successfully with English language songs on the *Billboard* charts.

Even some American artists recorded songs in foreign languages, either entirely or in part, and these efforts were rewarded with big sales and lofty chart rankings. The year with the most foreign language songs (three) was 1963.

The songs profiled herein contain some of the most beautiful melodies and vocals ever recorded, which shows that understanding song lyrics is not essential to deriving enjoyment from music.

To view the full lyrics to these songs, please log on to www.google.com, enter song titles & artist names and click Google Search.

To listen to these songs, please log on to www.youtube.com and enter song titles & artist names.

Nel Blu Di Pinto Di Blu (Volaré) [Domenico Modugno] – The title of this song, the first foreign language song to make a splash on the American charts during the rock era, translates to "In The Blue Sky Painted Blue (To Fly)." The artist is considered to be the first Italian *cantautore*, a musician who creates his own music, including lyrics and melodies, and sings while playing an instrument.

The song describes a dream in which a man paints his hands blue and sings as he flies through "the blue painted in blue."

The turning point in Domenico Modugno's career came in 1958, when he performed at the annual Sanremo Music Festival in Sanremo, Liguria, Italy. With Johnny Dorelli, he sang "Nel Blu Di Pinto Di Blu," which he had co-authored with Franco Migliacci. The song won the competition, and the subsequent recording sold more than 22 million copies worldwide.

In America, besides holding down the No. 1 spot on the charts for five weeks, the song won record of the year and song of the year at the first Grammy Awards. It was *Billboard's* top song for the year.

Modugno's song "Io" was translated into English for Elvis Presley and became a No. 12 hit under the title of "Ask Me" In 1964. Modugno later acted in 44 films and produced two of them. In the 1970s he took to acting on television and singing in modern operas.

In 1987 the man who was hailed as "the music genius of Italy" was elected to the Italian parliament.

Two years after Modugno's big hit, Bobby Rydell recorded the song in English under the title of "Volaré" and took it to No. 4 on the *Billboard Hot 100*. Dean Martin and Al Martino also made hit recordings of the song.

Nel Blu Di Pinto Di Blu (Volaré)
Songwriters: Domenico Modugno, Franco Migliacci
Peaked at No. 1 on Billboard Hot 100
Aug. 18, 1958
Sept. 1, 1958
Sept. 8, 1958
Sept. 15, 1958
Sept. 22, 1958

Domenico Modugno

Jan. 9, 1928-Aug. 6, 1994

Born in Polignano a Mare, Apulia, Italy, and died of a heart attack at his home on the island of Lampedusa, south of Sicily

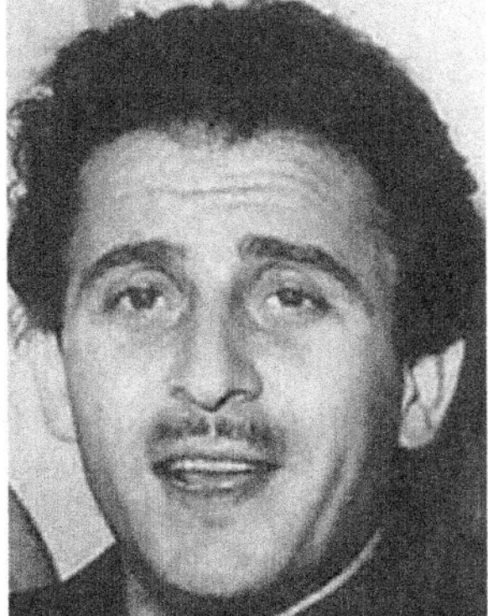

Domenico Modugno

La Bamba [Ritchie Valens] – This is a traditional Mexican folk song that was turned into a modest hit by a young Hispanic singer from Pacoima, Calif.

Ritchie Valens' career was only about eight months old when he died in an infamous plane crash with Buddy Holly and J.P. Richardson while on tour near Clear Lake, Iowa, on Feb. 3, 1959. He became considerably more popular after his death than he had been while alive.

Oddly, Valens's only two top 40 hits occupied both sides of the same 45 rpm record. The "A" side was "Donna," which spent two weeks at No. 2 before the "B" side, "La Bamba," began to chart on its own.

"La Bamba" is often played at weddings in the Mexican state of Veracruz, where the groom and bride do an accompanying dance. The recording that peaked at No. 22 on *the Billboard Hot 100* was infused with a rock beat provided by Carol Kaye (acoustic rhythm guitar), Earl Palmer (drums and claves), René Hall (electric guitar), Buddy Clark (acoustic bass) and Ernie Freeman (piano). Valens played the lead electric guitar.

Valens did not speak Spanish fluently but was said to be proficient in "Spanglish." His parents came from Mexican and native American backgrounds.

The lyrics begin with the narrator bragging to his fiancée, "I'm not a sailor, I'm a captain." The song is filled with the optimism of youth.

The song got a second wind in 1987, when the biopic *La Bamba* was released, telling Valens' life story to the world. It was the first Hollywood movie with a Hispanic subject, and it became a huge hit. The title song on the soundtrack was performed by Los Lobos from East Los Angeles, and the single spent three weeks at No. 1 and was the first *Billboard* No. 1 song with all Spanish lyrics. Valens appeared as himself in one movie, *Go, Johnny, Go!* released in 1959.

Internationally, the song had the best performance in Belgium, where it peaked at No. 13.

In 2019 the Valens version of "La Bamba" was selected by the Library of Congress for preservation in the National Recording Registry for being "culturally, historically or aesthetically significant."

Valens was the second of five siblings and grew up listening to mariachi music, flamenco guitar, jump blues and R&B. Naturally left-handed, he was so eager to learn guitar that he mastered the right-handed version of the instrument. He played in a local band known as the Silhouettes.

One of his high school classmates tipped off owner/president Bob Keane of Del-Fi Records in Hollywood about Valenzuela's talent. Keane auditioned him and then signed him to a recording contract on May 27, 1958. At that point Valenzuela shortened his name to Ritchie because "there were a lot of Richards out there." Keane shortened the last name to widen his audience appeal. By the fall of 1958, the demands of Valens's career forced him to drop out of school.

La Bamba

Songwriter: Traditional, produced by Bob Keane

Peaked at No. 22 on Billboard Hot 100

Feb. 2, 1959

Ritchie Valens

May 13, 1941-Feb. 3, 1959

Born Richard Steven Valenzuela in Pacoima, Calif., and died in a plane crash near Clear Lake, Iowa, while on tour with Buddy Holly and J.P. Richardson (the "Big Bopper")

Ritchie Valens

Wooden Heart [Joe Dowell] – This song got off the launching pad when Elvis Presley recorded it in 1960 for his film *G.I. Blues*. Presley's version hit No. 1 in the U.K. but wasn't released in America until 1964, when it appeared as the B-side of "Blue Christmas."

In the meantime, Joe Dowell recorded the song for his label, Smash Records. He aspired to write his own material, but his contract stipulated that he record songs that were owned by Smash's parent company, Mercury. His version of "Wooden Heart" became a million-seller and topped the *Billboard Hot 100* and the easy listening chart.

Dowell was handed the song when he walked into his first Smash recording session and had three hours to learn it. "I didn't have any idea what I was singing," he said. "I learned the song phonetically."

With four other competing versions out at the time, Dowell's recording was rushed to market in three days, and he was sent on a monthlong promotional tour. It paid off.

Most of the song's lyrics are in English, but there is a verse and some alternating lyrics in German. The song was based on the German folk song "Muss I Denn" (Must I Then), originating from the Rems Valley in Württemberg, southwest Germany. Friedrich Silcher wrote the original version.

Before Presley's version, Marlene Dietrich recorded the song in German some time before 1958. It appeared as the B-side of her 1959 single "Lili Marlene." Bobby Vinton recorded it in 1975, with certain lines sung in Polish.

Dowell had one more top 40 hit but, due to struggles with his management, he was dropped from his record label. He went on to record some folk and gospel music.

Wooden Heart

Songwriters: Fred Wise, Ben Weisman, Kay Twomey, Bert Kaempfert

Peaked at No. 1 on Billboard Hot 100

Aug. 28, 1961

Joe Dowell

Jan. 23, 1940-Feb. 4, 2016

Born Joseph Harry Dowell in Bloomington, Ind., and died in Bloomington, Ill.

Joe Dowell

Al Di Lá [Emilio Pericoli] – This song came to America via an Italian movie, *Rome Adventure* starring Troy Donahue and Suzanne Pleshette. The title translates to "Beyond."

If you like love ballads, this song is for you. The romantic words sung in Italian give the sound a great vibe.

Emilio Pericoli, like Domenico Modugno, had a strong tie to the Sanremo Music Festival. In 1961 Betty Curtis (real name Roberta Corti) won the competition with her rendition of "Al Di Lá," and Pericoli recorded his version the following year.

Once an aspiring accountant, he had no further success in English speaking countries, but he found a niche as a television actor in his homeland.

Billboard ranked the record at No. 48 on its 1962 year-end chart. Connie Francis, Jerry Vale, Al Martino, the Ray Charles Singers and Al Hirt also recorded the song.

Pericoli's version of the love song peaked at No. 2 on the Italian charts. On the *Billboard* adult contemporary chart it peaked at No. 3.

Al Di Lá

Songwriter: Carlo Donida

Peaked at No. 6 on Billboard Hot 100

July 7, 1962

Emilio Pericoli

Jan. 7, 1928-April 9, 2013

Born Emilio Pericoli in Cesenatico, Italy, and died in Savignano sul Rubicone, Italy

Emilio Pericoli

Sukiyaki [Kyu Sakamoto] – First released in 1961 in Japan, this song was introduced to America in the spring of 1963. It is the only song sung in a non-European language to top the *Billboard Hot 100.*

The melody hints of a sad-but-beautiful love song, but the lyrics were born of a different mindset. Lyricist Rokusuke Ei wrote the words while returning home from a protest of the Treaty of Mutual Cooperation and Security between Japan and the United States. He was feeling dejected about the failure of the protest movement. The lyrics were rendered generic on purpose so that they could refer to any lost love. This information was not imparted to American radio listeners, perhaps because disc jockeys had not been given that information.

The Japanese title is "Ue o Muite Arukō." The title "Sukiyaki" was chosen for releases in English speaking countries only because it is a short, catchy term that is readily recognizable as Japanese to those in the Western world. *Sukiyaki* actually refers to a Japanese hot-pot dish with cooked beef. A *Newsweek* columnist observed the re-titling was like issuing "Moon River" in Japan under the title of "Beef Stew."

Nonetheless, the record sold over 13 million copies worldwide, hitting No. 1 in Australia, Canada and Norway. It held down the No. 1 position in Japan for three months in 1961 and in the United States for three weeks in 1963.

In 1981, the Los Angeles duo A Taste of Honey hit No. 3 with the song, but the English lyrics of that version were totally unrelated to those in the original version.

Sakamoto joined his first band in Japan when he was 16. Besides vocals, he contributed on guitar, trumpet and piano. With the help of "Ue o Muite Arukō," he established a solo career in 1961. He had a follow-up to "Sukiyaki" with the song "China Nights," which peaked at a disappointing No. 58 in the U.S. He also acted in eight Japanese films.

He was the youngest of his father's nine children – his mother was his father's second wife. During the air raids on the greater Tokyo area in the summer of 1944, his mother Iku took her three children to live with their maternal grandparents in rural Kasama, Ibaraki Prefecture. They moved back to Kawasaki in 1949.

Sakamoto died near Mount Takamagahara at Ueno, Japan, with 519 other passengers in the plane crash of Japan Airlines flight 123, the deadliest single-aircraft accident at the time.

Sukiyaki

Songwriters: Rokusuke Ei, Hachidai Nakamura

Peaked at No. 1 on Billboard Hot 100

June 15, 1963

June 22, 1963

June 29, 1963

Kyu Sakamoto

Dec. 10, 1941-Aug. 12, 1985

Born Hisashi Sakamoto in Kawasaki, Kanagawa, Japan, and was raised as Hisashi Oshima

Kyu Sakamoto

Enamorado [Keith Colley] – What I originally thought was a love song by a Mexican man with an English-sounding name turned out to be a song by an American man from Spokane, Wash.

Colley's knowledge of the Spanish language was sketchy, at best, when he went into the recording studio to record his song "Enamorado" for Unical Records in 1963. The song, which had a pretty melody, was translated into Spanish to cover up the shallowness of the lyrical content. Colley's vocal interpretation was convincing.

The title means "in love."

The single became a regional hit in several U.S. markets. Such was the case in Chicago, where it peaked at No. 16, Los Angeles (No. 4) and Seattle (No. 5). It peaked at No. 66 on *Billboard's Hot 100.*

Unical hoped for more success using the "Enamorado" format and sent Colley back to the studio to record two more songs in Spanish. It was not to be, however, and neither song made a splash. The songs' names are not even in the public record today.

Colley moved on to Vee Jay Records and then Challenge Records without having any national hits. Then he shifted his focus to songwriting and cut demo recordings of many of his songs, backed by some of Los Angeles's finest session musicians. Those songs were picked up by such noted artists as the Newbeats, the Knickerbockers, the Sandpipers, Jackie DeShannon and the New Christy Minstrels.

As the 1960s were ending, Colley had turned toward the business side of the music industry, serving as artist and repertoire man and then an administrator for Four Star Publishing.

While attending the University of Washington, he recorded a version of "A Teenager in Love," which was played on local radio and helped get him signed to his first recording contract.

Almost 25 years later Linda Ronstadt would record two albums of Spanish language songs in a fashion similar to Colley's. Honoring her Mexican heritage, she took songs that her grandfather and father had taught her when she was a girl.

"I remember my dad singing in Spanish and playing on the guitar, harmonizing with his brothers and my grandfather singing and playing on the solo guitar," Ronstadt told *AARP Magazine.* "And then on Saturday afternoons my father would play records by Los Panchos, Trío Calaveras, Trío Tariácuri, Lola Beltrán, Mariachi Vargas. I loved all these records and I wanted to sing them, but only knew part of the words.

"I didn't speak very good Spanish as a child, so I thought Spanish was the language you sang in and English was the language you spoke. To me, Spanish was always a musical language."

Enamorado
Songwriter: Keith Colley
Peaked at No. 66 on Billboard Hot 100
Oct. 26, 1963

Keith Colley
Born Jarrell Keith Colley in Spokane, Wash., in 1941

Keith Colley

Dominique [The Singing Nun] – The story of the rise and fall of this singer and her songs could rival the plot of any television soap opera.

It began for the Belgian woman named Jeannine Deckers, who was an avid Girl Guide (as Girl Scouts are known in Europe). She liked to play her guitar and sing at evening scouting events. In 1959 she entered the Missionary Dominican Sisters of Our Lady of Fichermont, headquartered in Waterloo, where she took the religious name "Sister Luc-Gabrielle."

She liked to write and casually perform songs for her peers and visitors at the convent. They were so well received that her religious superiors encouraged her to record an album that they could sell to retreatants on site. After some delay, more than a dozen songs were recorded at Philips Records in Brussels in 1962. The melodies were simple and contained uplifting messages. Sister Luc-Gabrielle was accompanied by a chorus of four nuns and a new guitar, and she sang in the language of Belgian French.

The resulting album was so successful that Philips decided to release it commercially, and thousands of copies were sold throughout Europe. Philips gave the singer a new name – Sœur Sourire, or "Sister Smile."

The album was released internationally, and the artist became known as The Singing Nun in English speaking countries. It gathered little notice until music publisher Paul Kapp decided to release "Dominique" as a single in the United States. The song eulogizes the founder of the Dominican order.

The single became an instant smash, and Luc-Gabrielle became an overnight celebrity. Her song held down the No. 1 spot on the *Billboard Hot 100* for the final month of 1963, and she made a remote appearance from the convent on the *Ed Sullivan Show* on Jan. 5, 1964. Her album also charted at No. 1, making it the first time any artist had a No. 1 single and album simultaneously.

Within three years there was a movie about the Singing Nun's life. It starred Debbie Reynolds in the title role, marking the first time an artist who had recorded a No. 1 hit ("Tammy") played the part of an artist who had a No. 1 hit.

Soon after the release of the film, Luc-Gabrielle left the convent, contending that she had been forced out. She became a lay Dominican and served as a secular missionary. Upon her departure from the convent, Philips forced her to stop using the names Sœur Sourire and Singing Nun, so she continued performing under the name Luc Gabrielle.

In 1967 she released a song defending the use of contraception, which led to an intervention by the Catholic hierarchy in Montreal, Canada, where one of her concerts was canceled. Ultimately, an entire tour was scrapped. She published a book of inspirational verse in 1968, but it failed to attract readership.

In the late 1970s the Belgian revenue agency notified Deckers that she owed $63,000 in back taxes. She claimed that she had donated her music proceeds to the convent, which in turn gave her what it considered to be her fair share. Philips had received 95% of her revenues but did nothing to help her during the tax crisis.

In an attempt to relieve her financial woes, she released a disco synthesizer version of "Dominique" in 1982. This final attempt to revive her singing career failed.

In a suicide note, Deckers claimed she had "lost all courage in the face of a losing battle with tax people." She and her roommate, Annie Pécher, were found dead from overdoses of barbiturates and alcohol on March 29, 1985.

Dominique

Songwriter: Jeanine Deckers

Peaked at No. 1 on Billboard Hot 100

Dec. 7, 1963

Dec. 14, 1963

Dec. 21, 1963

Dec. 28, 1963

The Singing Nun (Sœur Sourire)

Oct. 17, 1933-March 29, 1985

Born Jeanne-Paule Marie Deckers in Laeken, Belgium, and committed suicide in Wavre, Brabant, Belgium

The Singing Nun

Guantanamera [Sandpipers] – This Cuban anthem goes back to at least 1929, and it broke into the American top 10 in 1966.

The title is the Spanish word for "woman from Guantánamo." The official writing credit has been bestowed upon Joséito Fernandez, who first popularized the song on radio.

The better-known lyrics are based on poetry by Jose Martí. The song's musical structure lends itself to improvised verses, thus making the song a vehicle for patriotic, humorous, romantic or social commentary in Cuba and other places where Spanish is spoken.

The Sandpipers, an easy listening trio formed in California and composed of members from Los Angeles (Jim Brady), Rochester, N.Y. (Mike Piano), and Seattle, Wash. (Richard Shoff), made it their first chart success. They started out as the Four Seasons in the early 1960s but changed their name to the Grads in the face of rising popularity by the New Jersey group led by Frankie Valli.

At a live performance in Lake Tahoe, Nev., the Grads caught the attention of A&M Records co-founder Herb Alpert, who signed them to his label. After one unsuccessful single, they decided on a name change, picking the term "Sandpipers" out of a dictionary. Their producer, Tommy LiPuma, recommended that they record "Guantanamera."

Female singer Robie Lester provided uncredited backing vocals.

The Sandpipers went on to record songs in other languages, such as English, French, Italian, Portuguese and Tagalog.

Other mainstream pop artists recorded "Guantanamera," including Julio Iglesias, Joan Baez, Jimmy Buffett, Trini Lopez, Gloria Estefan and Pete Seeger.

"Guantanamera" earned the Sandpipers a Grammy nomination in 1967 for best performance by a vocal group.

Guantanamera
Songwriter: Joseíto Fernandez
Peaked at No. 9 on Billboard Hot 100
Sept. 17, 1966

The Sandpipers
Jim Brady (Aug. 24, 1944-)
Mike Piano (Oct. 26, 1944-)
Richard Shoff (April 30, 1944-)
Formed in Los Angeles, Calif., in 1966, remaining active until 1975

The Sandpipers: Mike Piano, Jim Brady, Richard Shoff

Eres Tu (Touch The Wind) [Mocedades] – This is one of a handful of songs sung completely in Spanish that cracked the *Billboard* top 10. *Eres tu* means "It's you."

The song, written by Juan Carlos Calderón, was Spain's entry in the 1973 Eurovision Song Contest, and it placed second in the competition that was like *American Idol* and showcased the best in European music. The group that performed it, Mocedades, was from Bilbao, Spain, and Amaya Uranga sang lead on the track. Mocedades means "youths."

Uranga and her two younger sisters formed the core of the group. They started singing together in 1967, and their brothers and friends eventually joined them during rehearsals. They decided to name themselves *Voces y Guitarras* (Voices and Guitars), and their folk and spiritual renderings were influenced by the Beatles.

For a year they played gigs around their hometown before sending a demo tape to Calderón in Madrid. He took an interest in them from the start, and he renamed them Mocedades.

Calderón gave them "Eres Tu," and it was released as a single after the Eurovision competition. It became a huge international hit. The group would have other hit records, but none cracked the American market.

The "B" side of the single was titled "Touch The Wind," and it was sung in English with the same music but is otherwise completely unrelated to the "A" side. Most disc jockeys didn't seem interested in playing the "B" side, but I heard it a couple of times on St. Louis AM station KSD.

Eres Tu (Touch The Wind)
Songwriter: Juan Carlos Calderón
Peaked at No. 9 on Billboard Hot 100
March 23, 1974
March 30, 1974

Mocedades
Amaya Uranga (Feb. 18, 1947-)
Izaskun Uranga (April 17, 1950-)
Estibaliz Uranga (Dec. 9, 1952-)
Jose Ipina
Carlos Zubiaga
Javier Garay
Formed in Bilbao, Spain, in 1967

Mocedades

Before The Next Teardrop Falls [Freddy Fender] – Only one of three of this song's verses is sung in Spanish, but it is a noteworthy occurrence because the recording hit No. 1 on both the *Billboard* country and pop charts.

Tejano singer Freddy Fender was a mature 37 years old when this record took off. He had dropped out of high school at 16, and his music career was put on hold for three years while he was incarcerated in Louisiana for marijuana possession.

"Before The Next Teardrop Falls" was written in 1967 and got exposure from three country artists, including Charley Pride and Jerry Lee Lewis. In 1974 producer Huey Meaux asked Fender to do a vocal overdub for an instrumental version of the song, and Fender sang it in bilingual fashion, repeating the opening verse in Spanish as the second stanza.

"The recording only took a few minutes," Fender said. "I was glad to get it over with, and I thought that would be the last of it."

In January 1975 the recording was distributed to country radio stations and soared to No. 1. By spring it had been picked up by top 40 stations, and the pattern of success repeated itself on the *Hot 100. Billboard* ranked it as the No. 4 song for the year.

By the way, in 1975 there was a total of six songs that topped both the country and pop charts, which is quite unusual for one year. The other five songs were "(Hey Won't You Play) Another Somebody Done Somebody Wrong Song" by B.J. Thomas; "Thank God I'm A Country Boy" by John Denver; "Rhinestone Cowboy" by Glen Campbell; "I'm Sorry" by John Denver, and "Convoy" by C.W. McCall.

Fender also recorded a version fully in Spanish, titled *"Estare Contigo Cuando Triste Estas."* His career took an unprecedented upswing in 1975, ensuring his popularity in the pop, country and Tex-Mex genres for years to come.

His father was a Mexican immigrant. Freddy dropped out of school at the age of 16 and did a three-year enlistment in the U.S. Marine Corps. As a singer of rockabilly music throughout the South, he legally changed his name in 1958 to Freddy Fender – taking Fender from the name of the guitar manufacturer and Freddy because he liked the alliteration (and because it would sell better with gringos!)

He underwent a kidney transplant in 2002 and a liver transplant in 2004. However, he developed cancerous tumors on his lungs, and he died at his home in Corpus Christi, Texas, with his family by his bedside.

Before The Next Teardrop Falls

Songwriters: Vivian Keith, Ben Peters

Peaked at No. 1 on Billboard Hot 100

May 31, 1975

Freddy Fender

June 4, 1937-Oct. 14, 2006

Born Baldemar Garza Huerta in San Benito, Texas, and died in Corpus Christi, Texas

Freddy Fender

99 Luftballons [Nena] – This huge international hit got its lyrical storyline from the Cold War. It's about brinksmanship, fear, paranoia and the lost dreams of the German people following World War II.

While at a June 1982 concert by the Rolling Stones in West Berlin, Nena's guitarist Carlo Karges noticed that balloons were being released. As he watched them move toward the horizon, he noticed them shifting and changing shapes, where they looked like strange spacecraft. He thought about what might happen if they floated over the Berlin Wall to the Soviet sector.

With that scenario in mind, Karges wrote the original lyrics of "99 Luftballons" to tell a story of 99 plain party balloons being released into the air and showing up on radar as UFOs. A military commander sends aircraft to investigate, and a large show of power results after no threat is found. Nations along the border become worried, and defense ministers on both sides whip up a frenzy to try to grab power for themselves. A 99-year war is the end result, with much devastation for all but no winner. At the end, the narrator walks through rubble and finds a balloon, which she lets fly. This represents one surviving dream.

Band member Jörn-Ewe Fahrenkrog-Petersen, the keyboard player, composed the melody.

Epic Records had no intention of releasing the single in the United States. A disc jockey at Los Angeles radio station KROQ, however, found a copy and started playing it, sparking interest.

After the song became a hit in Europe, Nena recorded a version in English, "99 Red Balloons." The words of that version, by a different lyricist, are not an exact translation of the German lyrics. That version hit No. 1 in the U.K., Canada and Ireland.

Fahrenkrog-Petersen remarked, "We made a mistake here. I think the song loses something in translation and even sounds silly."

American and Australian listeners preferred the German version, as it hit No. 1 down under and peaked at No. 2 in the U.S. on *Billboard's Hot 100*. It was certified as a million-seller, and *Billboard* rated it the 28th biggest hit of 1984. It also ascended to No. 1 in Austria, Belgium, Japan, Netherlands, New Zealand, Sweden, Switzerland and, of course, West Germany.

Nena, a German singer-songwriter, actress and comedian with the birth name Gabriele Susanne Kerner, was 23 when she and her band recorded "99 Luftballons." She acquired her Spanish nickname, which means "little girl," while on vacation in Majorca with her parents as a child. She was lead singer of a band called The Stripes and moved from Hagen to West Berlin after the group broke up. It was there that she met the musicians who would join her in the band called "Nena."

"99 Luftballons" was Nena's only hit song in the English-speaking world, but they continued to enjoy success in Europe. The leader launched a solo career in 1989.

99 Luftballons

Songwriters: Uwe Fahrenkrog-Petersen, Carlo Karges

Peaked at No. 2 on Billboard Hot 100

March 3, 1984

Nena

Gabrielle Susanne Kerner [Nena] (March 24, 1960-) vocals
Carlo Karges (July 31, 1951-Jan. 30, 2002) guitar
Uwe Fahrenkrog-Petersen (March 10, 1960-) keyboards
Jürgen Dehmel (Aug. 12, 1958-) bass
Rolf Brendel (June 13, 1957-) drums
Formed in West Berlin, Germany, in 1982

Nena

Rock Me Amadeus [Falco] – This song became the first German language song to hit No. 1 on the *Billboard Hot 100.* It was sung by Austrian musician Falco, was inspired by the 1984 movie *Amadeus* and is about the life and popularity of classical period composer Wolfgang Amadeus Mozart.

The record was released in Europe in the original, German version in 1985. For international markets several different single and extended-play mixes were produced. None of them contained English-only lyrics, but the international single versions reduced the German lyrics.

For the version released in the United States, the song was remixed with an English background overlay.

The basic concept of the lyrics is the suggestion that Mozart was the musical rebel of his day.

In most countries this was Falco's only hit recording. It reached No. 1 in Austria, Germany, Canada, Ireland, New Zealand, South Africa, Spain, Sweden and the U.K.

"I was really impressed with the movie *Amadeus* and the way Milos Forman (the director) translated the rococo person (into) today's terms," Falco said. "If Mozart were alive today, he wouldn't be making classical music – he'd be an international pop star. And I felt it was time to write a song about him."

The song's video features Falco dressed in Mozart's period clothing, wearing a rainbow powdered wig. He passes through an 18th century audience in a concert hall but seems to feel more comfortable among 20th century leather-clad bikers.

Falco ended up a tax exile and died in a car crash in the Dominican Republic at age 40. His body was returned to Austria, where he was buried in Vienna.

Rock Me Amadeus

Songwriters: Falco, Rob Bolland, Ferdi Bolland
Peaked at No. 1 on Billboard Hot 100
March 29, 1986
April 5, 1986
April 12, 1986

Falco

Feb. 19, 1957-Feb. 6, 1998

Born Johann Hölzel in Vienna, Austria, and died in the Dominican Republic

Falco

Gangnam Style [Psy] – Exposure of this song's video on *YouTube* and other media outlets helped to propel it to staggering success worldwide. It became the first major hit in the United States sung in Korean.

Starting with its release in 2012, the video has been viewed more than 3.4 billion times. What makes the video so entertaining is the dance that the singer, Psy, does throughout the song. It is driven by a catchy beat.

Psy is the stage name for Park Jae-sang, who co-wrote the song and co-produced the recording.

The term "Gangnam style" refers to the lifestyle of people who live in the Gangnam district of the South Korean capital. These Seoul residents are said to be hip, trendy and classy.

The lyrics describe a female who is the perfect girlfriend. An article in the *Los Angeles Times* translated some of the lyrics thusly: "A lady who is warm like daylight, who knows how to enjoy a cup of coffee with ease, whose heart gets hotter as night gets near, a lady who has unexpected character."

The narrator has a few things to say about himself, like, "I am a man who gets hot in the daytime like you. I am a man who can have one shot of coffee before cooling it down, a man with a heart that explodes at night. I am that kind of man. I am (big brother), Oppa Gangnam Style!"

A testament of the song/video's viral impact came at the 2013 Phoenix Open golf tournament, when one of the PGA professionals celebrated a birdie by doing the Gangnam dance just off the side of the putting green. Serbian tennis pro Novak Djokovic and Filipino boxer Manny Pacquiao also have done the dance at international competitions.

While the recording peaked at No. 2 for several weeks on the *Billboard Hot 100*, it went to No. 1 in more than 30 other countries. The recording represented the culmination of a lengthy build-up of the South Korean music industry.

Gangnam Style

Songwriters: Park Jae-sang, Yoo Gun-hyung

Peaked at No. 2 on Billboard Hot 100

Oct. 6, 2012
Oct. 13, 2012
Oct. 20, 2012
Oct. 27, 2012
Nov. 3, 2012
Nov. 10, 2012
Nov. 17, 2012

Psy

Born Park Jae-sang in Gangnam District, Seoul, South Korea, on Dec. 31, 1977

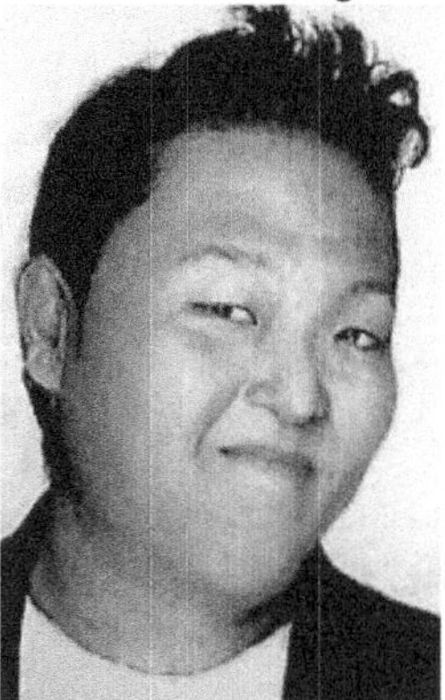

Psy

Chapter 10

End The War!

Songs of protest

Overview: War is hell. No one knows that better than many American men and women who were between the ages of 18 and 25 in the 1960s.

Some 3,403,000 American young men were sent to Southeast Asia after being conscripted into the U.S. armed forces in 1964-75. South Vietnam was under attack by North Vietnam, which wanted a unification under communist rule.

While Red China was supplying the North, the United States government, under the John Kennedy administration, vowed to help the South remain a democratic state. Lyndon Johnson escalated the war when he became president in 1963, and Richard Nixon kept it going from 1969 to '74. Finally, in 1975, the U.S. pulled out of Vietnam amid a collapse of the South's defense.

It was America's most unpopular war, and it provided fodder for many songwriters who felt compelled to protest it via song. While the United States government tried to tell the public that the war was about stopping the spread of communism in southeast Asia, it became a war to keep defense contractors in business. It also was the first war that the U.S. lost, which no one in government was willing to admit.

The draft was altered to a lottery system in 1969 and was abolished in 1973 as the nation went to an all-volunteer army.

The lottery was actually a two-part drawing that first randomly drew all 366 possible birth dates. Then, as a tie-breaker, it selected all 26 possible letters of the alphabet. My birth date, May 23, was drawn as No. 319, which effectively eliminated any possibility of me being drafted after my student deferment ended. In January 1970 the Selective Service System reclassified me, and I was free to pursue my career after I received my bachelor's degree. Only men with numbers 1-195 were considered for the draft.

For those who may be interested, the Selective Service System still exists as a contingency plan.

Of the dozens of war protest songs that have been recorded, here are a few of the most notable.

To view the full lyrics to these songs, please log on to www.google.com, enter song titles & artist names and click Google Search.

To listen to these songs, please log on to www.youtube.com and enter song titles & artist names.

Where Have All The Flowers Gone [Kingston Trio] – Although folk singer/songwriter Pete Seeger wrote this song in 1955, it was relevant in 1962, when the Kingston Trio recorded it as the U.S. involvement in Vietnam gained momentum.

His inspiration came from the novel *Quiet Flows The Don* by Russian author Mikhail Sholokhov. Seeger borrowed the melody from an Irish lumberjack song. Joe Hickerson added more verses in 1960, turning it into a song whose lyrics ran in a connecting circle.

The words that triggered Seeger's theme were: "Where are the flowers? The girls have plucked them. Where are the girls? They've all taken husbands. Where are the men? They're all in the army."

A powerful line in the song states, "Where have all the young men gone – gone for soldiers, every one." The number of military casualties in Vietnam exceeded 58,000, which is a staggering total. And, at the end, the communists took over the entirety of Vietnam.

Despite that fact, there has been no further spread of communism throughout the region.
The Kingston Trio's version rose to No. 21. Many other prominent artists around the world have recorded the song, but Johnny Rivers' rocking version was the only one that charted high as a single, reaching No. 26 in 1965.

The Kingston Trio, which was featured in Chapters 3 and 4, had a new member for the recording of "Flowers," as Dave Guard left and John Stewart replaced him.

Where Have All The Flowers Gone
Songwriter: Pete Seeger
Peaked at No. 21 on Billboard Hot 100
April 7, 1962

<u>Kingston Trio</u>
Nick Reynolds (July 27, 1933-Oct. 1, 2008)
Bob Shane (Feb. 1, 1934-Jan. 26, 2020)
John Stewart (Sept. 5, 1939-Jan. 19, 2008)
Formed in Palo Alto, Calif., in 1957

Kingston Trio: Bob Shane, Nick Reynolds, John Stewart

Eve Of Destruction [Barry McGuire] – You say that a record that is widely banned from radio play cannot hit No. 1 on the pop chart? This may be the only one in history that did!

The lyrics written by P.F. Sloan were unfiltered, presenting a raw, ugly picture of the state of war. McGuire, formerly of the New Christy Minstrels, gave it a powerful vocal.

"Eve Of Destruction's" content also referenced the ongoing civil rights movement, where Selma, Ala., had been a flashpoint of violence. There's also mention of "you're old enough to kill, but not for voting," which does not apply any more since the voting age has been lowered to 18.

Some participants in the radio embargo of the record claimed it gave aid and comfort to the United States' enemy in Vietnam. In the United Kingdom, the BBC placed it on a restricted list that forbade playing it on general entertainment programs.

Lyrics that probably helped get the record banned were "even the Jordan River's got bodies floating," "there'll be no one to save with the world in a grave" and "if the button is pushed there's no running away." Those words trigger some pretty grim thoughts.

There also is an indictment of American leadership: "Handful of senators don't pass legislation."

The Byrds had first crack at the song, but they rejected it. Jan & Dean recorded it for their 1965 album "Folk 'n Roll," and the Turtles put a version on their debut album in '65.

Sloan was just 19 when he wrote the song. On his website, this comment was posted: "The song 'Eve of Destruction' was written in the early morning hours between midnight and dawn in mid-1964. The most outstanding experience I had in writing this song was hearing an inner voice inside of myself for only the second time. It seemed to have information no one else could've had. For example, I was writing down this line in pencil, 'think of all the hate there is in Red Russia.' This inner voice said,

'No, no it's Red China!' I began to argue and wrestle with that until near exhaustion. I thought Red Russia was the most outstanding enemy to freedom in the world, but this inner voice said the Soviet Union will fall before the end of the century and Red China will engage in crimes against humanity well into the new century!

"This inner voice is inside of each and every one of us but is drowned out by the roar of our minds. The song contained a number of issues that were unbearable for me at the time. I wrote it as a prayer to God for an answer.

"I have felt it was a love song and written as a prayer because, to cure an ill you need to know what is sick. In my youthful zeal I hadn't realized that this would be taken as an attack on The System. Examples: The media headlined the song as everything that is wrong with the youth culture. First, show the song is just a hack song to make money and therefore no reason to deal with its questions. Prove the 19-year-old writer is a communist dupe. Attack the singer as a parrot for the writer's word.

"The media claimed that the song would frighten little children. I had hoped through this song to open a dialogue with Congress and the people. The media banned me from all national television shows. Oddly enough, they didn't ban Barry (McGuire). The United States felt under threat. So any positive press on me or Barry was considered un-patriotic. A great deal of madness, as I remember it. I told the press it was a love song. A love song to and for humanity, that's all. It ruined Barry's career as an artist and in a year, I would be driven out of the music business, too."

Sloan died of pancreatic cancer at the age of 70.

Eve Of Destruction
Songwriter: P.F. Sloan
Peaked at No. 1 on Billboard Hot 100
Sept. 25, 1965

<u>Barry McGuire</u>
Born Barry McGuire in Oklahoma City, Okla., on Oct. 15, 1935

Barry McGuire

I-Feel-Like-I'm-Fixin'-To-Die Rag [Country Joe & the Fish] – The first time I heard this song, I thought that it was the greatest anti-war song that I had ever heard. And that was four years after it had been written and first recorded.

An extended play disc in 1965 and an album in '67 were the first two appearances of the song. I didn't hear it until I listened to the Woodstock Soundtrack in '69.

The lyrics contain a lot of dark humor, but it is humor, nonetheless. "You can be the first ones on your block to have your boy come home in a box" – it just doesn't get much better than that. While smirking at the war effort, McDonald used the strongest possible language to drive home his points.

Let's hand it to Country Joe McDonald. If you're going to stick it to the military-industrial complex, why mince words? McDonald certainly didn't mince words when he wrote this song. Politicians, high ranking military officials and big corporations that profited from the war all were in McDonald's crosshairs. And the youngsters of the counterculture made it one of their favorite songs. McDonald, who grew up in Southern California and served in the U.S. Navy, said he wrote the lyrics in about 30 minutes.

Representing the men who were sent to Asia to fight the war, McDonald ended each verse with "whoopee, we're all gonna die." Death is a consequence that the politicians, generals and CEOs did not have to face.

For obvious reasons, "I-Feel-Like-I'm-Fixin'-To-Die Rag" never was issued as a single.

Representatives of CBS-TV's *Ed Sullivan Show* were at the 1968 Schaefer Summer Music Festival in New York City, where Country Joe & the Fish performed the song. They cancelled the band's scheduled appearance on the show and, not surprisingly, barred them from future shows.

"My most famous song really couldn't get airplay," McDonald told *Entertainment Weekly* in 2019. "It got me banned from municipal auditoriums for a long time after. So I paid a price. But I'm proud to say that I've carried with me the reality of the Vietnam War. I'm the elephant in the room."

I-Feel-Like-I'm-Fixin'-To-Die Rag

Songwriter: Joe McDonald

Included on the album "I-Feel-Like-I'm-Fixin'-To-Die"

Peaked at No. 67 on Billboard 200

Feb. 3, 1968

Country Joe & the Fish

"Country Joe" McDonald (Jan. 1, 1942-) vocals, acoustic guitar
Barry "the Fish" Melton (June 14, 1947-) lead guitar, vocals
Gary "Chicken" Hirsh (March 9, 1940-) drums
Bruce Barthol (Nov. 11, 1947-) bass
David Bennett Cohen (Aug. 4, 1942-) guitar
Formed in Berkeley, Calif., in 1965

Country Joe & the Fish

The Unknown Soldier [Doors] – The Doors were good at pushing the envelope with their lyrics. They did so with their 10-minute song "The End" from their first album. They did so with many of lead singer Jim Morrison's antics during their concerts, too. And they did so in 1968 with this song from their third album.

The anti-war track contains little to tie it to the Vietnam War, and that's the way the Doors wanted it. It was meant to be a universal statement about war. In a way, the Doors were at war with society in general with the subject matter they presented in their songs.

The middle section contains a military cadence count, drum rolls, officer's commands and sounds of a firing squad cocking rifles. Then there is a gunshot.

Ray Manzarek played some eerie organ riffs, which added to the spookiness of the simulated carnage.

The first verse, which is repeated as the last, says, "Breakfast where the news is read, television children fed." This is a statement about the way news of the Vietnam War was presented in the homes of ordinary American citizens.

At the end, the lyrics proclaim that "the war is over," while church bells peal and crowds cheer.

With producer Paul Rothchild seeking perfection, the track took over 130 takes to finish.

Still, it was a heavy scene – one that was too controversial for most radio stations, and many refused to play it. Despite that major obstacle, "The Unknown Soldier" crept into the pop top 40.

A promotional film was made to hype the song. It contains footage of fighting in Vietnam, and it shows Morrison walking along a beach near the burnt remains of the Pacific Ocean Park pier. He is tied to some timbers and then is executed, after which the other three Doors are shown walking along the beach without him.

The Unknown Soldier

Songwriters: Jim Morrison, Ray Manzarek, Robby Krieger, John Densmore

Peaked at No. 39 on Billboard Hot 100

May 4, 1968
May 11, 1968
May 18, 1968

The Doors

Jim Morrison (Dec. 8, 1943-July 3, 1971) vocals
Ray Manzarek (Feb. 12, 1939-May 20, 2013) keyboards
Robby Krieger (Jan. 8, 1946-) guitar
John Densmore (Dec. 1, 1944-) drums
Formed in Los Angeles, Calif., in 1965

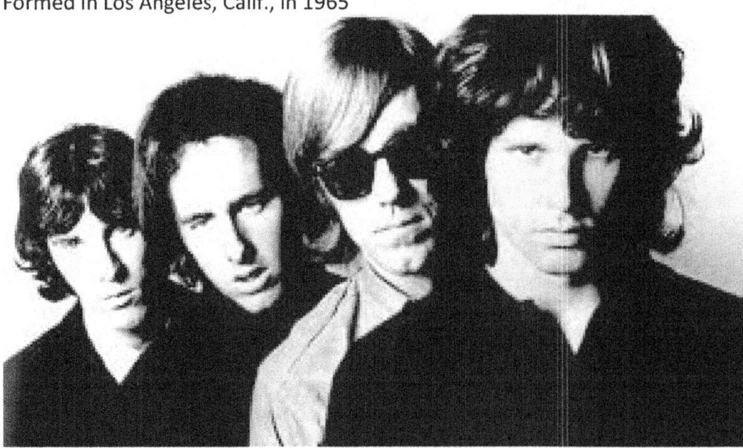

The Doors: John Densmore, Robby Krieger, Ray Manzarek, Jim Morrison

To Susan On The West Coast Waiting [Donovan] – Donovan is Scottish, not American. Yet, he chose to get involved with protest of the Vietnam War.

To be fair, this song wasn't bellicose in nature. The words are in the form of a letter from a soldier named Andy to his significant other, Susan. In criticizing the United States war effort he says, "Our fathers have painfully lost their way."

The Selective Service System drafted Andy and took him from his occupation, for the time being.

If nothing else, the song is a reminder of how much soldiers miss the loved ones they left behind to fight in the armed services, and vice versa. The loneliness must have been devastating.

There's one line in the song with which I take issue. It says, "To Susan on the West Coast waiting, from Andy supposedly hating." The Vietnam War was not fought over hatred of anything other than communism and political oppression. United States military forces were sent to Vietnam to stop the spread of communism into South Vietnam, which had been using a democratic system of government. I think it is misleading to infer that freedom fighters were combatting enemies just because they hated them personally.

According to the www.donovan-unofficial.com website, the female backing vocals on the track were provided by three fans, who had been waiting to see Donovan outside his recording studio. Their vigil was rewarded when he eventually invited them in to help with the singing.

To Susan On The West Coast Waiting
Songwriter: Donovan Leitch
Peaked at No. 35 on Billboard Hot 100
March 1, 1969
March 8, 1969

Donovan
Born Donovan Philips Leitch in Glasgow, Scotland, on May 10, 1946

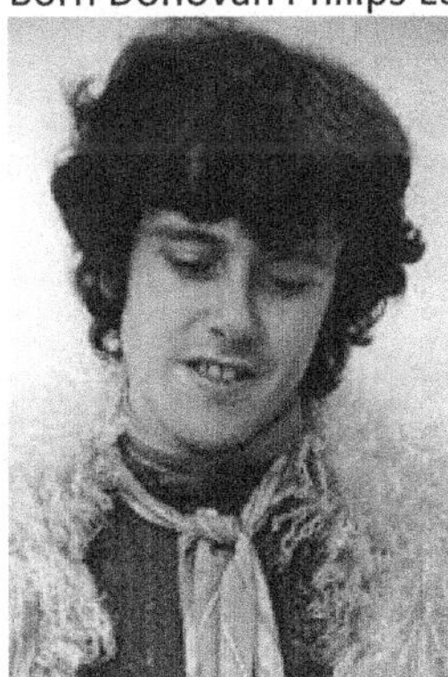

Donovan

Galveston [Glen Campbell] – Write an anti-war song without ever mentioning war or fighting? Songwriter extraordinaire Jimmy Webb did that in 1969, and Glen Campbell sang it to the top of the charts.

The absence of war rhetoric may have led some to errantly believe that the song was penned as an ode to a Texas city on the Gulf of Mexico. The original lyrics do not form a patriotic message either.

Webb wrote the tempo slower than Campbell's version. It's a sad story about a soldier who had to leave his beloved hometown and girlfriend to go to war.

"In actual fact ... it's about a guy who's caught up in something he doesn't understand and would rather be somewhere else," Webb said during the taping of a show on WFUV-TV.

Campbell learned the song from Don Ho when the Hawaiian entertainer made a guest appearance on Campbell's television variety show.

The second verse originally read:

Wonder if she could forget me
I'd go home if they would let me
Put down this gun
And go to Galveston

In Campbell's version those lines were changed to:

I still hear your sea waves crashing
While I watch the cannons flashing
I clean my gun
And dream of Galveston

As a boy, Webb joined his Baptist preacher father as he traveled from church to church in Oklahoma and Texas. The beauty of the seacoast, with its huge waves and avian life, struck a chord with Webb as he wrote "Galveston."

Campbell's music was closely identified with the country music genre, and the song went to No. 1 on the *Billboard Country Chart* and *Easy Listening Chart.* On the *Hot 100* it peaked at No. 4.

Country Music Television (CMT) ranks it as No. 8 on its list of 100 Greatest Country Songs.

Galveston
Songwriter: Jimmy Webb
Peaked at No. 4 on Billboard Hot 100
April 12, 1969

Glen Campbell
April 22, 1936-Aug. 8, 2017
Born Glen Travis Campbell in Billstown, Ark., and died in Nashville, Tenn., from complications of Alzheimer's Disease

Glen Campbell

Sweet Cherry Wine [Tommy James & the Shondells] – The lyrics of this protest song were a bit cryptic. For clarity, look back to Chapter 2, Rockin' Devotional. There we saw that Tommy James and his band had become Christians in the late 1960s.

James, in a 2010 interview with Christian Broadcasting Network, revealed that the "wine" in the title and lyrics is a metaphor for the blood of Jesus Christ. Others who listened to the song may have thought that the song was about enjoying recreational drugs. The psychedelic era was in full swing, after all.

The overall Christian message of the song, though, references war – "yesterday my friends were marching out to war, listen now, we ain't marching any more. No, we ain't gonna fight, only God has the right to decide who's to live and die."

Perhaps, rather than anti-war, it's a call for peace in the name of God.

James was raised a Catholic but said he became a born-again Christian after watching a Billy Graham sermon on television.

There was a consciousness that was raised during the Vietnam War that I think we are still struggling with. Is it OK to slaughter thousands of people, including civilians, during a political conflict? Is it right to punish young people for their refusal to participate in such fighting – for any reason? We need to resolve these questions before we send more of our youth to die in a war that doesn't involve the security of the United States.

Sweet Cherry Wine

Songwriters: Richard Grasso, Tommy James

Peaked at No. 7 on Billboard Hot 100

May 3, 1969

May 10, 1969

Tommy James & the Shondells

Tommy James (April 29, 1947-) vocals, guitar, tambourine

Eddie Gray (Feb. 27, 1948-) guitar

Peter Lucia (Feb. 2, 1947-Jan. 6, 1997) drums

Ron Rosman (Feb. 28, 1945-) keyboards

Mike Vale (July 17, 1949-) bass

Formed in Niles, Mich., in 1964

The Shondells: Ron Rosman, Mike Vale, Tommy James, Peter Lucia, Eddie Gray

Ruby, Don't Take Your Love To Town [Kenny Rogers & the First Edition] – This song looks at war from the point of a disabled veteran.

"It's hard to love a man whose legs are bent and paralyzed," the war vet says. He fears that his wife is getting dolled up to go look for love elsewhere.

Longtime country music star Mel Tillis wrote the song, and Johnny Darrell put a version on the country charts in 1967.

When the First Edition released their version in the summer of 1969, most listeners assumed the war in question was the Vietnam War, since the lyrics mention "that old crazy Asian War." But the war that Tillis had in mind was the Korean War of the 1950s.

According to *Songfacts,* Tillis's lyrics were inspired by a couple who lived near his Florida home. The man incurred injuries in Germany during World War II and recuperated in England. He married the nurse who was in charge of his care. After they moved to Florida, he had to make return trips to a hospital for continuing care. While he was hospitalized, his wife stepped out on him.

There were instances of Rogers performing the song in a lighthearted manner during his shows. Some observers felt that this was a slight toward injured veterans.

"Look, we don't see ourselves as politicians," Rogers told *Beat Instrumental* in 1970, "even if a lot of pop groups think they are in the running for a Presidential nomination. We are there primarily to entertain.

"Now, if we can entertain by providing thought-provoking songs, then that's all to the good. But the guys who said 'Ruby' was about Vietnam were way off target – it was about Korea. But whatever the message and however you interpret it, fact is that we wouldn't have looked at it if it hadn't been a good song. Just wanna make good records, that's all."

Rogers and his band had the biggest hit of all the artists who recorded the song, reaching No. 6 on the *Billboard Hot 100* and No. 2 on the U.K. singles chart.

Ruby, Don't Take Your Love To Town

Songwriter: Mel Tillis

Peaked at No. 6 on Billboard Hot 100

Aug. 2, 1969

Aug. 9, 1969

Kenny Rogers & the First Edition

Kenny Rogers (Aug. 21, 1938-March 20, 2020) vocals, bass

Mickey Jones (June 10, 1941-Feb. 7, 2018) drums

Thelma Camacho (1949-) vocals

Terry Williams (June 6, 1947-) guitar

Mike Settle (March 20, 1941-) guitar, backing vocals

Formed in Los Angeles, Calif., in 1967

First Edition: Mike Settle, Kenny Rogers. Mickey Jones, Thelma Camacho, Terry Williams

Give Peace A Chance [Plastic Ono Band] – This may be the highest charting recording that was created in a hotel suite.

The occasion was the second "bed-in" by John Lennon and his new wife, Yoko Ono, in 1969. The pair had staged their first bed-in during their March honeymoon in Amsterdam, Netherlands, as a way to call for an end to global wars. They stayed in bed for an entire week as a publicity stunt.

New York City was supposed to be the site of the second bed-in. However, the United States government would not admit Lennon into the country because of a marijuana conviction in 1968. Lennon and Ono went to the Bahamas to hold the event in May but found the heat to be stifling. They flew to Montreal, Quebec, Canada, instead and checked into four rooms at the Queen Elizabeth Hotel.

The bed-in there featured the newlyweds conducting interviews in bed, in their pajamas. Lennon's response to a reporter who asked why he was staying in bed: "Just give peace a chance."

On June 1, Lennon had a four-track tape recorder delivered to the suite. Invited guests who joined the recording session were comedian Tom Smothers, singer Petula Clark, psychologist Timothy Leary, actor Dick Gregory, disc jockey Murray Kaufman and cartoonist Al Capp (who did not sing). Producer André Perry served as recording engineer and set up four microphones.

With Lennon and Smothers playing acoustic guitar and Lennon singing lead, the ensemble sang "Give Peace A Chance," which Lennon had written earlier in the week. The aforementioned attendees added backing vocals, tambourine and hand claps. Perry did percussion.

Lennon shared songwriting credit with fellow Beatle Paul McCartney, per their years-long agreement. But this recording was done independent of the other Beatles, and Lennon later regretted that he didn't give Ono songwriting credit, since she helped him write it.

Lennon did not sing from printed lyrics and forgot some of the words. He mentions "masturbation" in the third verse, which he changed to "mastication" on the official lyrics to sidestep controversy.

The words declare that "everybody's talking about ..." various topics. But the focus steadily returns to the message of the title.

Lennon gave his handwritten lyrics as a memento to a teenage girl who had sneaked into the hotel with a friend. In 2008 the memento fetched $834,000 at auction.

After the original tape was polished in a studio, the single was released worldwide. It rose to No. 2 in the U.K. and No. 14 in the U.S.

The song was credited to the group Plastic Ono Band, but it was Lennon's first solo effort after playing in bands for about a dozen years. According to Ono, Lennon coined the name Plastic Ono Band from the plastic stands Yoko used during recording sessions. Other performances by the Plastic Ono Band included other, more legitimate musicians.

Lennon would eventually gain legal residence in the United States, but the Nixon administration vigorously tried to deport him because of his anti-war activism. Ironically, it was in the U.S. where Lennon met a violent death in 1980, when deranged fan Mark Chapman gunned him down in New York City outside of his apartment building.

Ono told *Uncut* in 1998, "I think we kind of made a point there. We thought that we were presenting a thought through an alternative theater setting, and that was the platform and the world was the theater."

Give Peace A Chance

Songwriters: John Lennon, Paul McCartney

Peaked at No. 14 on Billboard Hot 100

Sept. 6, 1969

Plastic Ono Band
John Lennon (Oct. 9, 1940-Dec. 8, 1980)
Yoko Ono (Feb. 18, 1933-)
Tom Smothers (Feb. 2, 1937-)
Petula Clark (Nov. 15, 1932-)
Timothy Leary (Oct. 22, 1920-May 31, 1996)
Dick Gregory (Oct. 12, 1932-Aug. 19, 2017)
Murray Kaufman (Feb. 14, 1922-Feb. 21, 1982)

The Plastic Ono Band records in a Montreal hotel suite

Fortunate Son [Creedence Clearwater Revival] – John Fogerty, guitarist, lead singer and songwriter for Creedence Clearwater Revival, was an Army veteran when he wrote this song. The anti-war spin he put on it: common people are conscripted to fight wars while those who have lives of privilege are exempt or placed in positions away from the battles.

Fogerty enlisted in the U.S. Army Reserve the same day he received a draft notice. He served stateside at three different forts in 1966-67. CCR drummer Doug Clifford also was a military reservist.

Rather than bash the fighting that was taking place in Vietnam, the lyrics take aim at inequality among classes.

"'Fortunate Son' wasn't really inspired by any one event," Fogerty wrote in a 2015 memoir. "Julie Nixon was dating David Eisenhower. You'd hear about the son of this senator or that congressman who was given a deferment from the military or a choice position *in* the military. They seemed privileged and, whether they liked it or not, these people were symbolic in the sense that they weren't being touched by what their parents were doing. They weren't being affected like the rest of us."

Julie, the daughter of President Richard Nixon, ended up marrying David, grandson of former Pres. Dwight Eisenhower.

With his anger mounting one day in 1969 as he thought about that union of privilege, Fogerty wrote the song in about 20 minutes, he said.

The single was issued as part of a double-A side single, backed with "Down On A Corner." On Nov. 22, 1969, "Fortunate Son" peaked at No. 14 on the *Billboard Hot 100.* The following week, *Billboard* changed its procedure for ranking two-sided hits, and the two songs became linked during the remainder of their chart run. They hit a peak position of No. 3 on Dec. 20, 1969.

The National Recording Registry of the Library of Congress listed the song for being "culturally, historically or aesthetically significant."

Fortunate Son

Songwriter: John Fogerty

Peaked at No. 14 on Billboard Hot 100

Nov. 22, 1969

Creedence Clearwater Revival

John Fogerty (May 28, 1945-) lead guitar, vocals

Tom Fogerty (Nov. 9, 1941-Sept. 6, 1990) rhythm guitar

Stu Cook (April 25, 1945-) bass

Doug Clifford (April 24, 1945-) drums

Formed in El Cerrito, Calif., in 1967

CCR: Stu Cook, Doug Clifford, John Fogerty, Tom Fogerty

American Woman [Guess Who] – It was the summer of 1969, and the Canadian band the Guess Who was heating up. They had two hit singles and two successful albums that year, and they were filling some time playing gigs in their homeland.

One night at a small venue in Scarborough, Ont., the band had left the stage while waiting for guitarist Randy Bachman to replace a broken string. He began playing a riff to tune his guitar, and he soon realized that it was something worth remembering. The rest of the four-man band returned to the stage and joined in, beginning a jam that would become the song "American Woman." Lead singer Burton Cummings improvised lyrics on the spot.

The musicians noticed a fan in the audience recording the show with a cassette tape machine, which was a new product at the time. They had their road manager get the tape so that could listen to what they had spontaneously created.

"We actually kind of learned it from that tape," Cummings said in an interview with Ray Shasho. "Otherwise nobody would have ever heard it again. I guess the music gods were smiling on us. The music gods probably sent that kid with the cassette machine."

The lyrics have been largely misunderstood. They have nothing to do with glorifying America or bashing American women.

Bachman, in a 2014 interview, called it "an anti-war protest song."

"We had been touring the States," Bachman told *Songfacts.* "This was the late '60s, one time at the US/Canada border in North Dakota they tried to draft us and send us to Vietnam. We were back in Canada, playing in the safety of Canada where the dance is full of draft dodgers who've all left the States."

One of the song's most poignant lines is "I don't want your war machines, I don't want your ghetto scenes."

The Guess Who first played the completed song at the Seattle Pop Festival later in 1969.

While the record was the Guess Who's first and only No. 1 song in the U.S., they played one show at which they were requested *not* to play it. Tricia Nixon, the 23-year-old eldest daughter of President Nixon, was a fan of the band and asked them to play at a reception on the White House lawn, July 17, 1970. The press liaison for First Lady Pat Nixon asked that the song be omitted from the set list because of the controversial lyrics.

"(The reception gig) left a bad taste in my mouth," Cummings told the *Winnipeg Free Press.* "They wanted a Commonwealth act (to greet Prince Charles and Princess Anne). We were the token Commonwealthers."

The recording has been used in several television commercials over the years.

American Woman

Songwriters: Burton Cummings, Randy Bachman, Garry Peterson, Jim Kale

Peaked at No. 1 on Billboard Hot 100

May 9, 1970
May 16, 1970
May 23, 1970

The Guess Who

Burton Cummings (Dec. 31, 1947-) vocals, keyboards
Randy Bachman (Sept. 27, 1943-) guitar
Garry Peterson (May 26, 1945-) drums
Jim Kale (Aug. 11, 1943-) bass
Formed in Winnipeg, Manitoba, Canada in 1965

The Guess Who: Jim Kale, Burton Cummings, Randy Bachman, Garry Peterson

War [Edwin Starr] – While some songs about war have had a message that wasn't clear or strong, this one came out blasting with both barrels. The message in a nutshell: war is destructive, war is horrible, war is good for nothing.

Two mainstays on the Motown songwriting staff, Norman Whitfield and Barrett Strong, wrote it. Whitfield was the producer.

The Temptations (see Chapter 6, Motown) were the first to receive the song. They recorded it early in 1970, and it was included on their album "Psychedelic Shack." Although many fans mailed in requests for Gordy/Motown to release the Temptations' version as a single, the corporation resisted, so as not to imperil the popular group's image.

"War" was the first politically oriented record released by the Motown Corp. The term "Vietnam War" is not mentioned in the lyrics.

The lyrics state, "They say we must fight to keep our freedom, but God knows there's got to be a better way." However, that "better way" was not suggested.

Edwin Starr, a little known solo artist, was next in line to record the anti-war anthem. His version was more powerful and forceful. His gritty vocal sent the single to No. 1 on the *Billboard Hot 100* and the *Canada RPM 100* in late summer of 1970. The next year Starr reaped a Grammy Award for Best R&B Male Vocal Performance.

Like John Fogerty, Starr logged service in the United States military.

Starr originally was under contract to Ric-Tic Records, but he came into the Motown stable when Motown bought Ric-Tic and its parent label, Golden World. His first hit on Gordy was "Twenty-Five Miles." Starr's follow-up to "War" was "Stop The War Now," which peaked at No. 26 on the *Hot 100.*

"War" has been used in several motion pictures and television shows. Bruce Springsteen and the E Street Band recorded a version in 1986 that hit No. 8.

Starr moved to England in 1973, and he died there in 2003 of a heart attack at the age of 61.

War

Songwriters: Norman Whitfield, Barrett Strong
Peaked at No. 1 on Billboard Hot 100
Aug. 29, 1970
Sept. 5, 1970
Sept. 12, 1970

Edwin Starr

Jan. 21, 1942-April 2, 2003
Born Charles Edwin Hatcher in Nashville, Tenn., and died of a heart attack in Chilwell, Nottingham, England

Edwin Starr

Stoned Love [Supremes] – Instead of an anti-war song, perhaps we could call this a pro-peace piece.

Kenny Thomas, who wrote it, used the term "stone love" to describe an unchanging brotherhood among people. The word "war" appears in the lyrics, but so do the words "love" and "peace."

The original title was "Stone Love" but, in the process of label printing at the record pressing plant, a typographical error turned it into "Stoned Love."

Thomas, a Detroit teenager who was discovered by Motown producer Frank Wilson via a radio talent show, played an unfinished version of the song in his living room in an informal audition for Wilson. Thomas preferred to have his name spelled backward on the 45 rpm label credit.

This was the Supremes' biggest single after the departure of Diana Ross, with Jean Terrell singing lead. According to *Wikipedia,* Motown president Berry Gordy hated the song. Yet, it became a No. 1 hit on the *Billboard Hot R&B Chart.*

"Stoned Love" was widely misinterpreted to be about drug use. According to *Songfacts,* however, it is about the need for love and compassion. "Stones are forever," Thomas said. "They don't break or come apart. Love will be here forever."

Two other R&B songs that came along later used the stone metaphor – "I'm Stone In Love With You" by the Stylistics in 1972 and "Stone Love" by Kool & the Gang in '86. There also was "Stone In Love" by the rock band Journey in 1981.

Stoned Love

Songwriters: Kenny Thomas, Frank Wilson
Peaked at No. 7 on Billboard Hot 100
Dec. 19, 1970
Dec. 26, 1970

The Supremes
Jean Terrell (Nov. 26, 1944-)
Mary Wilson (March 6, 1944-)
Cindy Birdsong (Dec. 15, 1939-)
Formed in Detroit, Mich., in 1959

The Supremes: Cindy Birdsong, Jean Terrell, Mary Wilson

What's Going On [Marvin Gaye] – This is perhaps the most touching war protest song of all. It invokes a family angle, with brothers dying, mothers crying and pleas for father not to escalate.

Marvin Gaye was not the sole contributor to the writing of the song, but he had a hand in writing this and all the other songs on his album of the same title.

"What's Going On" has a mournful feel, which connects the words to emotions that Gaye was trying to evoke. The song's message also sticks up for other youthful protesters – "don't punish me with brutality." Gaye served as producer.

The song received many accolades from the press and industry critics.

Obie Benson, a member of the Four Tops, got inspiration for the song when the group was on tour in Berkeley, Calif., in 1969. While there, he saw a violent police reaction to an anti-war demonstration. He began to ask himself questions about why the nation's leaders were sending the nation's youth far from home to fight in the unpopular Vietnam War, all the while attacking others in the streets of America.

Benson discussed his feelings with songwriter Al Cleveland, who put together a song that incorporated Benson's questions and concerns. He offered it to the Four Tops, but they refused it. In 1970 Benson passed it on to Gaye, who gave it a new melody and other revisions.

Most listeners probably never were aware that football players Lem Barney and Mel Farr of the Detroit Lions contributed backing vocals and part of the spoken interlude. The musicians were a mix of Motown house players and musicians whom Gaye had recruited.

After Gaye played the recording for Berry Gordy, the Motown head refused to release it, saying it was "the worst thing I ever heard in my life." Gaye's response was a "strike" during which he stopped recording any more material until Berry relented. The result was a No. 1 ranking on the *Billboard Hot R&B Chart* for five weeks early in 1971.

What's Going On

Songwriters: Al Cleveland, Renaldo Benson, Marvin Gaye
Peaked at No. 2 on Billboard Hot 100
April 10, 1971
April 17, 1971
April 24, 1971

Marvin Gaye

April 2, 1939-April 1, 1984

Born Marvin Pentz Gay Jr. in Washington, D.C., and died in Los Angeles, Calif.

Marvin Gaye

Bring The Boys Home [Freda Payne] – This million-seller was a no-frills plea for the military to return soldiers home from the war – alive. Vietnam is not mentioned in the lyrics, but there is no doubt that is the war in question.

The single was released on a Detroit label – Invictus, which was started by the Holland-Dozier-Holland songwriters after they left Motown. It was added to Freda Payne's album "Contact" after the song gained popularity in 1971.

Armed Forces Radio kept it off its playlist on the premise that it would be beneficial to the enemy.

The song was released at a time when American G.I.s were returning home in body bags in alarming numbers. Reportedly, a disproportionate number of the dead were African Americans.

The average age of those serving in Vietnam was 20.

The record apparently did no favors to Payne's career. She had three more singles hit the *Billboard Hot 100,* but none cracked the top 40. Her last entry on the R&B chart came in 1982.

As we consider the message of this song, we should remember that there were some counter-protest songs, as well. The most notable was the No. 1 hit "The Ballad Of The Green Berets" by Staff Sgt. Barry Sadler in 1966. The lyrics extol the virtues of bravery and defending people who are oppressed. Some of the phrasing includes "fearless men who jump and die" and "trained in combat hand to hand."

Then there was "Okie From Muskogee" by Merle Haggard in 1969. Some statements that song made included "we don't burn our draft cards down on Main Street," "we don't let our hair grow long and shaggy like the hippies out in San Francisco do" and "we still wave Old Glory down at the courthouse."

With its dynamic sound effects, "Sky Pilot" by Eric Burdon & the Animals put both a positive and negative spin on the war in 1968. The lyrics are about a military chaplain who gives his troops a blessing before they head off to battle.

The chaplain "tells them it's all right – he knows of their fear in the forthcoming fight."

But, as a young soldier returns from the fight, he "looks at the Sky Pilot so ill, remembers the words 'Thou Shalt Not Kill.'"

Bring The Boys Home

Songwriters: Angelo Bond, General Johnson, Greg Perry

Peaked at No. 12 on Billboard Hot 100

Aug. 7, 1971

Aug. 14, 1971

Freda Payne

Born Freda Charcilia Payne in Detroit, Mich., on Sept. 19, 1942

Freda Payne

Chapter 11

Pop turns back the clock

Songs that recall the days before the Rock Era

Overview: Music runs in cycles. Once a song has been recorded for the first time, it may be recorded by another artist within days, months or years, if it is popular enough.

In the 1950s, it was common for two or three versions of a song to be on the charts simultaneously. In the 1960s such an occurrence was rare. But the song "Go Away Little Girl" by Steve Lawrence was No. 1 in 1963, and Donny Osmond's version was No. 1 in 1971.

Another example is "The Locomotion." Little Eva's version was No. 1 in 1962, and Grand Funk Railroad's rendition was No. 1 in 1974.

Once the Rock Era began in 1955, songs that were decades old began to resurface in the form of fresh recordings by artists of the day. I'm talking about songs from the 1920s, '30s and '40s. Showing their resilience, these old songs, written by composers who had long since retired or died, took on new life and won new admirers.

To view the full lyrics to these songs, please log on to www.google.com, enter song titles & artist names and click Google Search.

To listen to these songs, please log on to www.youtube.com and enter song titles & artist names.

Deep Purple [Nino Temp & April Stevens] – The brother/sister duo took this old song and turned it into a No. 1 smash. It topped the *Billboard Hot 100* the week in November 1963 during which President John Kennedy was assassinated.

The song was composed in 1933 by pianist Peter DeRose. Sheet music sales for it were so brisk that Mitchell Parish added lyrics five years later.

Released in January 1939, a recorded version by Larry Clinton & His Orchestra (featuring vocalist Bea Wain) was No. 1 on the U.S. pop charts for nine consecutive weeks. Other prominent musicians had success with the song in the 1930s and '40s.

In the rock era, the Tempo/Stevens version was the biggest. This was a pivotal time in the history of rock and roll. Leading up to 1963, most of the popular acts on the charts were vocalists – typically solo males, with a few females and duos thrown into the mix. A band with members who played their own instruments and wrote most of their own material was a rarity. The Beach Boys from Hawthorne, Calif., were an example. "Go Away Little Girl" by Steve Lawrence and "Blue Velvet" by Bobby Vinton were two of the biggest songs of '63, but they basically belonged in the adult contemporary genre.

The Beatles had their first single released in the U.S. in late winter of 1963. I don't recall hearing on the radio, but years later I looked back at my WLS *Silver Dollar Surveys* and noticed it at about No. 35 at its peak position. Obviously, the time for the Beatles to bring their music to America was not ripe then. After the Kennedy death and the ensuing period of mourning, the time was perfect. We were ready for some new music – something uplifting. And, with the Beatles' help, 1964 was the year that the rock band format took off, and the rock landscape changed dramatically.

To give you some idea of what the state of rock was in 1963, "Deep Purple" was awarded a Grammy for Best Rock and Roll Record.

Stevens came up with the idea to record it, and Tempo did the arrangement. In October 1962 they went into the studio to record "Paradise." They had 14 minutes left in session time afterward, so they took a crack at doing "Deep Purple" unrehearsed. They nailed the song in two takes.

"Nino was supposed to sing the second chorus by himself," Stevens said. "He didn't know the words, so I started speaking them to him (into a live microphone)."

A friend who heard the demo thought her "narration" sounded great. "It took me two months to convince my brother," Stevens said. "He didn't want anyone talking while he was singing."

Ahmet Ertegun, the president of Atlantic/Atco Records who produced the recording, didn't like it and said it was the most embarrassing thing Nino and April ever had recorded. The recording sat on the shelf for a year.

It took a threat from Tempo to leave the label in order for Ertegun to relent. Ertegun said that if "Deep Purple" flopped, then Tempo could have his contract back. The rest is history. A year later the state of rock music had not changed much, and the public enthusiastically embraced the song.

A musical prodigy, Nino Tempo learned to play clarinet and tenor saxophone as a child. After his family relocated to California, he became a child actor and sought-after session musician. As a result of a Bobby Darin recording session, he made connections with Atlantic Records and contracted with its Atco subsidiary.

April Stevens originally used the stage name Carol Tempo but changed it to April Stevens after she recorded the song "No, No, No, Not That!" in 1949. Recording as a solo artist since she was 15, her most successful hit was "I'm In Love Again," which hit No. 6 on the pop chart in 1951.

Deep Purple

Songwriters: Peter DeRose, Mitchell Parish

Peaked at No. 1 on Billboard Hot 100

Nov. 16, 1963

Nino Tempo & April Stevens

Nino Tempo – born Antonio LoTiempo in Niagara Falls, N.Y., on Jan. 6, 1935

April Stevens – born Caroline LoTiempo in Niagara Falls, N.Y., on April 29, 1936

April Stevens and Nino Tempo

Ain't She Sweet [Beatles] – From their inception, the Beatles revered old songs. This one was composed in 1927 by Milton Ager with lyrics by Jack Yellen. The Beatles recorded it in Hamburg, Germany, on June 22, 1961. Pete Best, the original drummer, was still in the band then, and John Lennon did the lead vocal.

In the rock era, Gene Vincent recorded a version in 1956, but it wasn't released as a single. The Beatles performed it on stage during their Hamburg residency in the early '60s.

Ager wrote the song for his daughter Shana, who was known as the political commentator Shana Alexander during her adult life. The song quickly became a Tin Pan Alley standard.

I had to ask myself why the Beatles released this recording in America in the summer of 1964. It wasn't a song that they wrote. It wasn't a song that was contained on any of their popular albums. It had a sound akin to that of rock's early days of the 1950s. But I realized that the song didn't require any extra studio time, since it had been recorded three years earlier. It was an easy way to sell a few thousand more singles, since everything that the Beatles put out in '64 sold wildly.

Why didn't the song chart any higher than No. 19? One reason was the Beatles themselves. When "Ain't She Sweet" peaked, two other Beatles singles were ahead of it on the chart ("A Hard Day's Night" and "And I Love Her.")

The only other major country in which the song charted was Australia, where it reached No. 16.

Early lineups of the Beatles were known as the Quarrymen and the Silver Beatles. Ringo Starr replaced Best as drummer in 1962.

Ain't She Sweet
Songwriters: Milton Ager, Jack Yellen
Peaked at No. 19 on Billboard Hot 100
Aug. 22, 1964

The Beatles
John Lennon (Oct. 9, 1940-Dec. 8, 1980) rhythm guitar
Paul McCartney (June 18, 1942-) bass
George Harrison (Feb. 25, 1943-Nov. 29, 2001) lead guitar
Pete Best (Nov. 24, 1941-) drums
Formed in Liverpool, England in 1960

The Beatles: John Lennon, George Harrison, Paul McCartney, Pete Best

Tears [Ken Dodd] – Liverpool, England, native Ken Dodd revived this song that was first recorded by Rudy Vallee in 1929 and turned it into Britain's biggest hit of 1965. It spent five consecutive weeks at No. 1 on the U.K. pop singles chart and sold over a million copies in England alone.

There was a bit of irony in this accomplishment, with an entertainer who was primarily known as a comedian out-dueling his fellow Liverpudlians, the Beatles, on the British charts. The Fab Four had recently released the soundtrack from their second movie, "Help!" and were on top of their game.

Dodd had 18 hits on the U.K. top 40 between 1960 and 1981, which belies his image as a slapstick stand-up performer. Success in the United States eluded him, though. "Tears" stalled at No. 107 in the *Billboard* pop rankings, and he failed to crack the Hot 100 with any of his recordings. Dodd also dabbled in acting and appeared in stage plays and on BBC-TV.

"Tears" briefly appeared on the *Billboard Hot 100* in 1966 as a cover version by Bobby Vinton, peaking at No. 59.

In the book *1000 UK #1 Hits,* Dodd is quoted as saying, "It had been a waltz, and we thought we'd have a hit if we did it four beats to the bar. The disc jockeys hated it. They couldn't find words bad enough to say about it, but it didn't matter. The public was ready for a tuneful, singalong song, and you can't keep a good song down. You can be the squarest of squares but, if you make a good record, you can still get there."

Dodd's "Tears" was rated the No. 1 song for 1965 in the U.K. and four decades later still was one of the U.K.'s top 20 singles of all time.

His career in show business started in the mid-1950s, and he became known as "the last great music hall entertainer." Although primarily a stand-up comedian, he also recorded many serious songs. He was appointed an Officer of the Order of the British Empire in 1982, and he was knighted in 2017. He died at age 90 at his home in Knotty Ash, having been hospitalized with a chest infection.

Tears

Songwriters: Frank Capano, Billy Uhr

Peaked at No. 1 on U.K. pop chart

Sept. 30, 1965
Oct. 7, 1965
Oct. 14, 1965
Oct. 21, 1965
Oct. 28, 1965

<u>Ken Dodd</u>

Nov. 8, 1927-March 11, 2018

Born Kenneth Arthur Dodd in Knotty Ash, Liverpool, England, and died at his home there

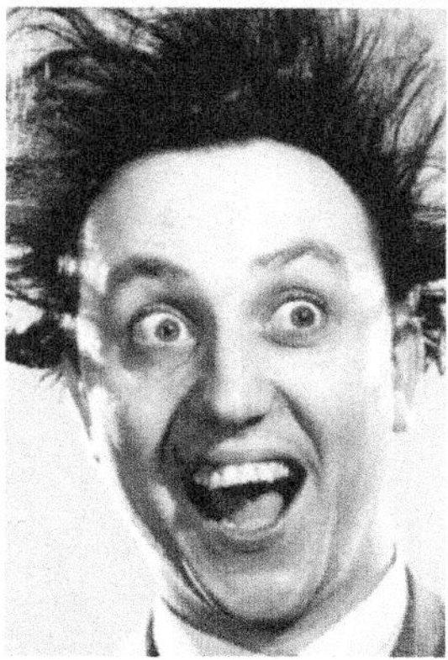

Ken Dodd

Some Enchanted Evening [Jay & the Americans] – This classic tune from the play/movie *South Pacific* is the biggest hit ever to come out of a Richard Rodgers/Oscar Hammerstein musical. *South Pacific* debuted in 1949, six years before the acknowledged beginning of the Rock Era.

Perry Como hit No. 1 with it in '49, and Bing Crosby took it to No. 3 that year. Many other major recording artists had success with it in ensuing years.

Riding a hot streak in 1965, the New York vocal group Jay & the Americans recorded it and watched it soar to No. 13 for two weeks. Lead singer Jay Black delivered a powerful lead vocal befitting the song's status as a showstopper.

In *South Pacific* the song is sung as a solo by the lead male character of Emile de Becque, who has fallen in love with Nellie Forbush.

The song enabled Jay & the Americans to showcase their incredible knack for supplying superb backing vocals behind a strong lead vocal.

The vocal group originally was an all-Jewish quartet. Black replaced John "Jay" Traynor as lead singer in 1963. Their chart career lasted from 1962 to '69.

Some Enchanted Evening

Songwriters: Richard Rodgers, Oscar Hammerstein

Peaked at No. 13 on Billboard Hot 100

Oct. 9, 1965

Oct. 16, 1965

Jay & the Americans

Jay Black (born David Blatt) (Nov. 2, 1938-)

Marty Sanders (born Martin Kupersmith) (DOB unavailable)

Howard Kane (born Howard Kirschenbaum) (DOB unavailable)

Kenny Vance (born Kenneth Rosenberg) (Dec. 9, 1943-)

Sandy Deanne (born Sandy Yaguda) (DOB unavailable)

Formed in Brooklyn, N.Y., in 1960

Jay & the Americans

Summertime [Billy Stewart] – George Gershwin composed this song in 1934 for the opera *Porgy and Bess,* which debuted the following year.

The song soon became a jazz standard, with more than 25,000 recorded versions.

Porgy and Bess was based on the novel *Porgy* by DuBose Heyward, who wrote the lyrics for "Summertime." The song is sung several times throughout the opera, the first time by Clara as a lullaby.

Abbie Mitchell, who played the role of Clara in the premier production of the opera, was the first to record it in 1935.

There were a number of versions recorded early in the rock era, but Billy Stewart's was by far the most successful, hitting No. 10 on the pop chart and No. 7 on the R&B chart in 1966. Stewart's recording was sung in the jazz scat style, using his voice to stutter, repeat lines and imitate instruments.

Living in an era of political incorrectness, Stewart's nickname was "Fat Boy." He was a very large man, and he also had recorded a song called "Fat Boy." He met his fate two months before his 33rd birthday in a single-car crash in broad daylight while traveling to do a concert.

Summertime

Songwriters: George Gershwin, DuBose Heyward, Ira Gershwin

Peaked at No. 10 on Billboard Hot 100

Aug. 27, 1966

Sept. 3, 1966

Billy Stewart

March 24, 1937-Jan. 17, 1970

Born William Larry Stewart II in Washington, D.C., and died near Smithfield, N.C., in a car crash with his three band members on the way to do a show in Columbia, S.C.

Billy Stewart

Winchester Cathedral [New Vaudeville Band] – The artists who created this hit were London studio musicians brought together by songwriter Geoff Stephens. His gem, with the first verse played solely by the instruments with vocal added on the second, was reminiscent of dance band music of the 1920s.

The vocal, provided by John Carter, hearkened back to a style made popular by Rudy Vallee. Without a microphone to amplify his voice, Vallee used to stroll through crowds at his shows while singing through a megaphone.

The recording became a transatlantic smash that held down the No. 1 position in the United States for three weeks while reaching No. 2 in Germany and No. 4 in the U.K. Global sales soared over three million copies.

Despite not being a rock and roll record, "Winchester Cathedral" won a Grammy Award in 1967 for Best Contemporary Song. It is one of the few charted songs to feature a bassoon.

After the song became an international hit, there was intense demand for the New Vaudeville Band to go on a concert tour. That meant a full-time band had to be assembled. Alan Klein was chosen to be the lead singer, and he was billed as "Tristram – Seventh Earl of Cricklewood." Original session drummer Henri Harrison also joined the troupe.

In 1967 the New Vaudeville Band issued an "On Tour" album. Three subsequent singles charted well in the U.K.

Winchester Cathedral

Songwriter: Geoff Stephens

Peaked at No. 1 on Billboard Hot 100

Dec. 3, 1966

Dec. 17, 1966

Dec. 24, 1966

New Vaudeville Band

London, England, studio musicians under the direction of producer Geoff Stephens (Oct. 1, 1934-)

John Carter [born John Nicholas Shakespeare] (Oct. 20, 1942-) – lead vocal

New Vaudeville Band

Hello Hello [Sopwith Camel] – At a time when the psychedelic rock era was beginning, this simple tune, backed with a honkytonk piano, had good traction on the charts as 1967 began.

Sopwith Camel has become known as the second San Francisco band to get a recording contract with a national record label (the Grateful Dead was the first) and the first such group to have a top 40 hit. Following them onto the charts in the next few months were Jefferson Airplane and Moby Grape.

When I hear "Hello Hello," I can visualize a singer sitting at a piano, garters on his sleeves and a straw skimmer on his head, singing the song on a vaudeville stage while his bandmates provide handclaps and finger snaps. It's just a basic love song – with a little applause and whistle at the end.

Sadly, the band was unable to repeat the success of their first album and single, and they disbanded later in 1967.

Hello Hello

Songwriters: Peter Kraemer, Terry MacNeil

Peaked at No. 26 on Billboard Hot 100

Feb. 11, 1967

Sopwith Camel

Peter Kraemer – vocals, saxophone
Terry MacNeil – guitar
William "Truckaway" Sievers – guitar
Martin Beard – bass
Norman Mayell – drums
Formed in San Francisco, Calif., in 1965

Sopwith Camel

Mairzy Doats [Innocence] – This song was written in 1943 and was a real blast from the past when it showed up on the airwaves in 1967. I'd heard the song years earlier when my mom sang it to me and my sisters.

The novelty song was first played on New York radio station WOR by Al Trace and his Silly Symphonists. Recorded versions were on the charts several times by various artists, and the Merry Macs took it to No. 1 in 1944.

One of the song's composers, Milton Drake, said the song is based on an English nursery rhyme. The story goes that one day Drake's daughter came home singing, "Cowzy tweet and sowzy tweet and liddle sharksy doisters."

This led to another form of gibberish that makes sense when enunciated differently.

Innocence had two previous songs that hit the *Billboard* top 40. The first, "New York's A Lonely Town," came when they were known as the Trade Winds in 1965. "Mairzy Doats" was their follow-up to "There's Got To Be A Word" earlier in 1967.

Innocence formed as the Videls in Providence, R.I. They changed their name to Innocence in 1966.

Mairzy Doats

Songwriters: Milton Drake, Al Hoffman, Jerry Livingston

Peaked at No. 75 on Billboard Hot 100

March 18, 1967

Innocence

Peter Anders (born Peter Andreoli)

Vincent Poncia Jr.

Artie Ripp

Formed in 1958 as the Videls in Providence, R.I.

Innocence

That Acapulco Gold [Rainy Daze] – This is another song that easily could pass for a burlesque comedy song in a vaudeville show. Without using the word "marijuana," it promotes the use of *cannabis*. This was long before some states passed laws legalizing marijuana for medicinal or recreational purposes.

"Acapulco Gold" is the name given to the strain of *cannabis* grown near Acapulco, Mexico, that has a brownish-gold color or a mixture of green and gold. It was favored in the 1960s as a plant that had better quality than those grown in California or Texas.

The record managed to rise to No. 70 on the national pop singles chart before radio station executives figured out the meaning of the lyrics and banned it from airplay. I remember hearing it a couple of times on Chicago's WLS, although it never cracked the station's top 40 list.

Besides the old-time sound of the instrumentation, some of the lyrics lend a retro feel to the song. With stripped-down production, it features organ, piano, minimal use of electric guitar and lots of backing vocals. We hear "hey diddle diddle" from an English nursery rhyme that goes back to at least the 16th century. There's also "twenty-three skidoo," a popular phrase that first caught on in 1906 and means leaving quickly, being forced to leave quickly by someone else, or taking advantage of a propitious opportunity to leave, that is, "getting [out] while the getting's good." The origin is uncertain.

The Denver, Colo., group the Rainy Daze started out as a band that covered other bands' hits and used their exposure as fraternity party entertainment to land an appearance on local TV. This allegedly caught the attention of legendary record producer Phil Spector, who offered a management contract.

That Acapulco Gold
Songwriters: Tim Gilbert, John Carter
Peaked at No. 70 on Billboard Hot 100
March 25, 1967

The Rainy Daze
Tim Gilbert – vocals, guitar
Kip Gilbert – drums
Mac Ferris – lead guitar
Sam Fuller – bass
Bob Heckendorf – keyboards
Formed in Denver, Colo., in 1965

The Rainy Daze

I Got Rhythm [Happenings] – For several years the New Jersey vocal group the Happenings crafted a nice recording career by putting their own stamp on songs that had been popularized by other artists. Four of those songs found their way into the *Billboard* top 20. Some of those songs went back decades.

"I Got Rhythm" had been published in 1930 after George and Ira Gershwin wrote it. The song was included in the musical *Girl Crazy* and became a jazz standard.

It also was included in the 1951 film *An American In Paris,* in which Gene Kelly sang it while tap dancing.

During the rock era the Happenings had the most success with it, taking it to No. 3 on the pop charts in the spring of 1967. Their follow-up was "My Mammy," a No. 13 hit that was written by Walter Donaldson, Joe Young and Sam M. Lewis and was first performed in 1918.

The Happenings cut their first record in 1961 but didn't get any action on the national charts until 1966, when their version of "See You In September" soared to No. 3. Their last entry on the *Hot 100* came in 1969. They originally were known as the Four Graduates, and tight vocal harmony was their hallmark.

I Got Rhythm
Songwriters: George Gershwin, Ira Gershwin
Peaked at No. 3 on Billboard Hot 100
May 27, 1967
June 3, 1967
June 10, 1967

The Happenings
Dave Libert
Bob Miranda
Tom Giuliano
Ralph DiVito
Formed in Paterson, N.J., in 1961

The Happenings

Ding Dong! The Witch Is Dead [Fifth Estate] – This well-known song comes from the 1939 motion picture *The Wizard of Oz.* The Connecticut band the Fifth Estate turned it into a sunshine pop hit midway through 1967.

In the movie, the song is sung by the Munchkins, Glinda and Dorothy Gale after Dorothy's house lands on the Wicked Witch of the East. It also celebrates the death of the Wicked Witch of the West, who was splashed with water.

While the song was the biggest hit in the career of the Fifth Estate, it also has been the highest American-charting recording of any Harold Arlen or *Wizard of Oz* song by any artist since the modern chart era began in 1940. The song was recorded in five different languages (Japanese, Italian, French, German and English) and released around the world.

The Fifth Estate also appeared in an episode of *Malibu U.,* an American variety show that starred Rick Nelson and aired on ABC-TV during the summer of 1967. Originally known as the D-Men, they changed their name in 1966.

"Fifth Estate" is a socio-cultural reference to groupings of outlier viewpoints in contemporary society and is mostly associated with journalists. It dates back to the 1960s counterculture and, in particular, the *Fifth Estate*, an underground newspaper first published in Detroit in 1965.

Ding Dong! The Witch Is Dead
Songwriters: Harold Arlen, E.Y. Harburg
Peaked at No. 11 on Billboard Hot 100
July 1, 1967

The Fifth Estate
Rick Engler – lead vocals, guitar, harmonica
Ken "Furvus" Evans – drums, vocals
Doug "Duke" Ferrara – bass, vocals
Wayne "Wads" Wadhams – piano, organ, harpsichord
Bill Shute – guitar, vocals
Formed in Stamford, Conn., in 1963

The Fifth Estate

Anything Goes [Harpers Bizarre] – This composition by Cole Porter goes back to 1934, when it was included in his musical *Anything Goes.* The version by Harpers Bizarre played over the opening credits of the 1970 film *The Boys in the Band.* The song made it to No. 43 on the pop chart and No. 6 on the Adult Contemporary list.

This is an abridged version of the original lyrics, which feature humorous references to various figures of scandal and gossip in the Depression Era. Some of these people included Samuel Goldwyn, Anna Sten, Max Gordon, Evalyn Walsh McLean and Lady Mendl. None of the verses containing these references made the 2 minute version recorded by Harpers Bizarre.

Hailing from Santa Cruz, Calif., Harpers Bizarre was led by Ted Templeman. After the group disbanded in 1970, he began a successful career as a record producer – his main clients were the Doobie Brothers and Van Halen.

In 1980, when I was a limousine driver in Phoenix, I drove Templeman around town for three days. He was accompanied by a new vocalist on the rise, Nicolette Larsen, and they stayed at the Arizona Biltmore Hotel. One of the reasons he came to Phoenix from Los Angeles was to see a concert by Van Halen, a band he produced.

While driving him through town one day, I asked Templeman what the job of a record producer entailed. I'm afraid he was dismissive of me. "A producer does whatever the recording artist wants to do in the recording studio," he replied.

Through a lot of reading and observation over many years, I have learned that producers control all aspects of a recording session from start to finish. They not only coach the musicians in the studio but also decide what instruments will be used. Producers have their fingerprints all over the sound of the finished product, so to speak.

A homophone, Harpers Bizarre is a takeoff of the women's fashion magazine *Harper's Bazaar*, which first was published in 1867. The band's first name was the Tiki's, and their first national hit was "59th Street Bridge Song (Feelin' Groovy)."

While returning to San Francisco after playing a show in Pasadena, Calif., Harpers Bizarre's TWA flight was hijacked. All of the passengers were safely released in Denver, but the plane and its crew continued to Rome, Italy, where the hijacker was apprehended.

Anything Goes

Songwriter: Cole Porter

Peaked at No. 43 on Billboard Hot 100

Sept. 23, 1967

Sept. 30, 1967

Oct. 7, 1967

Harpers Bizarre

Ted Templeman (Oct. 24, 1944-) vocals, drums, guitar

Dick Scoppettone (July 5, 1945-) vocals, guitar, bass

Eddie James (DOB unavailable) guitar

Dick Yount (Jan. 9, 1943-) bass, vocals

John Petersen (Jan. 8, 1945-Nov. 11, 2007) drums, percussion, vocals

Formed in Santa Cruz, Calif., as the Tikis in 1965

Harpers Bizarre

Loving You Has Made Me Bananas [Guy Marks] – This record was released in early 1968, but the song's feel takes us back to the 1930s or '40s. It is a parody of big band radio broadcasts that has a humorous side.

When I first heard it on the radio, I could barely believe my ears. This wasn't rock, and it wasn't pop. It was something from a time before I started listening to music, I thought. The words don't make sense, either. And that's when I realized that Guy Marks had adroitly turned back the clock with this humorous novelty song.

An album followed, containing more of Marks's vocals of songs in the same style.
The song was re-released in 1978, when it reached No. 25 on the U.K. singles chart.
Marks was an actor, singer, comedian and impressionist who made many appearances on TV variety shows and sitcoms in the 1960s and '70s.

Loving You Has Made Me Bananas

Songwriter: Guy Marks
Peaked at No. 51 on Billboard Hot 100
April 27, 1968
May 4, 1968

Guy Marks

Oct. 31, 1923-Nov. 28, 1987
Born Mario Scarpa in South Philadelphia, Pa., and died of cancer at the Atlantic City Medical Center in Pomona, N.J.

Guy Marks

Beer Barrel Polka (Bobby Vinton) – The music was composed by Czech Jaromir Vejvoda in 1927. Lyrics were added in 1934 by Vaclav Zeman, and in June 1939, Will Glahe's version was No. 1 on the *Hit Parade.*

The authors of the English lyrics were Lew Brown and Wladamir Timm. The song was widely popular with soldiers during World War II, and versions popped up in various languages.

It was an unlikely song to appear on mainstream pop radio in 1975, but Bobby Vinton wasn't shy about promoting the music of his heritage. The previous year he'd had a big hit with "My Melody Of Love," which contained English and Polish lyrics.

The polka is a Czech dance and genre of dance music, but it also is closely identified with Polish culture.

Vinton is of Polish and Lithuanian descent, and the family surname was Vintula until his father changed it.

Bobby got his college education at Duquesne University in Pittsburgh, where he graduated with a degree in musical composition and became proficient at playing piano, clarinet, saxophone, trumpet, drums and oboe. His first hit recording was the No. 1 song "Roses Are Red" in 1962.

Beer Barrel Polka

Songwriters: Jaromir Vejvoda, Vaclav Zeman
Peaked at No. 33 on Billboard Hot 100
April 19, 1975
April 26, 1975

Bobby Vinton

Born Stanley Robert Vinton Jr. in Canonsburg, Pa., on April 16, 1935

Bobby Vinton

Shaving Cream [Benny Bell] – The original version of this song was issued in 1946 on Benny Bell's Cocktail Party Songs label, with Phil Winston on vocals under the stage name Paul Wynn. Since Bell himself also recorded under that name, Winston's version often has been mistaken for Bell's.

Bell was 69 years old in 1975, when he finally received the mass appeal that had eluded him for decades. He truly was a leftover from an earlier era.

When I listen to this song I get a mental picture of a stage act at one of the Borscht Belt resorts of the Catskill Mountains in the 1940s.

After the syndicated *Dr. Demento Radio Show* began to play the song in the early 1970s, Vanguard Records reissued the recording early in '75, and it became a hit once again.

The underlying joke in this novelty song is that the singer is trying to avoid saying the obvious rhyming word *sh*** at the end of each verse. It makes the story of each verse nonsensical, but it's hilarious, nonetheless. The music is carried by vaudevillian horns.

"It was a simple concept that people could easily understand," radio personality Dr. Demento said. "And it was such a refreshing change from whatever was on the radio at the time."

As his song rose to No. 30 on the *Billboard* pop chart, there was a flurry of interest in Bell. But he had been burned by the music industry years before, and he failed to capitalize on it in a lasting way because he steadfastly refused to hire an agent or business manager. Those are roles that Bell filled for himself since the '40s.

Bell pursued a career in vaudeville and music and wrote approximately 600 songs. He also performed and recorded under the names of Benny Bimbo and Paul Wynn.

Shaving Cream

Songwriter: Benny Bell

Peaked at No. 30 on Billboard Hot 100

April 26, 1975

May 3, 1975

Benny Bell

March 21, 1906-July 6, 1999

Born Benjamin Samberg in New York City, N.Y., and died in his hometown

Benny Bell

(Ghost) Riders In The Sky [Outlaws] – This western classic was written in 1948, and a number of recorded versions were cross-over hits on the pop charts the next year. Vaughn Moore's version was No. 1 the week I was born in May 1949.

Southern rock band the Outlaws brought it back to the top 40 in 1981, inserting a lot of rock guitar into their arrangement. The original title was "(Ghost) Riders In The Sky: A Cowboy Legend."

Other artists who recorded the song throughout the years include Bing Crosby, Frankie Laine, Burl Ives, Marty Robbins, Johnny Cash, Eddy Arnold and Spike Jones & his City Slickers. Gene Autry sang it in the 1949 movie *Riders In The Sky,* and the man who wrote it, Stan Jones, recorded it for his 1957 album *Creakin' Leather.*

The fanciful lyrics tell of an aging cowboy who witnesses ghastly, damned cowboys chasing cattle across the heavens. One cautions him that, if he doesn't change his ways, he will be doomed to join them forever. Jones has said that, when he was 12 years old, an old cowboy friend told him the story.

Even though it's almost 6 minutes long, the Outlaws' version omits the final verse. The intro is 1 minute 16 seconds long, and the outro runs 1:51.

Interestingly, folk music veterans Peter, Paul & Mary recorded a parody of the song titled "Yuppies In The Sky" for their 1990 album *Flowers and Stones.*

The Outlaws experienced many personnel changes before they had their first national hit record in 1975. Their music falls mainly in the Southern rock genre, but it contains elements of country and rock with three- and four-part harmonies.

(Ghost) Riders In The Sky

Songwriter: Stan Jones

Peaked at No. 31 on Billboard Hot 100

March 7, 1981

The Outlaws

Rick Cua – vocals, bass
Freddie Salem – guitar, vocals
David Dix – drums
Billy Jones – guitar
Hughie Thomasson – guitar
Mike Duke – keyboards, vocals
Formed in Tampa, Fla., in 1964

The Outlaws

Puttin' On The Ritz [Taco] – Dutch vocalist Taco revived this Irving Berlin classic written in 1927 and turned it into a sizeable hit. A music video accompanied it, to be played on TV. It wasn't long before the video was pulled, however, because it featured some dancers in blackface.

The Harry Richman orchestra and chorus introduced the song in the 1930 musical film *Puttin' On The Ritz.* It was the first song in film to be sung by an interracial ensemble.

The title is derived from the expression to "Put on the Ritz," meaning to dress very fashionably." "Ritz" refers to the opulent Ritz Hotel in New York City.

The lyrics contain a reference to popular American film actor Gary Cooper, whose career spanned 1925-61.

The original version of Berlin's song included references to the then-popular fad of flashily dressed, poor black Harlemites parading up and down Lenox Ave. in Manhattan, "spending every dime for a wonderful time."

For the 1946 film *Blue Skies,* where it was performed by Fred Astaire, Berlin revised the lyrics to apply to affluent whites strutting "up and down Park Ave." In his video, Taco pays homage to Astaire with a tap dance solo in the middle of the song.

As the song rose to its peak on the 1983 charts, Berlin, 95, became the oldest living songwriter to have one of his compositions enter the *Billboard* top 10.

Taco was born abroad to Dutch parents. He spent much of his childhood moving around the world to the Netherlands, United States, Singapore, Luxembourg, Belgium and Germany. He graduated from the International School of Brussels, Belgium, in 1973 and afterward studied interior decoration and acting in Hamburg, Germany.

Puttin' On The Ritz

Songwriter: Irving Berlin

Peaked at No. 4 on Billboard Hot 100

Sept. 3, 1983

Sept. 10, 1983

Taco

Born Taco Ockerse in Jakarta, Indonesia, on July 21, 1955

Taco

Chapter 12

Folk Rock

The development of a popular hybrid

Overview: Folk music is centuries old. Generally speaking, it consists of simple melodies and lyrical stories which have been handed down orally from one generation to another. The authorship often is anonymous, and versions of the songs may have variances.

After rock music became the prevailing genre of popular music in the 1950s, it wasn't long before pop musicians began to write and record folk songs. After a few years, the predominant folk artist, Bob Dylan, introduced electrified instruments to his recordings. Hence, the sub-genre of folk rock officially was born in 1965 with "Like A Rolling Stone."

Soon the artists who were influenced by Dylan also used electronic instruments in their folky renderings.

Read on for descriptions of some of the top folk rock songs, both before and after 1965.

To view the full lyrics to these songs, please log on to www.google.com, enter song titles & artist names and click Google Search.

To listen to these songs, please log on to www.youtube.com and enter song titles & artist names.

Greenfields [Brothers Four] – This folk quartet proved very quickly that their kind of music could stand with the new sound called rock and roll. This, their second single, soared to No. 2.

The members met at the University of Washington in 1956, where they were members of the Phi Gamma Delta fraternity – hence the "brothers" connection to their name.

Their first professional performances were the result of a prank perpetrated by a rival fraternity, who set them up to play a bogus gig at the Colony Club in Seattle. Although the club's management didn't expect them to perform, they were allowed to audition and subsequently were hired. This was about a year before the Kingston Trio made their first recording.

The Brothers Four went to San Francisco in 1959, where they fell under the managerial wing of Dave Brubeck's manager, who secured them a contract with Columbia Records.

Following the million-selling success of "Greenfields" in 1960, the Brothers Four failed to chart any song higher than No. 26. But they had laid a good foundation for other folk rock acts that would follow in the 1960s and beyond. Their original lineup stayed intact until 1969, when Mike Kirkland left and was replaced by another University of Washington alumnus, Mark Pearson. Two of the original members still play with the group.

"Greenfields," a dark, brooding ballad about love lost, was written by the members of the folk trio the Easy Riders – Terry Gilkyson, Richard Dehr and Frank Miller.

Greenfields

Songwriters: Terry Gilkyson, Frank Miller, Richard Dehr

Peaked at No. 2 on Billboard Hot 100

April 18, 1960
April 25, 1960
May 2, 1960
May 9,1960

The Brothers Four

Bob Flick
John Paine
Mike Kirkland
Dick Foley
Formed in Seattle, Wash., in 1957

The Brothers Four

Michael [Highwaymen] – A year after "Greenfields" had its foray on the pop charts, the Highwaymen scored a No. 1 hit with "Michael."

The song is an adaptation of a 19th century folk song titled "Michael Row The Boat Ashore." It was sung by freed slaves who lived on islands off the coast of the state of Georgia as they traveled to work by boat to a plantation on the mainland each day during the Civil War years. The hit single was arranged by Highwaymen lead tenor Dave Fisher.

The stripped-down nature of the production allowed the vocals to carry a big wallop. A six string acoustic guitar and acoustic bass were the only instruments used. The whistling in the intro and outro by Steve Butts added a unique element.

Band member Steve Trott remarked, "Fisher put in a couple of minor chords that hadn't been there before, and that made all the difference." Recording of the song took only about 15 minutes, according to *Songfacts*.

Like the Brothers Four, the Highwaymen came together as college students. The five matriculated at Wesleyan University in Middletown, Conn., and their first genre was doo-wop music. Their follow-up to "Michael" was "Cotton Fields," which also was quite successful on the pop charts (No. 13).

The original members stopped performing in 1964 and went their separate ways in non-musical careers, with the exception of Fisher, who recruited four new members to keep the group going a few more years.

"Michael" was the first No. 1 hit for United Artists Records, which was one of the major labels for pop music throughout the 1960s.

Michael

Songwriters: Tony Saletan, Pete Seeger, Bob Gibson

Peaked at No. 1 on Billboard Hot 100

Sept. 4, 1961
Sept. 11, 1961

The Highwaymen

Dave Fisher (July 19, 1940-May 7, 2010)
Bob Burnett (Feb. 7, 1940-Dec. 7, 2011)
Steve Butts (DOB unavailable)
Chan Daniels (Jan. 1, 1940-Aug. 2, 1975)
Steve Trott (Dec. 12, 1939-)
Formed in Middletown, Conn., in 1958

The Highwaymen

Walk Right In [Rooftop Singers] – This song by a progressive folk-singing trio was another chart topper.

The Rooftop Singers were assembled by Baltimore native Erik Darling in June 1962, specifically to record an updated version of the 1929 country-blues song "Walk Right In." The other two members were Bill Svanoe and Lynne Taylor.

"When I heard that song (on a 30-year-old album), I said to myself, 'That's a hit,'" Darling said. He altered the lyrics from "everybody's talking about a two way woman" to "everybody's talking about a new way of walking."

The song became a crossbred phenomenon by hitting No. 1 on the *Billboard* pop chart (for two weeks) and the easy listening chart (five weeks), while also ascending the R&B chart to No. 4 and the country chart to No. 23. It was a million-seller that hit No. 1 in Australia and the top 10 in the U.K.

"Walk Right In" was recorded using two 12-string acoustic guitars, which were difficult to find in 1962. Darling ordered one from the Gibson Guitar Co., but recording was held up while the manufacturer built a left-handed model for Svanoe to play.

Gus Cannon wrote the song 33 years before the Rooftop Singers popularized it, and he no doubt was pleased with its new success. He had been forced to pawn his banjo the previous winter in order to pay his heating bill, and renewed interest in his music resulted in a recording contract for the 79-year-old musician.

The original lineup of the Rooftop Singers recorded two albums, and then Taylor resigned under pressure from her husband. The trio formally disbanded in 1967.

Walk Right In
Songwriters: Gus Cannon, Hosea Woods
Peaked at No. 1 on Billboard Hot 100
Jan. 26, 1963
Feb. 2, 1963

Rooftop Singers
Erik Darling (Sept. 25, 1933-Aug. 3, 2008)
Bill Svanoe (DOB unavailable)
Lynne Taylor (1928-1982)
Formed in New York City, N.Y., in 1962

Rooftop Singers: Bill Svanoe, Erik Darling, Lynne Taylor

Greenback Dollar [Kingston Trio] – Going back to 1958, the Kingston Trio was one of the most prolific folk groups. Author Joel Whitburn calls them "originators of the folk music craze of the 1960s."

Their last three top 40 hits came in 1963, just before the British Invasion dramatically changed the pop music landscape. This song was the first of those three.

A rift had opened within the trio, with Dave Guard on one side and Bob Shane and Nick Reynolds on the other. The result was Guard leaving the group in 1961, and he quickly was replaced by John

Stewart from southern California. After the Kingston Trio finally broke up, Stewart wrote a No. 1 song in 1967 for the Monkees, "Daydream Believer," and had a No. 5 solo hit in 1979, "Gold."

The theme of "Greenback Dollar" is remarkably similar to a song by the New Christy Minstrels that will appear a little later. It's about a guy with a devil-may-care attitude, and it was the lead-off single from the album "New Frontier."

Music critic Bruce Eder called the album "basically cheerful, optimistic music celebrating youth, nowhere more so than on John Stewart's title song, a bold, optimistic celebration of the Kennedy era."

"Greenback Dollar" had an alternate version to appease radio stations that objected to the term "give a damn." That version replaced the word "damn" with a sharp acoustic guitar lick. That was the only version I ever heard on Chicago radio station WLS.

Songwriter Hoyt Axton made the first recording of the song early in 1962.

Greenback Dollar

Songwriters: Hoyt Axton, Ken Ramsey

Peaked at No. 21 on Billboard Hot 100

March 16, 1963

<u>Kingston Trio</u>

Bob Shane (Feb. 1, 1934-Jan. 26, 2020)

Nick Reynolds (July 27, 1933-Oct. 1, 2008)

John Stewart (Sept. 5, 1939-Jan. 19, 2008)

Formed in Palo Alto, Calif., in 1954

Kingston Trio: John Stewart, Bob Shane, Nick Reynolds

Blowin' In The Wind [Peter, Paul & Mary] – Bob Dylan had a huge influence on the folk music movement of the 1960s, and he wrote this song in 1962 when he was 21 years old. He penned three other songs that appear in this chapter.

Peter, Paul & Mary were part of the Greenwich Village music scene in New York, as was Dylan. So, it was natural that they should record some of his songs. In fact, their follow-up to "Blowin' In The Wind" was another Dylan song, "Don't Think Twice, It's All Right."

"Blowin' In The Wind" generally is viewed as a protest song, but it asks rhetorical questions about peace, war and freedom. In 2004 it was ranked No. 14 on *Rolling Stone Magazine's* list of the 500 Greatest Songs of All Time.

Dylan's comments about the song in a publication in June 1962 went thusly: "There ain't too much I can say about this song except that the answer is blowing in the wind. It ain't in no book or movie or TV show or discussion group. Man, it's in the wind, and it's blowing in the wind. Too many of these hip people are telling me where the answer is but, oh, I won't believe that. I still say it's in the wind and, just like a restless piece of paper, it's got to come down some.

"But the only trouble is that nobody picks up the answer when it comes down, so not too many people get to see and know … and then it flies away. I still say that some of the biggest criminals are those that turn their heads away when they see wrong and they know it's wrong. I'm only 21 years old, and I know that there's been too many. You people over 21, you're older and smarter."

Peter, Paul & Mary's version of the song was the most commercially successful of hundreds of covers, peaking at No. 2 on *Billboard's Hot 100* and spending five weeks at No. 1 on the *Adult Contemporary* chart.

Blowin' In The Wind

Songwriter: Bob Dylan

Peaked at No. 2 on Billboard Hot 100

Aug. 17, 1963

Peter, Paul & Mary

Peter Yarrow (May 31, 1938-)

Paul Stookey (Dec. 30, 1937-)

Mary Travers (Nov. 9, 1936-Sept. 16, 2009)

Formed in New York City, N.Y., in 1961

Peter Yarrow, Paul Stookey, Mary Travers

Green, Green [New Christy Minstrels] – This vocal assemblage was a large-ensemble folk group that was founded by singer/guitarist Randy Sparks from the San Francisco Bay area. They were a high-profile act in the mid-1960s and were a big draw at concerts and on TV shows.

The 14-voice group was a conglomerate of a quartet, two trios and four individuals, including Dolan Ellis, who would become Arizona's official balladeer in 1966. Their debut album won a Grammy Award, and they recorded more than 20 albums in all. The rotating lineup has featured more than 300 singers over the years.

Sparks named the group after Christy's Minstrels, a group formed by Edwin Pearce Christy in 1842 that was known primarily for introducing many of Stephen Foster's compositions. Sparks' vision was to have the New Christy Minstrels showcase his own writing, which consisted of original songs and fresh adaptations of folk classics.

"Green, Green," written by Sparks and Barry McGuire, was one such song. The lyrics tell of a free-wheeling non-conformist who wants to roam and do his own thing. McGuire, who sang lead on the recording, would be a solo act within two years with a No. 1 single, "Eve Of Destruction."

Green, Green
Songwriters: Barry McGuire, Randy Sparks
Peaked at No. 14 on Billboard Hot 100
Aug. 17, 1963

New Christy Minstrels
Randy Sparks
Barry McGuire
Dolan Ellis
Jackie Miller
Nick Woods
Art Podell
Barry Kane
Larry Ramos
Clarence Treat
Gayle Caldwell
Formed in New York City, N.Y., in 1961

The New Christy Minstrels

Don't Let The Rain Come Down (Crooked Little Man) [Serendipity Singers] – The dawn of the Beatles era saw this folk rock song defy the Fab Four by challenging them on the charts. It was based on the English nursery rhyme "There Was A Crooked Man."

The humorous lyrics and the simplicity of the calypso tune made it a widely popular song. The Serendipity Singers' musical director, Bob Bowers, did the arrangement, along with Bryan Sennett and John Madden.

The song was first recorded as "Crooked Little House" by Jimmie Rodgers in 1960. Subsequent cover versions were released by the Brothers Four, Trini Lopez and Ronnie Hilton.

The Serendipity Singers started out as the Newport Singers at the University of Colorado. After the seven-member group left Colorado for New York City, they signed with manager Fred Weintraub, who recommended adding two members to round out their sound. He booked them into his Bitter End nightclub in Greenwich Village, and appearances on ABC-TV's *Hootenanny* and a contract with Philips Records followed.

Perhaps the crowning chart achievement for the song came on April 17, 1964, when it dislodged "Suspicion" by Terry Stafford from the No. 1 spot on the *WLS Silver Dollar Survey* in Chicagoland for one week.

The Serendipity Singers' name was sold in the 1970s, resulting in an all-new lineup.

Don't Let The Rain Come Down (Crooked Little Man)

Songwriter: Traditional, arranged by Bob Bowers

Peaked at No. 6 on Billboard Hot 100

May 2, 1964

May 9, 1964

The Serendipity Singers

Bryan Sennett

Brooks Hatch

Mike Brovsky

Jon Arbenz

Bob Young

Lynne Weintraub

John Madden

Tom Tiemann

Diane Decker

Formed in Boulder, Colo., and New York City, N.Y., in 1962-63

The Serendipity Singers

Laugh, Laugh [Beau Brummels] -- San Francisco's Beau Brummels, formed in 1964, did not set out to become a folk rock band, but their music leaned in that direction.

The local disc jockeys who owned Autumn Records were looking for acts to sign to their new label, and the Beau Brummels' music was meant to be an American answer to the Beatles.

The band's musical style blended Mersey beat music (from Liverpool) with folk music. While considered a rock outfit, the Brummels made extensive use of acoustic instruments, as was the case with most folk acts. They took their name from the Regency Era (1811-1820) Englishman Beau Brummel, who was an excessively well-dressed man.

"Laugh, Laugh" features a harmonica played by Declan Mulligan on the intro, middle and outro, and plenty of acoustic guitar was used throughout the song.

The producer of the recording was Sylvester Stewart, who at that time was an unknown in the music industry. About three years later he would be known as Sly Stone, the leader of the funk/soul band Sly & the Family Stone.

Guitarist Ron Elliott, who wrote the song, declared that Stewart was a positive influence on the band because of his talent, intelligence and experience.

While the single attained a peak position of No. 15 on the *Billboard* pop chart, it rose to No. 2 in Canada. One of the principals of Autumn Records, Tom Donahue, believed it could have been a No. 1 song if his company had stronger distribution.

In 1994 "Laugh, Laugh" was awarded inclusion in a Rock and Roll Hall of Fame exhibit of 500 Songs that Shaped Rock & Roll.

The Beau Brummels performed the song on television shows such as NBC's *Hullabaloo*, ABC's *Shindig!* and ABC's *American Bandstand.* They appeared as animated guests during Season 6 of *The Flintstones* under the moniker the Beau Brummelstones as they performed "Laugh, Laugh" on Bedrock's teen dance show, *Shinrock.*

Laugh, Laugh

Songwriter: Ron Elliott

Peaked at No. 15 on Billboard Hot

Feb.20, 1965

Feb. 27, 1965

Beau Brummels

Sal Valentino [born Salvatore Spampinato] (Sept. 8, 1942-) lead vocals

Ron Elliott (Oct. 21, 1943-) lead guitar, vocals

Ron Meagher (Oct. 2, 1941-) bass

Declan Mulligan (April 4, 1938-) harmonica, rhythm guitar

John Petersen (Jan. 8, 1942-Nov. 11, 2007) drums

Formed in San Francisco, Calif., in 1964

The Beau Brummels: Ron Elliott, Declan Mulligan, Sal Valentino, Ron Meagher, John Petersen

I'll Never Find Another You [Seekers] – Folk acts from foreign countries started entering the American charts in the mid-1960s. In this case it was the Seekers from Australia.

The quartet was named joint "Australians of the Year" in 1967, the year their song "Georgy Girl" reached No. 2 on the *Billboard Hot 100.*

Hailing from Melbourne, the group originally sang doo-wop music and was called the Escorts. In 1962 their lead singer left to get married, and he was replaced by Judith Durham as the name was changed to Seekers.

Like Peter, Paul & Mary, the Seekers featured spot-on harmonies and a strong female voice.

"I'll Never Find Another You" was written by Englishman Tom Springfield, who sang with his sister Dusty in a trio called the Springfields. The song was ranked as the second-best song in the U.K. for 1965. It reached No. 1 in Australia and the U.K. and was No. 2 in Ireland. It peaked at No. 4 in the U.S.

The song was revived by Sonny James in 1967 and hit No. 1 on the *Billboard Country Chart.*

I'll Never Find Another You

Songwriter: Tom Springfield
Peaked at No. 4 on Billboard Hot 100
May 15, 1965

The Seekers

Judith Durham (July 3, 1943-) vocals, piano, tambourine
Athol Guy (Jan. 5, 1940-) double bass, vocals
Keith Potger (March 21, 1941-) 12-string guitar, banjo, vocals
Bruce Woodley (July 25, 1942-) guitar, mandolin, banjo, vocals
Formed in Melbourne, Australia, in 1962

The Seekers: Keith Potger, Athol Guy, Judith Durham, Bruce Woodley

Like A Rolling Stone [Bob Dylan] – 1965 was an important year for Bob Dylan. That was the year that he began to abandon his style of all-acoustic folk music by introducing electric instruments into his songs. Hard core Dylan fans were not happy about that.

The change in style, however, quickly manifested itself in improved chart performances of his singles. "Like A Rolling Stone" became Dylan's biggest success on the singles chart by spending two weeks at No. 2. The song features an electric keyboard and electric guitar.

As we will see in the song profiles that follow, other recording artists were eager to employ his electric folk style on their songs in the late 1960s and 1970s. This marks Dylan as one of the most influential figures in pop/rock music history.

Like many of Dylan's songs, this one contained biting commentary. He based the lyrics on a short story he had written about a debutante who becomes a loner when she falls out of high society.

He got the idea from a 1949 Hank Williams song, "Lost Highway," which contains the line "I'm a rolling stone, all alone and lost."

It is rumored that the debutante actually was Edie Sedgwick, who ran with artist Andy Warhol's crowd. If that was true, then this barbed line was an accusation that Warhol mistreated her: "Ain't it hard when you discover that he wasn't really where it's at, after he took from you everything he could steal."

In its November 2004 issue, *Rolling Stone Magazine* rated the song No. 1 on its list of the greatest songs of all time.

Although Dylan was a prolific songwriter and recording artist, his genius was not reflected in success on the singles chart because most of his fans purchased his albums instead.

Columbia Records had reservations about releasing the song as a single because of the electrified sound and the length of 6 minutes 13 seconds. That was much longer than the normal length of radio hits at the time.

At an auction in 2014, Dylan's handwritten lyrics on note paper from the Roger Smith Hotel in Washington, D.C., fetched $2 million, a world record for a popular music manuscript.

Dylan was raised in Hibbing, Minn. He dropped out of the University of Minnesota after his freshman year and went to New York City to pursue his music career.

Like A Rolling Stone

Songwriter: Bob Dylan

Peaked at No. 2 on Billboard Hot 100

Sept. 4, 1965

Sept. 11, 1965

<u>Bob Dylan</u>

Born Robert Allen Zimmerman in Duluth, Minn., on May 24, 1941

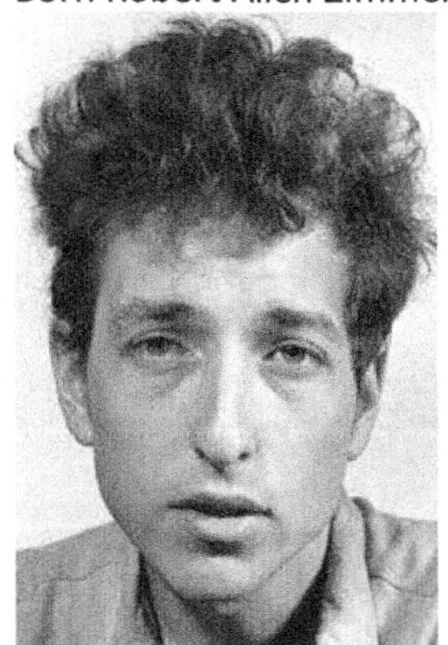

Bob Dylan

Mr. Tambourine Man [Byrds] – After Bob Dylan went electric, it wasn't long before some new American bands took his folk songs to the recording studio for more electrified treatment. The first was the Byrds, who formed in Los Angeles and visited the folk rock genre before moving on to psychedelic rock and country rock. Their star burned brightly as they recorded two No. 1 hits, but it burned out after a few short years.

There are those who would argue that this was the first folk rock song, since it contained the electric rock guitar.

One of the Byrds' members, Gene Clark, had been a member of the New Christy Minstrels. The Byrds' acknowledged leader, Roger McGuinn, had been with folk groups the Limeliters and the Chad Mitchell Trio.

When recording sessions for "Mr. Tambourine Man" commenced in January 1965, however, the Byrds had not yet gelled musically, and McGuinn was the only member to play on the song. Producer Terry Melcher brought in the consortium of top studio musicians known as the Wrecking Crew to play behind McGuinn's 12-string electric guitar and vocals by McGuinn, Clark and David Crosby.

The record was a smash on both sides of the Atlantic, hitting No. 1 in the USA and the U.K. The abstract lyrics penned by Dylan provided an intellectual and literary wordplay that was previously unfamiliar to rock music. It was the only song written by Dylan that reached No. 1 in America.

Folk guitarist Bruce Langhorne provided inspiration for the lyrics. Said Dylan, "Bruce was playing with me on a bunch of early records. On one session Tom Wilson (the producer) had asked him to play tambourine. And he had this gigantic tambourine. It was, like, really big. It was as big as a wagon wheel. He was playing, and this vision of him playing just stuck in my mind."

In the late 1960s the Beatles acknowledged the Byrds as creative competitors and named them as their favorite American band.

Mr. Tambourine Man

Songwriter: Bob Dylan

Peaked at No. 1 on Billboard Hot 100

June 26, 1965

The Byrds

Roger McGuinn (July 13, 1942-) lead guitar, vocals
Chris Hillman (Dec. 4, 1944-) bass, mandolin, guitar
David Crosby (Aug. 14, 1941-) guitar, keyboards, vocals
Michael Clarke (June 3, 1946-Dec. 19, 1993) drums, percussion
Gene Clark (Nov. 17, 1944-May 24, 1991) guitar, harmonica, tambourine
Formed in Los Angeles, Calif., in 1964

The Byrds: Chris Hillman, David Crosby, Roger McGuinn, Michael Clarke, Gene Clark

It Ain't Me Babe [Turtles] – The Turtles also were from Los Angeles, and at first they were known as the surf rock band the Crossfires. Acknowledging that the folk rock sound was trending, they turned their music in that direction and renamed themselves the Tyrtles.

The trendy spelling of their name didn't last, but the Turtles had a contract with new label White Whale Records and turned to Bob Dylan's "It Ain't Me Babe" for their first single. The recording made a quick climb up to No. 8 on *Billboard's Hot 100.*

In an irony of song titles, "It Ain't Me Babe" was rising at No. 21 while "I Got You Babe" was spending its third and final week at No. 1 for Sonny & Cher.

"It Ain't Me Babe" appeared on Dylan's fourth album, titled "Another Side Of Bob Dylan," which was released in 1964.

The song is about a man who is leaving a girlfriend because he is not prepared to be the kind of invincible hero and provider that she wants him to be. Dylan's biographers generally agree that the song's inspiration came from Dylan's former girlfriend Suze Rotolo, whom he dated from 1961 to '64. She is pictured walking with him in the cover photo of his album "The Freewheelin' Bob Dylan."

The popular singing duo Jan & Dean covered the song on their 1965 album "Folk 'N Roll."

The Turtles stayed on the pop charts through the end of the 1960s, placing nine singles in the top 40. Their biggest hit came in 1967, "Happy Together," which reached No. 1 on the *Hot 100.*

Howard Kaylan and Mark Volman still represent the Turtles as part of their annual nostalgia "Happy Together Tour" of 1960s-era pop stars.

It Ain't Me Babe

Songwriter: Bob Dylan

Peaked at No. 8 on Billboard Hot 100

Sept. 18, 1965

Sept. 25, 1965

<u>The Turtles</u>

Howard Kaylan (June 22, 1947-) vocals, keyboards

Mark Volman (April 19, 1947-) vocals, guitar, tambourine, keyboards

Don Murray (Nov. 8, 1945-March 22, 1996) drums

Chuck Portz (DOB unavailable) bass

Al Nichol (DOB unavailable) lead guitar, keyboards

Jim Tucker (Oct. 17, 1946-) rhythm guitar

Formed in Los Angeles, Calif., in 1965

The Turtles: Al Nichol, Howard Kaylan, Jim Tucker, Don Murray, Mark Volman, Chuck Portz

Homeward Bound [Simon & Garfunkel] – This was the second single in Simon & Garfunkel's chart career. As the follow-up to their No. 1 hit "The Sounds Of Silence," it became a No. 5 hit and validated the public's appreciation of the way the duo presented folk rock.

But the success story of native New Yorkers Paul Simon and Art Garfunkel was a fluke. They had started out in New York City singing as Tom & Jerry in the late 1950s. When that panned out, they both went off to college, Simon to NYU and Queens College and Garfunkel to NYU and Columbia.

They both continued to sing under various aliases and were active in the Greenwich Village folk scene. In 1964 they recorded an assortment of Bob Dylan songs, folk classics and Simon-penned originals. This collection would become their first album, "Wednesday Morning, 3 a.m." Then Simon moved to England, anticipating that the album would be a failure.

Months later a Boston radio station began to play "The Sounds Of Silence," which had a stripped-down, all acoustic production. Listener reaction was so positive that Columbia Records executives felt they would have a hit with it if they could electrify the track.

Tom Wilson, the producer of the original recording, was in the studio on June 15, 1965, with Dylan for the recording of "Like A Rolling Stone." When the recording of that song had been completed, Wilson asked the session musicians to record a new backing track for "Silence," using just an electric guitar, electric bass and drums. Four months later the reworked single was released. During the first week of January 1966, Simon, still in London, received a phone call from New York, informing him that "The Sounds Of Silence" was the No. 1 song in America.

"Homeward Bound" was kind of a musical step back and did not feature electrified instruments. It is an honest story about a troubadour who daily faces the hassles and boredom of a solitary life on the concert circuit. He wishes he were homeward bound, but that probably isn't going to happen soon.

Produced by Bob Johnston, it was released while its predecessor was at No. 1. It was recorded during the sessions for Simon & Garfunkel's second album, but it appeared on their third album, "Parsley, Sage, Rosemary and Thyme."

Simon wrote the song while in England. He had struck up a relationship with a ticket taker named Kathy Chitty at a club in Essex. But it became clear that Simon preferred to perform in London, which resulted in a sad farewell. After a performance in Liverpool, Simon was sitting in a rail station waiting for an early train to London. Missing Chitty, he began to write "Homeward Bound" on a scrap of paper.

Mention of Chitty appears in two other songs written by Simon: "Kathy's Song" (from the 1966 album "Sounds Of Silence") and "America" (from the 1968 album "Bookends.")

Homeward Bound
Songwriter: Paul Simon
Peaked at No. 5 on Billboard Hot 100
March 26, 1966
April 2, 1966

Paul Simon (Oct. 13, 1941-)
Art Garfunkel (Nov. 5, 1941-)
Formed in New York City, N.Y., in 1957 as Tom & Jerry

Art Garfunkel and Paul Simon

Ode To Billie Joe [Bobbie Gentry] – This song, which took the pop charts by storm in 1967, is closely associated with the country music genre. Its writer/singer is from Chickasaw County, Miss., near where

the story of the mysterious song is set.

The lyrics spin a story centered around the narrator, a teen girl who is part of a farm family in the Mississippi delta. As she, her brother and her father are called from the fields for their noon meal, the mother relays news she had just heard that a young man named Billie Joe McAllister, a friend of the family, has committed suicide by jumping off a nearby bridge.

The next few verses reveal an indifference among the family members, who are largely unmoved, although the news obviously has hit the narrator hard. Late in the song it is revealed that the local preacher recently saw the narrator with Billie Joe on the bridge, and the two were seen throwing "somethin' off the Tallahatchie Bridge."

The mystery remains twofold: what were the couple throwing off the bridge into the water below, and why did Billie Joe kill himself?

In a November 1967 interview, Gentry said that the question she had been asked most was what item was thrown from the bridge. Guesses ranged from an engagement ring to a draft card, a bottle of LSD tabs, flowers and an aborted baby. She said she knew the answer but would not reveal it. "Suppose it was a wedding ring," she posed.

A newspaper in England published a commentary about the song in 2017, which said, "Fifty years on, and we're no wiser as to why Billie Joe did what he did and, in the context of the song and Gentry's intentions, that's just as it should be."

"Ode To Billie Joe" originally was intended to be the "B" side of Gentry's first single, a blues number titled "Mississippi Delta." Gentry's original lyrics had 11 verses and ran over 8 minutes in length in adding to Billie Joe's story. Executives at Capitol Records recognized that the song would work best as an "A" side and cut the length in half to make it palatable for AM radio play.

"Those involved felt it had a number of drawbacks," Gentry has said. "They said it was too long, that it couldn't be categorized and aimed at a specific audience, that I was a female vocalist and soloist, and this was the day of group singers." At the end of the year, *Billboard* rated it as the No. 3 single of 1967.

The all-acoustic recording features a six-string guitar played by Gentry, four violins and two cellos.

The popularity of the song was so enduring that Warner Brothers hired an author to expand the story as a novel and screenplay in the mid-1970s. The result was a movie of the same name being released in 1976 and starring Robby Benson and Glynnis O'Connor.

Following the song's chart run, which saw it ascend to No. 1 only three weeks after its release, another phenomenon occurred. Several individuals visited the Tallahatchie Bridge, wanting to jump from it. Since it was only 20 feet from the bridge floor to the water, death or serious injury was unlikely. To curb the trend, the Leflore County board enacted a law to fine jumpers $100.

Gentry's parents divorced shortly after her birth, and her mother moved to California. She was raised by her paternal grandparents on a farm in Chickasaw County. She began teaching herself to play guitar, bass, banjo and vibraphone.

At the age of 13 she moved to Arcadia, Calif., to live with her mother. After she graduated from high school, she chose her stage name from the 1952 movie *Ruby Gentry*. She performed in a Las Vegas revue and then moved to Los Angeles to enter UCLA as a philosophy major. She later transferred to the Los Angeles Conservatory of Music.

After her early success as a recording star, she became one of three initial investors in the NBA Phoenix Suns expansion franchise. She remained a co-owner until 1987.

Ode To Billie Joe

Songwriter: Bobbie Gentry

Peaked at No. 1 on Billboard Hot 100

Aug. 26, 1967
Sept. 2, 1967
Sept. 9, 1967
Sept. 16, 1967

Bobbie Gentry

Born Roberta Lee Streeter near Woodland in Chickasaw County, Miss., on July 27, 1942

Bobbie Gentry

There Is A Mountain [Donovan] – This folky rock song came from the singer/songwriter who had more success on the American charts than other foreign folk artist. Donovan Leitch is a Scotsman who put 12 songs on the *Billboard* pop chart's top 40, including a No. 1, "Sunshine Superman."

Donovan did the vocals and played acoustic guitar. A flute, bongos and bass accompanied him.

The lyrics refer to a Buddhist mantra formulated by Qingyuan Weixin, a ninth century philosopher whose works were translated by D.T. Suzuki. Qingyuan wrote, "Before I had studied Ch'an (Zen) for thirty years, I saw mountains as mountains and rivers as rivers. When I arrived at a more intimate knowledge, I came to the point where I saw that mountains are not mountains, and rivers are not rivers. But now that I have got its very substance, I am at rest. For it's just that I see mountains once again as mountains, and rivers once again as rivers."

Fittingly, perhaps, the song played behind a television commercial in 2008 in which a silver Toyota RAV4 sport utility vehicle drives up a mountain, then down a mountain, then onto city streets and then up another mountain.

The quizzical lyrics did not hinder record buyers in 1967 as they conquered mountains and city streets to go buy a copy of the 45 rpm single. It rose to No. 11 in the U.S. and No. 8 in the U.K.

This is another folk-oriented song that employs a calypso beat, similar to "Crooked Little Man."

Donovan contracted polio as a child, which left him walking with a limp. His family moved to Hatfield, Hertfordshire, England, when he was young.

Influenced by his family's love of folk music, he began playing the guitar at age 14. Refining his craft by playing live performances and working on his songwriting, he got his first recording contract in 1964.

There Is A Mountain
Songwriter: Donovan Leitch
Peaked at No. 11 on Billboard Hot 100
Sept. 16, 1967
Sept. 23, 1967

Donovan
Born Donovan Philips Leitch in Glasgow, Scotland, on May 10, 1946

Donovan

Up On Cripple Creek [The Band] – Technically, The Band was not a foreign group. But only one of their members was a native-born American, while the others came from Canada.

Bob Dylan hired them to be his backing band in 1965, and they settled in Woodstock, N.Y., where Dylan had established a residence. It was only fitting that some of his folk influence rubbed off on them. The song was written by Robbie Robertson, the lead guitarist and primary songwriter of The Band.

Drummer Levon Helm, from eastern Arkansas, sang lead on this ditty about a truck driver who cavorts with a local girl named Bessie in Lake Charles, La. The song draws from The Band's musical roots of the American South, folk, country and bluegrass. A quirky aspect of the song is the use of a clavinet with wah-wah pedal (see Chapter 6, Motown), played by Garth Hudson.

Robertson has said of the song, "We're not dealing with people at the top of the ladder. We're saying, what about that house out there in the middle of that field? What does this guy think, with that one light on upstairs, and that truck parked out there?

"That's who I'm curious about. What is going on in there? And just following the story of this person, and he just drives these trucks across the whole country, and he knows these characters that he drops in on, on his travels. Just following him with a camera is really what this song is about."

"Up On Cripple Creek" was included in The Band's second of 10 studio albums that they recorded without Dylan. It was released late in 1969 and reached its peak on the *Billboard* pop chart at No. 25 in 1970. In Canada it peaked at No. 10.

The members of The Band originally were known as the Hawks, the backing band for local Toronto rockabilly singer Ronnie Hawkins.

Up On Cripple Creek
Songwriter: J. Robbie Robertson
Peaked at No. 25 on Billboard Hot 100
Jan. 3, 1970

The Band

Levon Helm (May 26, 1940-April 19, 2012) vocals, drums
Robbie Robertson [born Jaime Royal Robertson] (July 5, 1943-) guitar, vocals
Rick Danko (Dec. 29, 1943-Dec. 10, 1999) bass, fiddle
Richard Manuel (April 3, 1943-March 4, 1986) keyboards, drums, vocals
Garth Hudson (Aug. 2, 1937-) keyboards, saxophone, accordion, clavinet
Formed in Toronto, Ontario, Canada, in 1960

The Band: Richard Manuel, Levon Helm, Rick Danko, Garth Hudson, Robbie Robertson

The Night They Drove Old Dixie Down [Joan Baez]) – The "B" side of The Band's single "Up On Cripple Creek" was this song, which was written by Robbie Robertson with help from Levon Helm. Joan Baez made it the biggest "A" side of her career.

Baez sings the part of a male narrator, Virgil Caine, who is serving the Confederacy in the Civil War. Her version of the song is more up-tempo than that of The Band.

Robertson has said that he came up with the melody first and had no idea where the lyrics would go until a concept of a Civil War scenario came to him and he began to research the subject.

Helm, who died of cancer in 2012, wrote in his autobiography, "I remember taking (Robertson) to the (Woodstock) library so he could research the history and geography of the era and make General Robert E. Lee come out with all due respect."

The song's opening lines refer to one of George Stoneman's Union Army raids behind enemy lines, attacking the railroads of Danville, Va., near the end of the war in 1865.

Baez rode the song all the way up to No. 3 on the *Billboard Hot 100*, making it the biggest hit of her folk rock career. It is included in the Rock and Roll Hall of Fame's 500 Songs that Shaped Rock and Roll.

On the *Billboard Adult Contemporary* chart, it spent five weeks at No. 1. *Billboard* ranked it as the No. 20 song for 1971.

Inadvertently, Baez changed some the original lyrics. She later told a writer from *Rolling Stone Magazine* that she learned the song from listening to The Band's recording but had never seen the printed lyrics.

Baez's father was born in Mexico, and her mother was born in Scotland. The family moved from New York to California in the late 1940s so that her father could study at Stanford University.

Her first record album was released in 1960. Her folk songs often include themes of protest and social justice.

The Night They Drove Old Dixie Down

Songwriters: J. Robbie Robertson

Peaked at No. 3 on Billboard Hot 100

Oct. 2, 1971

Joan Baez

Born Joan Chandos Baez in New York City, N.Y., on Jan. 9, 1941

Joan Baez

Carefree Highway [Gordon Lightfoot] – A study of folk rock music would not be complete without including a song from Canadian troubadour par excellence Gordon Lightfoot. Practically any of his many recordings of the 1960s, '70s or '80s deserve inclusion here.

Lightfoot is unparalleled among Canadian folk rock singer/songwriters. He has placed 13 studio albums on the *Billboard 200* chart and 10 singles on the *Billboard Hot 100.*

"Carefree Highway's" title was inspired by a road of the same name in the Phoenix, AZ, area. The thoroughfare starts in the town of Carefree at Tom Darlington Drive and runs west along the north sides of Phoenix and Peoria, ending at U.S. 60 south of Wickenburg.

Lightfoot has said, "I thought it would make a good title for a song. I wrote it down, put it in my suitcase and it stayed there for eight months."

The term, as it is used in the song, refers to a state of mind where the narrator seeks to escape from mental torment over his failed relationship with a woman named Ann. Lightfoot has said that Ann was the name of a romantic interest he had at the age of 22.

"It was one of those situations," Lightfoot said, "where you meet that one woman who knocks you out and then leaves you standing there and says she's on her way."

The song was the follow-up to Lightfoot's only American No. 1 single, "Sundown," in 1974.

Some of the songs he has written have been recorded by such folk rock luminaries as Peter, Paul & Mary, Bob Dylan, Judy Collins, Neil Young, Marty Robbins and the Kingston Trio.

Carefree Highway
Songwriter: Gordon Lightfoot
Peaked at No. 10, 1974
Nov. 9, 1974
Nov. 16, 1974

<u>Gordon Lightfoot</u>
Born Gordon Meredith Lightfoot Jr. in Orillia, Ontario, Canada, on Nov. 17, 1938

Gordon Lightfoot

Chapter 13

The Stars of Blue-Eyed Soul

White singers with a black sound

Overview: The sound that black musicians contributed to music in the American South made rock and roll appealing. It was a trend that needed only a couple of years to take over the pop scene. The rhythms brought from Africa were a key ingredient.

White artists tried cashing in on the quality of the black sound. First they covered hits by black artists, putting their own stamp on such songs. Pat Boone, for example, had enormous success covering Fats Domino ("Ain't That A Shame") and Little Richard ("Long Tall Sally.") Ricky Nelson also covered Domino with "I'm Walkin'."

This practice wore thin after a while, and white artists began to realize that recording new material with black-sounding vocals was a viable path to success. A lot of the music recorded with this template came out of the doo-wop genre. Doo-wop is a style of vocal harmonizing that was started in the population centers of the northeastern states in the 1940s. It was characterized by a simple beat, multi-part harmonies and often no instrumentation. Typically, the songs are love songs.

By the end of the 1950s, singers like Dion DiMucci had refined a bluesy vocal sound that eventually became known as blue-eyed soul. Such artists didn't need to have blue eyes to fit into that classification – they just needed to be white singers who had that great black sound.

Recordings made by blue-eyed soul artists made a good alternative for record buyers who did not like the style of black artists of the day. In a way, this reflects a kind of racism, since record companies deliberately fed hit songs to white artists for the purpose of increasing sales.

A few of the best blue-eyed soul singers are profiled here.

Dion – Born and raised in the Bronx, N.Y., Dion DiMucci is the son of a Vaudeville entertainer, Pasquale DiMucci. As a boy he acquired an affection for his father's Al Jolson recordings, as well as country music that he heard on a local radio station he found by accident.

As a teenager singing on street corners and local clubs, Dion got into the doo-wop genre that was the rage in the late 1950s.

He survived gang membership and heroin addiction before he got the opportunity to record the song "The Chosen Few" for Mohawk Records. He was assigned a group of backing singers called the Timberlanes, whom he thought sounded "counterfeit." Dion responded by going into his neighborhood to find three guys who could serve as credible back-up vocalists – Angelo D'Aleo, Freddie Milano and Carlo Mastrangelo. The trio took the name the Belmonts, after Belmont Avenue in the Bronx, and the group became known as Dion & the Belmonts.

They ended up being the first group signed by Gene Schwartz on his new label, Laurie Records. They made seven top 40 recordings together between 1957 and 1960 before Dion decided it was time to go solo. Subsequently, his career kicked into overdrive, and he was one of the top male vocalists in the world until the British Invasion came along in 1964.

Dion signed with Columbia Records in 1962, and that major label showcased 20 of his soulful recordings on an album titled "Bronx Blues." This was the release that identified Dion as one of the first blue-eyed soul artists. Dion also was one of the first artists in the rock era to go by just his first name.

His biggest single was the No. 1 hit "Runaround Sue" in 1961. Dion, who married a woman named Sue, said that he wrote the song about a girl named Roberta.

After a forced four-year retirement due to the wild popularity of British music, Dion was living in Miami when Schwartz asked Florida record producer Phil Gernhard (see Chapter 3, Reality Meets Pop) to deliver to Dion a song titled "Abraham, Martin And John." Dion was at first reluctant to record a song about the assassinations of three men. But he relented when he saw the positive message in the song, and his single went to No. 4 on the *Billboard* pop chart in the fall of 1968. It was to be Dion's 21st and final top 40 hit.

Dion continued recording albums through the 1970s, '80s and '90s, on into the 21st century. Some received critical acclaim, while most were commercial failures.

Dion

Born Dion Francis DiMucci in the Bronx, New York City, N.Y., on July 18, 1939

Dion

Significant songs:

I Wonder Why [with the Belmonts]
No One Knows [with the Belmonts]
A Teenager In Love [with the Belmonts]
Where Or When [with the Belmonts]
Lonely Teenager
Runaround Sue
The Wanderer
The Majestic
Lovers Who Wander
Little Diane
Love Came To Me
Ruby Baby
Sandy
This Little Girl
Be Careful Of Stones that You Throw
Donna The Prima Donna
Drip Drop
Abraham, Martin And John

The Righteous Brothers – Two guys from Orange County, Calif., comprised this duo. The term "blue-eyed soul" came into common use after they became popular.

Bill Medley, from Santa Ana, was a member of the Paramours in the early 1960s, while Anaheim resident Bobby Hatfield was a member of the Variations. Medley and his guitar player joined with Hatfield and his drummer to form a new version of the Paramours. They released one single for Moonglow Records in 1962, "There She Goes (She's Walking Away)," but the group didn't have much success. After the Paramours broke up, Medley and Hatfield were left to perform as a duo.

They had contrasting vocal sounds, with Medley bellowing a baritone and Hatfield singing tenor. When they played at John's Black Derby nightclub in Santa Ana, the African-American Marines in the audience (stationed at El Toro Marine Corps Air Station) would shout at the end of the performance, "That's righteous, brothers!" That phrase turned their soulful sound into their new name.

They recorded a couple of singles that failed to catch on, but their big break came when they were part of an 11-act show at San Francisco's Cow Palace. It was there that they met producer Phil Spector, who was so impressed that he bought out the final two and a half years of their contract with Moonglow and signed them to his Philles label.

In late 1964 Spector brought New York songwriters Barry Mann and Cynthia Weil out to Los Angeles to write a song especially for the Righteous Brothers. They checked into the Chateau Marmont hotel on the Sunset Strip, rented a piano and began to write a ballad. They were inspired by their favorite song at the time, "Baby I Need Your Lovin'" by the Four Tops.

The result was "You've Lost That Lovin' Feelin'." The song was completed at Spector's house, where he, Mann and Weil wrote the bridge. By Feb. 6, 1965, the single was No. 1 on the *Billboard Hot 100.*

They had a second No. 1 single, "(You're My) Soul And Inspiration" in 1966.

"You've Lost That Lovin' Feelin'" also was a No. 1 song in the U.K. and entered the U.K. top 10 on three different chart runs. The song has been described by various music critics as "one of the best records ever made" and "the ultimate pop record."

Brian Wilson, the chief songwriter of the Beach Boys, called Mann and Weil to tell them, "Your song is the greatest record ever. I was ready to quit the music business, but this has inspired me to write again."

It was perhaps the best example of Spector's "wall of sound" technique, in which he had the instrumental tracks recorded first, adding layers of sound upon each other. When Medley and Hatfield began recording their vocals, they required about 40 takes which consumed about eight hours of studio time over two days.

Heretofore, Spector had worked with only black singers. Thanks to the blue-eyed soul sound of the Righteous Brothers, the white duo gave Spector the biggest hit he ever produced.

In December 1999, Broadcast Music Inc. ranked the song as the most-played on radio and television in the 20th century with 8 million airplays. That total had reached 15 million by 2011.

The duo had several other chart successes over the next few years, although they had periods where they did not perform together. They also were a highly popular concert act. I saw their show at the Orleans Showroom in Las Vegas. Shortly after that, Hatfield died of heart failure, reportedly brought on by cocaine ingestion on Nov. 5, 2003. He was 63.

Righteous Brothers

Bill Medley

Born William Thomas Medley on Sept. 19, 1940, in Santa Ana, Calif.

Bobby Hatfield

Aug. 10, 1940-Nov. 5, 2003

Born Robert Lee Hatfield in Beaver Dam, Wis., and died in Kalamazoo, Mich.

Bill Medley and Bobby Hatfield

Significant songs:

You've Lost That Lovin' Feelin'

(You're My) Soul And Inspiration

Just Once In My Life
Unchained Melody
Ebb Tide
Little Latin Lupe Lu
Go Ahead And Cry
Rock And Roll Heaven
Give It To The People
Dream On

The Walker Brothers – Like the Righteous Brothers, there were no blood relations in this group. And none of the three had a birth name of Walker. But before their singing careers were over, all three would change their name to Walker.

The Los Angeles trio formed in 1964 and consisted of Noel Scott Engel (Scott Walker), John Maus (John Walker) and Gary Leeds (Gary Walker). They had TV appearances on *Shindig!* and *Ninth Street A Go Go,* and they appeared in a movie, *Beach Ball.*

The Walker Brothers' business model was different from that of most American musicians. In 1965 they left their homeland and went to England to seek success. Leeds's stepfather provided financial backing for the trip.

They secured a contract with Philips Records and put several hits on the U.K. charts. Then they recorded a song by celebrated Brill Building songwriters Burt Bacharach and Hal David, "Make It Easy On Yourself." The song hit No. 1 in England and later was released in the U.S., where it peaked at No. 16. This was the Walker Brothers' first appearance on the American charts, which prompted many industry observers to assume that the group with the blue-eyed soul sound was British.

Their next single was "The Sun Ain't Gonna Shine (Anymore)," which also hit No. 1 in the United Kingdom and gained top 20 status on the American charts. The group's popularity soared in the U.K., and their fan club was said to be larger than that of the Beatles.

But the Walker Brothers seemed to have one fatal flaw: they sounded too much like the Righteous Brothers. Their success in the States died on the vine as the Righteous Brothers put hit after hit on the charts. The same fate befell several male vocalists who had sounded too much like Elvis Presley in the early 1960s.

The Walkers continued to have success on the other side of the pond in 1966 and '67, with heartthrob Scott Walker doing most of the lead vocals and taking a prominent role in their song choices and arrangements. But they had to leave England for six months in 1967 because of work permit problems.

As the direction of pop music moved into the psychedelic era, the Walker Brothers no longer were trending. After a U.K. tour at the end of 1967, followed by a tour in Japan in '68, they disbanded.

The Walker Brothers

Gary Leeds (March 9, 1942-)
Scott Engel (Jan. 9, 1943-March 22, 2019)
John Maus (Nov. 12, 1943-May 7, 2011)

The Walker Brothers: John Maus, Scott Engel, Gary Leeds

Significant songs:

Make It Easy On Yourself
The Sun Ain't Gonna Shine (Anymore)
No Regrets
My Ship Is Coming In
Another Tear Falls
(Baby) You Don't Have To Tell Me
Walking In The Rain
Stay With Me Baby
First Love Never Dies
Love Her
We're All Alone
Just Say Goodbye

Johnny Rivers – Born in New York City and raised in Baton Rouge, La., Johnny Rivers got the big break of his musical career in Los Angeles, where he was offered a contract in 1964 to play shows at the new Whisky A Go Go nightclub. The staples of his act were reworked songs that had been hits for artists like Chuck Berry, Harold Dorman, Willie Dixon and Pete Seeger.

Several of Rivers' shows were recorded and turned into "live" albums that were big sellers. Some of his tracks were recorded in a studio with crowd noise added. Most of his numbers were up-tempo and suitable for dancing.

But after two and a half years of milking this successful formula, Rivers was ready for a change. In 1966 he wrote and recorded the ballad "Poor Side Of Town, which became his only No. 1 hit. The next year he covered a couple of Motown classics, "Baby I Need Your Lovin'" (Four Tops) and "Tracks Of My Tears" (Miracles).

Those two smashes hit the top 10 and established Rivers as one of the giants of blue-eyed soul. In 1972, Rivers did a remake of Huey "Piano" Smith's "Rockin' Pneumonia and the Boogie Woogie Flu," which rose to No. 6 and cemented him as a top blue-eyed soul contributor.

Rivers' first two singles were "Memphis" and "Maybelline," which were written and originally made popular by Chuck Berry. On April 9, 2017, Rivers sang a song and accompanied himself on acoustic guitar at Berry's funeral in St. Louis, Mo.

"I grew up in Louisiana. If you think about it, all of my hits, except maybe 'Memphis,' were rooted in the blues," Rivers has said. "When I was at the Whisky, I was playing Fats Domino and Jimmy Reed songs. I was doing John Lee Hooker songs in 1964. Who was doing John Lee Hooker in 1964?

"People don't realize how much my music is rooted in the blues, because all my records hit pop. That's the way you had to do it, because a straight blues record wouldn't even get played on the radio at that time."

Johnny Rivers

Born John Henry Ramistella in New York City, N.Y., on Nov. 7, 1942

Johnny Rivers

Significant songs:

Memphis
Maybelline
Where Have All The Flowers Gone
Under Your Spell Again

Mountain Of Love
Midnight Special
Seventh Son
Baby I Need Your Lovin'
The Tracks Of My Tears
Summer Rain
Rockin' Pneumonia - Boogie Woogie Flu
Secret Agent Man
(I Washed My Hands In) Muddy Water
Poor Side Of Town
Blue Suede Shoes
Help Me Rhonda
Swayin' To The Music (Slow Dancin')

The Young Rascals – From 1966 to '69 this group duked it out, figuratively, with the Lovin' Spoonful for the title of best band in New York City. They were rockers who were heavily influenced by rhythm & blues music.

Three members – Felix Cavaliere, Eddie Brigati and Gene Cornish – had been members of Joey Dee's Starliters. Jazz drummer Dino Danelli had played with Cavalieri and Brigati in earlier years, and they asked him to join their new band in 1965. They wanted to name themselves the Rascals, but there already was a band called the Harmonica Rascals. Without their knowledge, Young Rascals was selected for them by the staff at Atlantic Records.

Their first No. 1 single was "Good Lovin'" in 1966, a song that had been recorded the previous year by a black group, the Olympics.

By the time their album "Groovin'" was released in 1967, the Young Rascals were at their soulful best. The title track spent four weeks at No. 1 and was powered by the soulful lead vocal of Cavalieri. It was knocked out of the top spot after two weeks, spent two weeks at No. 2, then went back to No. 1 for two more weeks.

After their first two singles, the Young Rascals were inspired by the Beatles to write their own songs.

On a tour of England in 1966, the Young Rascals found that members of such top British acts as the Rolling Stones, the Animals and the Beatles liked their brand of R&B and were attending their shows.

By 1968 Cavalieri, Brigati, Cornish and Danelli convinced Atlantic that they could legally drop the word "Young" from their name. The shortened moniker did not hurt their popularity, and they scored their third No. 1 song in the summer of '68, "People Got To Be Free."

Amid internal tensions, Brigati quit the group in 1970. Cornish left the following year, and the band officially folded in 1972.

The Young Rascals

Felix Cavaliere (Nov. 29, 1942-) vocals, keyboards
Eddie Brigati (Oct. 22, 1945-) vocals, tambourine, maracas
Dino Danelli (July 23, 1944-) drums
Gene Cornish (May 14, 1944-) guitar, harmonica
Formed in Garfield, N.J., in 1965

The Young Rascals: Gene Cornish, Dino Danelli, Felix Cavalieri, Eddie Brigati

Significant songs:

I Ain't Gonna Eat Out My Heart Anymore	It's Wonderful
Good Lovin'	A Beautiful Morning
Mustang Sally	People Got To Be Free
I've Been Lonely Too Long	A Ray Of Hope
Groovin'	Heaven
A Girl Like You	See
How Can I Be Sure	Carry Me Back

The Box Tops – This all-white band had a leg up on most other blue-eyed soul acts because they hailed from Memphis, the home of a lot of great soul and blues music.

Sun Records and Stax Records were the two major labels based in Memphis, and Stax and its affiliated label Volt recorded a lot of the great rhythm & blues music that came out of the 1960s and '70s.

The Box Tops also had a lead singer whose voice was dripping with soul. That young man was Alex Chilton, who had a voice so deep that it belied his age of 16 when he recorded the Box Tops' first song, "The Letter." It took the nation by storm in 1967, spending four weeks at No. 1 and finishing the year as *Billboard's* No. 2 song of '67.

The Box Tops started out as five friends who were in five different bands in high school. A local disc jockey introduced them to Dan Penn, who was writing and producing for acts at Memphis' American Recording Studios. On the day that they began sessions for "The Letter," they gathered at ARS but still didn't have a name.

Wayne Carson Thompson had written "The Letter" and was on hand to play guitar on the track. He related that one of the band members said, "Well, let's have a contest, and everybody can send in 50 cents and a box top." Penn looked at Thompson and knew at that instant that they had a name for the band.

While their singles were all original material, they sprinkled remakes of some of Memphis' soulful songs throughout their albums.

Rock critic Lester Bangs wrote, "A song like 'Soul Deep' is obvious enough, a patented commercial sound. Yet, within these strictures, it communicates with a depth and sincerity of feeling that holds the attention and brings you back often."

The Box Tops put seven hits in the *Billboard* top 40 and had their last hit in 1970. After that they broke up, and Chilton went on to a solo career and membership in a band called Big Star.

Chilton found himself in New Orleans in 1982, trying to prop up his music career by washing dishes in a restaurant, working as a janitor in a nightclub and trimming trees. He died of a heart attack in New Orleans in 2010 at the age of 59.

Original members Gary Talley and Bill Cunningham were part of a re-formed Box Tops that joined the Turtles' Happy Together Tour in 2017.

The Box Tops

Alex Chilton (Dec. 28, 1950-March 17, 2010) vocals
Bill Cunningham (Jan. 23, 1950-) bass, keyboards
Gary Talley (Aug. 17, 1947-) guitar
Rick Allen (Jan. 28, 1946-) bass
Thomas Boggs (July 16, 1944-May 5, 2008) drums
Formed in Memphis, Tenn., in 1967

The Box Tops

Significant songs:

The Letter
Neon Rainbow
Cry Like A Baby
Break My Mind
She Shot A Hole In My Soul
Sweet Cream Ladies, Forward March
Choo Choo Train
I Met Her In Church
I Shall Be Released
Together
I See Only Sunshine
Soul Deep

Daryl Hall and John Oates – Philadelphia was the home of this talented duo, and the City of Brotherly Love just so happened to be the home of many great soul artists in the 1960s and '70s. Some of the top groups were the Delfonics, the Stylistics, the Intruders, the Three Degrees, the O'Jays, the Spinners and Harold Melvin & the Blue Notes – all black artists.

These great acts served as inspiration for Hall & Oates, who met in 1967 in a service elevator when trying to sidestep a fight between rival black gangs at a record hop in the Adelphi Ballroom in Philadelphia. They both were attending Temple University at the time.

They officially became a recording act in 1970. "We basically tried to combine rhythm and blues and progressive music," John Oates said.

It took five albums before they released one that had a No. 1 single on it. The album was "Bigger Than The Both Of Us," and the 1977 single was "Rich Girl." They would record five more No. 1 hits before the end of 1984.

Daryl Hall's talent as a writer and singer was mostly responsible for the duo's success.

"We had to see what we were," Hall told *Creem Magazine* in explaining the lengthy wait for superstardom. "We made our mistakes in public, on record. We were in a learning process through the '70s, which were really not a very conducive time to do the kind of music we wanted to make."

The two found that renting an apartment in Greenwich Village, working at Electric Lady Studios in Manhattan and producing their own songs was a better way to get their vision of their sound onto record.

"We don't have to bother trying to communicate to other people," Hall told *Billboard.* "We always had a problem with it. That's one reason our sound kept changing so much, because the production style was changing so much." Hall & Oates also started recording with their own road band instead of session musicians.

Hall & Oates have sold about 40 million records, which makes them the best-selling duo in music history. *Billboard* has placed them at No. 15 on its list of the 100 greatest recording artists of all time.

After the release of their album "Big Bam Boom" in late 1984, Hall & Oates retired, sort of, citing the fact that they were on top of the pop music industry and had nowhere to go but down. The following year Hall released the second of his six solo albums (the first had been recorded in 1977 and was released by RCA in 1980.) He put two singles in the *Billboard* top 40.

They got back together to record albums in 1988, '90, '97, 2003 and '04, and they made a Christmas album in 2006. The single "Anything Your Heart Desires" hit No. 3 in 1988 and was their last top 10 song.

In the new millennium, Hall created a music show that was taped first in his home and then from his restaurant. It was called *Live From Daryl's House,* and it was carried first as an Internet webcast and then became a syndicated television show.

Each hour-long show featured a different guest solo singer or band playing with Hall and his band, along with a home cooked meal prepared by a chef who usually was from the New York City area.

Daryl Hall

Born Daryl Franklin Hohl in Pottstown, Pa., on Oct. 11, 1946

Vocals, guitar, keyboards

John Oates

Born John William Oates in New York City, N.Y., on April 11, 1948

Guitar, vocals

Daryl Hall & John Oates

Significant songs:

She's Gone
Sara Smile
Do What You Want, Be What You Are
Rich Girl
Back Together Again
It's A Laugh
Wait For Me
How Does It Feel To Be Back
You've Lost That Lovin' Feeling
Kiss On My List
You Make My Dreams
Private Eyes
I Can't Go For That (No Can Do)
Don't Hold Back Your Love
Did It In A Minute
Your Imagination
Maneater
One On One
Family Man
Say It Isn't So
Adult Education
Out Of Touch
Method Of Modern Love
Some Things Are Better Left Unsaid
Possession Obsession
Everything Your Heart Desires
So Close
Do It For Love

Boz Scaggs – It's hard to say what this guy calls his hometown – his father moved the family a lot because he was a traveling salesman. William "Boz" Scaggs spent his formative years in Plano, Texas, near Dallas. He learned to play guitar at the age of 12.

It was at St. Mark's School in Dallas that he met future rock star Steve Miller in 1959. Scaggs would team with Miller in bands while they attended the University of Wisconsin, and he appeared on the first two albums of the Steve Miller Band.

Also at St. Mark's, a schoolmate gave him the nickname "Bosley," which was shortened to Boz.

Scaggs left school in the mid-1960s to join the rhythm & blues scene in London, England, and moved on to Sweden to perform as a solo act. Back in the States, his early albums struggled to attract sales, but his material got progressively better.

The pinnacle of his career came in 1976 with the release of the album "Silk Degrees." It spawned four singles while peaking at No. 2 on the *Billboard 200* album chart. It also set up Scaggs with concert tours for months to come.

The single "Lowdown" sold over one million copies in the United States and won a Grammy Award for best R&B song.

Scaggs remained true to his blues roots throughout his career, and his 2015 album "A Fool To Care" hit No. 1 on the *Billboard* blues chart.

"As a guitar player, you can gravitate toward the blues because you can play it easily," Scaggs has said. "It's not a style that's difficult to pick up. It's purely emotive and dead easy to get a start with.

"I really just followed my musical instincts every step of my life.

"Quite frankly, I've always listened to the black side of the radio dial. Where I grew up, there was a lot of it, and there was a lot of live music around."

Boz Scaggs

Born William Royce Scaggs in Canton, Ohio, on June 8, 1944

Boz Scaggs

Significant songs:

Dinah Flo
You Can Have Me Anytime
It's Over
Lowdown
What Can I Say
Lido Shuffle
Hard Times
Hollywood
Breakdown Dead Ahead
JoJo
Look What You've Done To Me
Miss Sun

Robert Palmer – This Englishman was born in Yorkshire County but spent much of his youth in Scarborough. He took an interest in blues, soul and jazz music because that's what he heard on American Armed Forces Radio.

Palmer joined his first band at age 15. After stints in other bands, he became a solo artist in 1974 by signing with Island Records. He took up residency in New York City as a base for recording and touring before relocating to Nassau, Bahamas.

It was there, at Compass Point Studios, that Palmer recorded the album "Double Fun," a collection of Caribbean-influenced songs. One of them was "Every Kinda People," which got him on the American charts for the first time.

The 1980s saw an increase in Palmer's popularity. He became part of a supergroup called the Power Station with John Taylor, Andy Taylor and Tony Thompson and then recorded his first solo No. 1 hit, "Addicted To Love." A side benefit of that record was a 1987 Grammy Award for best male rock vocal performance.

Other successful singles followed, as well as notable music videos made for television. His suave appearance in immaculate suits and neckties prompted famous disc jockey Casey Kasem to call Palmer the "best-dressed man in rock and roll." *Rolling Stone* named him best-dressed male artist in 1990.

Concerned about the crime rate in Nassau, he moved to Lugano, Switzerland, in '87. He set up his own recording studio and crafted another hit album. "Heavy Nova" was a group of experimental songs that combined heavy rock with bossa nova rhythms and white-soul vocals.

Concerning the excesses of the rock and roll lifestyle, Palmer once said, "I loved the music, but the excesses of rock and roll never really appealed to me at all. I couldn't see the point of getting up in front of a lot of people when you weren't in control of your wits." His girlfriend at the time of his death, American Mary Ambrose, revealed that he liked to stay at home nights building model airplanes and trucks.

Palmer died of a heart attack on Sept. 26, 2003, in a Paris hotel room. He was 54. Reportedly, he was a heavy smoker.

Robert Palmer

Jan. 19, 1949-Sept. 26, 2003

Born Robert Allen Palmer in Batley, West Riding of Yorkshire, England, and died in Paris

Robert Palmer

Significant songs:

Sneakin' Sally Through The Alley
Every Kinda People
Bad Case Of Loving You (Doctor, Doctor)
Can We Still Be Friends
Some Guys Have All The Luck
Some Like It Hot [with Power Station]
Get It On (Bang A Gong)
You're Amazing
Addicted To Love
I Didn't Mean To Turn You On
Simply Irresistible
Communication [with Power Station]
Hyperactive
Early In The Morning
Tell Me I'm Not Dreaming
Mercy Mercy Me (The Ecology)

The Doobie Brothers – A familiar situation here: despite the familial wording in the band's name, there were no members named Doobie and no brothers.

They got their name from a guy who lived in the house where some of the members resided. One day he quipped, "Hey, you guys smoke so many joints, why don't you just call yourselves the Doobie Brothers?"

The band from San Jose, Calif., started out as a bunch of rockers in 1970 and first hit the pop charts in 1972. But they would not be able to stay that course.

On the eve of a concert tour in 1975, founder-guitarist-lead singer Tom Johnston was sidelined with bleeding ulcers. That forced the band to make an emergency hire, and Michael McDonald was brought in as Johnston's replacement. Keyboardist McDonald had played with Doobie guitar player Jeff Baxter in the band Steely Dan.

"In reality, I didn't really come with any expectations of even staying," McDonald told *Newsweek*. "I was just kind of hired on for a summer, a string of dates when (Johnston) had taken a medical leave. He was dealing with some pretty serious health issues. And they always kind of wished they had had a keyboard player. They were pretty much a guitar band, so rather than just hire another guitar player, they decided to go for keyboards.

"What started out as a temporary summer job became permanent employment with the band, and from that point on it was pretty much a group metamorphosis. My songs were maybe a little different than stuff they had done before, but we were always, collectively, a band. I would say that Jeff Baxter probably deserves as much credit as anyone for the change in direction of the band. Pat Simmons, also.

"The one thing the band was determined not to do was just try to fill the void, the great void, that was Tommy being gone with a Tommy soundalike or a Tommy wannabe, if you know what I mean. They figured, 'Hey, while we're at this juncture, we might as well just follow a musical path, whatever that is.'"

Although Johnston briefly returned to the Doobies in 1976, McDonald was on the way to transforming the band into an R&B driven group. Johnston went out on a solo career in '77, and McDonald remained as lead singer until the Doobie Brothers broke up in 1982.

With his soulful voice and his work on keyboards, McDonald dramatically changed the musical direction on the Doobies. And public response was positive. The first two albums with McDonald on board contained several hits, but the third was literally off the charts. "Minute By Minute" spent five weeks on top of the *Billboard 200* chart, and the single "What A Fool Believes" went to No. 1. Both the album and single won Grammy Awards.

The Doobies followed with another album, "One Step Closer," which produced another top 10 single for them. But the album could not match its predecessor. There was an over-saturation of the "McDonald sound" on the market, created in part by his numerous guest vocal appearances on records by Christopher Cross, Nicolette Larson, Kenny Loggins and others.

After the break-up, McDonald quickly embarked on a solo career. In 1986 he collaborated with Patti LaBelle on the No. 1 single "On My Own."

The Doobie Brothers (lineup 1976-1983)
Michael McDonald (Feb. 12, 1952-) vocals, keyboards
Patrick Simmons (Oct. 19, 1948-) guitar, piano, flute
Jeff "Skunk" Baxter (Dec. 13, 1948-) guitar
John Hartman (March 18, 1950-) drums
Bobby LaKind (Nov. 3, 1945-Dec. 24, 1992) congas, percussion
Tiran Porter (Sept. 26, 1948-) bass
Formed in San Jose, Calif., in 1970

Doobie Brothers: Jeff Baxter, John Hartman, Michael McDonald, Patrick Simmons, Tiran Porter, Bobby LaKind

Significant songs:

Listen To The Music
Jesus Is Just Alright
Rockin' Down The Highway
Long Train Runnin'
China Grove
Another Park, Another Sunday
Black Water
Take Me In Your Arms (Rock Me)
Takin' It To The Streets
It Keeps You Runnin'
Little Darling (I Need You)
Echoes Of Love
What A Fool Believes
Minute By Minute
Dependin' On You
Real Love
One Step Closer
You Belong To Me

Glenn Frey – After the Eagles broke up in 1980, founding member Glenn Frey did not sit moping for long. He got busy building a solo career, and he turned to his Michigan roots to flavor his new songs with Motown-inspired soul.

His first album, "No Fun Aloud" in 1982, gave Frey the freedom to express the way he felt about the music he had grown up with. Frey was born in Detroit and grew up in suburban Royal Oak.

Former Eagle Don Felder commented in *Rolling Stone*, "… Glenn wanted to go out and work by himself. He wanted to be free of that Eagles pressure cooker. It was an enormous amount of stress, and it wasn't sitting well with him. He wanted to go out and have fun and make his records, and even though it was a shock to us when he said he was leaving the band, I got it. That's what he wanted and needed to do."

And, speaking of busy, Frey did more than just create new music. In the 1980s he started working as a television and film actor and also did TV commercials. He even had time to squeeze in some concert tours.

Probably the pinnacle of Frey's blue-eyed soul works was the 1988 album "Soul Searchin'," a collection of songs that presented Frey at his soulful best. It was a stark contrast to his early days with the Eagles when he was co-writing and singing several of their country-rock songs.

His status as a blue-eyed soul star faded when the Eagles got back together in 1994. Their many concert tours over the next 20 years, however, would include some of Frey's solo gems, like "You Belong To The City."

Since 2009 Frey has been an inductee of the Michigan Rock and Roll Legends Hall of Fame.

Frey died in New York City from complications of rheumatoid arthritis, acute ulcerative colitis and pneumonia on Jan. 18, 2016. He was 67.

Glenn Frey

Nov. 6, 1948-Jan. 18, 2016

Born Glenn Lewis Frey in Detroit, Mich., and died In New York City, N.Y.

Glenn Frey

Significant songs:

I Found Somebody
The One You Love
Don't Give Up
Partytown
All Those Lies
Sexy Girl
The Allnighter
The Heat Is On
Smuggler's Blues
You Belong To The City
True Love
Soul Searchin'
Livin' Right
Part Of Me, Part Of You
I've Got Mine
Love In The 21st Century

Steve Winwood – Like Alex Chilton of the Box Tops, Englishman Steve Winwood was fronting a band that was on the American charts before his 18th birthday. Winwood sang lead for the Spencer Davis Group on several recordings in 1966-67, then he quit "because I didn't want to continue playing and singing songs that were derivative of American R&B," he told *Musician Magazine.*

With Spencer Davis Group, Winwood was best known for his gruff lead vocal on "Gimme Some Lovin'" in 1967. Before leaving the group, he made friends with Dave Mason and Jim Capaldi, with whom he would team up in the band Traffic. Psychedelic pop was their first direction, but Winwood steered Traffic in a more bluesy, soulful direction after Mason left.

He worked with Eric Clapton, Ginger Baker and Ric Grech in the short-lived band Blind Faith, providing keyboards. He is a multi-instrumentalist.

Winwood's second solo album, "Arc Of A Diver," got him noticed in the U.S. again in 1980. It spawned his first solo single hit, "While You See A Chance." Two albums later ("Back In The High Life") in 1986, he released the single "Higher Love," which became his first *Billboard* No. 1. Soul icon Chaka Khan added soaring backing vocals to that song and her drummer, John Robinson, played awesome timbale-style tom-tom percussion on the intro.

The title track from the 1988 album "Roll With It" became Winwood's second No. 1 single, spending four weeks at the top of the *Billboard Hot 100.* Trumpeter Wayne Jackson and saxophonist Andrew Love of the Memphis Horns added to the track's soulful sound.

Proving his soul chops once again, he recorded a version of "It's All Right" in 1994 for the album "A Tribute To Curtis Mayfield."

"It's not fair someone should have all that talent," recording engineer Terry Brown joked in an interview with *Uncut Magazine.* "Steve's singing is phenomenal, and his feel – it's just in his DNA – there's no doubt. It always seemed effortless."

Winwood has shunned the rock lifestyle in favor of a farm in Gloustershire County in southwest England. He also has a home in Tennessee, where he met his current wife, Eugenia. Their daughter Lilly also is a singer.

Steve Winwood

Born Stephen Lawrence Winwood in Handsworth, Birmingham, England, on May 12, 1948

Steve Winwood

Significant songs:

While You See A Chance
Arc Of A Diver
Valerie
Talking Back To The Night
Higher Love
Freedom Overspill
Roll With It
The Finer Things
Don't You Know What The Night Can Do?
Holding On
Hearts On Fire
One And Only Man
Another Deal Goes Down
Split Decision
Back In The High Life Again
Still In The Game

Michael Bolton – Connecticut native Michael Bolton took a shot at a career in hard rock music. He performed in a band called Blackjack, which lasted only from 1979-80. After that he decided to take his career in a different direction.

A talented songwriter, he first attracted attention when Laura Branigan made a hit out of his song "How Am I Supposed To Live Without You" in 1983.

Bolton hit the top 20 as a solo singer three times before he turned "How Am I Supposed ..." into a No. 1 smash. It came off "Soul Provider," an album which quickly established him as a blue-eyed soul star.

He also did a successful cover version of Otis Redding's "(Sittin' On) The Dock Of The Bay," which went to No. 11 on the *Hot 100.* Zelma Redding, Otis's widow, remarked that "it brought tears to my eyes. It reminded me so much of my husband that I know if he heard it, he would feel the same."

In 1991 Bolton garnered a second No. 1 hit with his version of Percy Sledge's "When A Man Loves A Woman." A Grammy Award for favorite pop/rock male artist followed in '92.

Bolton has performed with other soulful artists such as Ray Charles, Patti LaBelle, B.B. King and Percy Sledge. He also has shared the microphone with singers of various styles, such as Jose Carreras, Celine Dion, Placido Domingo, Luciano Pavarotti and Wynonna Judd. He has done his songwriting alone and as a collaborator.

Bolton's record sales are near the 60 million mark.

"People often ask, 'How do you feel that people are being conceived to your music?'" he told the *Independent* in England. "Well, I feel good about it. Naturally."

Michael Bolton

Born Michael Bolotin in New Haven, Conn., on Feb. 26, 1953

Michael Bolton

Significant Songs:

That's What Love Is All About
(Sittin' On) The Dock Of The Bay
Soul Provider
How Am I Supposed To Live Without You
How Can We Be Lovers?
When I'm Back On My Feet Again
Georgia On My Mind
Love Is A Wonderful Thing
Time, Love And Tenderness
When A Man Loves A Woman
Missing You Now [with Kenny G]
To Love Somebody
Said I Loved You ... But I Lied
Go The Distance

Chapter 14

The Art of Rock

Songs that reveal the artistic side of rock

Overview: When the Beatles returned to England following their 1965 North American concert tour, they had nothing planned except the production of a new album that was to be ready for the Christmas season. There were no film, concert or radio commitments on their calendar.

Since 1963 their manager, Brian Epstein, had scheduled a new album release each year for holiday purchases.

The summer of '65 had been stimulating for the Fab Four. They had met Bob Dylan while in New York and Elvis Presley while in Los Angeles, two musical icons whom they admired.

The Beatles took these meetings, as well as soulful songs they'd heard on American radio, as inspiration for their next record. Experiences that the foursome had gained through literature and drug use also found their way into the writing of the new work, which was to be titled "Rubber Soul."

Expanded use of the recording studio also was to be exploited, as the Beatles began to venture away from love songs to create music that had other themes – songs that contained a personal nature for the first time in the band's existence, and the four members were in complete creative control.

The two Beatles albums that followed "Rubber Soul" would show further development of what would become known as art rock – "Revolver" and "Sgt. Pepper's Lonely Hearts Club Band."

The songs that emerged from the sessions of autumn 1965 formed a stunning template for other artists who began to create thematic recordings with a sophistication that had never before been heard. Instrumentation that was unconventional for rock music became commonplace, and both British and American bands pushed the limits of recording studios. For the first time we heard sitar, Vox Continental organ, harmonium and stringed ensembles. Bells, maracas, cowbell and Hammond organ also were used throughout the 14 tracks of "Rubber Soul."

Magnetic tape recording was introduced in 1945, and multi-track recording was used almost immediately. Although we have studios using 24-track equipment today, four-track recorders were the state of the art in the 1960s. This limitation inspired musicians, producers (such as George Martin) and engineers (such as Norman Smith) to come up with gimmicks that would expand the listening experience.

The result of the "Rubber Soul" innovations was tracks of extraordinary length that sometimes told intricate stories. The following songs are great examples of rock music that truly displayed an artistic side of the genre.

To view the full lyrics to these songs, please log on to www.google.com, enter song titles & artist names and click Google Search.

To listen to these songs, please log on to www.youtube.com and enter song titles & artist names.

In My Life [Beatles] – John Lennon is responsible for most of the content of this song. There is some disagreement as to how much Paul McCartney contributed to the melody. A 2018 study that used bag-of-words modeling to analyze the song indicated that the music was entirely composed by Lennon. This method analyzes words, phrasing and chord progressions that a writer has used throughout his/her work in order to determine the likelihood of that person writing a particular piece.

The writing credit goes to both Lennon and McCartney, however, due to an arrangement the two Beatles made years previously.

The song was a departure for Lennon because it had lyrics that came from his personal life. Those lyrics drew from his childhood in Liverpool. It was practically the first Beatles song that didn't have to do with boy/girl relationships (I counted only two such songs that they recorded in 1963-65).

Like some other songs on the album "Rubber Soul," the Beatles used the recording studio as an instrument, tinkering with tape speeds, introducing new instruments and using other gimmicks. This strategy was a great innovation and one that Brian Wilson and the Beach Boys would embrace.

The song began as a poem describing a bus route Lennon used to take in Liverpool, and it named various sites along the ride. He later viewed the lyrics as "ridiculous" and reworked them to turn specific memories into a generalized evaluation of his past. According to Lennon's friend and biographer Peter Shotton, the line "some are dead and some are living" refers to Shotton and to deceased former Beatle Stu Sutcliffe, who died in 1962.

The Beatles' producer, the late George Martin, played the beautiful baroque piano solo on the instrumental break. The recording tape was run at half speed, and when it was played back at full speed it sounded like a harpsichord.

Lennon supplied the vocals (which were overdubbed) and rhythm guitar; George Harrison harmony vocal and lead guitar; McCartney harmony vocal and bass; and Ringo Starr drums, tambourine and bells.

Rolling Stone Magazine ranked the song No. 23 on its list of the "500 Greatest Songs of All Time." In 2000, *Mojo Magazine* ranked it as the best song of all time.

Like practically every Beatles album, "Rubber Soul" did not contain any single releases.

In My Life

Songwriters: John Lennon, Paul McCartney
Included on the album "Rubber Soul
Peaked at No. 1 on Billboard 200
Jan. 8-Feb. 12, 1966

The Beatles

John Lennon (Oct. 9, 1940-Dec. 8, 1980) rhythm guitar, vocals
Paul McCartney (June 18, 1942-) bass, vocals
George Harrison (Feb. 25, 1943-Nov. 29, 2001) lead guitar, vocals
Ringo Starr (July 7, 1940-) drums
Formed in Liverpool, England, in 1960. They officially went their separate ways in 1970.

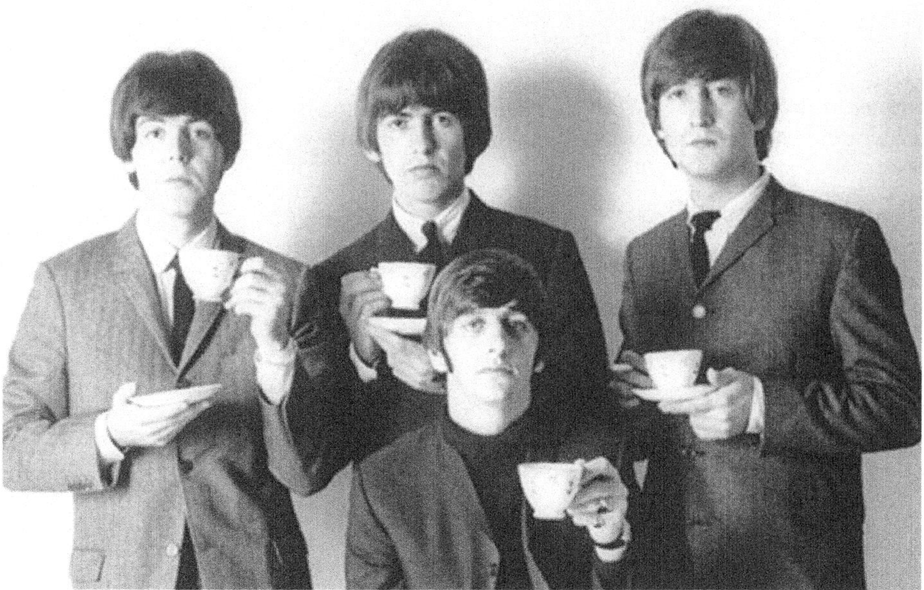

The Beatles: Paul McCartney, George Harrison, Ringo Starr (seated) and John Lennon

Summer In The City [Lovin' Spoonful] – With all of their first four singles having hit the top 10 on the pop charts, the Lovin' Spoonful were barely into the second six months of their recording career when they began working on their second album in spring 1966. Lead singer John Sebastian got help from his 14-year-old brother Mark in writing one of the songs for that album.

Mark had written a poem, which he showed to John. The beginning of the poem left the elder brother unimpressed, but a line later in the verse grabbed John's attention: " … but at night it's a different world." John proceeded to rework Mark's poem into a gritty, image-filled song lyric that became "Summer In The City." Bassist Steve Boone created the middle eight (eight bars in the middle of a conventionally structured pop song, generally of a different character than the other parts of the song.)

A heat wave in the summer of 1966 sent temperatures in New York City (home of the Lovin' Spoonful) to their highest since 1869. For 34 days the mercury reached 90 degrees or higher. The song fit the mood of the metropolis's weather perfectly.

With the help of producer Erik Jacobsen, a jagged electric piano riff was chosen to help convey the tension and edginess caused by lingering heat. Studio musician Artie Schroek provided this keyboard feature.

The lyrics show a dramatic shift in mood, as the heat of the day dissipates into a cooler night – one in which men can comb the cityscape for women to romance.

John Sebastian located an old-school radio engineer who provided a huge library of street sound effects that he had used for radio dramas. Sebastian called him "a hilarious old Jewish sound man." The band members listened to the tapes for hours, trying to find the perfect ones to use on "Summer." Eventually, just the right automobile horns were selected, and a jackhammer sound was added to fill out the urban ambience.

The instrumental break starts softly and then grows into a gridlock nightmare.

The song was recorded over the span of two days. The first session was for laying down the instrumental tracks, and the second saw vocals and sound effects added.

In a chart career that included 10 songs in the top 40, this was the only hard rock song recorded by Lovin' Spoonful. The group began as a jug band outfit called the Mugwumps, which also featured Cass Elliot and Denny Doherty – future members of the Mamas & the Papas.

They took their name from a lyric in the song "Coffee Blues" by Mississippi John Hurt. The song is a tribute to Maxwell House Coffee, and Hurt said that one spoonful of it was all he needed to feel alright – his "lovin' spoonful."

Summer In The City

Songwriters: John Sebastian, Mark Sebastian, Steve Boone

Peaked at No. 1 on Billboard Hot 100

Aug. 13, 1966

Aug. 20, 1966

Aug. 27, 1966

The Lovin' Spoonful

John B. Sebastian (March 17, 1944-) autoharp, harmonica, vocals
Steve Boone (Sept. 23, 1943-) bass
Zal Yanovsky (Dec. 19, 1944-Dec. 13, 2002) guitar
Joe Butler (Sept. 16, 1941-) drums, vocals
Formed in New York City, N.Y., in 1964

The Lovin' Spoonful: Joe Butler, John B. Sebastian, Zal Yanovsky, Steve Boone (standing)

Good Vibrations [Beach Boys] – Sometime around 1964-65 Brian Wilson, the de facto leader of the Beach Boys, could no longer stand going on tour with his band. Specifically, he had problems with flying in airplanes. So, he preferred to stay at home when the other Beach Boys toured so that he could productively use the time alone to write songs and produce records in the studios of Los Angeles.

Also around this time, Wilson began a friendly competition with the Beatles. He was respectfully jealous of the success of the album "Rubber Soul," and he vowed to produce an album that would surpass it in creative excellence. The release of the Beach Boys' "Pet Sounds" in early 1966 would be that album, and it briefly vaulted them ahead of the Fab Four. "Sgt. Pepper's Lonely Hearts Club Band" in 1967 would tilt the rivalry back in favor of the Beatles.

Starting on Feb. 17, 1966, Wilson began recording "Good Vibrations." Recording would conclude on Sept. 21, and the single was released on Oct. 10. Recording engineer Chuck Britz said that Wilson considered the song to be "his whole life performance in one track." More than 90 hours of tape was consumed during the sessions, and production costs reached $50,000, making it the most expensive song to record at that time.

Wilson would sit at a piano in the studio, recording a series of chord changes that he liked. Then he would convert the tape into an acetate disc, which he would take home and use to write the melody and lyrics. The song was a work in progress for months.

The theme of the song came to Wilson from words that his mother spoke to him when he was a child. She told him that dogs would bark at certain people because the animals could pick up bad vibrations from these people. Wilson wanted to title the song "Good Vibes," but lyricist Tony Asher advised him that it would be "lightweight use of the language." The two proceeded to write lyrics that were later discarded.

Beach Boy singer Mike Love wrote the final lyrics, claiming that they came to him while he was driving to the studio. He tapped into the cultural "flower power" movement of the day. Carl Wilson sang the verses, and Love's voice came in on the chorus.

After the song was recorded at Western Recorders, Brian Wilson laid down overdubs at RCA, Gold Star and Columbia studios. "Every studio has its own marked sound," he said in a *Rolling Stone* interview. "Using the four studios had a lot to do with the way the final record sounded."

Another thing that set the song apart from the pack was its use of an Electro-Theremin, which gave the song its eerie ambiance. Another important feature was the changes of tempo.

A plethora of top studio musicians contributed to the recording, including Hal Blaine, drums; Al De Lory, piano and harpsichord; Larry Knechtel, organ; Al Casey, guitar; Tommy Morgan, harmonica; Ray Pohlman, electric bass; Lyle Ritz, double bass; Jesse Ehrlich, cello; Jim Horn, piccolo; and Paul Tanner, electro-theremin.

"Good Vibrations" heralded a new sophistication in Beach Boys music, which would be seen in their next released album, "Smiley Smile."

Good Vibrations

Songwriters: Brian Wilson, Mike Love

Peaked at No. 1 on Billboard Hot 100

Dec. 10, 1966

The Beach Boys

Brian Wilson (June 20, 1942-) vocals, production, mixing

Carl Wilson (Dec. 21, 1946-Feb. 6, 1998) vocals, rhythm guitar, shaker

Dennis Wilson (Dec. 4, 1944-Dec. 28, 1983) Hammond organ

Mike Love (March 15, 1941-) vocals

Al Jardine (Sept. 3, 1942-) guitar [did not perform on "Good Vibrations"]

Bruce Johnston (June 27, 1942-) keyboards [did not perform on "Good Vibrations"]

Formed in Hawthorne, Calif., in 1961

The Beach Boys: Brian Wilson, Mike Love, Carl Wilson, Al Jardine, Dennis Wilson

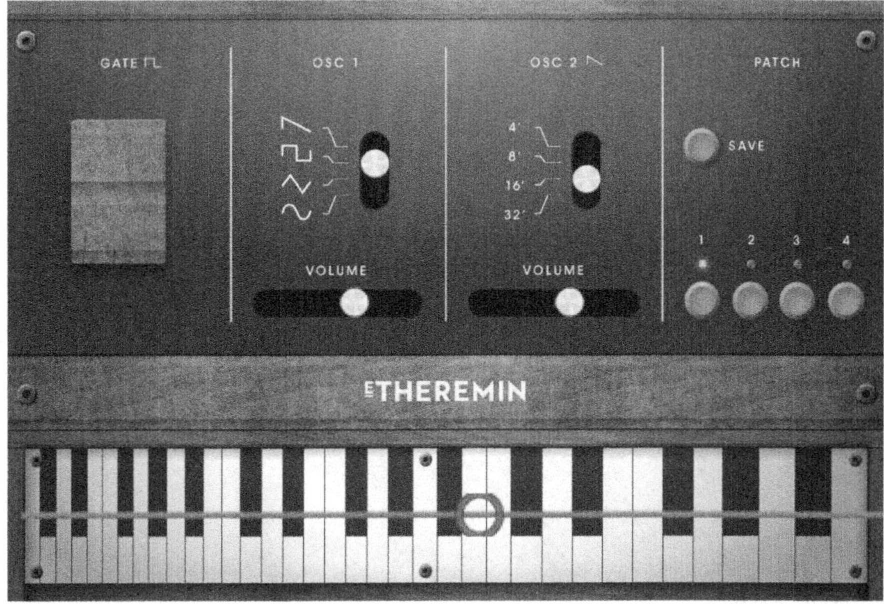

Example of an Electro-Theremin

Pretty Ballerina [Left Banke] – This was the second hit single in the brief chart career of the Left Banke. The band's style was termed by the music press as "Bach-rock" and "baroque rock." Sophisticated string arrangements were their hallmark.

"Pretty Ballerina" had a sound very much like the Left Banke's first hit, "Walk Away Renee." Keyboardist Michael Brown wrote both songs. The subject of both songs was Renee Fladen, who was the then-girlfriend of the Left Banke's bass player, Tom Finn. Brown was infatuated with her, and she was associated with the band for a few weeks. Brown wrote "Walk Away Renee" one month after he met her. He also wrote a third song about her, titled "She May Call You Up Tonight."

Talking about his unrequited love for the tall blonde, Brown said, "I was just sort of mythologically in love, if you know what I mean, without having evidence in fact or in deed ... But I was as close as anybody could be to the real thing."

With a haunting lead vocal by Steve Martin Caro, the recording also features a string quartet and oboe.

Henry Lookofsky, who was a session violinist and Brown's father, produced the recording and played on it, as well. His classical music influence on the Left Banke was huge.

Scoring two hits in the *Billboard* top 15, the Left Banke proved that chamber music could gain favor from a teen audience, even in the dawn of the psychedelic rock era.

The Left Banke soon splintered, and a reunion in 1969 was short lived.

They took their name from the Left Bank of the Seine River in Paris, France, a place where artists and wayfarers hang out. Although three of the original members are deceased, a version of the band was still active in 2019.

Pretty Ballerina

Songwriter: Michael Brown

Peaked at No. 15 on Billboard Hot 100

Feb. 25, 1967

March 4, 1967

The Left Banke
Michael Brown (April 25, 1949-March 19, 2015) keyboards, vocals
George Cameron (1947-June 24, 2018) drums, vocals
Tom Finn (DOB unavailable) bass
Steve Martin Caro (Oct. 12, 1948-) vocals
Jeff Winfield (Nov. 1, 1948-June 13, 2009) guitar
Formed in New York City, N.Y., in 1965

The Left Banke

Nights In White Satin [Moody Blues] – This song is a strong indicator that the Moody Blues were a band ahead of their time when they recorded this song on Oct. 8, 1967. The track has exceptional amounts of length and symphonic content.

As part of the British band's concept album "Days Of Future Passed," it was released in the United Kingdom on Nov. 10, 1967 and in the United States one day later. The album version was a robust 7 minutes 38 seconds, but there were two edited singles with lengths of 3:06 and 4:26.

On the initial chart run, ending in early 1968, "Nights In White Satin" peaked at No. 19 in the U.K. and No. 103 in the U.S. Listeners in the Netherlands thought quite highly of it, as it hit No. 1 there.

Later in '68 another single from the album, "Tuesday Afternoon (Forever Afternoon)," was released and reached a respectable No. 24 on the *Billboard Hot 100.*

Fast forward to 1972. Deram Records, a division of Decca, released the single again, and this time it rose to No. 2 on the *Hot 100* and No. 9 on the U.K. chart. By that time, such recordings as "Pretty Ballerina," "MacArthur Park" and "Hey Jude" had facilitated acceptance of longer, more artistic singles.

The London Festival Orchestra is credited with performing on the recording, but such a body did not exist. That was the name given to house musicians at the Decca studios. Symphonic sounds in the central part of the song were produced by Moody Blues keyboardist Mike Pinder on the Mellotron.

The album version has a spoken verse at the end titled "Late Lament." It was written by drummer Graeme Edge and recited by Pinder.

Guitarist Justin Hayward, who had joined the Moodies in 1966 after answering an ad in England's *Melody Maker Magazine,* wrote "Nights In White Satin" when he was 19. The lyrics, which were inspired by the gift of white satin bedsheets he received from a friend, are thought to be about an unrequited love.

"It was a series of random thoughts and was quite autobiographical," Hayward told *Daily Express Saturday Magazine* in 2008. "It was a very emotional time, as I was at the end of one big love affair and the start of another. A lot of that came out in the song."

This use of a personal theme mirrors that used by the Beatles in "In My Life."

The LP "Days Of Future Passed" marked a change of direction for the band, which had debuted as a blues/rock group in 1964. The songs of the themed album represent different times of the day.

Later songs that the Moody Blues recorded continued to present thoughtful lyrics and sophisticated instrumental arrangements. Some of the band's concert tours brought along orchestras to mimic the sounds that fans heard on records.

Speaking of "Nights," Hayward told writer Rob Hughes in 2017, "There's still so much emotion when we play it. It doesn't matter how well we do it in soundcheck, it's the audience that brings something magical to that song. The atmosphere in the room is suddenly different. There's a feeling to it that's quite electric."

"Nights In White Satin" has the distinction of having an amusement park ride named after it. During its brief lifespan in 2008, Hard Rock Park in Myrtle Beach, S.C., featured a ride with psychedelic visuals and stunning audio effects that ushered riders wearing 3-D glasses through a giant album cover. Onboard speakers reportedly were superb, and droplets of moisture, motion simulation and blasts of air added to the sensory experience.

Nights In White Satin

Songwriter: Justin Hayward

Peaked at No. 2 on Billboard Hot 100

Nov. 4, 1972

Nov. 11, 1972

The Moody Blues

Justin Hayward (Oct. 14, 1946-) guitar, lead vocals

John Lodge (July 20, 1945-) bass, backing vocals

Mike Pinder (Dec. 27, 1941-) keyboards, backing vocals

Graeme Edge (March 30, 1941-) drums, percussion, backing vocals

Ray Thomas (Dec. 29, 1941-Jan. 4, 2018) flute, backing vocals

Formed in Birmingham, England, in 1964

The Moody Blues: front – Mike Pinder, Graeme Edge; Rear – John Lodge, Ray Thomas, Justin Hayward

MacArthur Park [Richard Harris] – Los Angeles record producer Bones Howe was looking for a new song for the band The Association in 1967. He wanted a pop song with classical elements, different movements and changing time signatures. He delivered this request to Oklahoma native Jim

Webb, who had taken up residence in L.A., and Webb responded with a song that had all of those features.

Howe did not care for the ambitious cantata, though, and he rejected it. The lyrics played out a chapter in the 21-year-old Webb's personal life, as it symbolized the end of his romantic relationship with girlfriend Susie Horton. She worked for Aetna Life Insurance Co., whose L.A. offices were just across the street from MacArthur Park. Horton and Webb occasionally met there for lunch and spent many of their happiest times together there. Things that Webb did and saw are mentioned in the lyrics.

The song consists of four separate movements. There are some slow tempo and mid-tempo parts, but the song rocks out toward the end.

Irish actor Richard Harris was 37 when he met Webb at a fundraiser in East Los Angeles in 1967. He mentioned to Webb that he wanted to record an album, but Webb did not take him seriously. Harris had starred in the movie *Camelot* and had performed several numbers in the film.

Back home in England, Harris sent a telegram to Webb, inviting him to come to London and work on the album project as a writer. Webb flew to England and played Harris a number of possible songs, none of which seemed suitable for the album. The last one Webb offered was "MacArthur Park," and Harris chose it for his recording debut.

The track was recorded in Hollywood on Dec. 21, 1967. Orchestral parts were overdubbed on Dec. 29-30. Webb produced the record and played harpsichord. The album was given the title "A Tramp Shining," and the single was released in April 1968. It won a 1969 Grammy Award for Best Arrangement Accompanying Vocalists.

Throughout the various takes during the session, Harris persisted in singing the title phrase as "MacArthur's Park." Webb continually corrected him, but to no avail. The mispronunciation ended up on the take that was pressed onto vinyl.

"MacArthur Park" peaked at No. 2 on the *Billboard Hot 100*, but it went to No. 1 in Canada and Australia. In the U.K. it hit No. 4. Harris went on to record other albums and singles, but none matched the success of his first.

A disco version of the song was recorded by Donna Summer in 1978, and it went to No. 1 in the U.S. and Canada.

Harris had been diagnosed with Hodgkin's disease two months before his death, was hospitalized with pneumonia and spent his final three days in a coma.

Wanting to be a director, he moved to London at age 24 and enrolled in the London Academy of Music and Dramatic Art to take acting lessons. He was twice nominated for Academy Awards for acting and four times for Grammy Awards (winning once). His voice appeared on 14 record albums.

MacArthur Park

Songwriter: Jimmy Webb

Peaked at No. 2 on Billboard Hot 100

June 22, 1968

Richard Harris

Oct. 1, 1930-Oct. 25, 2002

Born Richard St. John Harris in Limerick, Ireland and died at a hospital in London, England

Richard Harris

Stairway To Heaven [Led Zeppelin] – This song from Led Zeppelin's untitled fourth album never was released as a single but became the most requested song on FM radio stations across America throughout the 1970s. It also is the most requested song in the history of Chicago AM station WLS.

This song is not to be confused with a song of the same title that was written and recorded by Neil Sedaka in 1960.

Although the album, commonly known as "Led Zeppelin IV," was released Nov. 8, 1971, it took until '73 for "Stairway To Heaven" to gain anthemic status. The band's guitarist, Jimmy Page, commented, "I knew it was good, but I didn't know it was going to be almost like an anthem … I knew it was the gem of the album, for sure."

The origins of the song go back to 1970, when Page and lead singer Robert Plant were hanging out at Bron-Yr-Aur, a remote cottage in Wales. Page said he wrote the music over a long period of time, with the first part coming at the cottage. He always kept a cassette recorder with him, and "Stairway" was formed from pieces of taped music.

Plant's lyrics were spontaneously improvised at Headley Grange, a recording and rehearsal venue in Hampshire County, England. Page was strumming a guitar, and Plant had pencil and paper in hand.

The song contains three sections, each one increasing in tempo and volume. It begins softly with acoustic guitar by Page and recorders, played by bassist John Paul Jones in Renaissance music style, before introducing electric instruments later. The final part includes a masterful guitar solo by Page, which was rated No. 1 by *Guitar World* magazine on its list of 100 Greatest Guitar Solos in Rock and Roll History. Overdubbing allowed the song to have an effect of layered guitars.

The track runs 8 minutes 3 seconds, with John Bonham coming in on drums at the 4:18 mark.

"Stairway" has received many accolades over the years, including a ranking of No. 31 on *Rolling Stone's* 500 Greatest Songs of All Time. On the 20th anniversary of the album's release, United States radio sources announced that the song had been played on air an estimated 2,874,000 times. By the year 2000, that number had risen to 3 million. It has sold more sheet music than any other rock song, still logging more than 10,000 in sales per year.

When asked why the song is so popular, Plant said it was because of its "abstraction." He added, "Depending what day it is, I still interpret the song in a different way – and *I* wrote the lyrics."

The lyrics seem to tell of a woman who thinks riches can buy her way into Heaven. Plant has commented that it was about "a woman getting everything she wanted without giving anything back."

Led Zeppelin's record label, Atlantic, sought to release the song as a single. The band's manager, Peter Grant, refused such requests in 1972 and '73 on the grounds that fans of the song should be forced to buy the entire album, thus enhancing profits. On the charts, the album hit No. 1 in the U.K. and Canada and No. 2 in the USA, Australia and Denmark. Sales in the USA have it at 23X platinum (over 23 million).

It should be mentioned that Plant and Page were sued for plagiarism over "Stairway To Heaven" in 2015. The suit was filed by a trustee for the estate of the late Randy Wolfe (aka Randy California), and it alleged that "Stairway" copied the 1968 instrumental song "Taurus" by the American band Spirit, of which Wolfe was a member. In 2016 a jury found in favor of Plant and Page.

However, in Sept. 2018 the 9th circuit court of appeals in San Francisco ordered a new trial, citing, among other things, the fact that jurors were not allowed to hear in court a recording of "Taurus."

Stairway To Heaven

Songwriters: Jimmy Page, Robert Plant

Included on the album "Led Zeppelin IV"

Peaked at No. 2 on Billboard 200

Dec. 18, 1971-Jan. 15, 1972

Led Zeppelin

Robert Plant (Aug. 20, 1948-) vocals
Jimmy Page (Jan. 9, 1944-) guitar
John Paul Jones (Jan. 3, 1946-) bass, keyboards, mandolin
John Bonham (May 31, 1948-Sept. 25, 1980) drums
Formed in London, England, in 1968. Their original name was the New Yardbirds, since Jimmy Page had been a member of the British band the Yardbirds.

Led Zeppelin: John Bonham, Jimmy Page, John Paul Jones, Robert Plant

Roundabout [Yes] – The term "progressive rock" or "prog rock" was starting to float around rock music circles about the time the English band Yes was formed. Hence, it is closely linked with Yes.

Although the band scored a No. 1 hit on the *Billboard Hot 100* in 1984 with "Owner Of A Lonely Heart," Yes might have had a greater presence on the charts if they'd had a more stable line-up. From their inception in 1968, they have had 19 different full-time members in a lineup that contained five at a time.

The release of the album "Fragile" in January 1972 was the band's break-through effort in the United States, and the single "Roundabout" garnered a lot of attention for the London-based outfit. "Your Move" had cracked the *Hot 100* in 1971 but suffered from lack of promotion, stalling at No. 40.

"Roundabout" ran 8 minutes 29 seconds in the album version, but much of its artistic beauty was sacrificed when it was trimmed to 3:27 on the U.S. single.

The full-length version features a 58-second intro. Written by lead singer Jon Anderson and guitarist Steve Howe, the song was conceived during a concert tour in Scotland, when Yes traveled from Aberdeen to Glasgow. According to Anderson, the band's vehicle drove through "maybe 40 or so" roundabouts along the route.

A roundabout is a circular feature that allows traffic to flow in multiple directions without the use of signal lights.

"In and around the lake" refers to Loch Ness. "Mountains come out of the sky, they stand there" describes nearby Highland mountains whose tops were obscured by clouds.

"Twenty four before my love you'll see I'll be there with you" was a message from Anderson to his then-wife Jennifer, telling her how many hours it would be until he returned home.

According to biographer Tim Morse, "Roundabout" was recorded in sections in a series of tape edits. This was a method that was new to the band.

Keyboard whiz Rick Wakeman had joined the band just prior to the recording of "Fragile," and he got the dramatic intro started by recording a note on piano and playing it backward. This created an effect that Howe described as if the sound were "rushing towards you." Much time and care was spent finding the right note and editing it correctly.

Wakeman also contributed parts on Minimoog synthesizer and Mellotron. Chris Squire played the bass part overdubbed with a Gibson ES-150 electric guitar. To augment Squire's work, Wakeman duplicated the bass line by playing arpeggios (broken chords) on a Hammond C3 organ with his right hand while playing the bass notes with his left.

Howe played both acoustic and electric guitars throughout the recording.

Once the instrumental tracks were finished, Anderson recorded his lead vocals. Later, the rest of the band sang harmonized backing vocals. Toward the end Anderson, Squire and Howe sang a three-part harmony that was repeated eight times.

As reported in the *Wall Street Journal,* in the background Wakeman can be heard singing the notes to "Three Blind Mice," which was placed "against the grain of what we were doing" to make it sound more intriguing. To close, Howe repeated his part of the acoustic guitar introduction but ended on an E major chord.

All in all, Yes and producer Eddie Offord made good use of the studio as an instrument.

"Roundabout," in its full-length version, was a major contributor to the rise of FM radio, whose popularity was surging in the early 1970s.

Roundabout

Songwriters: Jon Anderson, Steve Howe

Peaked at No. 13 on Billboard Hot 100

April 15, 1972

April 22, 1972

Yes

John Anderson (Oct. 25, 1944-) vocals

Chris Squire (March 4, 1948-June 27, 2015) bass, backing vocals

Steve Howe (April 8, 1947-) guitar, backing vocals

Rick Wakeman (May 18, 1949-) keyboards

Bill Bruford (May 17, 1949-) drums

Formed in London, England, in 1968

Yes: Chris Squire, Jon Anderson, Rick Wakeman, Steve Howe, Bill Bruford

Space Oddity [David Bowie] – One of Englishman David Bowie's signature songs and one of his greatest innovations, this song was first recorded in Feb. 1969. It was inspired by the 1968 Stanley Kubrick film *2001: A Space Odyssey.*

It was Bowie's first single to chart in the United Kingdom and reached No. 5 in its initial chart run. It received the 1970 Ivor Novello Special Award for Originality, given by the British Academy of Songwriters, Composers and Authors.

Bowie split with his record label, Deram, in June 1969, and his manager negotiated a one-album deal with Mercury and its U.K. subsidiary, Philips. Mercury executives had heard and liked an audition tape that included a demo of "Space Oddity." Bowie tried to find a producer for his album, and Beatles producer George Martin turned him down. Tony Visconti liked the demo tracks, but he considered the lead single ("Oddity") to be a "cheap shot" at the impending Apollo 11 space mission. Gus Dudgeon, who wound up producing Elton John's biggest hits in the 1970s, got the job.

On the extended version for the new album, Bowie sang lead and harmony vocals and played acoustic guitar and Stylophone (heard in the background during the first verse.) Rick Wakeman played Mellotron; Mick Wayne, guitar; Herbie Flowers, bass; and Terry Cox, drums. These studio musicians were paid barely more than £9 each. The U.K. release ran 4 minutes 33 seconds, while the version released in the U.S. was cut down to 3:26.

The single was released July 11, 1969, but BBC radio would not play it until the Apollo 11 crew had walked on the moon and safely returned to Earth.

Reception to the song in America was cool, as it stalled at No. 124 on the *Billboard* pop chart. It was rereleased in the U.K. by RCA in 1972 and became Bowie's first No. 1 single in his homeland. In early 1973 the single was rereleased in the U.S. and went to No. 15.

The lyrical term "whose shirt you wear" is English slang for "what soccer club you like."

German Peter Schilling recorded a sequel to the song (written by Schilling and David Harland Lodge) in 1983, titled "Major Tom (Coming Home)." In the lyrics of that song, the astronaut returns to Earth.

At London's Bromley Technical High School, Bowie studied art, music and design. He formed his first band age 15, the Konrads. To avoid being confused with future Monkees member Davy Jones, he changed his last name in the mid-1960's in honor of American pioneer Jim Bowie and the knife he popularized.

Bowie died in New York City, N.Y., of liver cancer. He had been diagnosed with the disease 18 months before his death but had not made that fact public.

Space Oddity

Songwriter: David Bowie

Peaked at No. 15 on Billboard Hot 100

April 7, 1973

<u>David Bowie</u>

Jan. 8, 1947-Jan. 10, 2016

Born David Robert Jones in Brixton, London, England, and died in New York City, N.Y.

David Bowie

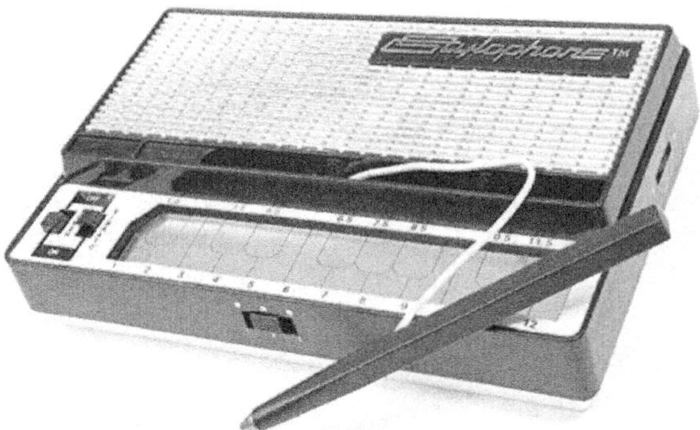

Example of a Stylophone

Example of a Mellotron

I'm Not In Love [10cc] – This is another instance of a band using the recording studio as an instrument, with stunning results. But in this case, the primary instruments used were the voices of the band members.

Members of 10cc, Eric Stewart and Graham Gouldman, took two or three days to write the song. Stewart got the idea for the lyrics when his wife of eight years kept asking him why he didn't tell her more often that he loved her. "I had this crazy idea in my mind that repeating those words would somehow degrade the meaning," he said. "So I told her, 'If I say every day I love you, Darling, I love you, blah, blah, blah,' it's not gonna mean anything eventually."

Originally, the song had a bossa nova beat and was played with guitars. The other two members of the band, Kevin Godley and Lol Crème, hated it and told Stewart to abandon the song. Their reaction to the demo recording was so negative that the band ultimately erased the tape. One thing kept it alive, though – members of the staff persisted in humming the melody around the recording studio.

10cc turned its attention to another song they wanted to put on an album, but they kept hearing staffers singing "I'm Not In Love" as they walked around Strawberry Studios. This led Stewart to approach the others in an attempt to revive the song. Godley, still skeptical, told him, "I tell you what, the only way that song is gonna work is if we totally f*** it up and we do it like nobody has ever recorded a thing before. Let's not use instruments. Let's try to do it all with voices."

Stewart was a bit taken aback, but he agreed to try Godley's suggestion of using voices as the focal point in a wall of sound. He spent three weeks recording Godley, Gouldman and Crème singing the phonetic sound "ahhh" 16 times for each note of the chromatic scale, building up to a choir-like total of 48 voices for each note of the scale.

Keeping the notes reverberating for an infinite length of time was a problem, but Crème suggested the use of tape loops. Stewart created loops of about 12 feet in length by feeding the loop at one end through the tape heads of the recorder in the studio and at the other end through a capstan roller fixed to the top of a microphone stand and tensioned by tape. By creating long loops, the blip caused by the splice in each loop could be drowned out by the rest of the backing track, providing the blips in each loop didn't coincide with each other.

Stewart then played each loop through a separate channel of the mixing board. This effectively turned the mixing board into a musical instrument, complete with all the notes of the chromatic scale. The four band members "played" these notes, fading up three or four channels at a time to create "chords" for the song's melody.

The instrumentation was added after the vocals had been recorded. This included a Fender Rhodes electric piano, played by Stewart; a Gibson 335 electric guitar, played by Gouldman for the rhythm melody; and a bass drum sound played by Godley on a Moog synthesizer. Crème played piano during the bridge and middle eight, where it replicated the melody of lyrics that had been discarded. The middle eight is the only part of the song that contains a bass guitar line, played by Gouldman. A toy music box was recorded and double-tracked for the middle eight and the outro.

Once the song was finished, Godley felt it was still lacking something. Godley remembered that he'd said something into the grand piano microphone when he was recording his solo – "be quiet, big boys don't cry." The band members agreed that would be a good insert for the break, if they only could find the right voice for it.

"Just at that point," Stewart said, "the door to the control room opened and our secretary Kathy (Redfern) looked in and whispered, 'Eric, sorry to bother you. There's a telephone call for you.' Lol jumped up and said, 'That's the voice, her voice is perfect!'"

They all agreed that Redfern had the perfect voice, but they had to coax the doubting, shy secretary into speaking the part. She used the same whispered voice she had used when she entered the control room.

10cc was in the process of leaving the UK Records label that had them under contract for the previous three years. They invited a representative of Mercury Records to come to the studio to listen to "I'm Not In Love," and he signed them to a five-year, five-album contract on the basis of one song.

So, what about the title and the lyrics? Gouldman commented, "… Eric came up with the title of that song, and it was the perfect title of an anti-love song. But, of course, is it an anti-love song? Is it 'I'm Not In Love' or 'I Am In Love?'"

The conflict comes from the title and helped make the song so poignant.

The song became the second No. 1 single in the U.K. for 10cc, and it also hit No. 1 in Canada. In the U.S. it was No. 2 for three weeks, and it peaked at No. 3 in Australia.

"I'm Not In Love" won Ivor Novello Awards in 1976 for Best Pop Song, International Hit of the Year and Most Performed British Work. It has appeared in 11 motion pictures and 12 TV shows.

Stewart, Godley and Crème played together in a band called Hotlegs in 1970-71, and Gouldman and Stewart were together in the Mindbenders before that. 10cc had its own recording venue – Strawberry Studios in Stockport – which was named after the Beatles' song "Strawberry Fields Forever."

I'm Not In Love

Songwriters: Eric Stewart, Graham Gouldman

Peaked at No. 2 on Billboard Hot 100

July 26, 1975
Aug. 2, 1975
Aug. 9, 1975

10cc

Graham Gouldman (May 10, 1946-) guitar, bass
Eric Stewart (Jan. 20, 1945-) vocals, guitar, keyboards
Kevin Godley (Oct. 7, 1945-) drums, percussion, vocals
Lol Crème (Sept. 19, 1947-) guitar, bass, keyboards, vocals
Formed in Stockport, England, in 1972

10cc: Kevin Godley, Lol Crème, Eric Stewart, Graham Gouldman

Could It Be Magic [Barry Manilow] – This song took a rather unique route to the No. 6 spot on *Billboard's Hot 100* chart on Sept. 20, 1975. It was recorded twice and released as a single thrice.

The first version in 1970 was attributed to a "ghost group" of studio musicians called Featherbed, which included the principal writer, Barry Manilow. Tony Orlando, then vice president at Columbia/CBS Music, contributed some of the lyrics and did the arranging and producing. The single was released in 1971 and did poorly. It had a bubble gum beat and cowbells and was up-tempo.

In subsequent interviews Manilow voiced pleasure at the record's failure, since he hated the arrangement so much. Up to that point Manilow had composed or arranged only commercial jingles, and he wasn't permitted to provide input for the production of the recording, which was released on Columbia subsidiary Bell Records.

Manilow arranged and produced the second version of "Could It Be Magic" in 1973. The melody was based on Frederic Chopin's Prelude in C Minor, Opus 28, Number 20 (first published in 1839). The tempo was slowed dramatically, and full orchestration replaced the pop elements that Orlando used. Adrienne Anderson reworked the lyrics, and the single was released a second time, under Manilow's solo name. The single failed to make an impact on the charts.

Meanwhile, Manilow kept busy as Bette Midler's producer and piano player.

Six months later Clive Davis took over Bell and merged it with Arista Records, along with all of the Columbia Pictures-owned labels. Most of the artists at Bell were dropped, but Arista kept Manilow because of "Could It Be Magic."

After Manilow hit No. 1 with "Mandy" and No. 12 with "It's A Miracle," Arista gave "Could It Be Magic" another chance by releasing it in the summer of 1975, on an album and as a single. It ended up being ranked as the 37th biggest hit of the year by *Billboard.*

The mention of "sweet Melissa" in the lyrics refers to Melissa Manchester, who at the time was an up-and-coming singer in the Arista family.

It ranks as one of the prettiest pieces in Manilow's catalog. Part of the pleasure of listening to a Manilow record is melodic craftsmanship, and "Could It Be Magic" boasts a superb arrangement that builds gradually to a trademark Manilow crescendo. So gradual that the song lasts nearly 7 minutes in its full-length version, spotlighting Manilow's piano work (in a pair of instrumental passages). The extra voices and horns are added gradually, at a pace that culminates in the peak it reaches after a few choruses. And then the whole song quickly is extinguished, ending on the somber piano notes that opened it.

Manilow studied at City College of New York, New York College of Music and the Julliard performing arts school. In the mid-1960s he became a writer and singer of commercial jingles. In the early '70s he became Midler's piano player, producer and musical director before launching his own solo singing career.

Could It Be Magic

Songwriters: Barry Manilow, Frederic Chopin, Adrienne Anderson

Peaked at No. 6 on Billboard Hot 100

Sept. 20, 1975

Sept. 27, 1975

Barry Manilow

Born Barry Alan Pincus in Brooklyn, N.Y., on June 17, 1943

Barry Manilow

Dream Weaver [Gary Wright] – Much as "Summer In The City" tried to transport its listeners to a hot urban street, this song attempted to take its listeners to a somnambulant world of dreams. And to contact with God.

Instrumentally, this was done by the artistic use of synthesizers, played by Gary Wright, who supplied all of the velvety vocals. The only other player on the track was drummer Jim Keltner. Wright has been recognized for his role in helping establish the synthesizer as a leading instrument in rock and pop music.

The expression "dream weaver" was popularized by John Lennon in lyrics from his 1970 debut solo album.

According to Wright, the song was inspired by *Autobiography of a Yogi* by Paramhansa Yogananda, a book which was given to Wright by George Harrison. Wright had played keyboards on Harrison's solo album "All Things Must Pass." Yogananda's poem "God! God! God!" refers to "the idea of the mind weaving dreams."

On his website Wright wrote about the development of the song. As he read the autobiography, he encountered the term "weaver of dreams." He wrote it in his journal of song titles and then forgot about it.

"Several months passed," Wright wrote, "and one weekend, while in the English countryside, I picked up my journal and came across the title 'Dream Weaver.' Feeling inspired, I picked up my acoustic guitar and began writing. The song was finished in an hour. The lyrics and music seemed to have flowed out of me as if written by an unseen source.

"After the record was released and became successful, many people asked me what the song meant. I really wasn't sure myself and would answer, 'It was about a kind of fantasy experience... a Dream Weaver train taking you through the cosmos.' But I was never satisfied with that explanation, and as years went by I began to reflect on what the song actually meant and then it came to me: 'Dream Weaver, I believe you can get me through the night...' was a song about someone with infinite compassion and love carrying us through the night of our trials and suffering. None other than God Himself."

The album "The Dream Weaver" was released about four months ahead of the single and sold over a million copies. Its jacket features a close-up photo of Wright with his eyes closed, ostensibly in a state of slumber.

Wright made his acting debut at age 7 in the television show *Captain Video and His Video Rangers,* and he also did TV and radio commercials and a Broadway show as a youth. He played with various local rock bands while in high school, and he was with the band Spooky Tooth before he began his solo music career.

Dream Weaver

Songwriter: Gary Wright

Peaked at No. 2 on Billboard Hot 100

March 27, 1976

April 3, 1976

April 10, 1976

Gary Wright

Born Gary Malcolm Wright in Cresskill, N.J., on April 26, 1943

Gary Wright

Bohemian Rhapsody [Queen] – If "Dream Weaver" sought to take its listeners to the land of nod, then this song brought its listeners into a virtual opera house. In fact, the title of the album that spawned the single is titled "A Night At The Opera."

The song is a six-minute suite, consisting of an intro, a ballad segment, an operatic passage, a hard rock part and a reflective ending.

Queen's lead singer and pianist, Freddie Mercury, wrote the song at his home in London. Roy Thomas Baker and Queen produced the recording. According to guitarist Brian May, most of Queen's material was written in the recording studio, "but this song was all in Freddie's mind" before the band started working on it in the studio.

According to Mercury's friend Chris Smith, Mercury started developing "Bohemian Rhapsody" in the 1960s. The song was completed and recorded in 1975, and it hit No. 1 in the U.K. that year. Its peak of popularity in most other parts of the world came in '76.

Music scholar Sheila Whiteley suggests that "the title draws strongly on contemporary rock ideology, the individualism of the *bohemian* artists' world, with *rhapsody* affirming the romantic ideals of art rock."

Commenting on bohemianism, Judith Peraino, associate professor of music at Cornell University, said, "Mercury intended ... (this song) to be a 'mock opera,' something outside the norm of rock songs, and it does follow a certain operatic logic: choruses of multi-tracked voices alternate with aria-like solos, the emotions are excessive, the plot confusing."

Mercury, May and drummer Roger Taylor sang the operatic parts for 10-12 hours a day during the recording sessions, and the entire piece took three weeks to complete. Some sections featured 180 separate overdubs. Since the technology of the day offered only 24-track analog tape, it was necessary for the three to overdub themselves many times to bounce the vocals down to successive sub-mixes. Tape segments had to be spliced into the correct sequence.

Again, we have here the use of the studio as an instrument.

The song has been affiliated with the genres of progressive rock, symphonic rock, hard rock and progressive pop. Its structure is highly unusual because of lack of a chorus, the presence of differing musical styles and lyrics that avoid conventional love-based narratives in favor of allusions to murder.

Bass player John Deacon performed on the track but did not contribute vocals.

"Bohemian Rhapsody" became one of the most decorated records in rock history. In 1976 the song hit No. 1 in Australia, Belgium, Canada, Netherlands and New Zealand. It peaked at No. 2 in South Africa and No. 9 in the U.S. After Mercury's death in 1991, the song went to No. 1 in the U.K. again for five weeks. It eventually became the U.K.'s third-best-selling single of all time.

After the song was used in the 1992 film *Wayne's World,* it went to No. 2 in the U.S. in a new chart run. It has been inducted into the Grammy Hall of Fame, and it appears high on several all-time lists of classic rock songs. In December 2018 it officially became the most-streamed song from the 20th century and the most-streamed classic rock song of all time.

Beach Boys leader Brian Wilson has praised it as being "the most competitive thing that's come along in ages … a fulfillment and an answer to a teenage prayer – of artistic music."

British record producer Steve Levine said that the recording "broke all sonic production barriers" in a fashion similar to "Good Vibrations" and "I'm Not In Love."

Queen released their first album in Britain in 1973 but did not make it big in America until 1975. They continued to release new material until 1991, the year that Mercury died of AIDS-related bronchial pneumonia.

Bohemian Rhapsody

Songwriter: Freddie Mercury

Peaked at No. 9 on Billboard Hot 100

April 24, 1976

May 1, 1976

Queen

Freddie Mercury [born Farrokh Bulsara] (Sept. 5, 1946-Nov. 24, 1991) vocals, keyboards
Brian May (July 19, 1947-) guitar, vocals
Roger Taylor (July 26, 1949-) drums
John Deacon (Aug. 19, 1951-) bass
Formed in London, England, in 1970

Queen: Roger Taylor, John Deacon, Freddie Mercury, Brian May

Telephone Line [Electric Light Orchestra] – An unanswered telephone call is the theme for this artistic triumph. The male caller lays out what he would say to his girlfriend if she would answer his call and talk with him. Apparently they'd had a bad spat.

Jeff Lynne, the writer, guitarist and leader of ELO, talked about the sound effects on the record. "To get the sound on the beginning, you know, the American telephone sound, we phoned from England to America to a number that we know nobody would be at, to just listen to it for a while. On the Moog (synthesizer), we recreated the sound exactly by tuning the oscillators to the same notes as the ringing of the phone." Lynne also served as producer.

The intro features a muted, mono telephone sound, which makes the listener feel as if he's listening through the telephone handset. This was a late addition to the production.

The recording had been completed, and Lynne was bringing the tape from England to California when he got the idea to add the effect to the finished product. So, it was at Cherokee Studios in Los Angeles that engineers Duane Scott and Kevin Gray were instructed to manually add the effect to the stereo master.

The song plays normally until the first vocal line of the first verse when the mono listening-on-the telephone effect cuts in. This continues, along with the ringback tone, until the "lonely, lonely, lonely, lonely nights" line. At that point stereo sound is slowly phased in, and the ringback stops.

The gentle doo-wop phrasing on the bridge references the sentimental songs of the 1950s. The lyric "blue days, black nights" may have been inspired by the Buddy Holly song "Blue Days Black Nights," which was the "B" side of his first single in 1956.

The backing track was recorded at Musicland Studios in Munich, Germany. The orchestra was recorded at De Lane Lea Studios in Wembley, England. The working title of the song was "Bad Salad Telephone," which is an anagram of "sad ballad."

ELO keyboardist Richard Tandy said of Lynne and the song, "I think everybody's had an experience where they've had a bad telephone call with somebody they care about and the way it gets to you. And I think he captured that."

Jim Beviglia, writing for *American Songwriter,* commented, "There have been some classic telephone songs in the rock era, but few have captured the helplessness of being on the lonely end of the receiver as well as 'Telephone Line,' a masterpiece of melancholy courtesy of Jeff Lynne and ELO."

By peaking at No. 7 on the *Billboard Hot 100*, "Telephone Line" became the second-most successful single for ELO in a career that saw 20 of their songs reach the top 40. By another measure it was their most successful hit: the record was in the *Hot 100* for 23 weeks, nearly a month longer than any of the band's other American releases.

Many of ELO's 7-inch singles were pressed on vinyl of various colors. This one was green, although there are many black copies in circulation.

The song was No. 1 in New Zealand (six weeks) and Canada, and it peaked at No. 8 in the U.K. In the year-end rankings for 1977, *Billboard* had it at No. 15.

Electric Light Orchestra took its name from the practice of combining electric rock instruments with orchestral instruments. "Light orchestras" were small orchestras popular in England in the 1960s. The orchestral strings on their recordings were provided in part by studio musicians.

In their widely acclaimed concert appearances in the late 1970s, ELO entered the stage by emerging from a huge spaceship, complete with fog machines and colored lasers. Their biggest world tour covered nine months, during which the band played 92 dates.

The band was formed out of Roy Wood and Jeff Lynne's desire to create modern rock songs with classical overtones. Lynne became the creative force and leader of the group, which disbanded in 1986 after Lynne lost interest in the project.

Telephone Line

Songwriter: Jeff Lynne

Peaked at No. 7 on Billboard Hot 100

Sept. 24, 1977

Oct. 1, 1977

Electric Light Orchestra

Jeff Lynne (Dec. 30, 1947-) vocals, guitar

Roy Wood (Nov. 8, 1946-) guitar, bass, keyboards, cello, drums, etc.

Bev Bevan (Nov. 25, 1944-) drums, vocals

Richard Tandy (March 26, 1948-) keyboards, synthesizers, guitar, bass

Kelly Groucutt (Sept. 8, 1945-Feb. 19, 2009) guitar, bass, vocals

Melvyn Gale (Jan. 15, 1952-) cello, keyboards

Mik Kaminski (Sept. 2, 1951-) violin

Hugh McDowell (July 31, 1953-Nov. 6, 2018) cello

Formed in Birmingham, England, in 1970

ELO: Mik Kaminski, Hugh McDowell, Bev Bevan, Jeff Lynne, Richard Tandy, Kelly Groucutt, Roy Wood

Chapter 15

The Psychedelic Years 1966-69

Songs that accompanied the drug culture

Overview: I found this definition for the word "psychedelic:" Relating to or denoting drugs, especially lysergic acid diethylamide (LSD), that produce hallucinations and apparent expansion of consciousness.

With the rise of the hippie counterculture and the widespread popularity and availability of recreational drugs, a strain of rock music arose in 1966 to accompany drug users on their trip to la-la land.

Most of these recordings featured extravagant use of electric guitar, electric keyboards and mystical lyrics, which accentuated the spacey activity going on in the heads of drug users. A lot of the psychedelic songs were hidden on albums, while many others were pressed into 45 rpm singles that sold well enough to have an impact on the pop charts.

During the four-year psychedelic era, there was a sort of role reversal. At first, songwriters and record producers broke out of the mold of conformity that had been the industry standard to create recordings that matched the drug culture. But, after a few months, the new individualism became the norm. Hence, one conformity was traded for another.

The psychedelic phase was played out by the end of 1969, when the music industry saw a new surge in rhythm & blues and mellow pop songs.

To view the full lyrics to these songs, please log on to www.google.com, enter song titles & artist names and click Google Search.

To listen to these songs, please log on to www.youtube.com and enter song titles & artist names.

Shapes Of Things [Yardbirds] – This may have been the first popular psychedelic song. The single was released on Feb. 25, 1966.

The Yardbirds, a blues-rock band from England, used some great guitar work by Jeff Beck with feedback from his speakers. Beck's innovations in the recording studio have been cited as being influential for Jimi Hendrix and Paul McCartney.

This was the first charted hit by the Yardbirds that was written by members of the band. The first recording sessions were held in Chicago, Ill., at Chess Studio while the Yardbirds were on an American concert tour in September 1965. Almost four months later, they did more work on the song in Hollywood at Columbia Studios and RCA Studios.

In the song's middle section, the beat goes into double time and the pace becomes almost frantic. This rhythmic strategy, called "rave-up," was featured in several of the Yardbirds' songs.

In regard to Beck's guitar work, music writer Keith Shadwick commented that it "suited Beck's taste for shaping and sculpting guitar sounds through the control and manipulation of sustain and, on occasion, feedback."

Beck said, "'Shapes Of Things' was the pinnacle of the Yardbirds. If I did nothing else, that was the best single."

The song's lyrics are a bit of a mixed bag, seeming to make statements about the ecology and the Vietnam War.

According to American author Richie Unterberger, "('Shapes Of Things') was arguably the first out-and-out psychedelic rock song, with its blistering feedback, veering tempos and stream-of-consciousness lyrics that owed nothing to traditional romantic themes."

The song did its best on the U.K. charts, where it peaked at No. 3. It reached No. 7 in Canada.

Shapes Of Things
Songwriters: Jim McCarty, Keith Relf, Paul Samwell-Smith
Peaked at No. 11 on Billboard Hot 100
May 14, 1966

The Yardbirds
Keith Relf (March 22, 1943-May 14, 1976) vocals, harmonica
Chris Dreja (Nov. 11, 1945-) rhythm guitar, bass
Jim McCarty (July 25, 1943-) drums
Jeff Beck (June 24, 1944-) lead guitar
Paul Samwell-Smith (May 8, 1943-) bass
Formed in London, England, in 1963

The Yardbirds: Chris Dreja, Keith Relf, Jim McCarty, Jeff Beck and Paul Samwell-Smith

Eight Miles High [Byrds] – On the heels of "Shapes Of Things" came this song, released less than one month later.

There were rumors that the song was about drug use, but the creation of the title was totally unrelated to that. The Byrds, from California, were on a plane ride to London, England, when Gene Clark asked bandmate Roger McGuinn how high the aircraft was. McGuinn replied, "Six miles." But the figure was changed to eight to play off the Beatles' song "Eight Days A Week."

Subsequently, members of the Byrds admitted that the song was inspired in part by their own drug use. Many of the lyrics refer to the band's stay in London.

The song has a complex structure that did not have a strong commercial appeal. McGuinn's licks on the 12-string Rickenbacker electric guitar are notable, but they did not add to the song's danceability.

Rhythm guitarist David Crosby, who contributed some of the lyrics, said the ending of the recording made him feel "like a plane landing."

The version that Columbia Records released was not the first version that the Byrds recorded. They went into RCA Studios in December 1965 and laid down the original track. But Columbia wouldn't release it because it wasn't recorded in a Columbia-owned studio. The final product was recorded the following month.

In describing the first recording, Crosby said, "It was a stunner. It was better, it was stronger. It had more flow to it. It was the way we wanted it to be."

After the single's release, a weekly industry newsletter, *Bill Gavin's Record Report*, carried allegations that the Byrds were advocating the use of recreational drugs through their music. The band's publicist issued a strong denial.

By the 1980s, however, Crosby was ready to admit, "Of course it was a drug song. We were stoned when we wrote it."

Clark's reaction was subtler. "It was about a lot of things," he said. "It was about the airplane trip to England. It was about drugs, it was about all that. A piece of poetry of that nature is not limited to having it have to be just about airplanes or having it have to be just about drugs. It was inclusive because in those days the new experimenting with all the drugs was a very vogue thing to do."

Nonetheless, after a few weeks of radio play "Eight Miles High" was banned by many stations. The record climbed to No. 14 and then faded quickly. Additionally, Columbia failed to give the record much promotional assistance and, frankly, the song was well ahead of its time.

American author Dominic Priore has said, "Prior to 'Eight Miles High' there were no pop records with incessant, hypnotic basslines juxtaposed by droning, trance-induced improvisational guitar."

Eight Miles High

Songwriters: Gene Clark, Roger McGuinn, David Crosby
Peaked at No. 14 on Billboard Hot 100
May 21, 1966

The Byrds

Roger McGuinn (July 13, 1942-) vocals, guitar
Gene Clark (Nov. 17, 1944-May 24, 1991) guitar, tambourine, vocals
David Crosby (Aug. 14, 1941-) guitar, keyboards, vocals
Michael Clarke (June 3, 46-Dec. 19, 1993) drums, percussion
Chris Hillman (Dec. 4, 1944-) bass, guitar
Formed in Los Angeles, Calif., in 1964

The Byrds: David Crosby, Chris Hillman, Roger McGuinn, Michael Clarke, Gene Clark

Psychotic Reaction [Count Five] – This band from San Jose, Calif., managed to combine its garage rock sound with psychedelic elements in its lone chartbuster.

Founded in 1964, Count Five were known in their early days for wearing capes on stage, a la Count Dracula. They were originally known as the Squires. After some personnel changes, they changed their moniker to Count V.

Guitarist John "Sean" Byrne came up with the idea for "Psychotic Reaction," and it became the focal point of the band's live performances in 1966. Over time, they were able to refine it. The song features prominent fuzz guitar and harmonica, and it uses changes in tempo to move from vocal parts to instrumental rave-ups, similar to the Yardbirds. In an interview, Byrne said that the Yardbirds' rendition of "I'm A Man" influenced Count Five's treatment of their own hit.

Finding a record label proved to be difficult for Count Five, but fledgling Double Shot Records in Hollywood finally decided to take a chance on them. Their total output was one great single and a so-so album of the same name.

"Things just didn't turn out right for us. We could've done the *Ed Sullivan Show*," Byrne told the *San Jose News*, "but they turned us down as being too weird."

Count Five would have a handful of other singles, but none saw the light of day in most markets across the nation. Double Shot dropped them in 1969, and the band's final demise came when its members decided to return to college, thereby avoiding being drafted into the Army. After all, the Selective Service System was looking for a lot of bodies to put into uniform in Vietnam.

Suffering from diabetes and cirrhosis, Byrne died at the age of 61.

Psychotic Reaction

Songwriters: Kenn Ellner, Roy Chaney, John "Sean" Byrne, John Michalski

Peaked at No. 5 on Billboard Hot 100

Oct. 15, 1966

Oct. 22, 1966

Count Five

John "Sean" Byrne (Nov. 16, 1947-Dec. 15, 2008) vocals, rhythm guitar

Kenn Ellner (1948-) harmonica, tambourine, vocals

John "Mouse" Michalski (1949-) lead guitar

Roy Chaney (1948-) bass

Craig "Butch" Atkinson (March 17, 1947-Oct. 13, 1998) drums

Formed in San Jose, Calif., in 1964

Count Five: Kenn Ellner, Roy Chaney, John Michalski, Craig Atkinson, John Byrne

I Had Too Much To Dream (Last Night) [Electric Prunes] – Another garage rock band, this one from Los Angeles, hit big with a career-defining hit. It was released in November 1966.

The roots of the Electric Prunes go back to L.A.'s Taft High School, where they were known as the Sanctions.

After the band was introduced to producer Dave Hassinger in '66, he suggested they change their name. The Electric Prunes moniker was a joke at first, but he got the members to agree with his suggestion by saying, "It's the one thing everyone will remember. It's not attractive, and there's nothing sexy about it, but people won't forget it."

I once heard a disc jockey joke that the Electric Prunes were "the first band on the run."

Hassinger didn't think the band could write its own songs. For the Prunes' second single, he went to songwriters Nancie Mantz and Annette Tucker for "I Had Too Much To Dream."

"I came up with the title one day and called Nancie," Tucker said. "She loved it, and we wrote it the next day in one-half hour. The words were there, and my melody came easily. I was influenced by the Rolling Stones at the time, and that is how I heard the song being recorded. Nancie and I envisioned this as a rock song."

An oscillating reversed guitar opens the song, and it originated from rehearsals at Leon Russell's house. "We were recording on a four-track," lead singer James Lowe explained, "and just flipping the tape over and re-recording when we got to the end. Dave cued up a tape and didn't hit 'record,' and the playback in the studio was way up – ear-shattering jet guitar. Ken (Williams, lead guitarist) had been shaking his Bigsby wiggle stick with some fuzztone and tremolo at the end of the tape.

"Forward, it was cool. Backward, it was amazing. I ran into the control room and said, 'What was that?' They didn't have the monitors on, so they hadn't heard it. I made Dave cut it off and save it for later."

A Bigsby wiggle stick is an accessory designed by guitar maker Paul Bigsby that, when connected to an electric guitar, produces a vibrato sound.

The lyrics describe how a guy feels after waking up from dreaming about an ex-lover. But the guitar riffs definitely brand the recording as psychedelic.

After riding up the *Billboard Hot 100* to No. 11 with "I Had Too Much To Dream," the Electric Prunes followed up with "Get Me To The World On Time," which peaked at No. 27. The remainder of their recording career was fairly undistinguished.

I Had Too Much To Dream (Last Night)
Songwriters: Annette Tucker, Nancie Mantz
Peaked at No. 11 on Billboard Hot 100
Feb. 11, 1967

The Electric Prunes

James Lowe (May 29, 1947-) vocals, rhythm guitar
Mark Tulin (Nov. 21, 1948-Feb. 26, 2011) bass
Ken Williams (DOB unavailable) lead guitar
Michael "Quint" Weakley (DOB unavailable) drums
Formed in Los Angeles, Calif., in 1965

The Electric Prunes

Light My Fire [Doors] – Hearing only the edited version of this song on AM radio in 1967, I never viewed it as a psychedelic track. But a few weeks later I started my freshman year in college, and my opinion of the song changed.

It seemed like every room in the dormitory had at least one copy of the Doors' eponymous first album in it, and I heard the full-length version of "Light My Fire" for the first time. At 7 minutes and change, the album track was a wormhole of instrumental delights. There was Ray Manzarek's Vox Continental keyboard. And there was Robby Krieger's Gibson SG electric guitar. Separately and together. John Densmore's drumming was steadily spot-on all the way through.

I never ingested drugs while listening to the track, but it could have been a wild trip if I had. My schoolmates and I never tired of hearing it play over and over.

Krieger was largely responsible for the writing, although the whole band got credit. Lead singer Jim Morrison contributed the second verse.

"Light My Fire" became the first song with psychedelic tendencies to hit No. 1 in America, spending three weeks atop the *Billboard Hot 100* during 1967's Summer of Love.

The song had been recorded the previous year, and Elektra Records held it until April 24, 1967. It turned the Doors from a band with a small cult following in Los Angeles into a nationally celebrated group.

Krieger told *Uncut Magazine*, "I asked Jim what I should write about. He said, 'Something universal, which won't disappear two years from now. Something that people can interpret themselves.'

"I said to myself that I'd write about the four elements: earth, air, fire, water. I picked fire, as I loved the Stones' song 'Play With Fire.' And that's how that came about."

In a recording career that lasted until Morrison's death in 1971, the Doors never had a bigger hit.

Elektra founder Jac Holzman told *Mojo Magazine,* "We had that huge problem with the time length – 7 and a half minutes. Nobody could figure out how to cut it. Finally I said to (producer Paul) Rothchild, 'Nobody can cut it but you.'

"When he cut out the solo, there were screams. Except from Jim. Jim said, 'Imagine a kid in Minneapolis hearing the cut version over the radio. It's going to turn his head around.' So they said, go ahead, release it. We released it with the full version on the other side." The cut version was only 2:52 in length.

Once the song's popularity took hold, many radio stations began to play the album version.

"Light My Fire" charted at No. 2 in Canada but got only as high as No. 49 in the U.K.

Light My Fire

Songwriters: Jim Morrison, Robby Krieger, John Densmore, Ray Manzarek

Peaked at No. 1 on Billboard Hot 100

July 29, 1967

Aug. 5, 1967

Aug. 12, 1967

The Doors

Jim Morrison (Dec. 8, 1943-July 3, 1971) vocals

Ray Manzarek (Feb. 12, 1939-May 20, 2013) keyboards

Robby Krieger (Jan. 8, 1946-) guitar

John Densmore (Dec. 1, 1944-) drums

Formed in Los Angeles, Calif., in 1965

The Doors: John Densmore, Jim Morrison, Robby Krieger, Ray Manzarek

White Rabbit [Jefferson Airplane] – It's fitting that a song like this would be included on an album titled "Surrealistic Pillow." The lyrical content fits right in with the name of Jefferson Airplane's second album.

Lead singer Grace Slick wrote the song when she was a member of a band called the Great Society. Slick joined the Airplane as the replacement for Signe Anderson, who left to give birth to her first child.

Imagery from Lewis Carroll's *Alice's Adventures in Wonderland* and its sequel *Through The Looking Glass* is woven throughout the lyrics. Slick has revealed that *Alice in Wonderland* often was read to her during her childhood – a memory she carried into adulthood.

According to author Rob Hughes, Slick wrote the song after ingesting LSD. Characters that she brought into the lyrics include the Red Queen, Alice, the caterpillar, the White Knight and the dormouse. The title never is mentioned in the lyrics, although one line says, "if you go chasing rabbits …"

With guitar chords making gentle changes in a slow tempo, the song creates a sedated mood. A nod to Ravel's "Bolero" also is evident in the rhythm.

Slick and her band were free spirits – a voice of the counterculture that came out of San Francisco in 1967.

"It wasn't actually a big hit," Jefferson Airplane bassist Jack Casady said of the song, "but it was within the culture of the times. It became the signature for the people who were doing the things it had reference to. But does it work on different levels other than just a drug song? Yeah, it does."

Slick told writer Mark Paytress, "In all those children's stories, you take some kind of chemical and have a great adventure. *Alice in Wonderland* is blatant. Eat me! She gets literally high, too big for the room. Drink me! The caterpillar is sitting on a psychedelic mushroom smoking opium."

In the song's final line, "feed your head" is a plea to liberate brains, as well as the senses.

The song peaked at No. 8 in the U.S. but was No. 1 in Canada and No. 3 in the Netherlands.

White Rabbit

Songwriter: Grace Slick

Peaked at No. 8 on Billboard Hot 100

July 29, 1967

Aug. 5, 1967

Jefferson Airplane

Grace Slick (Oct. 30, 1939-) vocals

Jorma Kaukonen (Dec. 23, 1940-) guitar, vocals

Marty Balin (Jan. 30, 1942-Sept. 27, 2018) vocals, guitar

Paul Kantner (March 17, 1941-Jan. 28, 2016) guitar, harmonica, vocals

Jack Casady (April 13, 1944-) bass

Spencer Dryden (April 7, 1938-Jan. 11, 2005) drums

Formed in San Francisco, Calif., in 1965

Jefferson Airplane: (back) Jack Casady, Grace Slick, Marty Balin
(front) Jorma Kaukonen, Paul Kantner, Spencer Dryden

Lucy In The Sky With Diamonds [Beatles] – There is more than one song on the album "Sgt. Pepper's Lonely Hearts Club Band" that can be considered psychedelic. But "Lucy" is a prime example.

As with all the tracks on the album, the song was not released as a single. But with over 32 million copies sold worldwide, there is universal familiarity with the track. Additionally, Elton John recorded the song in 1974 and had a No. 1 hit with it.

The sound is ethereal, and the lyrics are filled with wild imagery. Paul McCartney played a Lowrey organ, George Harrison played a tambura and there were sound distortions and echoes that enhanced the psychedelic feel.

The whole concept started when John Lennon's 3-year-old son Julian came hold from nursery school and showed him a drawing he had done. It was a depiction of his classmate Lucy O'Donnell, and he called it "Lucy – In the sky with diamonds. "I used to show Dad everything I'd built or painted at school, and this one sparked off the idea," Julian said years later.

Lennon retreated to his piano and began to write a song from this inspiration. His lyrics were also inspired by the literary works of Lewis Carroll, including *Alice In Wonderland*, which he had enjoyed.

McCartney helped Lennon finish the song, and he contributed the lyrics "newspaper taxis" and "cellophane flowers."

The album was released in the U.S. at the beginning of June 1967, and it didn't take long for speculation about the meaning of the song's title to start. The conventional opinion was that Lucy/Sky/Diamonds must surely stand for LSD, the hallucinogenic drug. The U.K. release of "Sgt. Pepper" had come the previous month, and a BBC radio ban came almost immediately.

Lennon, however, said that the song "wasn't about that at all" and "it was purely unconscious that it came out to be LSD. Until someone pointed it out, I never even thought of it. I mean, who would even bother to look at initials of a title? It's not an acid song."

In later years Harrison said "Lucy" was one of the few songs from "Sgt. Pepper" that he liked, and he said he was satisfied with his Indian music-inspired contributions.

Lucy In The Sky With Diamonds

Songwriters: John Lennon, Paul McCartney
Included on the album "Sgt. Pepper's Lonely Hearts Club Band
Peaked at No. 1 on Billboard 200
July 1-Oct. 7, 1967

The Beatles

John Lennon (Oct. 9, 1940-Dec. 8, 1980) keyboards, rhythm guitar, vocals
George Harrison (Feb. 25, 1943-Nov. 29, 2001) guitar, sitar, vocals
Paul McCartney (June 18, 1942-) bass, keyboards, vocals
Ringo Starr (July 7, 1940-) drums, vocals
Formed in Liverpool, England, in 1960

The Beatles: John Lennon, Paul McCartney, Ringo Starr, George Harrison

Purple Haze [Jimi Hendrix Experience] – Perhaps the first power trio ever, Jimi Hendrix and his two mates recorded this classic in early 1967. The song was contained on the album "Are You Experienced?"

Having left New York City for London in 1966, Hendrix was little known in the States. Along with his appearance at the Monterey Pop Festival, this album was like a coming out party for him in the U.S.

What most people don't know is that the very psychedelic-sounding "Purple Haze" wasn't about an LSD trip. "I dream a lot, and I put my dreams down as songs," Hendrix said in a 1967 interview before the song had been finished. "I wrote one called 'First Look Around The Corner' and another called 'The Purple Haze,' which was about a dream I had that I was walking under the sea."

Like the other songs on "Are You Experienced," this one was recorded a piece at a time with Hendrix on guitar, Noel Redding on bass and Mitch Mitchell on drums. Band manager Chas Chandler served as producer and found it more efficient to work alone with Hendrix in sessions for "Purple Haze." Three different studios in London were used.

"With 'Purple Haze,' Hendrix and I were striving for a sound and just kept going back in, two hours at a time, trying to achieve it," Chandler explained. "It wasn't like we were there for days on end. We recorded it, and then Hendrix and I would be sitting at home saying, 'Let's try that.' Then we would go in (to the studio) for an hour or two.

"That's how it was in those days. However long it took to record one specific idea, that's how long we would book. We kept going in and out."

With Hendrix's bluesy, innovative guitar work on display for the first time, the song also marked the first time that the Octavia guitar effects unit was ever used. It was designed for Hendrix by his British sound technician, Roger Mayer, and it reproduces the input signal from a guitar one octave higher or lower and mixes it with the original while adding distortion fuzz.

In creating a background track that has a distant sound, Chandler put a pair of headphones around a microphone for playback that had an echo effect.

It was a revolutionary sound – one that may have been a little too far ahead of its time. On the *Billboard Hot 100*, the single languished at No. 65. But "Purple Haze" had a better fit for album-oriented rock, and "Are You Experienced?" zoomed up to No. 5 on the *Billboard 200.* Hendrix, in fact, had eight albums that peaked in the top five of the album charts.

Rolling Stone Magazine has ranked the song No. 17 on its 500 Greatest Songs of All Time. But the fledgling publication's first impression of "Are You Experienced?" was less than favorable in 1967.

Wrote John Landau, "Despite Jimi's musical brilliance and the group's total precision, the poor quality of the songs and the inanity of the lyrics too often get in the way. Above all, this record is unrelenting, violent, and lyrically, inartistically violent at that. Dig it if you can, but as for me, I'd rather hear Jimi play the blues."

Purple Haze

Songwriter: Jimi Hendrix

Peaked at No. 65 on Billboard Hot 100

Oct. 14, 1967

Oct. 21, 1967

Jimi Hendrix Experience

Jimi Hendrix (Nov. 27, 1942-Sept. 18, 1970) guitar, vocals
Noel Redding (Dec. 25, 1945-May 11, 2003) bass, vocals
Mitch Mitchell (July 9, 1946-Nov. 12, 2008) drums
Formed in London, England, in 1966

Jimi Hendrix Experience: Noel Redding, Hendrix, Mitch Mitchell

Incense And Peppermints [Strawberry Alarm Clock] – In a strange twist of fate, this record was released before the band that recorded it got its final name.

The Los Angeles band had four singles under its belt with the name Thee Sixpence. The fourth had an A-side of "Birdman Of Alcatrash" and a "B" side of "Incense And Peppermints." During sessions for the "B" side, members of the band were disenchanted with the lyrics, which had been written by John S. Carter (co-writer on "That Acapulco Gold" for Rainy Daze; see Chapter 11).

The words had no cohesion, and the lines ended with meaningless words that happened to rhyme.

The lead vocal was sung by a visitor to the session, Greg Munford, who was a friend of the band. The band members provided backing vocals, and Munford never joined the band.

Veteran producer Frank Slay denied writing credits to band members Mark Weitz and Ed King, even though the song was based on their instrumental concept. All-American Records released it in April 1967.

After local L.A. disc jockeys got hold of the single, they began to play "Incense And Peppermints" instead of the "A" side. Believing that a national hit was at stake, Uni Records picked up the record for distribution and promoted "Incense" as the "A" side after re-releasing it in May.

By the time of the second pressing, the band had changed its name to Strawberry Alarm Clock because another band in the area had a name similar to Thee Sixpence.

The electric guitars, electric keyboard and lyrics made the hit song fit right in with the psychedelic genre of the time.

Keyboardist Weitz gave this account of the song's evolution to *Songfacts:* "I came up with the idea and actual music to the then untitled song. I wrote the intro (the oriental sounding riff), the verses and the ending, while Ed King, at my request for some help on completing the song, co-wrote the bridge and, of course, the lead guitar parts.

"At the time when the music was recorded at Art Laboe's Original Sounds studio in Hollywood, there was only a temporary title to the song, and lyrics had not yet been written. Our producer, Frank Slay, decided to send the fully mixed music track (recorded on 8 tracks of mono) to Carter, a member of the band The Rainy Daze, who Slay also produced at the time.

"John Carter was solely responsible for conjuring up the lyrics and the controversial melody line extracted out of the finished musical track. Frank Slay ultimately credited that melody line solely to the writing team of John Carter and Tim Gilbert. To this day, they have received 100 percent of the royalties."

The singers were trying to sound British on the track, which sounded a bit corny but worked, nonetheless. The single hit No. 1 and was a million seller.

Incense And Peppermints

Songwriters: John S. Carter, Tim Gilbert
Peaked at No. 1 on Billboard Hot 100
Nov. 25, 1967

The Strawberry Alarm Clock

Ed King (Sept. 14, 1949-Aug. 22, 2018) lead guitar, vocals
Lee Freeman (Nov. 8, 1949-Feb. 14, 2010) rhythm guitar, harmonica, vocals
Randy Seol (DOB unavailable) drums, vocals
Mark Weitz (DOB unavailable) keyboards, vocals
Gary Lovetro (DOB unavailable) bass
Formed in Los Angeles, Calif., in 1967

The Strawberry Alarm Clock

I Can See For Miles [The Who] – This was the most successful single on the American charts for the Who, a band that generated most of its sales from albums.

What makes it a psychedelic song is the ethereal vocal harmonies and Pete Townshend's strong guitar solo on the break. There also is some fabulous crashing by drummer Keith Moon. The title itself could make a drug user think he could see for miles while listening to the song.

The recording was done in London and New York, and it was mastered in Los Angeles. Some of the cutting edge studio techniques used by the Beatles and the Beach Boys were employed during production.

The single peaked at No. 9 on the *Billboard Hot 100* and at No. 10 in the U.K., but that wasn't good enough for Townshend, who wrote the song. He had penned "I Can See For Miles" in 1966 and kept it as "an ace in the hole," thinking it would be the Who's first No. 1 single. He's been quoted as saying, "To me it was the ultimate Who record, yet it didn't sell. I spat on the British record buyer." He called it "remarkable" and considered it one of his best works.

According to *Songfacts,* Townshend put together the lyrics shortly after meeting his future wife, Karen. It served as a reminder that he could keep an eye on her even when he was miles away on tour with the Who. The couple were married 1968-2009.

As quoted in *Rolling Stone*, Townshend said, "The words, which aging senators have called 'drug oriented,' are about a jealous man with exceptionally good eyesight. Honest."

I Can See For Miles
Songwriter: Pete Townshend
Peaked at No. 9 on Billboard Hot 100
Dec. 2, 1967

The Who
Pete Townshend (May 19, 1945-) guitar, vocals
Roger Daltrey (March 1, 1944-) vocals
Keith Moon (Aug. 23, 1946-Sept. 7, 1978) drums, vocals
John Entwistle (Oct. 9, 1944-June 27, 2002) bass, vocals
Formed in London, England, in 1964

The Who: Pete Townshend, John Entwistle, Keith Moon, Roger Daltrey

Just Dropped In (To See What My Condition My Condition Was In) [First Edition] – On their way to becoming a successful folk/pop group in the late 1960s, the First Edition with Kenny Rogers on lead vocals made this psychedelic production their first hit in '68.

Music fans who didn't already know, might be aghast to learn that the song first was recorded by Jerry Lee Lewis a few months earlier and was written by country songsmith Mickey Newbury. It appeared on Lewis's 1967 album "Soul My Way."

The First Edition was produced by Mike Post, who at first didn't see any value to having Rogers on board. "I didn't know what he brought to the party," Post said. "Shows what I know."

Most members of the First Edition had left the New Christy Minstrels to seek greater artistic freedom.

When one more song was needed to fill out the First Edition's first album, Rogers brought in "Just Dropped In," which Post called "dope and roll." A psychedelic handling of the song was chosen, and it became a top-five hit.

The song, which was intended to caution against the use of drugs, got a tepid reception from the public at first. Then the First Edition lip-synched the song behind a psychedelic video on the Smothers Brothers Comedy Hour on CBS-TV, and the record took off.

Top session musicians like Glen Campbell and Hal Blaine played on the track. The guitar solo played by Campbell was heavily compressed with a tremolo effect added for the psychedelic sound. The lyrics are filled with contradictory statements and warped imagery that give the feeling of a person on a drug trip.

One of the lines apparently is a nod to the Byrds' song in this chapter: "I tripped on a cloud and fell eight miles high."

Just Dropped In (To See What Condition My Condition Was In)

Songwriter: Mickey Newbury

Peaked at No. 5 on Billboard Hot 100

March 16, 1968

March 23, 1968

The First Edition

Kenny Rogers (Aug. 21, 1938-March 20, 2020) vocals, bass

Mickey Jones (June 10, 1941-Feb. 7, 2018) drums

Thelma Camacho (1949-) vocals

Terry Williams (June 6, 1947-) guitar

Mike Settle (March 20, 1941-) guitar, backing vocals

Formed in Los Angeles, Calif., in 1967

The First Edition: Mike Settle, Terry Williams, Thelma Camacho, Kenny Rogers, Mickey Jones

A Question Of Temperature [Balloon Farm] – With this song, a band from New Jersey proved that there was room in psychedelic pop for another garage rock outfit.

Members Don Henny and Ed Schnug played together in a band called Adam, whose only single was a song aptly titled "Eve." Proving that they really had a sense of humor, all of the musicians adopted the first name Adam.

After that group broke up, Henny and Schnug joined Mike Appel and Jay Saks in the Balloon Farm, a name they borrowed from a New York City nightclub. Their first single was "A Question Of Temperature," which was recorded in 1967 and broke onto the national charts in '68. Shnug, Appel and Henny wrote it.

The song had a pulsating beat and featured a fuzz guitar, echoes and a few psychedelic sound effects. The 45 rpm record also had a typographical error on the label, at first – "Tempature." Later pressings of the single corrected the mistake but, you have to admit, that was a unique way to put a psychedelic feel into the record.

The production may have been low tech, but the record crawled into the national top 40.

"I came up with the framework for the song and the guitar riff, and then everybody pitched in with the rest of the music," Appel told writer Mike Stax. "I think, being a wordy guy, I wrote the lyrics."

A follow-up single, "Hurry Sundown," didn't do so well. Laurie Records dropped the band before it could assemble enough recordings for a full album.

Proving that they had resilience, the members of Balloon Farm popped up later in 1968 with the name Huck Finn and a single, "Two Of A Kind."

After he wrote some songs for the Partridge Family, Appel became Bruce Springsteen's first manager.

A Question Of Temperature

Songwriters: Mike Appel, Ed Schnug, Don Henny

Peaked at No. 37 on Billboard Hot 100

March 23, 1968

March 30. 1968

April 6, 1968

The Balloon Farm

Mike Appel (Oct. 27, 1942-) guitar, vocals

Ed Schnug – keyboards

Don Henny – drums

Jay Saks – bass

Formed in New Jersey in 1967

The Balloon Farm

Pictures Of Matchstick Men [The Status Quo] – If you like guitar riffs that feature the use of lots of wah-wah pedal, this is a song for you. It is one of the few contributions to psychedelic rock by a British band.

Interestingly, only the mono version of the single has the wah-wah, while the stereo version omitted it.

The original intent was for this song to be the "B" side to "Gentleman Joe's Sidewalk Café," according to lead singer/guitarist Francis Rossi of the Status Quo. The two tracks changed place at the last minute in 1968.

Rossi later remarked, "I wrote it on the bog. I'd gone there, not for the usual reasons ... but to get away from the wife and mother-in-law. I used to go into this narrow frizzing toilet and sit there for hours, until they finally went out. I got three quarters of the song finished in that khazi. The rest I finished in the lounge."

According to *Songfacts*, Rossi said the song "... was basically about my ex-wife. I'd just got married, and I thought, 'Oh, this is a mistake. What have I done?'"

A fan of Jimi Hendrix, Rossi was inspired by the chord structure of "Hey Joe" when he wrote this song.

"Matchstick men" refers to paintings by British artist L.S. Lowry, who had painted scenes of life in the industrialized towns of northern England during the mid-20th century. He characterized humans as stick-like people.

After "Pictures Of Matchstick Men" began its trek up the charts, the Status Quo went on an extensive tour of Europe. The single rose to No. 12 on the *Billboard Hot 100*, but the band missed a good opportunity to promote their music in the U.S. because they did not tour in America.

The single reached No. 7 on the British charts and No. 8 in Canada.

Pictures Of Matchstick Men

Songwriter: Francis Rossi

Peaked at No. 12 on Billboard Hot 100

Aug. 3, 1968

The Status Quo

Francis Rossi (May 29, 1949-) lead guitar, vocals
Alan Lancaster (Feb. 7, 1949-) guitar, bass
Roy Lynes (Oct. 25, 1943-) keyboards
John Coughlin (Sept. 19, 1946-) drums
Formed in London, England, in 1962

The Status Quo

Hurdy Gurdy Man [Donovan] – For this song, Scotsman Donovan Leitch deviated from his normal, folky formula and turned toward psychedelia.

Donovan wrote the song while he was with the Beatles, studying transcendental meditation in Rishikesh, India. The recording features prominent drum licks and distorted electric guitar. Donovan played acoustic guitar and a four-string tambura that George Harrison had given him.

Rishikesh, in the foothills of northern India's Himalayas, has been known as the Yoga Capital of the World.

"I was intrigued by the Maharishi Mahesh Yogi's teachings of transcendental meditation, which were also followed by the Beatles," Donovan told the *Daily Mail Weekend*. "I went with the Beatles and George's wife, Pattie Boyd, Cynthia Lennon and Jane Asher to stay with the Maharishi in the Himalayas for three months. For a while, Mia Farrow and her sister Prudence shared the bungalow next to mine. She inspired John Lennon to write 'Dear Prudence.'

"'Hurdy Gurdy Man' was influenced by the sounds I heard there."

Lyrically, we find the narrator being visited via dream by the Hurdy Gurdy Man and his wingman, the Roly Poly Man. They come "singing songs of love," and we hear some other mystical phrasing.

According to Jimmy Page's website, he played guitar on the track. Other information on the Internet points to Alan Parker as the author of the guitar solo. Donovan has said that he wanted Jimi Hendrix to play, but he wasn't available.

A hurdy-gurdy is a stringed instrument that dates back to medieval times. It generates sound through a hand crank with a rosined wheel rubbing against the strings. The wheel's function is much like that of a violin's bow, and single notes sound much like those of a violin. Notes are selected by pushing buttons. Through the years it has been played by people from all walks of life, from beggars to members of nobility.

Hurdy Gurdy Man

Songwriter: Donovan Leitch

Peaked at No. 5 on Billboard Hot 100

Aug. 3, 1968

Donovan

Born Donovan Philips Leitch in Maryhill, Glasgow, Scotland, on May 10, 1946

Donovan

Journey To The Center Of The Mind [Amboy Dukes] – If one song can legitimize the career of a guitar virtuoso, this may be such a song.

Almost overnight, Ted Nugent became a household name in the summer of 1968 because of his stellar work on "Journey To The Center Of The Mind." It was a springboard to other fine songs that carried the stamp of his axe work throughout his career.

The song is about psychedelic drugs, and lyrics were written by the Amboy Dukes' rhythm guitarist, Steve Farmer. Nugent, who always has led a straight-arrow lifestyle as far as drug use, claims he did not know the meaning of the song. He thought it was about looking within oneself.

Nugent believed that taking recreational drugs makes a person less than what he was before. Although he wore long hair in the 1960s and looked like a hippie, he had no desire to dabble in that lifestyle. The band even turned down an invitation to play at the Woodstock festival in 1969 because Nugent didn't like hippies.

Getting back to Nugent's guitar work – it was strong, imaginative and vital to the success of "Journey." After the Amboy Dukes broke up in 1975, he fronted his own band using other lead singers. His name was on the docket because his guitar work was the key ingredient in his songs.

Nugent dubbed his group the Amboy Dukes because he liked the name. Apparently he knew nothing of the street gang of the same name from Perth Amboy, N.J., which appeared in a novel by Irving Shulman. The band formed in Chicago and later made Detroit their home base.

While continuing to play rock music in the 21st century, Nugent has become an activist for bowhunting and conservative politics.

Journey To The Center Of The Mind
Songwriters: Steve Farmer, Ted Nugent
Peaked at No. 16 on Billboard Hot 100
Aug. 24, 1968
Aug. 31, 1968

The Amboy Dukes
Ted Nugent (Dec. 13, 1948-) lead guitar, vocals
Steve Farmer (Dec. 31, 1948-) guitar, vocals
Dave Palmer (DOB unavailable) drums
John Drake (DOB unavailable) lead vocals
Andy Solomon (DOB unavailable) keyboards, vocals
Greg Arama (Aug. 17, 1950-Sept. 18, 1979) bass
Formed in Chicago, Ill., in 1964

The Amboy Dukes

Time Has Come Today [Chambers Brothers] – This quintet contributed to the psychedelic era in a rather unusual fashion.

The Chambers Brothers recorded this song in 1966, early in the era, but didn't see it hit the charts until late in '68 near the end of psychedelia's popularity. Oddly, the brothers were from Mississippi and began as a gospel group, but they recorded a psychedelic anthem.

A short, 3 minute version of the song bombed in '66, but the band played the long version in its live shows. When their album "The Time Has Come" was released, it contained a version that ran 11:06, which made for great listening in collegiate dorm rooms and apartments. My roommate during sophomore year had a copy.

Joe Chambers wrote most of the lyrics after class at UCLA, tripping on LSD, according to *Songfacts*. Willie wrote the melody and came up with the line "my soul has been psychedelicized."

Columbia Records president Clive Davis told the Chambers Brothers that they couldn't record the song because it was too incendiary for the political climate of the day. It seemed to be calling for a black revolution throughout the nation. "It's too profound a statement for four black guys to be saying to the world," Davis said.

With producer David Rubinson, the band surreptitiously made the recording in one take. Davis didn't find out about it until it had been mixed, printed and released. After he found out, he fired every employee who had been involved in the process, according to *Songfacts*.

The single was re-released in 1968 and spent several weeks at No. 11 on the *Billboard Hot 100*.

The alternate striking of two cowbells replicates the ticking of a clock. There are changes in tempo, reverb and echo effects, all of which make it a great psychedelic song.

Time Has Come Today

Songwriters: Willie Chambers, Joseph Chambers

Peaked at No. 11 on Billboard Hot 100

Sept. 28, 1968
Oct. 5, 1968
Oct. 12, 1968
Oct. 19, 1968

The Chambers Brothers

George Chambers (Sept. 26, 1931-) bass
Lester Chambers (April 13, 1940-) harmonica
Willie Chambers (March 3, 1938-) guitar
Joseph Chambers (Aug. 22, 1942-) guitar
Brian Keenan (Jan. 28, 1943-Oct. 5, 1985) drums
Formed in Los Angeles, Calif., in 1954

The Chambers Brothers

In-A-Gadda-Da-Vida [Iron Butterfly] – Not very many albums in the history of pop music have one song occupying an entire side. But the Iron Butterfly pulled off that feat in 1968 with "In-A-Gadda-Da-Vida." The album version of the title song eclipses 17 minutes.

Lyrics? I don't think the band spent much time on them. They're simple, only 30 different words in number and appear only at the beginning and end of the song. Instrumental jamming takes up the rest of the time.

Ron Bushy, the band's drummer, related that singer/organist Doug Ingle wrote the song one night while he was drinking an entire gallon of wine. Ingle, thoroughly intoxicated by then, played the song for Bushy, who wrote down the lyrics. Ingle was slurring his words so badly that Bushy interpreted "In The Garden of Eden" as "In-A-Gadda-Da-Vida."

An executive at Atco Records decided to use the butchered title because it sounded mystical. The Beatles' recent visits to India and adoption of some Eastern spirituality was well known throughout the industry, and every band wanted something in common with the Beatles.

It didn't take long for Iron Butterfly to decide to convert a 1½-minute ballad into a lengthy jam. British guitarist Jeff Beck maintains that he saw Iron Butterfly play at a club in April 1967, when an entire set consisted of 35 minutes of "In-A-Gadda-Da-Vida." Guitar and keyboard play take up most of the time, but bass and drum solos also appear.

The band was doing a run-through of the song for a sound check, with tape rolling in the studio control room, while the band waited for producer Jim Hilton to arrive. After the rehearsal was completed, Hilton and engineer Don Casale determined that the quality was good enough, and they allowed to it stand as a usable take.

The single issue of the song was boiled down to 2:53 in the U.S., and all solos were edited out. There were other versions of varying lengths released internationally.

Iron Butterfly was scheduled to play at Woodstock the year after their signature song hit it big, but their demands got in the way. Their manager insisted on a helicopter ride from New York LaGuardia Airport to the festival site some 100 miles away, as well as an immediate start time upon arrival, immediate payment at the conclusion of their set and a prompt return ride via copter. The festival organizers did not capitulate, and the band was left off the program.

In-A-Gadda-Da-Vida

Songwriter: Doug Ingle

Peaked at No. 30 on Billboard Hot 100

Oct. 26, 1968

Nov. 2, 1968

Iron Butterfly

Doug Ingle (Sept. 9, 1945-) organ, lead vocals

Ron Bushy (Sept. 23, 1945-) drums

Lee Dorman (Sept. 15, 1942-Dec. 21, 2012) bass

Erik Brann (Aug. 11, 1950-July 25, 2003) guitar

Formed in San Diego, Calif., in 1966

Iron Butterfly: Doug Ingle, Ron Bushy, Lee Dorman, Erik Brann

White Room [Cream] – Wah-wah pedal and some great imagery are the hallmarks of this hit from the British power trio Cream. It was possibly guitar wizard Eric Clapton's first experience with the wah-wah.

The song was recorded for the studio half of the 1968 double album "Wheels Of Fire," which featured live tracks on the other disc. The first sessions were held in 1967.

Poet Pete Brown contributed the lyrics. They speak of depression and hopelessness. "It was a meandering thing about a relationship I was in and how I was at the time," Brown told *Songfacts*. "There was this kind of transitional period where I lived in this actual white room and was trying to come to terms with various things that were going on.

"It's a place where I stopped – I gave up all drugs and alcohol at that time in 1967 as a result of being in the white room, so it was kind of a watershed period. That song's like a kind of weird little movie – it changes perspective all the time. That's probably why it's lasted. It's got a kind of mystery to it."

Clapton's guitar solo on the break got a ranking of No. 2 on *Guitar World's* greatest wah-wah solos of all time. Lead singer Jack Bruce composed the melody.

According to Brown, the "goodbye windows" in the lyrics are "just people waving goodbye from the windows of trains." "Black roof country" is the area near railroads, where steam trains leave soot and ash on the roofs of houses.

The single was released after Cream broke up. It peaked at No. 1 in Australia, No. 2 in Canada and New Zealand and No. 28 in the U.K.

White Room

Songwriter: Pete Brown, Jack Bruce

Peaked at No. 6 on Billboard Hot 100

Nov. 9, 1968

Nov. 16, 1968

Nov. 23, 1968

Cream

Jack Bruce (May 14, 1943-Oct. 25, 2014) bass, vocals

Eric Clapton (March 30, 1945-) guitar, vocals

Ginger Baker (Aug. 19, 1939-Oct. 6, 2019) drums, vocals

Formed in London, England, in 1966

Cream: Eric Clapton, Ginger Baker, Jack Bruce

Crimson And Clover [Tommy James & the Shondells] – This song had a title before it had a melody or lyrics, and it moved Tommy James & the Shondells out of the two-minute love song formula that had worked well for them for three years.

Supposedly, the title combination came to James as he was waking, uniting his favorite color, crimson, and his favorite flower, clover.

The track was recorded in late 1968 and was one of the first songs recorded on 16-track equipment.

Besides an echo effect on the opening vocal, what really makes this a great psychedelic song is the extended instrumental in the middle section of the album version. It is there that we hear lots of intricate guitar with wah-wah pedal and more echoed vocals. A tremolo (trembling) effect was used on both guitar and vocals.

These studio gimmicks turned a No. 1 single into a psychedelic era masterpiece. The single ran 3:23, but the album version clocked in at 5:25.

The single went to No. 1 in Canada, New Zealand, South Africa and Switzerland and No. 2 in Belgium and Germany. It did not chart in the U.K.

The Shondells had been out on the campaign trail with presidential candidate Hubert Humphrey for several weeks in 1968. By the time they got off the road, they discovered that many of the top recording acts that had specialized in making singles had disappeared and were replaced by musicians who were marketing great albums.

James decided that his band needed to make the transition from specializing in singles to making albums that would sell. "Crimson And Clover" became the name of the album that would carry a great single and help them through the transition.

"When we went into the studio to do it, we actually finished the record in about 5½ hours," James was quoted in *Songfacts*. "And, of course, we had done everything – we wrote the song, we produced the record, we did all the things we had to do. We designed the album cover, we got to the point where we almost took the creative process right on into the retail store.

"It was amazing. One of the things that was great about Roulette (Records) is that they allowed us the freedom to do these things. There was never any hand around our throat. At least not for that reason. There was never anybody who was really leaning on us. We had all the budgets, what we needed, we could take our time. Whatever we could become, Roulette allowed us to be.

"So, I'm thankful for that. And we had the public's attention long enough to morph into the second phase of our career. 'Crimson and Clover' allowed us to go on and have a Phase 2 of our career selling albums. And no other record we ever did would have done that."

While the band was in Chicago to do a show, James went to the WLS studios to do a radio interview. He had a rough mix of "Crimson And Clover" with him, and James played it for the program director. Unbeknownst to James, his recording was being taped. By the time James had left WLS and was in his car, a disc jockey was playing the song on the air as a "world exclusive."

The record broke so fast in Chicago that there was no time to do a final mix. The rough mix ended up being pressed onto vinyl.

Crimson And Clover

Songwriters: Tommy James, Peter Lucia

Peaked at No. 1 on Billboard Hot 100

Feb. 1, 1969

Feb. 8, 1969

Tommy James & the Shondells

Tommy James (April 29, 1947-) vocals, guitar, tambourine
Eddie Gray (Feb. 27, 1948-) guitar
Peter Lucia (Feb. 2, 1947-Jan. 6, 1997) drums
Ron Rosman (Feb. 28, 1945-) keyboards
Mike Vale (July 17, 1949-) bass
Formed in Niles, Mich., in 1964

The Shondells: Peter Lucia, Mike Vale, Tommy James, Ron Rosman, Eddie Gray

Hot Smoke & Sasafrass [Bubble Puppy] – A psychedelic song with a misspelled word in the title? That would be this one.

The correct spelling is "sassafras," but what do you want – good spelling or good music?

The band's name fit the psychedelic theme. Supposedly it came from "Brave New World" by Aldous Huxley, in which a children's game called centrifugal bumble-puppy was played.

The song title was a misheard phrase from the TV show *The Beverly Hillbillies,* in which Granny Clampett yelled at her grandson, "Hot smokin' sassafras, Jethro, can't you do anything right?"

Sassafras is a North American tree whose leaves can be used to make medicinal tea.

Mystical lyrics joined with dual lead electric guitar work to make this a psychedelic hit, as it ascended to No. 14 on the *Billboard Hot 100.*

Formed in 1964 in Houston, Bubble Puppy got its big break when it joined a concert tour to open for The Who, and that led to a recording contract with the label International Artists.

With Bubble Puppy riding high on the strength of its one hit, producer Peter Asher sought to bring the band to Apple Records. But the band could not break its contract, and IA would not lease the song to Apple.

The band left the Lone Star State for Los Angeles and played under a different name in an effort to circumvent its contract. But it was all for naught, and Bubble Puppy disbanded in 1970.

Hot Smoke & Sasafrass

Songwriters: Rod Prince, Roy Cox

Peaked at No. 14 on Billboard Hot 100

April 12, 1969

Bubble Puppy
Rod Prince – lead guitar
Roy Cox – bass
Todd Potter – lead guitar
David "Fuzzy" Fore – drums
Formed in San Antonio, Texas, in 1967

Bubble Puppy

Whole Lotta Love [Led Zeppelin] – Blues rock was Led Zeppelin's calling card, but guitarist Jimmy Page, who produced this song, turned it into a psychedelic carnival.

A freeform middle section with sound distortions and Robert Plant's orgasmic moans give the song a strong psychedelic feel. There's even a backward echo, which resulted from Plant's voice bleeding over onto the tape from a previous take. This mistake was accentuated, adding reverb to make the vocal sound as if Plant were foreshadowing his words from afar.

Although the song wasn't released as a single in the U.K., it was Led Zeppelin's highest charting single in the U.S., reaching No. 4. It went to No. 1 in Australia and Germany.

Atlantic Records made a chopped-up version of the song for release in the U.K., but Page nixed it. "I played it once, hated it and never listened to the short version again," Page told the *Wall Street Journal.*

Unfortunately for Led Zeppelin, the lyrics were a little too similar to a 1962 song by Willie Dixon, "You Need Love." These similarities led Dixon to sue Led Zeppelin in 1985, and the band settled out of court for an undisclosed amount.

"You only get caught when you're successful," Plant told *Musician Magazine.* "That's the game."

The lyrics have a bit of lewdness, as the song's narrator declares to his girl that "I'm gonna give you every inch of my love."

Drummer John Bonham delivered a big sound from his kit. To accomplish this, the band used the big room at Olympic Studios in London, which had a 28-foot ceiling. Engineer George Chkiantz put the drum kit on a platform and positioned microphones in unconventional places around the room.

Page also used a theremin, an instrument that the Beach Boys used in the recording of "Good Vibrations" in 1966.

The track was taped on an eight-track recorder. Page waited for the band to come to New York on tour because he wanted producer/engineer Eddie Kramer to work his magic on it. Kramer had relocated to New York City from London in 1968.

The following year Kramer and his crew recorded the entire Woodstock festival in three-plus days of near-sleeplessness.

Whole Lotta Love

Songwriters: John Bonham, Willie Dixon, John Paul Jones, Robert Plant, Jimmy Page

Peaked at No. 4 on Billboard Hot 100

Jan. 31, 1970

Led Zeppelin

Jimmy Page (Jan. 9, 1944-) guitar
Robert Plant (Aug. 20, 1948-) vocals
John Paul Jones (Jan. 3, 1946-) bass, keyboards
John Bonham (May 31, 1948-Sept. 25, 1980) drums
Formed in London, England, in 1968

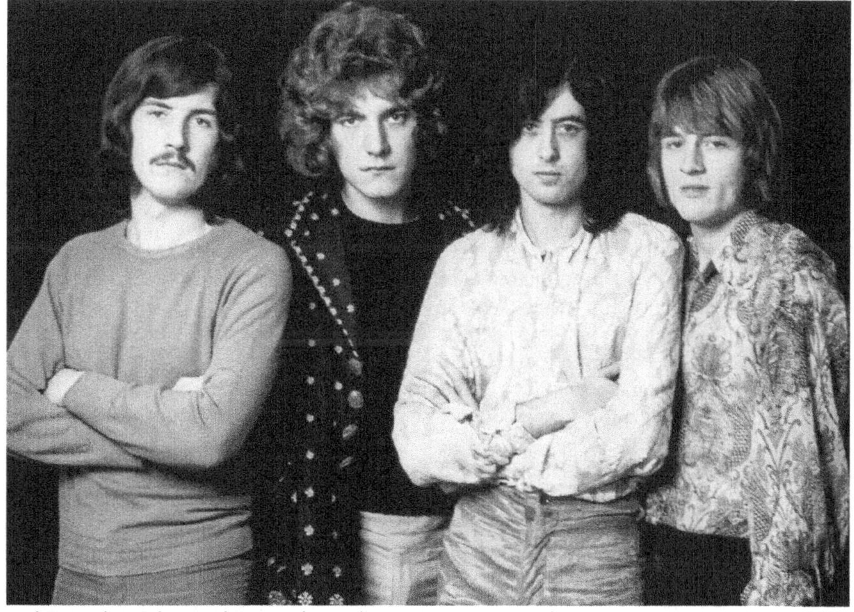

Led Zeppelin: John Bonham, Robert Plant, Jimmy Page, John Paul Jones

Chapter 16

Happily Ever After

Songs that tell a story

Overview: Storytelling is an art. Telling a good story in the span of a three-minute recording takes real talent.

Several songwriters have pulled off the feat of telling entertaining stories in their musical works. They have told tales that listeners can hear repeatedly without getting weary of the story. Many have attached a pleasant melody, while others are spoken word songs with background instrumentation.

Just remember – these are more like dime store novels rather than *War And Peace.*

The following are some of my favorite story songs.

To view the full lyrics to these songs, please log on to www.google.com, enter song titles & artist names and click Google Search.

To listen to these songs, please log on to www.youtube.com and enter song titles & artist names.

The Battle Of New Orleans [Johnny Horton] – The date was Jan. 8, 1815, when Gen. Andrew Jackson led American forces against the British near New Orleans, La. The battle turned into a rout for the home team, and it turned out to be the final clash in the War of 1812.

A folk song called "The Eighth of January" sprang from that victory and became a favorite of American fiddle players. In 1955 Jimmy Driftwood wrote lyrics for the song and gave it a new title. Country singer Johnny Horton turned it into a huge crossover hit on the pop charts.

The humorous twist of the lyrics helped give the record enduring popularity. After the patriots fired their "squirrel guns" on the British, the red coats "ran through the briars and they ran through the brambles" to escape the onslaught. "They ran so fast that the hounds couldn't catch 'em."

Driftwood was a schoolteacher from Snowball, Ark. After "The Battle Of New Orleans" became a smash, he quit his job to concentrate on music because his songwriting was in high demand.

Logging six weeks at No. 1 on the *Hot 100,* "The Battle Of New Orleans" became *Billboard's* top song for 1959. Horton placed two more history-themed songs in the top five the following year: "Sink The Bismarck" and "North To Alaska."

Horton did not live to see the end of 1960. While driving home to Shreveport, La., from a performance in Austin, Texas, he was killed in a car crash on a foggy highway on Nov. 5, 1960.

The Battle Of New Orleans

Songwriter: Jimmy Driftwood

Peaked at No. 1 on Billboard Hot 100

June 1, 1959
June 8, 1959
June 15, 1959
June 22, 1959
June 29, 1959
July 6, 1959

Johnny Horton

April 30, 1925-Nov. 5, 1960

Born John LaGale Horton in Los Angeles, Calif., and died in a car crash near Milano, Texas

Johnny Horton

Big Bad John [Jimmy Dean] – This 1961 song is like the ultimate ode to a co-worker. And its creator wrote it on a 90-minute flight.

Jimmy Dean, who was a country artist, made this a spoken-word recording, with back-up singers singing the title at the end of each verse.

The narrator is a miner, and Big Bad John is a strong, silent guy who comes to work at the mine each day, having earned the respect of others through his imposing size. One day a mine shaft caves in, and John saves the other miners by holding up a beam long enough for them to escape.

Ultimately, Big John is buried in the rubble, never to be seen again. The mine is closed forever, but John is memorialized by a plaque in front of the entrance.

Inspiration for the title character came from 6-foot-5 actor John Minto, with whom Dean had worked in during a summer stock production. He wasn't a husky guy, but Minto was the only person in the troupe who was taller than Dean. Jimmy started calling him "Big John."

The record-buying public loved the story so well that it became a No. 1 pop and country hit. Jimmy Dean went on to sell a fortune in sausages, and the company that bears his name was still in business in 2020.

Part of Dean's legacy is the variety show he hosted on ABC-TV from 1963 to '66, in which he introduced new stars like Roy Clark and Roger Miller. Another part is the pork sausage company that still bears his name.

Big Bad John

Songwriter: Jimmy Dean

Peaked at No. 1 on Billboard Hot 100

Nov. 6, 1961
Nov. 13, 1961
Nov. 20, 1961
Nov. 27, 1961
Dec. 4, 1961

Jimmy Dean

Aug. 10, 1928-June 13, 2010

Born Jimmy Ray Dean in Plainview, Texas, and died at his home in Varina, Va.

Jimmy Dean

Don't Go Near The Indians [Rex Allen with the Merry Melody Singers] – This Old West yarn was recorded by cowboy actor/singer Rex Allen, a native of southeast Arizona. The story is set in Cochise County, Ariz.

The narrator recounts the days of his youth, when he had a natural desire to spend time outdoors, wear moccasins and "hear wild stories about the Indians." In the chorus, however, his father warns him "don't go near the Indians."

As the boy matures into manhood, his hair turns black. There are lot of eligible white girls in his community, but they don't interest him. One day he goes onto the nearby Indian reservation, where he sees the beautiful native American Nova Lee drawing water from a creek. He falls head-over-heels in love and wants to marry her.

He tells his father of his plans to ask for the girl's hand in marriage, and that's when the truth comes out. His dad tells him that, years ago, the Indians and whites were in conflict. A brave scalped his young son and, in retaliation, he stole the Indian's little boy – who is the narrator.

Nova Lee cannot become the narrator's bride because she is his sister. Wow!

And that's where the story ends. It was cutting-edge stuff for 1962.

Allen's great voice got him much work in Hollywood as narrator for Disney films and nature documentaries. He became a successful country music singer and, in the age of the singing cowboy, starred as himself in 19 western movies.

He was not quite 79 years old when he died from injuries sustained when his caregiver accidentally struck him with a car in his driveway.

Don't Go Near The Indians

Songwriter: Lorene Mann

Peaked at No. 17 on Billboard Hot 100

Oct. 20, 1962

Rex Allen

Dec. 31, 1920-Dec. 17, 1999
Born Rex Elvie Allen in Willcox, Ariz., and died in Tucson, Ariz.

Rex Allen

Haunted House [Jumpin' Gene Simmons] – A ghost popped up in this song – a specter that haunts the house that the narrator has just purchased.

The narrator runs down a list of antics that the ghost uses to scare him and get him to move out. Bells ring, chains rattle and the ghost reveals himself having "one big eye and two big feet."

Later, the ghost drinks hot coffee from the spout of a coffee pot, drinks hot grease from a frying pan and eats raw meat from the narrator's hand. "Now, you better run, and don't be here when the mornin' come," the ghost says.

Through all the scare tactics, the narrator remains firm. "Say yes, I'll be here when the morning comes. I'll be right here, and I ain't gonna run."

The lyrics mention the word "haint," which is an old Southern word for ghost or evil spirit.

According to *Songfacts,* Simmons attributed the success of the record to overexposure of British rock songs in 1964. "Haunted House" originally was recorded by Johnny Fuller in 1958.

A native of Mississippi, Simmons worked as an opening act for Elvis Presley in Tupelo early in his career and dabbled in the rockabilly genre. "Haunted House" was his biggest hit.

According to *Wikipedia,* the bass player of the rock band Kiss, Gene Simmons, took his stage name in honor of Jumpin' Gene.

Haunted House

Songwriter: Robert Geddins
Peaked at No. 11 on Billboard Hot 100
Sept. 26, 1964

Jumpin' Gene Simmons

July 10, 1933-Aug. 29, 2006
Born Morris Eugene Simmons in Itawamba County, Miss., and died in Tupelo, Miss.

Gene Simmons

Leader Of The Pack [Shangri-Las] – There are a lot of things going on in the lyrics of this song. We have teen romance, parental rejection of a boyfriend, teen angst, death and life in the aftermath.

The lyrics open with the protagonist, Betty, talking with her girlfriends about her boyfriend, Jimmy. She confirms that she is going out with him and that she will be seeing him that night. Their love is so innocent – they met at the candy store, where "he turned around smiled at me … that's when I fell for the leader of the pack." Jimmy is the member of a motorcycle gang.

The couple's bliss doesn't last, as Betty's father tells her to dump Jimmy. The news doesn't sit well with him, of course. He asks her why, "but I could do was cry." He gives her a kiss goodbye and rides off on a rainy night.

"I begged him to go slow," Betty says. "Whether he heard, I'll never know."

The recording is peppered with cool sound effects, including motorcycle revs. As Jimmy's motorcycle crashes, we hear the sound of skidding tires and an impact with an unknown object.

Betty turns into an object of curiosity for her schoolmates. "At school, they all stop and stare. I can't hide my tears, but I don't care." Jimmy will live on as a monument in her heart.

The Shangri-Las were two pairs of sisters from Queens, New York: Mary and Betty Weiss and Marge and Mary Ann Ganser. Mary was only 16 when she sang lead on the track. She was too young to join a promotional tour to Great Britain following the chart run of the song.

Mary Ann died of encephalitis in 1971, and her twin Marge died of breast cancer in 1996.

Recording engineer Joey Veneri brought his motorcycle to the studio, where it was placed in an echo chamber in a hallway to record the revving sound.

Brill Building songwriter Ellie Greenwich (see Chapter 9, Brill Building) contributed to the song. She told author Fred Bronson, "There were only two songs in my whole career that I actually walked out of the studio and … had a gut feeling (they) would be Number One. 'Chapel Of Love' was one, and 'Leader Of The Pack' was the other."

Leader Of The Pack

Songwriters: Jeff Barry, Ellie Greenwich, George Morton

Peaked at No. 1 on Billboard Hot 100

Nov. 28, 1964

The Shangri-Las

Elizabeth "Betty" Weiss (Nov. 27, 1946-)
Mary Weiss (Dec. 28, 1948-)
Marguerite "Marge" Ganser (Feb. 4, 1948-July 28, 1996)
Mary Ann Ganser (Feb. 4, 1948-March 14, 1970)
Formed in New York City, N.Y., in 1963

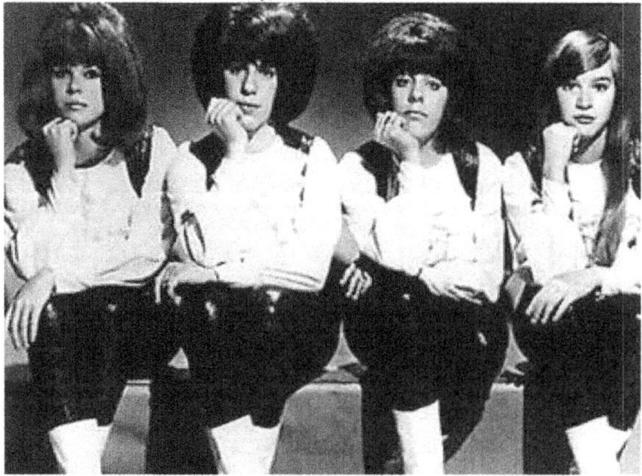

Shangri-Las: Betty Weiss, Mary Ann Ganser, Marge Ganser, Mary Weiss

Laurie (Strange Things Happen) [Dickey Lee] – This is another eerie story about a young man who apparently has an encounter with a ghost.

He meets a young lady – "an angel of a girl" – at a dance, and he is smitten with her. He proceeds to walk her home, whereupon she mentions that it's her birthday. Then she becomes very cold and asks to borrow his sweater.

The fellow kisses her good night on her doorstep and starts to leave. But he remembers his sweater and knocks on the door to retrieve it. The girl's father comes to the door, but he rebuffs the boy by telling him he couldn't have been with his daughter because she had died one year earlier on her birthday.

"A strange force" draws the boy to the local cemetery, where he finds his sweater on the girl's grave.

Memphis psychologist Dr. Milton Addington wrote the song after he read an article that 15-year-old Cathie Harmon submitted to a local newspaper. It is speculated that Harmon's writing was inspired by the legend of Resurrection Mary, a Chicago ghost whose lore rose out of the 1930s. People claimed to have seen the shy woman in a white dress as they drove past Resurrection Cemetery.

Addington shared his songwriting royalties with Harmon. Dickey Lee, who recorded the song, also is a native Memphian. He included the song on his 1965 album "Laurie and the Girl from Peyton Place."

Comedy recording artist Ray Stevens arranged the recording, which peaked at No. 14 on the *Billboard Hot 100.*

Laurie (Strange Things Happen)

Songwriters: Milton Addington, Cathie Harmon

Peaked at No. 14 on Billboard Hot 100

July 10, 1965

Dickey Lee

Born Royden Dickey Lipscomb in Memphis, Tenn., on Sept. 21, 1936

Dickey Lee

Harper Valley P.T.A. [Jeannie C. Riley] – A sassy widow with a strong backbone is the centerpiece of this story.

The woman, Mrs. Johnson, has a teen daughter attending Harper Valley Junior High School. One day the girl brings home a note to her mother from the school's Parent Teacher Association. The short missive accuses Mrs. Johnson of wearing dresses that are too short, drinking and running around with men "and going wild." In summary, the P.T.A doesn't believe she is being a good role model for her daughter.

At a scheduled meeting that same afternoon, the P.T.A. members are floored when Mrs. Johnson shows up and asks to address the body. She doesn't hold anything back in branding some of them as hypocrites.

She reveals one man, who is married, has asked her out seven times. She wants to know why another man's secretary had to move out of town, and she chides a woman for not keeping her window shades pulled completely down.

Mrs. Johnson accuses an absent man of missing the meeting because he stayed at a bar too long. She accuses another woman of having gin on her breath. In closing, she labels Harper Valley a "little Peyton Place" filled with hypocrisy.

In the last verse we find out that the narrator is actually Mrs. Johnson's daughter, who sounds proud of the way her mother fought back.

When Jeannie C. Riley was recording the song, someone in the studio suggested after the first take that the final line could be changed. It originally read, "That's the day my mama put down the Harper Valley P.T.A."

A current NBC-TV comedy show, *Rowan and Martin's Laugh-In,* had popularized the slogan "sock it to me." So, Riley then sang the line as "the day my mama socked it to the Harper Valley P.T.A."

Riley, a Texan who moved to Nashville, worked as a secretary while cutting demo records in an attempt to forge a recording career. Shelby Singleton, who bought Sun Records from Sam Phillips, heard her voice on a tape and judged it to be the right sound for the song written by Tom T. Hall.

By far Riley's biggest hit, "Harper Valley P.T.A." sold over six million records and topped both the pop and country charts. A Grammy award for Best Country Vocal Performance, Female followed.

Harper Valley P.T.A.
Songwriter: Tom T. Hall
Peaked at No. 1 on Billboard Hot 100
Sept. 21, 1968

Jeannie C. Riley
Born Jeanne Carolyn Stephenson in Stamford, Texas, on Oct. 19, 1945

Jeannie C. Riley

Rocky Raccoon [Beatles] – This entertaining tale from the Beatles' White Album wasn't a single. No tracks from that hit album were released as singles. But "Rocky Raccoon" stands as one of the most amusing of the bunch.

Paul McCartney wrote some great rhymes and used a lot of descriptive words to weave a story of betrayal, confrontation and defeat for the title character. According to the *Beatles Interview Database*,

McCartney originally named the protagonist Rocky Sassoon but changed it to Rocky Raccoon "because it sounded more like a cowboy."

At the onset we learn that Rocky is from the "Black Mountain Hills of Dakota." His girlfriend Magill (aka Lil and Nancy) runs off with a guy named Dan. Rocky doesn't take this snub lying down and goes to town to get revenge on the interloper.

In the local hotel, Rocky bursts into Nancy and Dan's room to confront him. He draws his gun, but Dan gets off the first shot. Rocky collapses in the corner of the room. A drunken doctor comes to assist Rocky, but the wounded cowpoke says his injury is minor.

Back in his room Rocky finds a Gideon's Bible, thinking that a previous tenant of the room named Gideon left it for him. That's all he has to help him regroup. End of story.

My father was a member of Gideons International in the 1980s. The evangelical Christian organization, founded in 1899, is renowned for distributing free Holy Bibles worldwide. The most notable recipients of their Bibles are hotels, which typically place one in each guest room.

On their famous trip to India to study transcendental meditation in early 1968, John Lennon, Donovan Leitch and McCartney were "sitting around enjoying ourselves" when Paul began to strum the chords of "Rocky Raccoon" as he was messing around with a guitar. The three started making up words to the song and, fortunately, wrote them down.

"I like talking-blues, so I started off like that, then I did my tongue-in-cheek parody of a Western and threw in some amusing lines," McCartney said. "I just tried to keep it amusing, really. It's me writing a play, a little one-act play giving them most of the dialogue."

Despite its status as one of 30 album tracks, "Rocky Raccoon" is well known to legions of music fans around the world. The White Album was No. 1 on the *Billboard 200* for nine weeks in 1969 and topped the U.K. album chart for eight weeks. It sold over 12 million copies in the United States alone.

Rocky Raccoon

Songwriters: John Lennon, Paul McCartney

Included on the album "The Beatles"

Peaked at No. 1 on Billboard 200

Dec. 28, 1968-Feb. 1, 1969

Feb. 15-March 1, 1969

The Beatles

Paul McCartney (June 18, 1942-) vocals, acoustic guitar

John Lennon (Oct. 9, 1940-Dec. 8, 1980) harmonium, harmonica, backing vocals, bass

George Harrison (Feb. 25, 1943-Nov. 29, 2001) backing vocals

Ringo Starr (July 7, 1940-) drums

Formed in Liverpool, England, in 1960

The Beatles: Paul McCartney, Ringo Starr, John Lennon, George Harrison

A Boy Named Sue [Johnny Cash] – A spoken word recording can be just as entertaining as one that has singing, especially when an artist like Johnny Cash is reading the story with his clever inflections.

This story-song took the country by storm in the summer of 1969 after it was recorded for a "captive" audience at San Quentin State Prison in Marin County, Calif. The song is punctuated by guitar picking and strumming and low key drumming in the background.

The narrative opens with the main character describing how his father deserted the family when he was a young boy, leaving him and his mother only "this old guitar and an empty bottle of booze." But the worst transgression of the runaway dad was naming the youngster Sue.

This leads to a lot of problems for the kid, with townsfolk laughing at him and other youths taunting him into fights. All of these travails help him grow into a tough young man. But he roams from town to town to hide the shame of his name, and he vows to search for his dad and "kill the man that gave me that awful name."

His opportunity comes one summer in Gatlinburg, Tenn., where he spots that "dirty, mangy dog that named me Sue," dealing cards in a saloon next to a muddy street. An old photo helps him confirm his elder's identity.

The young man issues a greeting – "My name is Sue! How do you do? Now you gonna die!" Then a fight ensues. There is punching, kicking, biting and knife play as the two crash through the saloon's wall into the quagmire of the street. The old man goes for his gun, but Sue draws his first.

Dad has no choice but to compliment Sue on the great fight and explain why he named him as he did. He says he knew that he wouldn't be around to help his son grow up, so he gave him a girl's name, knowing he'd have to get tough or die.

Sue is disarmed by this revelation, throws down his gun and embraces his father. He goes away with a new perspective on the situation, but he declares that if he ever has a son he will name him "Bill or George – anything but Sue!"

Shel Silverstein wrote the gem, and it brought the veteran writer into the national limelight for the first time.

Cash came back with another humorous, spoken song in 1976, "One Piece At A Time."

A Boy Named Sue

Songwriter: Shel Silverstein

Peaked at No. 2 on Billboard Hot 100

Aug. 23, 1969

Aug. 30, 1969

Sept. 6, 1969

<u>Johnny Cash</u>

Feb. 26, 1932-Sept. 12, 2003

Born J.R. Cash in Kingsland, Ark., and died at Baptist Hospital in Nashville, Tenn.

Johnny Cash

Taxi [Harry Chapin] – Native New Yorker Harry Chapin wrote and sang this story that takes place in San Francisco. If there is a better story-song in the history of pop music, I don't know what it is.

The narrator is a cab driver. On this rainy night he has time to pick up one more fare before he goes home. A woman flags him down, and he picks her up.

Her destination is a home in a nearby ritzy neighborhood. She looks familiar to the driver, but she tells him he is mistaken when he asks if they'd met before.

Finally, she checks the name on his displayed hack license, which confirms that she does indeed know who he is. "How are ya, Harry?" she says to her former boyfriend. He says, "How are you, Sue?"

We learn that years earlier she planned to be an actress, and he wanted to learn to fly. Their break-up, it is presumed, came when she pursued her acting career, while he went to do his thing. The aviation angle hints at Chapin's education at the U.S. Air Force Academy.

The song then enters its middle section, during which bass player John Wallace sings a verse in beautiful falsetto.

As the cab enters Sue's estate through a gated entry, it is more of an insult than anything when she hands Harry a $20 bill for a $2.50 fare and tells him to keep the change. After thinking about it for a moment, he deposits the money into his shirt.

Exiting the vehicle, Sue says, "We must get together." But Harry know that isn't going to happen because the two now live in different worlds.

The irony of the story comes at the conclusion: both of the former lovers got what they'd asked for. Sue is "acting happy inside her handsome home," and Harry is "flying in my taxi, taking tips and getting stoned." It's a brilliant ending to a great story.

Chapin was a champion of the fight against world hunger, and he was posthumously awarded the Congressional Gold Medal. His life ended in a fiery car crash on the Long Island Expressway in 1981.

Taxi

Songwriter: Harry Chapin

Peaked at No. 24 on Billboard Hot 100

June 3, 1972

June 10, 1972

Harry Chapin

Dec. 7, 1942-July 16, 1981

Born Harry Forster Chapin in New York City, N.Y., and died in a car crash in Jericho, N.Y.

Harry Chapin

Uneasy Rider [Charlie Daniels] – Country fiddler Charlie Daniels made this his first hit single. He had worked as a session musician in Nashville in the mid-1960s, and he released his first album in 1971.

There would be other story songs in Daniels' career, but this one from 1973 was special because it came out of nowhere to cross over to the pop charts and make a name for him.

With a lot of country-style guitar picking in the background, Daniels speaks the tale of a guy driving across country from east to west. The origin of the journey is unknown, but the destination is Los Angeles and the route goes through Mississippi. Daniels's home state is North Carolina, so perhaps that's where he started.

A tire on his car starts to whine, and the narrator is forced to pull over in Jackson, Miss., after the tire blows. The spare is flat, and he can't find a service station, so the car crawls down the shoulder of the road until he arrives at a bar called the Dew Drop Inn. He tucks his long hair under his hat, goes in to ask for change to telephone a service station nearby, then orders a beer while he waits for a mechanic to come.

He hopes he'll get out of the bar before his hippy appearance gets him into trouble with the conservative local residents, but a patron comes in and wants to know "who owns this car with the peace sign, mag wheels and 4-on-the-floor?" On his way out the door he encounters several big men and a drunk woman.

One of the three orders him to tip his hat to the woman and, when he does, his hair falls out. The narrator knows that trouble is coming, so he's got to think fast. He kicks one of them in knee, then accuses him of being an undercover FBI agent, among other things. The guy protests vehemently, but the "uneasy rider" doesn't wait around to argue.

As he runs into the parking lot, he sees that a mechanic is just finishing the tire replacement. He throws him $20 and jumps into his Chevy, starting the engine immediately. His instinct is to flee the scene, but he can't resist chasing his pursuers around the parking lot while "slinging gravel and putting a ton of dust in the air."

The narrator zooms away and doesn't slow down for two states.

As a final thought, he says he thinks he'll reroute his trip through Omaha, ostensibly to avoid encounters with any more redneck hillbillies.

The hippy hero of the song is kindred to the central characters in the 1969 film *Easy Rider,* who also had problems with conservative Southerners as they rode their motorcycles through the deep South from west to east.

Uneasy Rider

Songwriter: Charlie Daniels

Peaked at No. 9 on Billboard Hot 100

Aug. 11, 1973

Aug. 18, 1973

Aug. 25, 1973

Charlie Daniels

Oct. 28, 1936-July 6, 2020

Born Charles Edward Daniels in Wilmington, N.C., and died of a stroke in Nashville, Tenn.

Charlie Daniels

Billy, Don't Be A Hero [Bo Donaldson & the Heywoods] – The English songwriting team of Mitch Murray and Peter Callander seemed to have a fascination for writing songs about American history. They wrote successful songs like "The Ballad Of Bonnie And Clyde" and "The Night Chicago Died" (see Chapters 3 and 4).

The saga of "Billy" was set in the Civil War, and it too was a big hit. Cincinnati band Bo Donaldson & the Heywoods sang it to the top of the *Billboard Hot 100* in 1974, and sales surpassed three million copies.

The story opens with "soldier blues" parading through town, and the anonymous narrator spots Billy waiting to join the unit. His fiancé tearfully sees him off with the caveat, "Billy, don't be a hero, don't be a fool with your life … come back and make me your wife."

Next thing we know, the Union soldiers are cornered on a battlefield. The sergeant exhorts his troops to hang on, and then he asks for a volunteer to ride out and bring back reinforcements. Billy's hand goes up quickly, as he forgets his sweetheart's admonishment.

In the final verse, the narrator relates that he heard the fiancé received a letter, presumably from the government. It explained how Billy died and said that she should be proud of his bravery. "I heard she threw the letter away" is the final line. Obviously, she would rather have Billy back than keep a memory of his valor.

British band Paper Lace recorded the song first and took it to No. 1 in the U.K., Australia and Ireland. The Heywoods' version was No. 1 in the U.S. and Canada. It was the second single by the Heywoods, and they would have one more top 40 hit, "Who Do You Think You Are," before they permanently faded into obscurity.

Billy, Don't Be A Hero

Songwriters: Mitch Murray, Peter Callander

Peaked at No. 1 on Billboard Hot 100

June 15, 1974

June 22, 1974

Bo Donaldson & the Heywoods

Robert "Bo" Donaldson – keyboards

Mike Gibbons – lead vocals, trumpet

David Krock – bass, backing vocals

Rick Joswick – lead vocals, tambourine

Gary Coveyou – saxophone, flute, backing vocals

Baker Scott – guitar

Richard Brunetti – drums

Formed in Cincinnati, Ohio, in 1965

Bo Donaldson & the Heywoods

Wildwood Weed [Jim Stafford] – It was weeks after I first heard this record before I realized that it was spoken, not sung. My attention had been riveted on the words. Comedian Jim Stafford, who had a summer variety show on ABC-TV in 1975, recorded it.

This is probably the most hilarious counterculture recording ever. It recounts how a farm boy and his brother accidentally discover marijuana growing on their property. The narrator picked up a weed one day to have something to chew, and "things got fuzzy, things got blurry, then everything was gone."

After his brother Bill asks to give it a try, he disappears for the rest of the day. He is found the next morning, naked and singing atop a windmill.

The use of these magical plants gets to be a habit for the farmers, but they find no harm in using them. They find it to be a means to "take a trip and never leave the farm."

Their fun appears to come to an end, however, when a federal agent driving past the farm see the plants. He proceeded to dig and burn the marijuana growth until it's all gone.

But the kicker is revealed as the narrator concludes, "We just smiled and waved, sittin' there on that sack of seeds." It sounds like they'll have fresh pot next year.

A country flavor is maintained throughout the song by acoustic guitar picking, banjo strumming and jewsharp twanging. The record reached only No. 57 on the country chart but topped out at No. 7 on the pop chart. Naturally, some radio stations refused to play it because of its thinly veiled references to marijuana. If the song had been released five years earlier, it might have qualified for inclusion in Chapter 15, The Psychedelic Years.

Musically, "Wildwood Weed" takes its structure from the Carter Family's song, "Wildwood Flower." Stafford credits that in the first line of the recording.

Wildwood Weed

Songwriter: Don Bowman

Peaked at No. 7 on Billboard Hot 100

Aug. 24, 1974

Aug. 31, 1974

Jim Stafford

Born James Wayne Stafford in Winter Haven, Fla., on Jan. 16, 1944

Jim Stafford

Third Rate Romance [Amazing Rhythm Aces] – Stop me if you've heard this one. A guy meets this gal in a restaurant, and they end up in a motel …

That sounds like the start of a joke, but it's actually the plot of this 1975 story song. There is no mention of casual sex in the lyrics, but the implication is undeniable.

In the story, the pair of strangers are in a "ritzy restaurant," where they don't have much to talk about but are reading each other's mind. They're both thinking the same: let's hook up and get it on tonight.

Both have very low standards. She says, "You don't look like my type, but I guess you'll do." He responds, "I'll even tell you that I love you, if you want me to."

They drive to a cheap motel, where he signs the register and she opens the door. The woman's unconvincing line is, "I've never really done this kind of thing before, have you?" His answer, which is more honest, is, "Yes, I have, but only a time or two."

Musically, the song's signatures are a four-note sequence that is repeated throughout, and the chorus "third rate romance, low rent rendezvous."

The record had a good showing on both the *Billboard* pop and country charts, peaking at No. 14 and 11, respectively. In Canada it hit No. 1 on both pop and country charts.

Memphis, Tenn., was home base for the Amazing Rhythm Aces. Their sound was characterized as "roots music," a blend of country, rock, blues, folk and Latino genres. They released 18 albums over the span of 30 years. "Third Rate Romance" was their biggest single.

Third Rate Romance

Songwriter: Russell Smith

Peaked at No. 14 on Billboard Hot 100

Sept. 13, 1975

Sept. 20, 1975

<u>The Amazing Rhythm Aces</u>

Russell Smith (June 17, 1949-July 12, 2019) vocals, guitar

Jeff "Stick" Davis (Oct. 17, 1949-) bass

David "Butch McDade (Feb. 24, 1946-Nov. 29, 1998) drums

Billy Earheart III (Feb. 21, 1954-) piano

Barry "Byrd" Burton (Sept. 7, 1946-March 10, 2008) guitar

James Hooker (July 20, 1948-) piano

Formed in Memphis, Tenn., in 1972

The Amazing Rhythm Aces

Lyin' Eyes [Eagles] – This compelling story is the product of two great musical minds, Glenn Frey and Don Henley, who were the backbone of the Eagles. Their inspiration came one night in 1975 in West Hollywood, Calif., when they were visiting their favorite eating/drinking establishment.

As Frey and Henley conversed about beautiful women who cheat on their husbands, they looked across the room and spotted a pretty young woman sitting with an older, overweight, affluent-looking man. Frey remarked, "She can't even hide those lyin' eyes."

In a conversation with filmmaker/writer Cameron Crowe, Frey said, "The story had always been there. I don't want to say it wrote itself, but once we started working on it, there were no sticking points. Lyrics just kept coming out, and that's not always the way songs get written."

The story opens with a statement about the wiles of attractive, urbane women. Then it focuses on one of those gorgeous women who is in a marriage of convenience. She lives in the lap of luxury, but she doesn't love her aged husband. With a lie that she's going out to visit a sick friend, she gets in her car to go to "the cheating side of town," where her young lover waits.

The woman tells him their time together must be brief but, perhaps being overly optimistic, she says soon she'll come back to stay.

The final verse sees her pouring a drink during a spate of retrospection. She thinks about her life and how it could have been with a more attractive husband. In marrying a rich man, she wonders if she had been tired or just lazy. She had a scheme to score a life of ease, but she's still the same tramp that she's always been.

The single became the first Eagles song to score on the pop and country charts, and it earned a Grammy award for Best Pop Performance by a Group and a nomination for Record of the Year.

Lyin' Eyes

Songwriters: Don Henley, Glenn Frey
Peaked at No. 2 on Billboard Hot 100
Nov. 8, 1975
Nov. 15, 1975

The Eagles

Glenn Frey (Nov. 6, 1948-Jan. 18, 2016) vocals, acoustic guitar
Don Henley (July 22, 1947-) drums, backing vocals
Randy Meisner (March 8, 1946-) bass, backing vocals
Bernie Leadon (July 19, 1947-) lead guitar, mandolin, backing vocals
Don Felder (Sept. 21, 1947-) guitar
Formed in Los Angeles, Calif., in 1971

The Eagles: Don Henley, Don Felder, Glenn Frey, Bernie Leadon, Randy Meisner

Convoy [C.W. McCall] – Cashing in on a fad can be lucrative for recording artists. Chubby Checker did so with a dance craze that helped him create one of the biggest hits of all time, "The Twist." It had two chart runs and hit No. 1 both times. Ray Stevens took advantage of the 1974 streaking fad with a chart-topper, "The Streak."

In late 1975, an Omaha advertising agency director named Bill Fries changed his identity to C.W. McCall and recorded a spoken word song about the Citizen Band radio craze, "Convoy." The recording was a smash on the *Billboard Hot Country Songs*, spending six weeks at No. 1, but it also crossed over to the pop chart, where it became the second No. 1 single of 1976.

The story centers around an over-the-road trucker, whose CB call sign (handle) is Rubber Duck. He leaves Los Angeles on a cross-country trip to the East Coast, using his radio to organize other truckers into a convoy. The lyrics are filled with CB jargon, which trucking professionals had developed into their own language since the Citizen Band radio was introduced in 1958.

Cities are renamed in CB lingo – Los Angeles is "Shaky Town;" Flagstaff is "Flag Town;" Chicago is "Chi-Town." State troopers are known as "bears," logbooks are "swindle sheets," a weigh station is a "chicken coop" and the lead vehicle in the convoy is the "front door."

Two of Rubber Duck's cohorts are Pig Pen and Sodbuster.

As the size of the convoy swells to a thousand rigs, law enforcement along the route is stepped up. But there is no stopping the rogue consortium, and they proceed to cross a bridge without paying toll.

The song is interspersed with Rubber Duck's conversations on the radio, which sound like they're coming out of a small mobile speaker. An unidentified backing singer handles the choruses.

It's all in good fun, and no violence is reported. The story caught the imagination of many listeners, and sales of CB equipment spiked over the period of several months.

As the CB craze swelled in 1975, the communications device clearly no longer was a tool for professional truckers. The radios' popularity spiked as a result of the 1973 oil embargo by the Organization of Arab Petroleum Exporting Countries.

The embargo originally targeted the United States, United Kingdom, Canada, Netherlands and Japan and later included Portugal, Rhodesia and South Africa. The Arabs targeted these nations because they supported Israel against a coalition of Arab nations in the Yom Kippur War of October 1973. Israel won the war, fighting mainly against Egypt and Syria.

The U.S. had become dependent upon foreign oil for gasoline and heating oil because demand far outpaced domestic production. These were the days before the Alaska pipeline, the North Dakota oil boom and fracking dramatically increased U.S. crude oil production.

The reaction by many States was to lower highway speed limits in order for vehicles to save fuel. The National Maximum Speed Law of 1974 restricted the maximum speed on interstate highways to 55 mph. But it wasn't long before highway users were using their CBs to thwart speed enforcement by broadcasting the locations of state troopers and other enforcers.

Fries created his alter-ego while creating an advertising campaign for the Mertz Baking Co. He recorded the commercial's theme song and released it on his private label. After the recording sold 30,000 copies in three weeks, MGM Records signed McCall to a contract.

A movie titled *Convoy,* based on the song and starring Kris Kristofferson and Ali McGraw, was released in 1978. McCall recorded six albums between 1975 and '79.

After his recording days ended, McCall was elected mayor of Ouray, Colo., a position he filled for six years.

This was the last No. 1 record released on MGM. The label was sold to Polygram and henceforth carried only adult contemporary artists.

Convoy

Songwriters: Bill Fries, Chip Davis

Peaked at No. 1 on Billboard Hot 100

Jan. 10, 1976

C.W. McCall

Born William Dale Fries Jr. in Audubon, Iowa, on Nov. 15, 1928

C.W. McCall

Lucille [Kenny Rogers] – Here's a compressed soap opera played out in three verses. Like "Lyin' Eyes," this one has to do with marital infidelity.

In time, the late Kenny Rogers would prove to be a masterful storyteller with songs like "The Gambler" and "Coward Of The County." This song was his first major hit after he left the First Edition to go solo.

The opening scene is a barroom in Toledo, Ohio, where a woman sits down and takes off her wedding ring. The narrator notices her and moseys over to chat her up. They consume a few drinks before she loosens up and says she's tired of living on dreams. She wants to have some fun and escape the dreary life in which she has been entrapped.

Then a huge man enters the bar. "He looked like a mountain," the narrator says, and with big, calloused hands, he looks out of place. The narrator believes this guy is about to pummel him.

The big guy starts to shake, however, and it's apparent that he is hurting inside. "You picked a fine time to leave me, Lucille," he blurts, "with four hungry children and a crop in the field."

After the farmer departs, the narrator orders more drinks. Soon the beautiful Lucille is ready to have sex with him, and silently they walk to a nearby hotel.

The narrator cannot receive Lucille's advances, however, because the words of her husband still ring in his ears. That's how the story ends.

Rogers' mother was named Lucille, but that's not how the song got its title. My research turned up three widely different stories behind the creation of the song, and I am unable to say which is correct. Roger Bowling and Hal Bynum wrote it.

Version 1: According to *Songfacts,* songwriter Bynum was having marital difficulties when he was writing this tune. As his wife was about to depart on an out-of-town trip, he also was fighting off the temptation of another woman's advances. Bynum told his wife, "You picked a fine time to leave me." With the help of lyricist Bowling, he changed the scenario to a barroom encounter after seeing a couple arguing outside the Greyhound bus depot in Toledo.

Version 2: According the KXRB website, Rogers was near Tulsa, Okla., in the summer of 1958 to help his uncle cut hay. One day he heard a heart-broken man on television wail something like, "You picked a fine time to leave me, Lucille, with four hungry children and a crop in the field. We've had some good times and some bad times…" The words stayed with Rogers for years, and he felt there was a great song hidden behind those few lines. He finally turned to Bowling and Bynum to create the story song. (*Wide Open Country* identifies the relative Rogers was visiting as his father, not uncle.)

Version 3: According to *USA Today Network,* Bynum was in the Navy, on shore leave in Norfolk, Va. As he sought out a bar, he encountered a blind man on the street, playing and singing with a donation cup dangling from the end of his guitar. Bynum fell in behind him and listened to his song. It stayed with him, and years later after Nashville music publisher Paul Richey teamed Bynum with Bowling, they polished up the song and presented it to Rogers.

"Lucille" peaked at No. 5 on the *Billboard Hot 100,* No. 1 on the *Billboard Hot Country Songs* and was No. 1 pop and country in Canada. It also was No. 1 in the U.K., Yugoslavia and South Africa.

Lucille

Songwriters: Roger Bowling, Hal Bynum

Peaked at No. 5 on Billboard Hot 100

June 18, 1977

June 25, 1977

Kenny Rogers

Aug. 21, 1938-March 20, 2020

Born Kenneth Ray Rogers in Houston, Texas, and died at his home in Sandy Springs, Ga., under hospice care

Kenny Rogers

Copacabana (At The Copa) [Barry Manilow] – What we have here is a saga of innocent young love, power, lust, violence and tragedy. And all are brilliantly packaged with an economy of words.

The seeds were sown in Brazil when singer Barry Manilow and songwriter Bruce Sussman were staying at the Copacabana Hotel in Rio de Janeiro. They had a discussion over whether a song had ever been titled "Copacabana," according to the book *Copa: Jules Podell and the Hottest Club North of Havana.*

Upon returning to New York City, Manilow suggested that Sussman and Jack Feldman write a story song for him. After they did so, Manilow composed the melody.

"I remember putting the lyric on the piano's music stand, punching the 'Record' button on my tape deck and writing the song in less than 15 minutes," Manilow wrote in the liner notes for the album "Even Now."

The setting for the story is the Copacabana nightclub, which opened on E. 60th St. in Manhattan in 1940. Lola works there as a showgirl, and she tries hard to excel. Her boyfriend Tony works there, too, tending bar. They're in love.

One night a big shot named Rico comes into the club and is escorted to a VIP table. After he gets a look at Lola doing her thing, he calls her to his table following her number. Like the lout that he is, he puts his hands on her. Tony sees this, and he launches an attack on Rico. Punches fly, chairs are smashed and then a gunshot rings out.

Who takes a bullet? Unfortunately, it's Tony.

When the lyrics return after the instrumental middle part, we see that 30 years have passed. The Copacabana no longer is a nightclub but has become a discotheque. Lola, still in her dancer's costume, sits at the bar and drinks herself into inebriation. As the lyrics state, "She lost her youth and she lost her Tony, now she's lost her mind."

It's a spicy tale with a sad ending.

The storyline contained so much passion that it was turned into a TV movie and a stage musical. The song earned Manilow a Grammy Award for Best Pop Vocal Performance, Male.

Canada's dance chart and the French pop chart both saw the song go to No. 2.

Manilow had charted all three of his No. 1 singles by the time this record came out in 1978, but he stayed on the charts into the mid-1980s.

Copacabana (At The Copa)

Songwriters: Bruce Sussman, Jack Feldman, Barry Manilow

Peaked at No. 8 on Billboard Hot 100

Aug. 12, 1978

Aug. 19, 1978

Barry Manilow

Born Barry Alan Pincus in Brooklyn, New York, on June 17, 1943

Barry Manilow

Wet Dream [Kip Addotta] – At 4 minutes 54 seconds, this is one of the longer stories to be recorded. But it's worth every hilarious moment.

Kip Addotta was a comedian who released several albums. "Wet Dream," a spoken word record, was released as a single in 1984 on the Laff label, but it failed to crack the *Billboard Hot 100.* It's a shame it didn't get better promotion.

The story has a nautical/aquatic/marine theme with puns, double entendres and homophones used in practically every line. The inferences get a little bawdy, but there's no blatant indecency.

The narrator is a guy named Marlon who is driving through downtown Atlantis. After he experiences car trouble, he walks into a tavern called the Oyster Bar, where he has some adventures.

He meets a cute female, whom he tries to romance. But her sizeable "boyfriend" gets in the way. A fight ensues, with the other guy getting in the first punch before Marlon lays him out with a left hook.

The way is clear for Marlon to woo his quarry. "From then on, we had a whale of a time," he says. "I took her to dinner, I took her to dance, I bought her a bouquet of flounders."

For all his trouble, our hero winds up with a communicable disease.

Sound effects on the record include bubbling noises and a simulated ambulance siren. Instrumental background is provided by Rick Johnston with an electrified keyboard, bass and drums. A female vocalist sings the choruses.

Addotta released albums with titles like "I Hope I'm Not Out Of Line," "The Comedian Of The United States," "Life In The Slaw Lane" and "I Saw Daddy Kissing Santa Claus." He made numerous appearances on NBC-TV's *The Tonight Show Starring Johnny Carson* as well as other televised variety, comedy and game shows.

Wet Dream

Songwriters: Kip Addotta, Biff Manard

Included on the album "Comedian Of The United States"

Neither the single nor the album charted

1975

Kip Addotta

June 16, 1944-Aug. 13, 2019

Born Francis Kip Addotta in Rockford, Ill., and died in Los Angeles, Calif.

Kip Addotta

Chapter 17

Ramble On

Songs about people on the move

Overview: Travel is a common theme in music. In the various genres of rock, songwriters have chosen many different ways to describe the travel experience.

In this chapter there will be people traveling by ship, riverboat, airplane, balloon, train, bus, motorcycle, car and truck – even by foot. Each will have their own outlook on the business of moving people.

The reasons for doing the travel also are explained from song to song. Enjoy the travelogue!

To view the full lyrics to these songs, please log on to www.google.com, enter song titles & artist names and click Google Search.

To listen to these songs, please log on to www.youtube.com and enter song titles & artist names.

Walking To New Orleans [Fats Domino] – The title reveals the mode of transportation in this song. It's the "shoe leather express."

The narrator is hoofing it back to his home in the Big Easy on a melancholy trip to be reunited with his girlfriend. "You used to be my honey," he says, "till you spent all my money."

The idea for the song came from Bobby Charles, a songwriter whose "Before I Grow Too Old" had been recorded by singer Fats Domino. Charles idolized Domino and visited his dressing room while Fats was on a concert tour in Lafayette, La., and Domino proceeded to invite him for a visit at his home in New Orleans.

Charles replied something like, "I don't have a car. If I go, I'd have to walk."

The thought lingered on Charles' mind, and eventually he took pen to hand and wrote the song in about 15 minutes.

The recording zoomed all the way to No. 2 on the *Billboard Hot R&B Songs*, while stopping at No. 6 on the *Hot 100.* It sold over 2 million copies.

Domino, sometimes referred to as the "Architect of Rock and Roll," had a king-sized chart career. He put 37 songs in the pop top 40, starting in 1955. Some of his memorable hits were "I'm In Love Again," "Blueberry Hill" and "Blue Monday."

Although he was one of the pioneers of rock, Domino's popularity had faded by the early 1960s. Perhaps this was because he was already in his late 20s when he made his first rock hits. Nonetheless, he influenced many musicians who came after him, including Elvis Presley.

"This gentleman was a huge influence on me when I started out," Presley told an interviewer in 1957. "A lot of people seem to think I started this business. But rock and roll was here a long time before I came along. Let's face it, I can't sing it like Fats Domino can. I know that."

Walking To New Orleans

Songwriters: Bobby Charles, Robert Guidry, Fats Domino, Dave Bartholomew

Peaked at No. 6 on Billboard Hot 100

Aug. 15, 1960

Fats Domino

Feb. 26, 1928-Oct. 24, 2017

Born Antoine Domino Jr. in New Orleans, La., and died at his home in Harvey, La.

Fats Domino

Travelin' Man [Ricky Nelson] – This song is about a sailor, ostensibly a merchant seaman. Shamelessly, he is not faithful to any woman.

The narrator lists Hong Kong, Germany, Mexico, Alaska and Hawaii as the ports where he keeps girlfriends. I have to admit that this guy has some exotic tastes in women. "A girl in every port was the idea," writer Jerry Fuller told writer Paul Sexton.

Fuller wrote the song one day in Hollywood while in his car, waiting for his wife. He had an eye toward Sam Cooke recording it. Cooke's manager, J.W. Alexander, didn't think much of it, though, and did not keep the demo.

According to *Songfacts,* Nelson's bass player, Joe Osborn, was in the next room and heard the recording through the wall. He proceeded to request it from Alexander, who retrieved the acetate from a trash basket and gave it to him.

Eventually, it wound up in Ricky Nelson's camp, and he turned it into the second No. 1 hit of his illustrious recording career in 1961.

Later that year Nelson changed his stage name to "Rick Nelson." He had grown up in the public eye as an actor on the radio and television series *The Adventures of Ozzie and Harriet,* starting at age 8. He began recording music at about the age of 17 in 1957.

The Jordanaires, who backed Elvis Presley on many of his recordings, appeared on "Travelin'Man," which sold over 6 million copies.

The "B" side of the 45 rpm single was "Hello Mary Lou," which also charted at *Billboard* No. 9. In Chicago it was a No. 1 hit.

Travelin' Man

Songwriter: Jerry Fuller

Peaked at No. 1 on Billboard Hot 100

May 29, 1961

June 12, 1961

Ricky Nelson

May 8, 1940-Dec. 31, 1985

Born Eric Hilliard Nelson in Teaneck, N.J., and died in a plane crash near DeKalb, Texas

Ricky Nelson

Six Days On The Road [Dave Dudley] – This is a real trucker's anthem, repeating the feelings and sentiments of many over-the-road drivers who are happy to return home after days away.

Truck drivers are famous country music lovers, and this song is right up their alley. It peaked at No. 2 on the *Billboard Hot Country Songs* chart while still getting good action on pop radio stations.

Bill Dahl, writing for *Allmusic,* said "Six Days On The Road" is the "ultimate overworked rig driver's lament."

Country music writer Bill Malone wrote that it "strikingly captures the sense of boredom, danger and swaggering masculinity that often accompanies long-distance truck driving. (Dave Dudley's) macho interpretation, with its rock and roll overtones, is perfect for the song."

The lyrics lay bare the realities of truck driving life: breaking speed laws to save time, taking "uppers" to stay awake while driving, having a logbook that isn't up to date and carrying an overweight load. There also is the mention of temptations of sex with women along the route, although the narrator declares, "I could have a lot of women, but I'm not like some other guys."

Dudley, a native of Wisconsin, had a short career as a baseball player but went into country music after an arm injury made it impossible to continue. Another injury, suffered in 1960 when he was struck by a hit-and-run driver, set back his music career a few months.

"Six Days On The Road" became Dudley's signature song, but he also recorded "Truck Drivin' Son-Of-A-Gun" and "Trucker's Prayer."

Six Days On The Road

Songwriters: Earl Green, Carl Montgomery

Peaked at No. 32 on Billboard Hot 100

Aug. 3, 1963

Dave Dudley

May 3, 1928-Dec. 22, 2003

Born David Darwin Pedruska in Spencer, Wis., and died in Danbury, Wis., after suffering a heart attack

Dave Dudley

No Particular Place To Go [Chuck Berry] – This ditty about a romantic drive in an automobile helped Chuck Berry regain a foothold on the charts. He dropped out of sight in 1962 when he began to serve a prison sentence of 1½ years after being convicted of violating the Mann Act.

The narrator of the tale is out to romance his girlfriend while cruising the town. In the final verse, the couple decide to park and go for a walk in a park. However, a safety device that was patented in 1958 – the seat belt – foils their plans when the man is unable to unfasten his girl's lap belt.

Thereafter, with chagrin showing in his voice, the narrator says that he is resigned to "cruising and playing the radio with no particular place to go."

Berry used the term "calaboose" to describe the confinement of the seat belt. It's a slang term for "prison." He also recycled the melody of his earlier hit "School Days" to power this song.

Starting in 1955, Berry racked up 14 top 40 hits, but he had to wait until 1972 for one of them to hit No. 1 – "My Ding-A-Ling."

No Particular Place To Go

Songwriter: Chuck Berry

Peaked at No. 10 on Billboard Hot 100

July 11, 1964

Chuck Berry

Oct. 18, 1926-March 18, 2017

Born Charles Edward Anderson Berry in St. Louis, Mo., and died in Wentzville, Mo.

Chuck Berry

Yellow Submarine [Beatles] – The concept of underwa travel was floated by the Beatles in this hit. It became the highest charting Fab Four single with Ringo Starr on lead vocal.

Paul McCartney came up with the idea for the song, and John Lennon made a lesser contribution. According to his autobiogra, /, Donovan Leitch added the line "sky of blue, sea of green."

Two years later it became the title song of an animated feature film, which contained other Beatles songs.

Undersea life in the yellow vehicle is "a happy place, that's all," McCartney has said. "You know, it was just ... we were trying to write a children's song. That was the basic idea. And there's nothing more to be read into it than there is in the lyrics of any children's song."

Sound effects help the song come alive. Lennon blew bubbles, Alf Bicknell rattled chains and Brian Jones clinked glasses. McCartney and Lennon spoke through tin cans to replicate the sound of a captain's order coming through an intercom.

The record was so successful that it won the Ivor Novello Award (highest certified sales in Great Britain) for 1966.

It hit number one in Australia, Austria, Belgium, Canada, Ireland, Netherlands, New Zealand, Norway, Sweden, West Germany and the U.K.

Yellow Submarine

Songwriters: John Lennon, Paul McCartney

Peaked at No. 2 on Billboard Hot 100

Sept. 17, 1966

The Beatles

Paul McCartney (June 18, 1942-) bass, backing vocals
John Lennon (Oct. 9, 1940-Dec. 8, 1980) backing vocals, acoustic guitar, sound effects
George Harrison (Feb. 25, 1943-Nov. 29, 2001) backing vocals, acoustic guitar, tambourine
Ringo Starr (July 7, 1940-) lead vocal, drums
Formed in Liverpool, England, in 1960

The Beatles: Ringo Starr, Paul McCartney, George Harrison, John Lennon

Up - Up And Away [5th Dimension] – Flight in a hot air balloon was advocated by this hit song of 1967. It was one of the first successes that got songwriter Jimmy Webb noticed.

The lyrics paint a pleasant picture of gliding and floating in a "beautiful balloon," where the "world's a nicer place."

The 5th Dimension, signed to Johnny Rivers' new Soul City label, used the song to launch a stellar recording career that lasted nine years. In 1975 Marilyn McCoo and husband Billy Davis Jr. broke away from Florence LaRue, Ron Townsend and Lamont McLemore to form a duo.

The sub-genre of sunshine pop was big in '67, and "Up – Up And Away" was a major component. The song was honored repeatedly at the 1968 Grammy Awards, winning trophies for Record of the Year, Song of the Year, Best Pop Performance by a Duo or Group with Vocals,
Best Performance by a Vocal Group, and Best Contemporary Single.

Fittingly, LaRue married the 5th Dimension's manager, Marc Gordon, while in a hot air balloon 50 feet off the ground at the Century Plaza Hotel in Los Angeles in 1969. McCoo and Davis also were joined in wedlock that year.

According to *Songfacts,* Webb got inspiration for the lyrics from a hot air balloon that his friend flew on promotions for a radio station.

Up - Up And Away

Songwriter: Jimmy Webb

Peaked at No. 7 on Billboard Hot 100

July 8, 1967
July 15, 1967
July 22, 1967

The 5th Dimension

Billy Davis Jr. (June 26, 1938-)
Marilyn McCoo (Sept. 30, 1943-)
Ron Townson (Jan. 29, 1933-Aug. 2, 2001)
Lamonte McLemore (Sept. 17, 1939-)
Florence LaRue (Feb. 4, 1944-)
Formed in Los Angeles, Calif., in 1965 as the Versatiles

5th Dimension: Florence LaRue, Ron Townson, Marilyn McCoo, Lamonte McLemore, Billy Davis Jr.

Born To Be Wild [Steppenwolf] – They aren't mentioned anywhere in the lyrics, but this song is strongly connected to motorcycles.

"Get your motor running, head out on the highway. Looking for adventure and whatever comes our way." What else could those words refer to?

The single was released in 1968, but the biker connection was cemented in '69 when the movie *Easy Rider* gave it a prominent part in the soundtrack.

The phrase "heavy metal thunder" made its first appearance in the lyrics and later became associated with hard rock music. Author William Burroughs first used "heavy metal" in his 1961 book *The Soft Machine.*

Mars Bonfire, who wrote the song, related to *Songfacts*, "I was walking down Hollywood Boulevard one day and saw a poster in a window saying 'Born to Ride' with a picture of a motorcycle erupting out of the earth like a volcano with all this fire around it. Around this time I had just purchased my first car, a little secondhand Ford Falcon. So, all this came together lyrically: the idea of the motorcycle coming out, along with the freedom and joy I felt in having my first car and being able to drive myself around whenever I wanted.

"'Born To Be Wild' didn't stand out initially. Even the publishers at Leeds Music didn't take it as the first or second song I gave them. They got it only because I signed as a staff writer. Luckily, it stood out for Steppenwolf. It's like a fluke rather than an achievement, though."

The "fluke" turned into a No. 2 smash on the *Billboard Hot 100.* It went all the way to No. 1 in Canada.

"Born To Be Wild" has been licensed for use in many television shows and movies. The band rejected a request from Paris Hilton's reality show *The Simple Life 2* in 2004. Steppenwolf's John Kaye told the *Toronto Star,* "There are certain things even a rock-and-roller will not stoop to."

Born To Be Wild

Songwriter: Mars Bonfire

Peaked at No. 2 on Billboard Hot 100

Aug. 24, 1968

Aug. 31, 1968

Sept. 7, 1968

Steppenwolf

John Kay (April 12, 1944-) lead vocals

Goldy McJohn (May 2, 1945-Aug. 1, 2017) keyboards

Jerry Edmonton (Oct. 24, 1946-Nov. 28, 1993) drums

Michael Monarch (July 5, 1950-) guitar

Rushton Moreve (Nov. 6, 1948-July 1, 1981) bass

Formed in Los Angeles, Calif., in 1967

Steppenwolf

Proud Mary [Creedence Clearwater Revival] – Picture yourself on a river, one big enough to have paddleboat travel. That's the place where this song can take you.

The opening guitar licks mimic the rhythmic churning of a paddlewheel, and the lyrics proclaim, "big wheel keep on turning, Proud Mary keep on burning."

The narrator is using the boat to leave the town where he has been "working for the man every night and day." He never sees the good side of this city until he is down river looking back, happy to be out of there.

Guitarist/vocalist John Fogerty of CCR originally conceived the song about a cleaning lady named Proud Mary when he was serving in the Army National Guard. Bass player Stu Cook suggested a river travel aspect while watching an episode of the television series *Maverick,* which was about a riverboat gambler.

In a great career of "almost No. 1 hits," this was the first of five Creedence singles that peaked at No. 2. The song attracted 35 cover versions in 1969 and over 100 overall. Ike & Tina Turner's version hit No. 4 in 1971.

The CCR version hit No. 1 in Austria, South Africa and Yugoslavia.

Proud Mary
Songwriter: John Fogerty
Peaked at No. 2 on Billboard Hot 100
March 8, 1969
March 15, 1969
March 22, 1969

Creedence Clearwater Revival
John Fogerty (May 28, 1945-) lead vocals, guitar
Tom Fogerty (Nov. 9, 1941-Sept. 6, 1990) rhythm guitar, backing vocals
Stu Cook (April 25, 1945-) bass, backing vocals
Doug Clifford (April 24, 1945-) drums, backing vocals
Formed in El Cerrito, Calif., in 1967

CCR: Doug Clifford. Stu Cook, John Fogerty, Tom Fogerty

Leaving On A Jet Plane [Peter, Paul & Mary] – This is a bittersweet song about a touring musician who has to leave his lover to fly off and earn a living. The recording was placed on Peter, Paul & Mary's "Album 1700" in 1967 and then sat dormant for two years.

Mary Travers was assigned the lead vocal, so the song is sung from a female perspective. A then-unknown John Denver wrote the song in an airport in 1966, so it bears a naturally male point of view.

As the troubadour prepares to depart, there is confession: "There's so many times I've let you down, so many times I've played around."

We also hear promises: "Every place I go I'll think of you, every song I sing I'll sing for you. When I come back, I'll wear your wedding ring."

The narrator speaks of dreams for the future, and then there are final kisses and hugs. The song ends on a hopeful note: "Tell me that you'll wait for me … oh babe, I hate to go."

Air travel had become commonplace in the 1960s, and it made possible long tours for entertainers who had to do one-night stands to make a living. This song captured the personal side effect of these travels in the relationships with loved ones.

Leaving On A Jet Plane
Songwriter: John Denver
Peaked at No. 1 on Billboard Hot 100
Dec. 20, 1969

Peter, Paul & Mary
Peter Yarrow (May 31, 1938-)
Paul Stookey (Dec. 30, 1937-)
Mary Travers (Nov. 9, 1936-Sept. 16, 2009)
Formed in New York City, N.Y., in 1961

Peter, Paul & Mary

Vehicle [Ides Of March] – A guy is dating a girl for several months, and then she breaks up with him. Yet, she calls him up from time to time to ask him to drive her to modeling classes and other appointments. He always says yes.

Instead of "Vehicle," the song could have been titled "Tool."

This was the real-life scenario in which singer/guitarist Jim Peterik found himself in the late 1960s. It inspired him to write the biggest song that his band, the Ides Of March, ever recorded.

Peterik was 18 when he wrote the song, and his vehicle was a cherry 1964 white Plymouth Valiant with mag wheels.

It all worked out for Peterik, though, as he and the on-and-off girlfriend eventually got married.

The opening line of the song originally was, "I got a set of wheels, pretty baby, won't you hop inside my car?" Peterik was influenced to change it after he saw a government-issued pamphlet of about the dangers of drug use and how strangers could lure teens into their cars to supply them with illicit drugs.

Peterik told *Songfacts,* "To me, the dichotomy is kind of cool. To me, the first line is the most important of all. The original line had nothing going for it. It had no scansion, it had no rhythm to it. When I came across, 'I'm the friendly stranger in the black sedan, won't you hop inside my car,' all other concerns went out the window."

The Ides Of March seemed to have caught lightning in a bottle in the recording studio when they did the "Vehicle" sessions in 1970. Then one of the engineers accidentally pushed a button on the console that caused 13 seconds of tape to be erased. Luckily, the engineer retrieved 13 seconds from the tape of a previous take and seamlessly spliced it into the good version. The day was saved!

The girl I was dating in the first half of 1972 was a friend of the band, and we went to see them play on the Ides of March (March 15) at their high school alma mater, Morton East in Berwyn, Ill. Then we partied with them afterward.

We went to several gigs to see the Ides Of March, and I got to know the band members and their manager. When I found myself unemployed that summer, Peterik offered me a job as a roadie. I was grateful, but I turned it down because I wanted to use my time to find another job in journalism.

That proved to be a good decision, because I was back in the newspaper business within three months. The Ides, on the other hand, broke up the following year.

Vehicle

Songwriter: Jim Peterik
Peaked at No. 2 on Billboard Hot 100
May 23, 1970

The Ides Of March

Jim Peterik (Nov. 11, 1950-) lead guitar, vocals
Larry Millas (March 5, 1949-) keyboards, guitar, vocals
Bob Bergland (March 14, 1949-) bass, tenor saxophone
Mike Borch (Aug. 25, 1949-) drums
Ray Herr (Sept. 24, 1947-March 29, 2011) rhythm guitar, vocals
John Larson (Nov. 6, 1949-Sept. 21, 2011) trumpet
Chuck Soumar (1953-) trumpet
Formed in Berwyn, Ill., in 1964

The Ides Of March

Hitchin' A Ride [Vanity Fare] – If you have no money to ride a train or other public transportation, what do you do? Many of us have gone to the roadside and stuck out a thumb.

In earlier chapters, Mitch Murray and Peter Callander came to the fore as British songwriters with big hits to their credit ("The Ballad Of Bonnie And Clyde," "The Night Chicago Died" and "Billy, Don't Be A Hero"), and this was another one of their gems. Vanity Fare from Kent, England, made "Hitchin' A Ride" their second international smash.

The narrator in this song is standing in the rain after midnight, trying to hitch a ride so he can reunite with his girlfriend. Many a young man can relate to that predicament. Unfortunately, hitchhiking has become a thing of the past because it is no longer safe.

A million seller, this song soared to No. 5 on the *Billboard Hot 100,* No. 2 in South Africa, No. 3 in Canada and No. 16 in the U.K.

Hitchin' A Ride
Songwriters: Mitch Murray, Peter Callander
Peaked at No. 5 on Billboard Hot 100
June 27, 1970
July 4, 1970

<u>Vanity Fare</u>
Trevor Brice (Feb. 12, 1945-) vocals
Tony Goulden (Nov. 21, 1942-) guitar
Dick Allix (May 3, 1945-) drums
Tony Jarrett (Sept. 4, 1943-) bass
Barry Landeman (Oct. 25, 1947-) keyboards
Formed in Kent, England, as the Avengers in 1966

Vanity Fare

Me And You And A Dog Named Boo [Lobo] – Here's a fanciful cross-country romp by a freewheeling guy, his girlfriend and their dog. Their old car takes them from Georgia to Minnesota to California.

The love of travel is what keeps this trio going, and they don't seem to stay in one place for long.

There's a bit of mischief along the way, as the hungry travelers are caught stealing eggs from a henhouse near St. Paul, Minn. "Old McDonald made us work, but then he paid us for what it was worth," declares the narrator. The payment turns out to be a tank of gas for the car.

The allure of Los Angeles tempts the threesome to settle there, but somehow the car convinces them to get back on the road after about a month.

Lobo made this record his first hit single, and he parlayed the early '70s trend of soft rock into a career that saw four No. 1 songs on the *Billboard Easy Listening Chart* (which eventually became the *Adult Contemporary Chart*).

Me And You And A Dog Named Boo

Songwriter: Kent Lavoie

Peaked at No. 5 on Billboard Hot 100

May 15, 1971

May 22, 1971

Lobo

Born Roland Kent Lavoie in Tallahassee, Fla., on July 31, 1943

Lobo

The City Of New Orleans [Arlo Guthrie] – This is a graphic description of a passenger train journey from Chicago, Ill., to New Orleans, La. The route is still in the Amtrak system, and it began in 1947 as part of the Illinois Central Railroad's service.

In 1971 Amtrak renamed the route the Panama Limited, which it was called when Arlo Guthrie recorded the song in 1972. Amtrak restored the name City of New Orleans in 1981.

As the 15-car train rolls south, we hear mention of "houses, farms and fields … and graveyards of rusted automobiles." It's a smorgasbord for a passenger's eyes.

Inside the train we find a card game in progress in the club car and a bottle inside a paper bag being passed from one rider to another. Mothers with babies in tow can let the swaying cars rock the little ones to sleep.

Sometime after nightfall the train enters Memphis, where some cars are changed. The train is a little more than halfway to its destination.

According to *Spotlight Central*, songwriter Steve Goodman ran across Guthrie in the Quiet Knight club in Chicago one evening. For the cost of a beer, Guthrie allowed Goodman to play him the song, which he liked. He made it the only *Billboard* top 40 hit of his recording career.

The lyrics end with the line "this train's got the disappearing railroad blues." Nobody has been doing wholesale destruction of railways, but that line may refer to the loss of popularity of rail transportation because of the rise of airline and interstate highway usage. It also may be a way of noting that a number of small communities like Cairo, Ill., and Batesville, Winona, Durant and Canton, Miss., have lost their rail service.

Words from the chorus, "Good morning, America, how are you," have a lasting legacy. They inspired names for enduring daybreak television shows such as *Good Morning America* and *Good Morning Arizona.*

The City Of New Orleans
Songwriter: Steve Goodman
Peaked at No. 18 on Billboard Hot 100
Oct. 28, 1972

Arlo Guthrie
Born Arlo Davy Guthrie in Brooklyn, N.Y., on July 10, 1947

Arlo Guthrie

Ramblin Man [Allman Brothers Band] – "I was born in the back seat of a Greyhound bus," the narrator declares. Now that's a real rambling man!

The American South is the venue for this song. The narrator's father was a gambler in Georgia, as revealed in the first verse. The final verse sees the narrator leaving Nashville to go to New Orleans. It sounds like a fun romp through Dixie. "They're always having a good time down on the bayou."

Though we know that his birthplace was a bus on U.S. Route 41, his mode of transportation as an adult is unspecified. He's just "trying to make a living and doing the best I can." He tells his girl, "When it's time to leave, I hope you'll understand that I was born a ramblin' man."

Guitarist Dickie Betts wrote the song and provided the lead vocal. The record charted in the fall of 1973, and it was the first time the Allman Brothers scored high on the pop singles chart.

Betts took the theme from his personal life, in which his father moved the family frequently. "When I was a kid, my dad was in construction and used to move the family band and forth between central Florida's east and west coasts," he wrote in the book *Anatomy of a Song*. "I'd go to one school for a year and then the other the next. I had two sets of friends and spent a lot of time in the back seat of a Greyhound bus. Ramblin' was in my blood."

Betts had a friend named Kenny Harwick in the late 1960s. One day Harwick asked him, "How are you doing?" Then he quickly answered his own question with "I bet you're just trying to make a living and doing the best you can." The words stayed with Betts for three years before he finished the lyrics to "Ramblin Man" in Macon, Ga.

The ABB lost a founding member when Duane Allman died following a motorcycle accident in Macon in 1971. Bass player Berry Oakley died in a similar fashion in 1972, three blocks from where Allman crashed and 49 weeks before "Ramblin Man" peaked at No. 2 on the *Billboard Hot 100.*

Ramblin Man
Songwriter: Dickey Betts

Peaked at No. 2 on Billboard Hot 100
Oct. 13, 1973

Allman Brothers Band
Gregg Allman (Dec. 8, 1947-May 27, 2017) keyboards, guitar
Dickey Betts (Dec. 12, 1943-) guitar, vocals
Berry Oakley (April 4, 1948- Nov. 11, 1972) bass
Butch Trucks (May 11, 1947-Jan. 24, 2017) drums
Chuck Leavell (April 28, 1952-) keyboards
"Jaimoe" Johanson (July 8, 1944-) drums
Formed in Jacksonville, Fla., in 1969

Allman Brothers Band

Midnight Train To Georgia [Gladys Knight & the Pips] – The veteran soul singers from Atlanta rode the rails to No. 1 with this 1973 smash. It was their second single with "train" in the title, as they'd released "Friendship Train" in 1969.

The lyrics are about a guy who has been overwhelmed by his job in Los Angeles and has decided to return to his roots in Georgia. The narrator, his girlfriend, is going to join him on the eastbound midnight train since "I'd rather live in his world than live without him in mine."

It's a message of love, devotion and faithfulness. A lot of listeners related to that theme, and the record became Gladys Knight's biggest hit and signature song.

Written by Mississippi native Jim Weatherly, the song originally was titled "Midnight Plane To Houston," and Weatherly recorded the first version. According to the *Billboard Book of Number 1 Hits,* Weatherly remarked, "It was based on a conversation I had with somebody … about taking a midnight plane to Houston. I wrote it as kind of a country song.

"Then we sent the song to a guy named Sonny Limbo in Atlanta, and he wanted to cut it on Cissy Houston. He asked if I minded if he changed to title to 'Midnight Train To Georgia.' I said, 'No, I don't mind. Just don't change the rest of the song.'"

Weatherly's publisher forwarded the song to Gladys Knight & the Pips, who kept the title the same as Houston's version.

Knight had her public singing debut in church at age 4. She formed a vocal group called the Pips with some cousins, and they earned their first recording contract in 1957 when Gladys was 13. Their first chart success was the No. 6 hit "Every Beat Of My Heart" in 1961.

Midnight Train To Georgia
Songwriter: Jim Weatherly
Peaked at No. 1 on Billboard Hot 100
Oct. 27, 1973
Nov. 3, 1973

Gladys Knight & the Pips
Gladys Knight (May 28, 1944-)
Merald "Bubba" Knight (Sept. 4, 1942-)
William Guest (July 2, 1941-Dec. 24, 2015)
Edward Patten (Aug. 27, 1939-Feb. 25, 2005)
Formed in Atlanta, Ga., in 1952

The Pips: William Guest, Bubba Knight, Gladys Knight, Edward Patten

Movin' On [Bad Company] – Another typical, dreary day on the road for a rock star – that's what we have in the words of this song.

Paul Rodgers sang a good lead vocal, and Mick Ralphs played a great lead guitar. The song was contained on Bad Company's debut album, which was recorded in 1973 and released in '74. It was the British band's second single release. The critically acclaimed eight-song LP hit No. 1 on the *Billboard 200* chart.

There is a taxi to ride, a plane to catch, schedules to be met, hotel to check into, etc. The tour goes from town to town with little fanfare, aside from the shows that are to be performed.

It's a message of isolation and loneliness for a touring musician, who finds that fame isn't always the exhilarating, satisfying experience that most people think it is. Bad Company was a new band when this song was recorded, but its four British members had been in other bands previously.

The song made a decent showing on the *Hot 100,* peaking at No. 19.

Movin' On
Songwriter: Mick Ralphs

Peaked at No. 19 on Billboard Hot 100
March 1, 1975
March 8, 1975

Bad Company
Paul Rodgers (Dec. 17, 1949-) vocals, keyboards, guitar
Simon Kirke (July 28, 1949-) drums, vocals
Mick Ralphs (March 31, 1944-) guitar, keyboards, vocals
Boz Burrell (Aug. 1, 1946-Sept. 21, 2006) bass, guitar, vocals
Formed in London, England, in 1973

Bad Company: Paul Rodgers, Simon Kirke, Mick Ralphs, Boz Burrell

Black Water [Doobie Brothers] – When I was about 19 years old I had a fantasy about building a raft, which I would toss into the Mississippi River somewhere off the Illinois shore and proceed to float down to New Orleans.

I never got to live out that fantasy, but the Doobie Brothers helped me relive my mental images of the trip when they released this song as a single in early 1975.

The track had been hiding on the album "What Once Were Vices Are Now Habits" and on the "B-side" of "Another Park, Another Sunday" since being recorded in 1974.

"That's a story that could have happened back then but never would happen now," Doobie guitarist Tom Johnston told *Songfacts*. "Roanoke, Virginia (radio station WROV-AM) picked up that tune and started playing it in heavy rotation, and somebody in Minneapolis who, I guess, knew somebody in Roanoke, heard the song and decided to follow suit. And it ended up becoming our first No. 1 single.

"That was Pat's (Simmons) first single. And, oddly enough, it was never looked at as a single by the record company."

Simmons is a longtime lover of Delta blues music, and he used a 1971 visit to New Orleans to grab the vibe and turn it into song. Several images in the lyrics of "Black Water" come from his personal experiences. Some of the lyrics formed in his mind while he was riding a streetcar through the university district.

The basic guitar riff for the song came to Simmons while he was relaxing between takes at the Warner Brothers recording studio in 1973. "What is that?" producer Ted Templeman asked through the intercom. Simmons replied, "It's just a little riff I came up with that I've been tweaking with."

Prophetically, Templeman said, "I love that. You really should write a song using that riff."

Black Water
Songwriter: Patrick Simmons
Peaked at No. 1 on Billboard Hot 100
March 15, 1975

The Doobie Brothers

Tom Johnston (Aug. 15, 1948-) vocals, guitar, harmonica
Patrick Simmons (Oct. 19, 1948-) vocals, guitar, piano, flute
Tiran Porter (Sept. 26, 1948-) bass, vocals
John Hartman (March 18, 1950-) drums, percussion
Michael Hossack (Oct. 17, 1946-March 12, 2012) drums
Formed in San Jose, Calif., in 1970

The Doobie Brothers: Michael Hossack, Patrick Simmons, Tom Johnston, Tiran Porter, John Hartman

Roll On Down The Highway [Bachman-Turner Overdrive] – Twelve years after "Six Days On The Road" drove up the charts, a Canadian band delivered another song about truckers. This one was pure rock, though, rather than country.

Some themes that we saw in "Six Days" are present here. Truckers are pushing speed limits in order to save time, and law enforcement is a constant threat to write them up. Time is money for these road professionals, and they're trying to make good use of it.

Randy Bachman, a guitarist who helped form Bachman-Turner Overdrive after he left the Guess Who, was under contract to write songs for the Ford Motor Company's commercials. The automotive giant didn't pick up any of his compositions, but "Roll On" was born out of an idea from one of the rejected numbers.

"It's like getting an assignment," Bachman told *Songfacts.* "Write a new commercial for Ford, and you'll get paid $100,000. Well, I'd sit down and write a commercial for Ford, 'Let It Roll Down The Highway.' Ford never picks it up, and I have a song called 'Roll Down The Highway.'"

Drummer Robbie Bachman, Randy's brother, helped develop the idea into this song. It was contained on an album titled "Not Fragile," which was the antithesis of a 1972 album by Yes, which was titled "Fragile."

Randy Bachman left the Guess Who at the height of their popularity in 1970. Differences with lead singer Burton Cummings reportedly centered around Bachman's conversion to Mormonism. The next year he formed the band Brave Belt, which evolved into BTO.

The year 1974 was particularly good for BTO, as they placed "Let It Ride," "Takin' Care Of Business" and "You Ain't Seen Nothing Yet" in the *Billboard* pop top 40.

Roll On Down The Highway

Songwriters: Fred Turner, Robbie Bachman

Peaked at No. 14 on Billboard Hot 100
March 1, 1975
March 8, 1975

Bachman-Turner Overdrive
Randy Bachman (Sept. 27, 1943-) guitar, vocals
Fred Turner (Oct. 16, 1943-) bass, vocals
Tim Bachman (Aug. 1, 1951-) guitar
Robbie Bachman (Feb. 18, 1953-) drums
Formed in Winnipeg, Manitoba, Canada, in 1973

BTO: Robbie Bachman, Randy Bachman, Tim Bachman, Fred Turner

Drivin' My Life Away [Eddie Rabbitt] – This looks like another trucker song, although some music industry observers believe it is about roadies who travel in support of touring artists. The track was part of the soundtrack for the 1980 feature film *Roadie* starring Meat Loaf and Art Carney.

Whatever the case, highway travel is the bread and butter of the lyrics. There is mention of rainy weather, truck stops and driving through mountain passes. A cute young female also tries to con the narrator into giving her a ride. "Said I wouldn't be sorry," he says. But the girl obviously is underage.

The up-tempo song reached No. 5 on the pop chart and No. 1 on the country chart, establishing Eddie Rabbitt as a crossover artist. His next single, "I Love A Rainy Night," garnered the top spot on both the pop and country charts.

What keeps the driver going? A life that is better than the one he has. "Ooh, I'm driving my life away, looking for a better way for me," he says.

Rabbitt, who got his start in the music business as a songwriter, got an early boost from Elvis Presley, who recorded his "Kentucky Rain" in 1970.

Drivin' My Life Away
Songwriter: Eddie Rabbitt

Peaked at No. 5 on Billboard Hot 100
Oct. 4, 1980
Oct. 11, 1980

Eddie Rabbitt
Nov. 27, 1941-May 7, 1998
Born Edward Thomas Rabbitt in Brooklyn, N.Y., and died of lung cancer in Nashville, Tenn.

Eddie Rabbitt

Sailing [Christopher Cross] – Sailing in a small craft can be a dicey means of travel or recreation. Bad weather on open waters is a constant threat, and emergencies often are fatal because help can be far away.

Emerging artist Christopher Cross examined the upside of sailing on this 1979 recording. It was the only No. 1 song from his highly acclaimed debut album, and it was one of the first songs recorded using digital equipment.

Memories of summer days spent sailing with a friend off the coast of Texas sparked the creation of the song.

"It's not far down to paradise, at least not for me, and if the wind is right you can sail away and find tranquility," says the first verse. The mood builds from there with a slow tempo that feels relaxing. There are no squalls in this song, which I once read is the perfect cure for stress for anyone stuck in rush hour traffic on a hot day.

Relating how the song came to be, Cross told *Songfacts,* "I was just at home sitting in this cheap apartment, sitting at the table. I remember coming up with the verse and chorus, and the lyrics to the first verse of the chorus all came out. These tunings, like Joni (Mitchell) used to say, they get you in this sort of trance, so all that came out at once: 'It's not far down to paradise...' The chorus just sort of came out.

"So I got up and wandered around the apartment just thinking, 'Wow, that's pretty f'ing great.' I just thought, 'That's really cool.' So then I sat down and had to try to come up with other stuff to make the rest of the song, but I thought I had something there.

"It took about two years before I came up with the bridge that changes all the keys to where it lifts, but it was a pretty special moment."

Cross said he didn't think the song would be a hit because "it was way too introspective."

Sailing
Songwriter: Christopher Cross

Peaked at No. 1 on Billboard Hot 100
Aug. 30, 1980

Christopher Cross
Born Christopher Charles Geppert in San Antonio, Texas, on May 3, 1951

Christopher Cross

Walking In Memphis [Marc Cohn] – Memphis, Tenn., is comprised of 324 square miles. That can make for a lot of legwork if someone has to get around on foot.

Singer/songwriter Marc Cohn used some shoe leather and a few personal experiences to craft this song in 1991.

"It's 100 percent autobiographical," Cohn told the *Chicago Tribune*. "The moment I wrote it, I had no idea I was writing a hit, but I knew I was writing something that deeply defined so many facets of me – my conflicting feelings about religion, about my own state, my humor about it, my acceptance about everybody in terms of what they believe … it's not a religious thing for me, it's just deeply moving."

The personal experience is similar to the one that John Lennon used to work up "In My Life" (see Chapter 14, The Art of Rock).

Cohn, who was having trouble writing songs that he valued, made a trip to Memphis from New York City in 1985, looking for inspiration. Among other places, he visited the Full Gospel Tabernacle Church to hear Rev. Al Green preach. Green was a highly successful secular R&B singer in the 1970s.

Other places in Memphis mentioned in the song are Beale St. (where many restaurants and nightclubs are located), Union Avenue (home of Sun Studio) and Graceland. Elvis Presley gets a nod, and so does Muriel Wilkins, who did piano/vocal shows on Friday nights at the Hollywood Café in nearby Tunica, Miss. She died in 1990.

Also mentioned is W.C. Handy, a blues composer and musician who plied his trade in Memphis during the first half of the 20th century.

I have been to Memphis, and I found that the major musical points of interest are pretty well spread out. But, if I had to walk from one to another to another, it would be worth it.

Memphis is the place where Delta blues, country music and mainstream pop came together to form rock and roll.

Walking In Memphis
Songwriter: Marc Cohn
Peaked at No. 13 on Billboard Hot 100
July 6, 1991
July 13, 1991

Marc Cohn

Born Marc Craig Cohn in Cleveland, Ohio, on July 5, 1959

Marc Cohn

GLOSSARY

a cappella – without instrumental accompaniment

arpeggio – a group of notes played one after the other, up or down in pitch. The player plays the notes of a particular chord individually rather than together.

audio feedback – the ringing noise (often described as squealing, screeching, etc.) sometimes present in sound systems. It is caused by a "looped signal," that is, a signal which travels in a continuous loop.

B side – the side of a 45 rpm record that receives little or no promotion because the issuing label is reserving that attention for the other side (A side)

backward echo (reverse echo) – a sound effect created as the result of recording a reverberated signal of an audio recording played backward. The original recording is then played forward accompanied by the recording of the reverberated signal which now precedes the original signal. The process produces a swelling effect preceding and during playback.

bag of words model – a simplifying representation used in natural language processing and information retrieval, which can be used to identify the author of certain text or lyrics according to habitual phrasing

bar – the line marking the division between two measures of music

baroque – a period or style of Western art music composed from approximately 1600 to 1750. During the Baroque era, professional musicians were expected to be accomplished improvisers of both solo melodic lines and accompaniment parts. Baroque music expanded the size, range and complexity of instrumental performance.

bassline – the term used in many styles of music for the low-pitched instrumental part or line played by a rhythm section instrument such as the electric bass, double bass, cello, tuba or keyboard or synthesizer

beat – the audible, visual or mental marking of the metrical divisions of music

break – a solo passage, usually from 2 to 12 bars, during which the rest of the instruments are silent

bridge – a musical passage that connects two sections of a song. For example, a bridge often connects the verse to the chorus of a song. It can also sit between the last two chorus sections to add variation.

British Invasion – a cultural phenomenon of the mid-1960s, when rock and pop music acts from the United Kingdom and other aspects of British culture became popular in the United States

bubblegum – upbeat pop music that is considered to be disposable, contrived or marketed for children and adolescents. The term also refers to a pop subgenre, originating in the United States in the late 1960s.

cadence – a sequence of notes or chords comprising the close of a musical phrase

call and response – pertaining to a style of singing in which a melody sung by one singer is responded to or echoed by one or more singers

cantata – a medium-length narrative piece of music for voices with instrumental accompaniment, typically with solos, chorus, and orchestra

chord progression – the foundation of Western popular music styles (e.g., pop music, rock music) and traditional music (e.g., blues and jazz). In these genres, chord progressions are the defining feature on which melody and rhythm are built.

claves – a percussion instrument consisting of a pair of short dowels about 20–30 mm thick. Traditionally they are made of wood. When struck they produce a bright clicking noise. Claves are sometimes hollow and carved in the middle to amplify the sound.

coffeehouse – a cafe or other place where coffee is served, sometimes also offering informal entertainment

cover version – a recording or performance of a previously recorded song made especially to take advantage of the original's success

crescendo – the loudest point reached in a gradually increasing sound

demo – the recording of a song or piece of music that aims to demonstrate the capabilities of a musical group or performer or as preparation for a full recording

doo wop – a style of pop music marked by the use of close harmony vocals using nonsense phrases, originating in the U.S. in the 1950s

double-A side – a 45 rpm record on which both sides receive equal promotion by the label that issues it

Electro-Theremin – an electronic musical instrument controlled without physical contact by the user. Its controlling section usually consists of two metal antennas that sense the relative position of the thereminist's hands and control oscillators for frequency with one hand, and amplitude (volume) with the other. The electric signals from the theremin are amplified and sent to a loudspeaker.

falsetto – a method of voice production used by male singers, especially tenors, to sing notes higher than their normal range

fuzz box – a small amplifier that is designed to be overdriven, thus producing a raspy, "fuzz" tone

genre – a category of artistic composition, as in music or literature, characterized by similarities in form, style or subject matter

gold record – a 45 rpm single that attains one million in sales or a 33 rpm album that attains 500,000 in sales

glam rock – a style of *rock* music that developed in the United Kingdom in the early 1970s performed by musicians who wore outrageous costumes, makeup, and hairstyles, particularly platform shoes and glitter

groupie – a person, especially a young woman, who regularly follows a pop music group or other celebrity in the hope of meeting or getting to know them or have sex with them

hair band – a subgenre of heavy metal, which features pop-influenced hooks and guitar riffs, and borrows heavily from the fashion and image of 1970s glam rock

handbell – a bell designed to be rung by hand

harmonium – a keyboard instrument that is a lot like an organ. In a foot-pumped harmonium, the player presses two pedals with his or her feet, one at a time. This is joined to a mechanism which operates a bellows, sending air to the reeds.

harmony – any simultaneous combination of tones, or the simultaneous combination of tones, especially when blended into chords pleasing to the ear; chordal structure, as distinguished from melody and rhythm

hip hop – also called rap, it is a genre of popular music developed in the United States by inner-city African- Americans and Latino-Americans in the Bronx borough of New York City in the 1970s

homophone – each of two or more words having the same pronunciation but different meanings, origins, or spelling

Ivor Novello Award – Named after the entertainer Ivor Novello, it is an award for songwriting and composing. They have been presented annually in London by the Ivors Academy (formerly the BASCA) since 1956.

Jew's harp – also known as the jaw harp, mouth harp, gewgaw, Ozark harp, Galician harp, it is a lamellophone instrument, consisting of a flexible metal or bamboo tongue or reed attached to a frame

jug band – a band that uses primitive or improvised instruments, such as an empty jug, to play blues or folk music

guitar lick – a short section of lead guitar playing, either used as a fill or as a characteristic repeated element of a song. Licks can even serve as choruses, but are usually incorporated to introduce the lead guitar prior to a solo.

LP – a long playing record made of vinyl, spinning at a 33 rpm turntable speed

measure – in musical notation, a bar (or measure) is a segment of time corresponding to a specific number of beats in which each beat is represented by a particular note value and the boundaries of the bar are indicated by vertical bar lines

Mellotron – an electro-mechanical musical instrument developed in Birmingham, England, in 1963. The instrument is played by pressing its keys, each of which pushes a length of magnetic tape against a capstan, which pulls it across a playback head. Then as the key is released, the tape is retracted by a spring to its initial position. Different portions of the tape can be played to access different sounds.

Minimoog – an analog synthesizer first manufactured by Moog Music between 1970 and 1981. The Minimoog was designed as an affordable, portable, simplified instrument which combined the most useful components in a single device.

mixing board (or console) – an electronic device for combining sounds of many different audio signals. Inputs to the console include microphones being used by singers and for picking up acoustic instruments, signals from electric or electronic instruments, or recorded music. Depending on the type, a mixer is able to control analog or digital signals. The modified signals are summed to produce the combined output signals, which can then be broadcast, amplified through a sound reinforcement system or recorded.

Moog synthesizer – a music synthesizer that consists of separate modules – such as oscillators, amplifiers, envelope generators, filters, noise generators, ring modulators, triggers and mixers—which create and shape sounds, and can be connected via patch cords. It can be played using controllers including keyboards, joysticks, pedals, and ribbon controllers. Its oscillators can produce waveforms of different timbres, which can be modulated and filtered to produce more combinations of sounds.

movement – a self-contained part of a musical composition or musical form overdubbing – a technique used in audio recording where a passage has been pre-recorded, and then during replay, another part is recorded to go along with the original. The overdub process can be repeated multiple times.

platinum record – a 45 rpm single that attains two million in sales or a 33 rpm album that attains one million in sales

power trio – a rock and roll band format having a lineup of electric guitar, bass guitar and drum kit (drums and cymbals), leaving out the second rhythm guitar or keyboard instrument that are used in other rock music bands that are quartets and quintets

progressive rock – a form of rock music that evolved in the late 1960s and early 1970s as part of a "mostly British attempt to elevate rock music to new levels of artistic credibility." The term "art rock" is often used interchangeably with "progressive rock."

ragtime -- a musical style that enjoyed its peak popularity between 1895 and 1919. Its cardinal trait is its syncopated or "ragged" rhythm.

rave-up – extended guitar **soloing**, feedback and assorted abstract musical departure

rhythm & blues – a style of music that combines soulful singing and a strong backbeat, which was the most popular music created by and for African-Americans between the end of World War II (1945) and the early 1960s

riff – a short repeated phrase in popular music, typically used as an introduction or refrain in a song

scat vocals – vocal improvisation with wordless sounds, nonsense syllables or without words at all

slide guitar – a particular technique for playing the guitar that is often used in blues-style music. It typically involves playing the guitar in the traditional position (flat against the body) with the use of a tubular "slide" fitted on one of the guitarist's fingers. The slide may be a metal or glass tube, such as the neck of a bottle.

Spanish guitar – a type of acoustic guitar that is strung with nylon strings. It is typically used to play either classical music or traditional music which is either Spanish or Spanish in origin

string ensemble – a music group consisting solely of stringed instruments

studio group – a conglomeration of musicians who play only on recordings in a studio, as opposed to playing in concerts before an audience

Stylophone – a miniature electronic musical instrument producing a distinctive buzzing sound when a stylus is drawn along its metal keyboard

sunshine pop – a subgenre of *pop* music that originated in Southern California in the mid-1960s. Rooted in easy listening and advertising jingles, sunshine pop acts combined nostalgic or anxious moods with "an appreciation for the beauty of the world."

super group – a musical performing group whose members have successful solo careers, are members of other groups or are well known in other musical professions

synthesizer – an electronic musical instrument, typically operated by a keyboard, producing a wide variety of sounds by generating and combining signals of different frequencies

tambura – a stringed instrument that is played as a folk instrument in the Balkan peninsula. It has doubled steel strings and is played with a plectrum, in the same manner as a mandolin.

tape loops – loops of magnetic tape used to create repetitive, rhythmic musical patterns or dense layers of sound when played on a tape recorder. They were used among contemporary composers of 1950s and 1960s, who used them to create phase patterns, rhythms, textures, and timbres. Popular composers and producers of the 1960s and 1970s, particularly in psychedelic, progressive and ambient genres, used tape loops to accompany their music with innovative sound effects.

tremolo – a wavering effect in a musical tone, produced either by rapid reiteration of a note, by rapid repeated slight variation in the pitch of a note, or by sounding two notes of slightly different pitches to produce prominent overtones

upright piano – a musical instrument in which the soundboard and plane of the strings run vertically, perpendicular to the keyboard, thus taking up less floor space than the normal grand piano

vibrato – a rapid, slight variation in pitch in singing or playing some musical instruments, producing a stronger or richer tone

volume swell – a musical crescendo commonly associated with the electric guitar. It alters the tone of a note, reducing the treble tones of the pick or finger strike, allowing the softer tone that follows to sustain.

Vox continental organ – a transistorized combo organ that was introduced in 1962 by the musical equipment manufacturer Vox. Having a characteristic bright but thin, breathy sound, the "Connie," as it was affectionately known, was designed for touring musicians.

wah-wah pedal – a type of electric guitar effects *pedal* that alters the tone and frequencies of the guitar signal to create a distinctive sound, mimicking the human voice saying the onomatopoeic name "wah-wah."

waltz time – dance music in triple meter, often written in ¾ time. A waltz typically sounds one chord per measure, and the accompaniment style particularly associated with the waltz is to play the root of the chord on the first beat, the upper notes on the second and third beats.

ABOUT THE AUTHOR

Readers have been enjoying Larry Coffman's writing for most of his adult life. It began with his high school experience as a sportswriter and progressed through his education at Bradley University, where he earned a degree in journalism. He had a career as a daily newspaper reporter, columnist and editor.

As a freelance writer Larry has consistently demonstrated a way with words. He spent 16 years writing feature stories for the website of the Acoustic Storm, an internationally syndicated weekly radio program, producing dozens of articles on acoustic rock music.

In an effort to personally get in touch with music, Larry has visited several key locations where rock history was made.

Made in the USA
Monee, IL
14 August 2020

38194585R00184